# THE TURKS IN WORLD HISTORY

**The Mounted Archer, Hero of the Steppes.**

Steppe warriors were famous since ancient times for their ability to rotate in the saddle at full gallop and fire an arrow to the rear with deadly accuracy—the so-called Parthian shot. Made with great skill from wood, horn, and sinew, compound bows of this type set distance records still unsurpassed in modern times. From Topkapī Palace Museum, Hazine 2165, fol. 42b, anonymous miniature, possibly sixteenth century.

# THE TURKS
# IN WORLD HISTORY

# CARTER VAUGHN FINDLEY

OXFORD
UNIVERSITY PRESS

2005

# OXFORD
UNIVERSITY PRESS

Oxford   New York
Auckland   Bangkok   Buenos Aires   Cape Town   Chennai
Dar es Salaam   Delhi   Hong Kong   Istanbul   Karachi   Kolkata
Kuala Lumpur   Madrid   Melbourne   Mexico City   Mumbai   Nairobi
São Paulo   Shanghai   Taipei   Tokyo   Toronto

Copyright © 2005 by Oxford University Press, Inc.

Published by Oxford University Press, Inc.
198 Madison Avenue, New York, New York 10016

Library of Congress Cataloging-in-Publication Data
Findley, Carter V. [date]
The Turks in world history / Carter Vaughn Findley.
p.   cm.
Includes bibliographical references and index.
ISBN 0-19-516770-8; 0-19-517726-6 (pbk.)
1. Turkic peoples—History.   I. Title.
DS26.F563 2004
909'.04943—dc22      2004041578

9 8 7 6 5 4 3 2 1

Printed in the United States of America
on acid-free paper

In Memory of

ANDREAS TIETZE

26 April 1914–22 December 2003

# PREFACE

Chapters 1 through 3 of this book originated as the Leon Poullada Memorial lectures at Princeton University in December 1999. Carl Brown asked me if I could prepare a series of lectures on a panoramic subject. I am grateful to him for insisting when I replied that the only such subject I had in mind was the Turks in world history. I am also indebted to those who attended and asked questions.

The idea for such a book came to me forty years ago as a first-year graduate student in Middle Eastern studies at Columbia University. The courses that I took with Kathleen Burrill, Tibor Halasi-Kun, Ehsan Yarshater, and J. C. Hurewitz introduced me simultaneously to the literature on the Islamic history of the Middle East, especially in the Seljuk and Ottoman periods, and on the Turkic peoples in Inner Asia. The Middle Eastern and Inner Asian literatures differed in ways that created more cognitive dissonance than I could resolve at the time. Not only did the geographical purviews of area studies programs divide Inner Asia and the Middle East between different programs, but also most of the literature on the Middle East was recognizably the work of historians, whereas that on the Turks in Inner Asia bore the (to me) alien stamp of philologists. Who was I to argue with people who knew so much more than I did? But much of this literature, especially that on Inner Asia, could charitably have been described as not very "user-friendly," except that the term had still not been invented. As I entered a new field of study, I discovered highly technical studies, produced by scholars scattered across the Middle East, Soviet Union, Europe, and North America. The authors had been trained in different ways, carried out their research under very different conditions, responded to different priorities, and were not all talking to each other. If history was a field of the humanities, and if the humanities were supposed to enlarge one's sense of what it meant to be a human being, was there some reason that the history of the Turks was not or could not be written in such a way? It did not seem to me that the authors had bad intentions—far from it—but rather that they had not yet succeeded in bringing the Turks' history to life as part of the history of humanity. Secretly doubting myself for asking such questions in my moments of discouragement, I formed the idea for an interpretive essay on "the Turks in history." Could I write something like that some day? Other necessities intervened, until the invitation from Carl Brown in 1999 brought this idea back to the forefront.

Of the many things that happened in the intervening years, two have particular significance for this study. Having always been excited by macroconceptual approaches to the organization of knowledge, as well as by the microfocused empiricism basic to historical research, I started teaching world history around 1980 alongside my courses in Middle Eastern and Islamic subjects. Initially, I did not anticipate significant synergies between my world history teaching and my research. However, broadening one's field of vision inevitably affects one's perception of any particular object. Where this study is concerned, that happened when I realized that the comparative history of Eurasia provided the ideal terrain on which to advance beyond the old fragmentation that divided the study of the Turks between disciplines and area-studies fields. In his great book on pre-Ottoman Turkey, Claude Cahen wrote in 1968 that in the history of the Turks "there is just as much to claim the attention of historians as in the history of other peoples"; however, "this expectation has not altogether been fulfilled."[1] The same could still be said. No one book can change that, but the growing interest in world history provides an arena where the history of the Turkic peoples can be seen entire and its importance more fully realized.

The other development that did most to prepare me to write this book was the publication of Peter Golden's *Introduction to the History of the Turkic Peoples* in 1992. This book is a study of the Turkic peoples, great and small, from their origins through the sixteenth century. For me as a scholar who has spent most of his life on the historically oriented, Ottoman-Islamic, Middle Eastern side of Turkish studies, Golden's work came along just at the right time to reignite my interest in the Inner Asian side of the field. Golden's book led me back to some of the works and issues I had studied as a first-year graduate student. His generous guidance has also led me forward to other major works published since 1992.

This book is intended for nonspecialists who want to know more about this important part of the history of humanity. The book's chief goal is to suggest ways of organizing and interpreting the evidence. How can the chronological flow be divided into meaningful periods? What are the major long-term continuities? What are the sharpest discontinuities? What are the most distinctive large-scale patternings in politics, culture, society, or economy, and how do things differ for Turkic peoples who somehow avoid incorporation into these patternings? A short book cannot answer all such questions to the satisfaction of learned experts. However, if it enables nonspecialist readers better to understand an important realm of human experience, and if it stimulates them to further inquiry, then the book will have accomplished its most important goal.

Many others have aided me in reaching this point. I am indebted to the History Department, College of Humanities, and Mershon Center at Ohio State University for supporting this project. It is a pleasure also to acknowledge the advice and assistance of Thomas Allsen, June Anderson, Lisa Balabanlılar, Nina Berman, Günhan Börekçi, Cynthia Brokaw, Carl Brown, Emma Bunker, Filiz Çağman, Zeynep Çelik, Wellington Chan, David Christian, Samuel Chu, Howard Crane, Stephen Dale, Walter Denny, Devin DeWeese, Nicola Di Cosmo, Ding Xueyun, Boğaç Ergene, Susan Ferber, Peter Golden, John Guilmartin, Aylin Güney, Andras Hamori, Şükrü Hanioğlu, Chang Hao, Jane Hathaway, Metin Heper, Asım Karaömerlioğlu, Adeeb Khalid, Ayşe Koçoğlu, Kong Qun, Bernard Lewis, Nathan Light, Heath Lowry, Lu Minghui, William McNeill, Ilber Ortaylı, Kenneth Pomeranz, Serdar Poyraz, Christopher Reed, Günsel Renda, Michael Rogers, Safa Saraçoğlu, Irvin Schick, Dona Straley, Ayfer Karakaya Stump, Talat Tekin, Mete Tunçay, Ufuk Ulutaş, Patrick Visel, Susan Whitfield, Eugene Whitmore, Vincent Wilhite, Charles Wilkins, Bin Wong, and Tsing Yuan. I am indebted most of all to my wife, Lucia Findley, for keeping our hearth fires steadily alight—to use a metaphor that will come up in the following chapters—while pursuing a full professional life of her own.

Scholars of Turkish lost their greatest colleague and gentlest friend when Andreas Tietze died in December 2003. This book is dedicated to his memory.

# CONTENTS

# ABBREVIATIONS USED IN THE NOTES

| | |
|---|---|
| *CHEIA* | Denis Sinor, ed., *The Cambridge History of Early Inner Asia* |
| *ESHOE* | Halil İnalcık and Donald Quataert, eds., *An Economic and Social History of the Ottoman Empire, 1300–1914* |
| EN | www.eurasianet.org |
| *EI2* | *Encyclopedia of Islam*, 2nd ed. |
| *HEO* | Robert Mantran, ed., *Histoire de l'Empire ottoman* |
| *HTPPP* | Hans Robert Roemer, ed., with the assistance of Wolfgang-Ekkehard Scharlipp, *History of the Turkic Peoples in the Pre-Islamic Period; Histoire des Peuples Turcs à l'Époque Pré-Islamique* |
| *İA* | *İslâm Ansiklopedisi*, 13 vols. |
| *IPMCC* | Bernard Lewis, ed. and trans., *Islam from the Prophet Muhammad to the Capture of Constantinople*, 2 vols. |
| *NYT* | *New York Times* |
| *TL* | Lars Johanson and Éva Á. Csató, eds., *The Turkic Languages* |
| *WSJ* | *Wall Street Journal* |

# NOTE ON USAGE

In a work for nonspecialist readers, simplicity and consistency seem like the best policy in representing names and terms from Turkic and other languages, even though there is no way to apply that policy without doing some injustice to the cultural and linguistic diversity of a large part of the world. As a result, the use of diacritical signs will be minimized. In the vocalization of terms and names from other languages, the Ottoman Empire will, in a manner of speaking, conquer all. The letter *q* as scholars use it in transliterating Turkic languages, Arabic, and Persian will become *k* (Kur'an instead of Qur'an; Kazak instead of Qazaq). In Mongolian names and terms, where some scholars use *q*, others use *kh*. This study will follow the latter usage: thus Khubilai Khan instead of Qubilai Qan.

In discussion of the late Ottoman Empire and Turkish Republic, the rendering of Turkish names and terms reflects modern Turkish usage, including the following features:

c, C   like *j* in English

ç, Ç   like *ch* in English

ğ      the "soft *g*." Depending on the adjoining letters, this is dropped, pronounced like *y* in English, or treated as lengthening the preceding vowel. Soft *g* does not appear at the beginning of words in Turkish. Thus, in loanwords from Arabic, whereas ğ is used to represent medial *gh* (the Arabic letter *ghayn*), initial *ghayn* becomes *g* in Turkish, whence Turkish *gazi* for Arabic *ghazi*.

ı, I    has no consistent orthographic representation in English. Spreading the lips as if to say "easy" and then trying to say "cushion" produces the Turkish word *kışın*, "in winter."

i, İ    like *i* in English "bit"

ö, Ö    like *ö* in German or *eu* in French *peur*

ş, Ş    like *sh* in English

ü, Ü    like *ü* in German or *u* in French

In the rendering of Chinese names and terms, the currently preferred Pinyin transliteration has been taken as the standard. Inasmuch as transliterations according to the formerly preferred Wade-Giles system are still widely encountered, an effort has been made, at the first appearance of each such name or term, to give both the Pinyin version and then in parentheses the Wade-Giles version. Chinese specialists do not need this; the point is to help everybody else.

# THE TURKS IN WORLD HISTORY

# INTRODUCTION

S ince the collapse of the Soviet Union, influential analysts have capti-
vated public opinion with prognostications of a future to be dominated
by a clash of civilizations. The clash, they say, will be fought out along "fault
lines" between civilizations. The West, consisting of western Europe and
North America, will be in the leading position, not only in terms of material power but also as the champion of universal values. The other civilizations have attempted to become modern without becoming Western, but
only Japan has thus far succeeded in doing so. Of the remaining civilizations, that of Islam is the largest competitor to the West. To the extent that
Muslims experience blockages or frustrations in their attempts to become
modern without becoming Western, we are told that one result is "conflict
along the fault line between Western and Islamic civilizations," where "conflict has been going on for 1,300 years." In such a perspective, to ask "what
went wrong?" in the history of Islamic civilization became a question for
expert analysis, in reflection not just on the terrorist attacks of 11 September 2001 but on centuries past.[1]

Despite their wide resonance among government leaders and the general public, such analyses need to be questioned on a number of grounds.
They imply a hardness of edge and an internal consistency that would enable civilizations to clash like tectonic plates, grinding against one another
at fault lines. The elision of difference between Western and universal values concedes no principled position to others for whom Western morals
and values, known worldwide less through statements of high principle than
through film and television, offer plentiful reasons for wanting to become
modern without becoming Western. If others criticize the West for double

3

standards in application of its high principles, moreover, the answer seems to be "Double standards in practice are the unavoidable price of universal standards in principle."[2]

The concept of civilization basic to the "clash" theory is also an old-fashioned, essentializing one that underestimates the extent to which each civilization, however much binds it together, is a site of contestation, difference, and inequality of access to its refinements. Diversity and contestation within civilizations consequently stand in the way of their clashing as coherent blocs, raising the likelihood that events like 11 September 2001 do not represent civilizations in any aggregate sense. Emphasizing the boundedness of civilizations impedes recognizing the extent to which people, ideas, goods, and contagions move across civilizational boundaries, with or without conflict, and the extent to which migration and hybridity contribute to the development not just of civilizations but also of a modernity that is increasingly a global (and not just Western) reality.[3] Failing to adapt to global modernity, or lashing out violently against its manifestations, is not peculiar to any one civilization, as examples of religiously and politically motivated extremist violence generated from within societies ranging from the United States and Japan to Israel and Palestine prove.[4] People throughout history have struggled to assert their identity. Today, they do this in the face of processes of globalization that can no longer be thought of solely as "made in the West" but rather as "universal" in the sense of being operative globally.

The subject of this book may appear remote from heated topical debates at the time of writing. Those are debates about civilizations, their clashes and competitions. This is a book about the Turks, a group of peoples definable by their languages and by certain shared elements of culture and history but otherwise astonishingly diverse among themselves. In their civilizational commitments, they have undergone profound conversions over time. In almost any period, one group of outsiders or another has not considered them particularly civilized at all. Such perceptions have to do largely with their historically nomadic lifestyle. In a sense, the Turks migrated among civilizations as they moved across Eurasia. Yet while doing so, they maintained their identity. They also proved that they could remain committed to a particular civilization over very lengthy periods and contribute greatly to its advancement. Although it started long before today's arguments about clashing civilizations, the two-thousand-year story of their expansion across Eurasia may shed a valuable light on the processes by which a large and diverse group of people established, transformed, and projected its identity across space and time. The fact that much of Turkic history unfolded on or near frontier zones between Islamic and European civilization may certainly throw light on the extent to which those zones have or have not been sites of millennial conflict.


## Of Buses, Caravans, and Carpets

I n talking about Turkish origins and identity from the vantage point of modern Turkey, I once suggested playfully to a Turkish friend that the whole phenomenon of Turkishness (*Türklük*) resembled a bus traveling across Asia from East to West.[5] The trip took a long time, and there were many stops. At each stop, people got on and off. They loaded and unloaded bags and bundles as they did so. Many of the travelers cared little about the beginning and ending points of the bus route. Many intended to go only short distances. The idea that what they shared with all the other passengers on the bus was more significant than their differences probably never crossed their minds. Occasionally, the bus broke down and had to be repaired with parts found along the way. By the time the bus reached Turkey, it was hard to know which, if any, of the passengers or parcels had been on board for the whole trip. The bus, too, was no longer the same as when it set out. Yet this was still the "Trans-Asian Turkish Bus."

My Turkish friend got a laugh out of the bus image and later repeated it to other friends. Further thought, however, made clear that the bus image is only a starting point. The contemporary Turkish Republic arguably has a history going back in time in three directions: the Anatolian heritage, extending back long before the Turks arrived there; the Islamic heritage, reaching back to seventh-century Arabia; and the Turkic or Turko-Mongol heritage, going back to the earliest Turks and their precursors in Inner Asia. The image of the bus evokes only the third of these. Moreover, the contemporary Turkish Republic is not the only vantage point from which to think about the history of the Turks. The bus route that led to modern Turkey was not the only one for the Turks. If we look at the historical trajectory of the Turkic peoples not from the vantage point of today's Turkey but from that of their historical starting points, we see not one route ending in the West but radiating routes beginning in eastern Inner Asia, interconnecting along the way, and ending at points all across Eurasia or even—since the 1960s—around the world. Nor surprisingly, this network approximates the trans-Asian trade routes of earlier centuries. Thinking of earlier centuries also suggests replacing the bus with other modes of travel: pastoralist migrations and merchant caravans. "[T]his world is like a wayside hostelry (*ribat*); the sons of Adam are like a caravan; some stop, some pass on," in the ponderous wisdom of Ebulgazi's heroic account of Oghuz Khan, forefather and Islamizer of the Oghuz Turks, whose descendants expanded and peopled the western Turkic world, from Turkmenistan to the Ottoman lands.[6]

To put it another way, the image of a bus traveling to Turkey facilitates discussion of what is *Turkish*—now conventional scholarly usage in English for the people, language, and culture of the Turkish Republic—but does not include all that is *Turkic*—the corresponding term applicable to all Turks everywhere, including the Turkish Republic. The image of caravans starting from Inner Asia facilitates discussion of everything Turkic. The Turkish-Turkic distinction does have a guilty history. Russian imperialists had political motives to draw a distinction between the Turks of the Russian and the Ottoman Empires. Scholarly usage later redrew the distinction to address the fact that there is a country called Turkey, but not all the Turks live there. Not surprisingly, modern Turkish, as spoken in Turkey, entered the post-Soviet period with no conventional way to distinguish "Turkish" and "Turkic." To make up for this, the term *Türki* has made something of a comeback in referring to the Eastern Turkic world. Some nationalists detest such distinctions among Turks; others do not want their distinctness smothered under encompassing labels.[7] The fact that all speakers of Turkic languages are Turks does mean that the terminological distinction can be difficult to sustain in practice. This study will use the two terms pragmatically, when making the distinction seems to add clarity, referring to the Turks of Turkey as "Turkish" and to all Turks everywhere as "Turkic."

More interesting than the bus or caravan are the travelers and their baggage. If we try to picture the baggage of the Turkic trans-Asian caravan, it is easy to see brightly woven textiles, both as the contents and as the outer wrappings of bags and bundles. Joseph Fletcher, a historian of Inner Asia, in fact developed a textile metaphor to discuss the history of that region in global context.[8] He pictured horizontal continuities—phenomena experienced simultaneously by societies that were not necessarily in communication with each other—as the weft, and vertical continuities—phenomena that survived through time—as the warp. To picture the working through this warp and weft of the interlinkages that tied the early modern world together, he used the image of "needlepoint," picturing cross-cultural phenomena like inter-regional religious or commercial networks as colored threads worked through the weave of horizontal and vertical continuities.

In talking about the Turkic peoples, the varied techniques for weaving and knotting kilims and carpets offer a more natural image, although embroideries were no doubt included in some of the bundles on the bus. In carpets and kilims, not only the warp and weft but also the designs woven or knotted over them belong to schools and traditions that can be traced across space and time and studied in detail. Carpet knots, for example, can be rendered as colored squares on a sheet of graph paper, which can then be given to a weaver to reproduce. Today, we would want to computerize such a graphic; manipulate the design, changing the color, scale, and relative prominence of different motifs; and put images of different types of carpets on a website. Those who wished could use it to compare carpets from different periods and collections, have distinctive elements of each design type pointed out to them, pursue links to other types of carpets or to explanatory information about the places or peoples among whom that type of carpet was produced, and electronically manipulate their favorite design types.

Long before computers and websites, some of the passengers on the Turkish bus—women with carpet weaving under their fingers, men with long experience in the trade—could see in their mind's eye some of the same continuities and mutations that such a website could reveal to the uninitiated. The thought of women weavers and men traders opens up questions about the Turks' social and economic history. The higher status of women in pastoral-nomadic, as compared to agrarian, societies has been noted throughout history. The fact that the women produced all the value-added products from the nomads' herds, from dairy products to textiles and carpets, probably had much to do with this.

As physical objects, too, carpets exemplify in microcosm important traits that are paralleled in the genesis of peoples, languages, and cultures. Art knows no borders, say the art historians: the carpet weaver's inspiration can come from many sources. However, she works with materials that set limits at all stages of the production process—shearing, spinning, dying, and weaving. If the weaver belongs to a nomadic people, her loom has to be one that can be taken apart for transport. Art may be boundless, but the same cannot be said for either the weaver's loom or her technique. She has to tie the vertical warp threads at the top and bottom of the loom before she can weave. With a loom that permits her to roll her work as she goes, she can make shorter or longer carpets on the same loom. After she finishes, she will cut the warp threads to make a fringe. She must also tie them to keep the carpet from unraveling at the ends. At the warp ends, then, carpets do have a certain unboundedness. In contrast, the side posts of the weaver's loom set limits that she can exceed only by weaving a carpet in two panels and stitching them together after both are completed. As she weaves, the return of her shuttle or spindle after each pass through the warp produces well-defined selvages that will not unravel easily.

Most likely, the weaver is weaving a carpet with multiple, repeated motifs—typically the geometrical, often octagonal configurations known in Turkish as *gül* ("flower"). So basic to the carpet tradition as to have defined what one expects to see in a Turkish rug, the *güls* are thought to have originated from the *tamgha*, or brand, that symbolized each Turkic tribe's identity. The carpets historically expressed the different Turkic tribal identities in the most literal sense.[9] As the weaver works her way up the carpet, she will not find it difficult to keep the width of her *güls* the same. However, she will find it hard to control their height. Carpets with some *gül* motifs shorter or longer than others, although equal in width, are countless, displaying what might happen when a woman's concentration lapsed or she let her inexperienced daughter take over for a while. When two carpets were woven to be stitched together lengthwise to form a wider rectangle, even an experienced weaver would have great difficulty producing two panels of exactly the same length in which all the *güls* matched their mates on the other panel. Human failing and fantasy worked together to give character and originality to each carpet.

Only under the supervised conditions of court workshops, or later under the more or less industrial conditions of production symbolized by the knot diagrams drawn on graph paper, could such limitations be overcome. No doubt, the weavers found working under those conditions much less fun. As in other art forms, the fascination of the carpet weaver's art springs from the necessity to express the tetherless soaring of her imagination through the discipline and material constraints of the medium. As collectors know, the imperfections of carpets are part of their fascination.

To the extent that the imperfections reflect the conditions of work in nomadic tents or village households, they also point to another reason that carpets, more than other art forms, preeminently symbolize Turkic identity. Most other art forms, among which calligraphy and the arts of the book historically predominated, depended heavily on palace patronage. Although it could be refined in palace workshops, carpet weaving was basically a folk art rooted in the socioeconomic realities of everyday life. As compared to other art forms, carpet weaving was much more likely to continue in periods of crisis and was much more adaptable to the way in which the Turkic peoples emerged and spread across the map.

If most Turkish carpets were made by anonymous women, who used the carpets? Turkish carpets have adorned palaces, as well as village houses and nomadic tents. People have prostrated themselves on carpets or otherwise used them in worship in mosques, synagogues, and churches. People have sat or lain on Turkish carpets to commit every sin imaginable. Visually spectacular, these versatile textiles are more than mere symbols of Turkic identity and history.

The story of the Turks in Eurasian history in many ways corresponds to these bus, caravan, and carpet images. By any means of conveyance, what united the Turkic peoples above all was the cultural baggage that they carried as they spread across Eurasia. This cultural complex was characterized by long-term continuity, as well as by great potential both to absorb exogenous elements and to transform itself. This was also a cultural complex characterized by dominant and secondary motifs that shifted, in different times and places, from background to foreground and later shifted again. However, they did so in a dialectical fashion that led, not back toward starting points that became irrecoverable with time, but forward toward reworkings of the design.

This book will look for continuities and distinctive designs in the history of the Turkic peoples. Chronologically, a comprehensive discussion of the Turks in world history requires considering the pre-Islamic Turks and their precursors (through the eleventh century C.E.); the entry of the Turks and the Mongols, with whom the Turks shared a great deal, into the Islamic world (eleventh to fourteenth centuries); the last great age of indigenous Asian empire building (fourteenth to eighteenth centuries); and finally the modern period. As this journey progressed through time, civilizations sometimes clashed; at other times they fused and metamorphosed. As noted, Turkic history contains both remarkably long continuities and great transformations. Two such transformations stand out as particularly significant: the Turks' entry first into Islam and then into modernity. The remainder of this introduction traces the natural and the sociocultural settings in which the Turks' history unfolded.

## Natural Ecology: The Terrain Where the Carpets Are Woven

Viewed from a satellite in space, the most striking terrain feature on earth is "the belt of desert that stretches, nearly unbroken, from northwest Africa to China."[10] This arid belt breaks down into a hotter, southward-lying zone to the west and a colder, northward-lying zone to the east. The hotter, southwestern region stretches from the Atlantic coasts of Morocco and Mauretania eastward to Iran, Pakistan, and northwestern India. Within the southerly zone, the term *Middle East* defines the region consisting of Southwest Asia and Egypt, with Turkey, Iran, and the Arabian peninsula at the other corners. The colder, northerly, eastern belt of desert lies in Inner Asia, spanning historical West Turkistan (now Turkmenistan, Uzbekistan, Tajikistan, Kazakhstan, and Kyrgyzstan), East Turkistan (China's Xinjiang province, the historic Uyghur country), and part of Mongolia. Toward the east, the northerly belt of aridity is also much more broken by mountain chains than is the southern, westerly one. The place where the two belts most nearly join, and where the topography permits easiest movement from one to the other, roughly coincides with present-day Turkmenistan.

Advancing southward from the African desert zone or northward from the Inner Asian one, similar bioclimatic progressions to zones of lesser aridity appear. In Africa, the progression moves southward from desert to a band of short grasses, to the savanna of grass and scrub, and to the tropical rainforest. In Inner Asia, the progression moves northward from the desert zone of Turkistan to the steppes (mostly short grasses but with some long-grass prairie), then to the boreal forest (*taiga* in Russian), and finally to the tundra, the opposite, Arctic extreme corresponding to the equatorial extreme of the tropical rainforest in Africa. Whereas the term *Central Asia* has long been used to refer to the historically Islamic zone of desert and steppe, the term *Inner Asia* may be used to refer to the entire region from Tibet to the Arctic Sea, spanning all these zones.[11] To take in more westerly historical sites in this northerly zone, such as the Crimea, it makes more sense at times to refer to Inner Eurasia.

In the northerly arid region, significantly, as we move to the north, the zones of diminishing aridity tend to become much wider in their extent from east to west than is the Central Asian desert. Whereas the desert extends from the Caspian Sea to China and Mongolia, the steppe zone of short grasses immediately to its north extends as far west as the Wallachian plain and far enough to the east to wrap a southward-reaching arm around the eastern end of the desert zone. The eastern end of the Inner Asian steppe, what is now Mongolia and environs, provided the stage for the earliest documented Turkic history.[12] At the northern edge of the steppes, patches of long-grass prairie, although thinner in north-south extent than the short-grass steppe and discontinuous from east to west, extend from the Hungarian plain in the West to Manchuria in the East. The nearly continuous cover of grasses made the steppes historically into the zone of choice for *pastoral nomadism*, a mobile way of life based on animal husbandry and on seasonal migration by families with their flocks from pasture to pasture in an annual cycle.[13] Upon reaching the Mongol-ruled steppes north of the Black Sea, Ibn Battuta, the fourteenth-century Moroccan traveler, was surprised to see both wheeled wagons and grasslands luxuriant enough that "no one . . . gives forage to his beast." Wheeled vehicles had virtually disappeared in the Arab lands because of the camel's efficiency as a beast of burden, but they never disappeared from the steppes.[14] Later, the richness of the steppe soils would prove irresistibly tempting to Slavic farming populations, a fact reflected in the very name of the Ukraine (from Slavic *ukraina*, "frontier"). The steppes' gentle relief made them easy to traverse, and the scarcity of navigable rivers—either because those in the most arid regions never reach the ocean

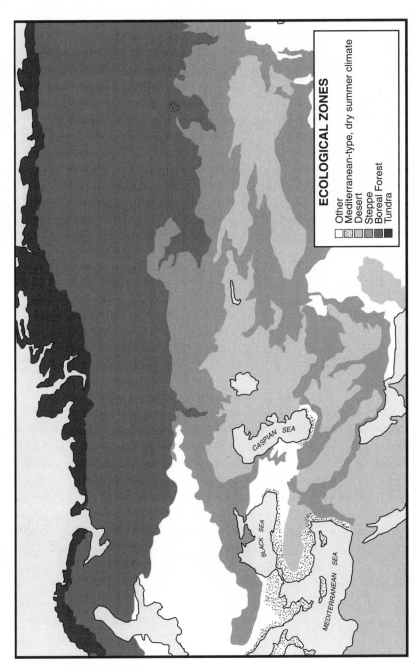

**Map of Major Eurasian Ecological Zones.** The map shows Eurasian ecological zones important for the history of the Turkic peoples. Map by Ron McLean, Digital Media Creation Services, Ohio State University.

**ECOLOGICAL ZONES**

- Other
- Mediterranean-type, dry summer climate
- Desert
- Steppe
- Boreal Forest
- Tundra

CASPIAN SEA

BLACK SEA

MEDITERRANEAN SEA

**Nomadic Camp Scene.** At lower right a traveler unpacks while conversing with a squatting figure. Two famished-looking dogs play, while two horses graze. Above, the traveler's weapons appear stacked, a man blows on a fire, and two other figures appear to wash clothes. This anonymous painting, possibly produced somewhere between Herat and Tabriz, fifteenth or sixteenth century, invites comparison with those attributed to the so-called Ustad Mehmed Siyah Kalem (Master Mehmed the Black Pen, or the Draftsman; compare figures on pages 31, 36, and 63). From Topkapı Palace Museum, Hazine 2153, f. 8b.

or because many further north flow toward the Arctic Ocean—made movement by land a necessity in most places. The boreal forest, source of the furs historically coveted in Eurasian trade, stretches furthest of any of the northern zones, 10,000 kilometers from Norway to the Pacific.

In addition to its north-south zonal differentiation, the northern arid zone also displays significant variations from east to west. Both winter cold and aridity increase toward the east. One reason for the temperature difference is that the Mongolian steppes, at 1,500 meters above sea level or more on average, are higher than the Turkic steppes to the west, which are near sea level.[15] The east-west difference in aridity gains in significance from the climatological law that the *amount* of annual precipitation and its *variability* bear an inverse relationship to each other.[16] Sharp variations in the amount of moisture also lead to frequent shifts in boundaries between zones. One of the most important east-west differentials is the predominance of the east as a site of nomadic state formation. In addition to ecological factors, this seems to be true because Mongolia, while open to the north, confronted

China to the south, with its highly developed and populous agrarian society. Elsewhere along the arid zone, agrarian society was limited to "island" oases in a sea of aridity. The societies and economies of China and the steppe lands interacted in significant ways, but normally, Mongolia's only outlet for expansion was the Jungarian (Zungharian) corridor, which extended westward between the Tienshan and Altai mountains. High pressures could be built up on the Mongolian steppe, and consequently Mongolia became the classic site for Inner Asian state formation. However, although it was possible to form a state on the Mongolian steppe, even aggressive mobilization of the caravan trade scarcely made it possible to maintain a state there. This left little choice other than expansion and conquest to the west.[17] To the west, the sprawl of the steppes and the absence of large-scale agrarian societies created an opposite set of conditions, at least until the sixteenth century, when Russian expansion began.

If the endless capacity of the "barbarian" world to produce one invading "horde" after another convinced the Romans that there was a "people hatchery" or "workshop of peoples" (*officina gentium*) out there somewhere,

**Turkic Nomad Family on the Steppe, 1905–15.** Photographed by Sergei Mikahilovich Prokudin-Gorskii, probably on the Kazakh steppe. From Library of Congress, Prokudin-Gorskii Collection, LC-DIG-prok-01854.

then the land that ended up being known as Mongolia was most deserving of those names.[18] However, it only became the Mongol homeland around 1000–1200 C.E. Before that, what is now Mongolia was a Turkic homeland and the site of the earliest Turkic empires (552–840). For the steppe world as a whole, "the elongated steppe zones, the isolated oases, and the major mountain passes and corridors of Inner Asia have been the overland equiva- lents of ocean routes, ports-of-call, and canals," the site of countless journeys, in all directions, rivaling in length the maritime ventures of the European age of exploration.[19]

The most legendary of routes crossing this landscape is the so-called Silk Road, a term invented in the nineteenth century. In reality, it was not a single route but a network of them, generally oriented east and west but with branches in all directions—toward India, Iran, or northern Eurasia.[20] Between China and Samarkand in Central Asia, the traveler had a choice between a route that went north of the Tienshan mountains through Jungaria, or south of them through the Tarim basin and its city-states. From Samarkand, the most important crossroads, there was a choice of routes in all direc- tions, including westerly or southwesterly routes leading toward Anatolia and Syria. The distance from China's Gansu (Kan-su) province to the Black Sea was 7,000 kilometers; some destinations were even farther. At the slow pace of a camel caravan, the trade routes were more like relay routes, with few travelers covering the whole distance. When they did, their experiences seemed incredible to their fellows at home, as in the case of Marco Polo, the thirteenth-century Venetian. Although silk may have been the most prized good, Chinese porcelain, Siberian furs, Baltic amber, pharmaceuti- cals, and slaves were always traded over these routes. Not only trade routes, they also transmitted ideas and faiths. Until the sixteenth century, the Silk Route network remained the world's most important system of communi- cation and exchange. For a thousand years it was controlled primarily by the Turks and Mongols.

One of the places to which the western end of the Silk Road led was Anatolia, the Asian part of today's Turkish Republic. In terms of vegetation and temperature, Anatolia resembles a western extension of the northern arid zone's steppes and grasslands, with the valuable addition of well-watered, highly productive, coastal agricultural regions. However, this Anatolian extension is cut off from the rest of the northern arid zone by mountains and seas. It is cut off, that is, except for people who have migrated from Inner Asia into Iran. To a people habituated to life in the northern arid zone who had ventured into Iran, Anatolia must have offered an enticing vista.[21] As a matter of historical fact, centuries passed after the rise of Islam and the early Islamic conquests before Anatolia was opened to Muslim settlement

**Textile Merchant in his Shop, Samarkand, 1905–15.** A study in reds, the color version of this photograph shows that the textiles are richly colored and elaborately patterned. The merchant embodies the modern importance of the textile trade in one of the major centers of the historic Silk Routes. From Library of Congress, Prokudin-Gorskii Collection, LC-DIG-prok-01725.

and expansion. When this occurred, in the aftermath of the Battle of Manzikert, or Malazgird (1071), the conquerors were no longer the predominantly Arab forces of the early Islamic conquests, from the hot, southerly part of the arid zone, but rather Turks whose recent conversion to Islam had opened the gates of the Middle East to their in-migration. Anatolia became the place, then, where the Turks interwove their Inner Asian nomadic heritage, their Islamic heritage, and the ancient Mediterranean heritage of agrarian civilization.

Only a few short, foolish steps lie between describing these environments and advancing environmentally determinist arguments about them. Yet environmental factors and human responses to them clearly help to create the vertical and horizontal continuities in the fabric of history and, at times, to rend the fabric. Perhaps the oldest conflict in history is that between steppe and sown, between agrarian societies and those, necessarily reliant on pastoralism, in zones too arid for agriculture. The Chinese, for example, found it difficult to sustain military campaigns in the steppe region.[22] The nomads could conquer an agrarian society but could not rule it without adapting to its culture. Another salient feature of the arid zone is that particular peoples are closely associated with its southern and northern parts. The southern part has been particularly associated with the Semitic peoples and cultures, including the three genetically related monotheistic religions that emerged in Palestine and Arabia. From the seventh century C.E. on, with the prestige of Islam behind it, Arabic expanded remarkably, at the expense of other languages.[23] In contrast, the northern arid zone, dominated in ancient times by Indo-Iranian peoples, increasingly became the land of the Turks (*Turkistan*) from the sixth century C.E. onward. There, while Turko-Iranian symbiosis persisted, it was the Turkic languages that "over the last two millennia have been steadily advancing." Where different populations came into contact, "Turkic speech has usually prevailed," with the result that "linguistic assimilation has been a crucial element in the ethnogenesis of the Turkic peoples."[24] Of the three monotheistic religions, Judaism and Christianity have very different histories, but Islam historically spread in the arid zone, ultimately including its northerly and its southerly bands, as well as extensions into other regions. Environmental factors did not predetermine these outcomes, but they defined the terrain on which they occurred and on which the fabric of Turkic history has been woven.

## Sociocultural Ecology: The People Who Wove the Carpets

S ome of the travelers on the trans-Eurasian Turkic bus or caravan in earlier times would not necessarily have thought that they belonged to the same category of people. This raises questions of unity and diversity among the Turkic peoples, offering fascinating insights into how fluid categories such as culture and ethnicity can be and how unobtrusively people can slip across civilizational "fault lines," spanned by networks like the Silk Routes. In recent years, the Turks, like peoples everywhere, have become increasingly determined to define and assert their identity. The result is a heightened sense, for some, of what is shared and, for others, of what differs.[25]

Linguists insist that the unity of the Turkic peoples is most apparent in language. Some scholars go so far as to say that no factor unites all Turks but language.[26] Although the often-mentioned genetic connections between

Turkic languages and a larger Altaic family including Mongolian and Tungusic are controversial, the resemblance among the Turkic languages is unmistakable. They have differentiated to a point where not all Turkic languages are mutually intelligible; yet they still resemble each other more closely than do Indo-European languages. Resemblances across time, between the earliest written Turkic and the modern languages, are conspicuous. Spoken mostly in Inner Asia, the Turkic languages divided in the course of their historical evolution into several groups, three of which have large numbers of speakers. One of these large linguistic groups is the southeastern one, found in Central Asia astride the Chinese border, including Uyghur and Uzbek. The northwestern group is another large one, including languages spoken from the Crimea to the Volga-Ural region and the Kazakh steppe, such as Crimean Tatar, Kazan Tatar, Bashkir, Kazakh, and Kirghiz. The southwestern language group, that of the Turkic influx into the Middle East, includes Türkmen, Azeri, and Turkish. All these groups include other languages spoken by small numbers of speakers. A fourth regional grouping, the northeastern, consists entirely of languages spoken by small Siberian peoples, the most numerous being the Sakha, commonly known via Russian as Yakuts. Two final groups consist of isolated languages with archaic features: Chuvash in Russia, and Khalaj in Iran.

Although it is not a total exaggeration to say that language is the only thing that unites all Turkic peoples, other important commonalities apply to the vast majority. Linguists' efforts to deduce what the original, undifferentiated "proto-Turkic" language must have been like lead to the conclusion that it was spoken in western and central Siberia and to the south, roughly between 3000 and 500 B.C.E.[27] The few words so widely found among Turkic languages as to imply that they go back to proto-Turkic indicate that the earliest Turks knew about ironworking, agriculture, and some aspects of horticulture; lived in tents and practiced animal husbandry; were organized in clans and tribes; had religious specialists of the type known as shamans; and had a decimally organized numeral system. None of these features is uniquely Turkic, but all of them are of lasting importance among Turks. In historical times, another common trait that stands out, even as Turkic peoples became differentiated, is the wide-ranging resemblances among their orally transmitted folk literatures. The heroic epics differ in the presence or absence of Islamic themes; yet Islamization is never complete. Elements from the pre-Islamic past persist in a jumble that the epics' original audiences perhaps did not even recognize as such.[28]

Not surprisingly, pan-Turkic nationalists have found much more in common among Turks than have linguists. Some of their insights are memorable. Yusuf Akçura (1876–1935) drew a connection between the heritage of the Turks as warlike nomads and their attachment to their language and customs, rather than to any specific territory.[29] Among these customs he listed patriarchy; the holding of land in common; the attribution to the *khan*, or leader of the community, of very great power but also the limitation of that power by law (*yasak*, *töre*); the existence of an aristocracy; the tendency to form states; and extreme tolerance in religion. If studied exhausitively, Turkic societies show variations around these norms. For example, Turkic nomads often did not want to be ruled by states, whereas the Ottoman sultans formed elites to serve them but resisted the rise of any aristocracy independent of their control. Still, Akçura not only sums up persistent traits but also offers insights into why movables (language and culture) more than immovables (territories) shaped the identity of these historically nomadic people.

Appreciation of how much diversity outweighs uniformity among the Turks only requires looking beyond the largest and best-known Turkic peoples.[30] It is when the small peoples from the Turkic peripheries are taken into account that language seems like the only common thread. Even in religion, not all Turks are Muslims. Not only was there a time when none of them were, but also some have never been. Historically, Turkic non-Muslims have included Orthodox Christians (the Gagauz of the Danubian delta, the Chuvash of the Volga region, and the Yakuts and smaller peoples in Siberia), Buddhists (the Tuvans of Siberia or the Yellow Uyghurs of Gansu Province, China), and a few Jews (the Karaim of eastern Europe). The traditional Inner Asian cults, commonly referred to as shamanism, survive in many places, often submerged in other religions. In post-Soviet Siberia, 300 years after their forced conversion, the Yakuts and others have completely rejected Orthodox Christianity in favor of a revived shamanism.[31]

Moreover, Turks do not all physically look alike. They never did. The Turks of Turkey are famous for their range of physical types. Given the Turks' ancient Inner Asian origins, it is easy to imagine that they once presented a uniform Mongoloid appearance. Such traits seem to be more characteristic in the eastern Turkic world; however, uniformity of type can never have prevailed there either. Archeological evidence indicates that Indo-Europeans, or certainly Europoid physical types, inhabited the oases of the Tarim basin and even parts of Mongolia in ancient times. In the Tarim basin, persistence of these former inhabitants' genes among the modern Uyghurs is both observable and scientifically demonstrable.[32] Early Chinese sources describe the Kirghiz as blue-eyed and blond or red-haired. The genesis of Turkic ethnic groups from earliest times occurred in confederations of diverse peoples. As if to prove the point, the earliest surviving texts in Turkic languages are studded with terms from other languages.

Although the nomadic lifestyle is typical for peoples of desert and steppe, Turks have also differed historically in their modes of adapting to their natural environment. The interests of livestock herders and farmers conflict in many respects, but their modes of production have historically complemented each other in others. However, any assumption that Turks were exclusively pastoral nomads, living from animal husbandry, and that they did not engage in agriculture, handicrafts, and trade would be overstated even for prehistoric times, to judge from the vocabulary of proto-Turkic. The proportion of Turks leading sedentary as opposed to migratory lifestyles no doubt grew over time. In Inner Asia, the Uzbeks and the Uyghurs have been sedentary for centuries, while the Kazakhs, Turks of southern Siberia, and Yakuts further east preserve nomadic traits most fully. In the Middle East, pastoral nomadism, agriculture, and urban life coexisted for thousands of years before Turks migrated into the region. Since about the fifteenth century, not only has sedentarization increased, but so has detribalization, the result being that significant numbers of Turks began to live not as members of a specific clan or tribe but as generic Tatars in the Volga region or generic Turks in the Middle East. For such people, a return to nomadic life would be impossible. Detribalization in some places, alongside numerical expansion of tribes in others, marked the varied trails by which different Turkic peoples later made their way into modernity.

Although the Turkic peoples are famous as empire builders, here again the diversity among them could not be wider. Turks often created or served major empires. Yet Turks living as pastoral nomads commonly preferred a stateless or politically decentralized existence and tended to resist state domination for all they were worth, as nomads commonly have done. Scholars often approach this seeming paradox by looking for factors, both internal to the nomadic society or external, that caused or facilitated empire building in specific cases. Instead of thinking in terms of the presence or absence of states, it may make more sense to see here two alternate modes of politics, which defined key questions and sought to answer them on two different scales. In the micropolitics of tribal life, the khan and elders of the kin group would make the decisions about migration, grazing grounds, marriage or other relationships, dispute resolution, and defense or attack against outsiders. In the macropolitics of state formation, historically, some combination of need and opportunity precipitated the formation of a larger entity, in most basic form a tribal confederation, in which a dominant leader would emerge over the khans. To consolidate his power, these dominant rulers had to develop additional institutions. The earliest to appear clearly in historical sources was the ruler's retinue or bodyguard, recruited and trained in a way designed to separate the retainers from their own tribes and make them loyal only to their ruler. Micropolitical decentralization and macropolitical empire building are each as characteristic of Turkic history as the other, even if historians and nationalists like Yusuf Akçura usually find the empires more interesting.

Over the centuries, then, not all the travelers on the trans-Eurasian caravan and bus routes were Turks, and those who were did not necessarily realize that they had much in common. Where social organization is visualized in terms of kinship, whether the kinship is literal or figurative, the meaningful "we" is characteristically the kin group itself, and wider groups that might be imagined in terms of language or religion tended historically to be seen as "they." In Inner Asia, too, nomads might dismiss the sedentary folk as peddlers or traders; the term *sart*, which originally meant "caravan leader" and later became a pejorative term for "trader," would make the point. The townsman might shoot back at the nomad with *kazak*, pejoratively implying not just "nomad" but also "vagabond" or even "thief." An Uzbek might travel next to a Kazakh or a Turkmen but not want his daughter to marry one.[33] In the Ottoman Empire, those well versed in the Ottoman court culture reserved the word "Turk" for boorish peasants. Holy men, perhaps not all Muslim, would accompany the travelers. Among the Muslims, differences of sect (both Sunnis and Shi'is) or of affiliations with the Islamic mystical orders would create a variegated picture. Differences of language and dialect would lead at times to miscommunication but probably also reinforce a sense of commonality. Yet the most learned or the most widely experienced travelers in the caravan might have inklings of the modern linguists' inclusive view of what held so many people together. Today, amid grandiose scenarios of civilizations clashing at fault lines that supposedly divide them, the journey of the Turkic peoples may have important lessons to teach about how such a large human collectivity was formed, has made its way in world history, and actually has crossed major civilizational thresholds, transforming itself without ever losing its identity.

# ONE

# The Pre-Islamic Turks and Their Precursors

## Before There Were Turkish Carpets: Prehistory of the Turks

The origins of the Turkic peoples are not well documented. Yet the Turks or their precursors already had a greater-than-regional role in Eurasian history before their name appears in historical sources. Their Inner Asian homeland also felt the impact of major historical currents originating outside it. Manifold illustrations of these points emerge from the prehistory of the Turks and from what is known about the social, economic, and political forms of the societies that preceded them. Although linguists hypothesize that proto-Turkic, of which no direct evidence survives, was spoken as early as 3000–500 B.C.E., the Turks did not indisputably appear in history until the sixth century C.E., when Chinese sources mention a people in Mongolia and southern Siberia called the Tujue (T'u-chüe), whom modern scholars identify as Turks.[1]

Peoples sharing at least some of the same traits had appeared in historical sources by the third century B.C.E. The best known of these are the Xiongnu (Hsiung-nu), as they are known in Chinese sources. The Xiongnu have been widely, although not universally, regarded as precursors of the Turkic and Mongol peoples, even if they are not well enough documented to permit firm proof of connections in language and ethnicity.[2] The Xiongnu were heirs, in turn, to a tradition of steppe life formulated in the first millennium B.C.E. among other steppe peoples whose ethnolinguistic identity was predominantly Indo-European. The most notable of these were the Scythians, as the Greeks called them (Sakas to the Iranians), who developed adaptations to the steppe environment that endured for 2,000 years. The

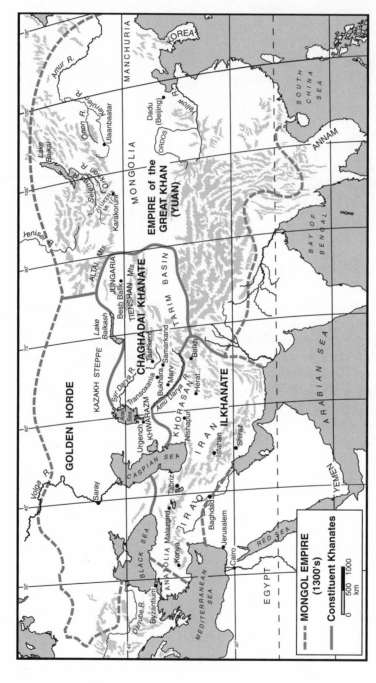

Map of The Early Turkic World. The map identifies sites mentioned in chapters 1 and 2, with the approximate outer limits of the Mongol Empire and its constituent khanates (as of about 1300). Then and earlier, states did not have precisely defined borders. Map by Ron McLean, Digital Media Creation Services, Ohio State University.

Sakas' adaptations to life in the steppes had roots, in turn, in prehistoric times. To account for the rise of the Turkic peoples and cultures thus requires thinking in terms of the following periodization: the prehistory of Inner Asia, the Scythian florescence of the first millennium B.C.E., that of the Xiongnu at the beginning of the common era, and finally the Turkic peoples prior to their conversion to Islam.


## Prehistory of Inner Asia

Although even earlier periods left important legacies, including the earliest human migrations into the region and probably also their shamanic cults, specific innovations of the *neolithic* or "new stone age" (roughly eighth to third millennia B.C.E.) opened new possibilities for the peoples of the Inner Asian arid zone to adapt to their environment.[3] In world history generally, the neolithic period is noted for the rise of agriculture, which in turn made possible rapid growth in population and the rise of civilization. Archeological evidence shows that agriculture began to spread into Inner Eurasia in this period, for example, along the southern border of modern Turkmenistan around 7000 B.C.E. The aridity of the region restricted agriculture to Inner Asia's oases and river valleys. Yet the agricultural potential of Inner Asia has always been significant. Over long centuries, the region produced wheat and rice and was famed for its fruits—apples, peaches, pomegranates, apricots, cherries, melons, and grapes (and wine).[4] The ability of Inner Asia's agricultural zones to produce a surplus supported the rise of towns and cities as early as the third millennium B.C.E. Over time, these became centers of trade and handicrafts, and a "distinctive oasis culture" developed.[5] The Inner Asian landscape did not consist only of steppe and desert, the people were not ignorant of agriculture, and the oft-cited "trading and raiding" were not the only way for steppe peoples to obtain agricultural products, although those activities did figure prominently in their history.

By the fourth millennium B.C.E., however, lifeways based on the domestication of animals, rather than plants, had begun to prove more widely adaptable than agriculture in a region where aridity was the norm. The enduring "contrast between pastoralist Inner Asia and agricultural Outer Eurasia" was beginning to emerge.[6] Cattle, sheep, and goats had been domesticated by 6000 B.C.E. Although these animals, especially sheep, were most significant for making the arid zones economically productive, a second wave of innovation in the steppes had greater significance for mobility and warfare. Horseback riding, selective horse breeding, and the wheel all appear to have been developed between 4000 and 2000 B.C.E. in the

steppes between the present-day Ukraine and the Russian-Kazakh border, subsequently spreading from there. The two-humped Bactrian camels of Central Asia were also domesticated in the third millennium B.C.E.;
so, further south, were the one-humped dromedaries of Arabia.[7] Developing techniques to take advantage of the milk, wool, and traction power
of the animals increased the versatility of the region's peoples, enabling
them to expand as pastoral nomads into zones too arid for agriculture. As
they developed the military potentials of a form of pastoralism dominated
by the horse, the nomads of Inner Asia also perfected "the most mobile
and militaristic of all major forms of pastoralism."[8]

The neolithic equestrian culture of the steppes spread far and wide, more
or less in association with speakers of Aryan or Indo-Iranian languages. The
fact that both Iranians and Indians called themselves Aryans implies that "they
once were an undivided people living together on the steppes of south Russia
and Siberia before moving south."[9] The first prehistoric culture to extend
all across the steppe from the Urals to western China was the Andronovo
culture, successor to the Indo-Aryan Sintashta-Petrovka culture (2100–
1700 B.C.E.).[10] Burials found in the Tarim basin, radiocarbon datable to 2000–
400 B.C.E. and containing well-preserved, desiccated corpses with distinctly
Caucasian features, imply that Indo-Europeans then inhabited that region,
now part of China's Xinjiang province. Moreover, the graves contain plaid
textiles of a characteristically northern European type and long, black,
brimmed "witch" or "wizard" hats of a type identified with early Iranians.
These people appear to be the ancestors of the Tokharians, who later inhabited the region and left behind manuscripts in an Indo-European language with traits resembling those of languages like Celtic and Germanic
from the far western end of the Indo-European world. The Turkic "bus"
was not the first of its kind to traverse Eurasia, nor were carpets the only
noteworthy textiles transported in the baggage. The spread of the Indo-
Iranian peoples in prehistoric times "can be compared with the later expansion of the Turkish peoples," the cardinal difference being that the Turkic
expansion "can be seen in the full light of history."[11]

The peoples of the steppes enter history in the first millennium B.C.E.,
when written sources produced in other cultures, including Herodotus'
*Histories*, began to describe them. They are identified particularly with tribes
known to Greeks as Scythian and to Iranians as Saka. An extremely widespread culture—from the Danube to Mongolia and southward into Iran—
and a new political and military configuration characterized this florescence
of the warlike steppe peoples.[12] Although the causes of its emergence—
climatic, demographic, or technological—are debated, essential elements of
this "Scythic" cultural complex are clear from historical and archeological

evidence.[13] Whereas the Sakas, or at least their leadership, were Indo-Iranian, the same culture spread eastward, both among the Altaic peoples from whom Turks and Mongols would emerge and into northern China.

This cultural complex is often identified with the "Scythian triad" of goods found in burial mounds: weapons of bronze and iron, horse gear, and art featuring animal motifs, although archeological evidence now shows that important parts of this complex predated the Scythians.[14] Much of the art that has survived is in metals, including bronze, iron, and gold; indeed, "all the steppe peoples displayed a proficiency in metal-working."[15] In addition to the "triad," this cultural complex also included other elements. The Scythians already lived in domed, felt-covered tents, but they had not yet developed the collapsible ones later used by Turks and Mongols and consequently had to transport their dwellings on wagons. In a practice suggestive of the water taboo later observed by the Mongols, Saka men "never let water near their bodies at all" but relied for cleanliness or ritual purification on steam baths, made by placing hot stones inside a tent and throwing water and hemp seeds onto them to create an intoxicating steam; the women made a paste of pounded aromatics and water, applied it, and took it off the next day, "becoming shining clean."[16] Like the Sakas' "animal art" and their avoidance of water, their religious practices, including a cult of ancestor gods, are evocative of the forms of spirituality common to this region and often misleadingly grouped together as "shamanism." The development of distinguishable regional styles makes clear that animal art was not an undifferentiated category and so proves that this cultural legacy evolved as it spread.[17]

Their textiles offer significant evidence on the Sakas' artistic and technological development. Their domed, felt tents show that they knew how to make felt, an unwoven fabric produced by matting fiber; among later steppe peoples, the Mongols also practiced felt making but not weaving. The ancient animal art includes appliqué images and three-dimensional animal figures in felt. Excavation of a burial mound at Pazyryk in the Altai range in Siberia in 1949 revealed evidence of a culture of Scythian type frozen in the permafrost. The most remarkable find was an elaborate woven carpet, nearly two meters square and thought to have been produced around 383–32 B.C.E. in the transitional zone between Iran and Central Asia (today's Turkmenistan). Showing that art has no borders, the design of the carpet features motifs common in Iran and Central Asia. Among other reasons for believing that the carpet was woven far from where it was found, panels depicting horses and riders show blankets on the horses' backs but no saddles: the Pazyryk people already used saddles, unlike peoples further west. The carpet was woven with a type of knot that is now considered distinctively

Turkish and is called the Gördes knot, after a town in Turkey. Comparison with other ancient carpet fragments shows that differences in weaving techniques had already developed and spread widely in Eurasia 2,500 years ago. Whatever the exact origin of the Pazyryk carpet, it is "perhaps not as important as the fact that the pile carpet technique developed so early and spread so rapidly throughout the nomadic civilizations of the Steppe Corridor, reaching a very high level of sophistication comparable to the greatest masterpieces of more recent times."[18] Otherwise, the near total lack of surviving carpets, from this time until about the thirteenth century C.E., means that all references to carpet making as a metaphor for the elaboration of Turkic identities during the intervening centuries are indeed symbolic.[19]

Critical in defining the steppe culture of Saka times were new developments that increased the military effectiveness of the man on horseback. The compound bow, made of wood, horn, and sinew and shaped in a complex curve that reduced its height while increasing its draw length, made it possible to shoot powerfully and accurately from horseback, so enabling mounted archers to dominate the steppes and extend beyond them. As nomadic warriors, they made use of the small, tough Przhevalski horses, which are able to survive on the steppes, in contrast to the large horses that could transport a man in armor but could not survive year-round on the steppes without being stabled and fed. Scythian material culture also included a specific type of short sword or dagger, along with the complex horse harness, vessels and weapons of bronze and iron, and animal art.

As in other aspects of their culture, the Scythians set precedents for later steppe societies in war and politics. Prowess in war was the key to prestige. Although there is evidence of differentiation of gender roles, women performed male tasks, including fighting, when needed. Burials of women often included full sets of weapons. Herodotus relates that Scythian men drank the blood of the first enemy they slew, took scalps, brought severed heads to their commanders, and gained a share of the loot by doing so.[20] Scythian military tactics, combining mobility, skill in mounted archery, and deceptive maneuvers such as ambushes and feigned retreats, set standards that remained the key to victory on the steppes until the advent of effective gunpowder weapons. Mounted archers were famous for their skill in rotating in their saddles, at full gallop, and firing an arrow to the rear with deadly accuracy. Later centuries would identify this skill with Turks and Mongols, but its historic origins among Indo-Iranian peoples are implied in the phrase "Parthian shot." Now that the Parthians, ancient Iranian inhabitants of today's Turkmenistan, are long forgotten, the term is more often heard as "parting shot." While some use of armor and heavy cavalry occurred in Saka times, the development of bows that could pierce early forms of armor, and the dependence of heavy cavalry on large horses that had to be stall-fed and stabled during the winter, left the advantage with the archers mounted on the tough little horses of the steppes.

Although the steppe empire had not yet emerged as a form of political organization, evidence on the Scythians indicates that some of the practices and ideas that could make it possible to weld a tribally organized, warlike, nomadic society into a large confederation did appear in this period.[21] The concept of charismatic ruling clans, whom Herodotus calls the Royal Scythians, was already present. The vast scale of elite burials indicates that steep social stratification accompanied the concept.

In the Scythian period, Indo-Europeans still dominated the steppes, and their culture had spread more widely still, turning into a common cultural inheritance for later rulers of the steppes, whatever their ethnolinguistic origins. Here lies the relevance of a Latin expression often applied to the succession of nomadic powers on the steppes: *translatio imperii*, "transfer of command." Tools and techniques for mastering the steppes were there for whoever was powerful enough at a given time to take advantage of them, a fact resulting in long continuities, punctuated by abrupt ruptures.

At the same time, interactions with nonnomadic peoples also profoundly affected the steppes. Zoroaster, or Zarathustra as he is known in the sacred texts of the religion he founded, probably lived in the eastern part of the Iranian world (today's Afghanistan, Tajikistan, and Uzbekistan) around 1000 B.C.E. Rejecting the old cults, he proclaimed the worship of one "wise lord," Ahura Mazda. Zoroastrianism became the official religion of the Sassanians, the last pre-Islamic dynasty of Iran, and was widely followed in Central Asia.[22] Earlier, the Achaemenian Empire of Iran attempted to establish suzerainty in Central Asia, introducing into the region coinage, a postal relay system for official communications, and the Aramaic script, which was destined for long use among the languages of the region. In the 320s B.C.E., Alexander of Macedon also campaigned into Central Asia, with such results as the introduction of Greek settlers, the founding of new cities and states, and extensive influence of Greek language, culture, and art, especially in Bactria (roughly, modern Tajikistan), where a Greco-Bactrian state lasted into the mid-second century B.C.E. Probably woven in the borderlands between Iran and Central Asia about the time of Alexander's campaigns, the Pazyryk carpet proves that carpets were already woven and exchanged across vast distances.[23]

Until the first century C.E., then, Central Asia was still predominantly inhabited by Indo-Europeans. As yet uninterrupted by the spread of other languages and peoples into the region, Indo-Europeans prevailed more or less continuously from India and Iran to Europe. Archeological analysis of skeletal remains and artifacts from what later became Mongolia shows, however, that already by the second millennium B.C.E. two worlds coexisted and mingled there and that Mongoloid types had begun to expand westward. As peoples of eastern Inner Asia, including Turks, continued expanding westward, epochal "transfers of command" would occur. In the process, much of the old would be absorbed and retained, culturally and even genetically, and symbiotic relationships would develop with descendants of the former masters of the steppes. Whatever clashes of civilizations occurred as the steppe world became Turkistan, this symbiosis quickly became proverbial. An eleventh-century Central Asian work on Turkic languages quotes a proverb that states the Turkish-Iranian symbiosis with a suitable "hat" image: "just as a hat cannot be without a head, a Turk cannot be without a Tat (Iranian)."[24] Before the Turks, however, the next stage in the ethnocultural transformation of the steppe was dominated by their precursors, the Xiongnu.

## The Xiongnu

The Xiongnu are important particularly because they created the first empire on the steppes. Their precedent-setting example of the shift from the micropolitics of decentralized tribal life to the macropolitics of empire defined the model on which their Turko-Mongol successors built. By the late fourth century B.C.E., Chinese chroniclers' attention began to be taken up in a sustained way by Inner Asian nomads on their northwestern borders. In an apparent paradox, the disunited China of the Warring States period (480–221 B.C.E.) was able to cope with these people without great difficulty, whereas after unification (221 B.C.E.), the Han dynasty (202 B.C.E.– 9 C.E.) could not defend its borders effectively and had to accept humiliating treaties. The explanation of the seeming anomaly, it has been argued, is that China's unification was preceded by aggressive Chinese expansion into the northern frontier region. One part of this expansion was the building of northern walls, of which the first emperor, Qin Shihuangdi (Ch'in Shihhuang-ti), unified the northern set and demolished those further south. Another aggressive move was the controversial decision of the state of Chao to adopt cavalry in 307 B.C.E.: "I changed our garments to those of the mounted archers to guard our borders"—better garments for riding and shooting.[25] In this perspective, China's wall-building appears not as a defensive policy but as an aggressive, expansionist one.

The Xiongnu thus created the first Inner Asian empire in response to China's expansion into the nomads' territory. The Xiongnu were a confederation of tribal peoples. As usual in tribal societies, their confederation and even the member tribes were probably polyethnic in origin. They would have been united more by politics than by common descent, although that would have provided the idiom for imagining their common identity, much as nationalism would do for their modern descendants. It has been widely held that the Xiongnu, or at least their ruling clans, had or were acquiring a Turkic identity, or at least an Altaic one. However, what is known, via Chinese sources, of the Xiongnu kingly language leaves this point open to doubt. By the end of the Xiongnu period, however, the Altaic peoples would be the ones most identified with the equestrian culture earlier developed among the Indo-European peoples of Inner Asia. Furthermore, the earliest clearly Turkic peoples appeared on the peripheries of the late Xiongnu Empire. Peoples associated with it also spread far to the west, if, as often thought, what Europeans called the Huns were an extension of the Xiongnu. If not their ethnic progenitors, then, the Xiongnu had manifold ties to the later Turks.[26]

To ask how the Xiongnu Empire formed is not only to inquire into relations between China and the steppe peoples but also to examine the first recorded instance of the oscillation between tribal micropolitics and imperial macropolitics, which would become one of the most prominent patterns in the metaphorical carpets of Turkic history. In the Xiongnu case, the shift from statelessness to empire has been analyzed in terms of crisis, militarization, and centralization.[27]

Scholars have long argued that crises of different sorts precipitated the formation of nomadic empires. The crisis might come from within the society, as in the case of factors like drought that threatened the survival of flocks and people; unmanageable conflicts among tribes; or the emergence of a charismatic leader, unifying ideology, or both, as seen in the rise of Islam in Arabia in the seventh century C.E. Alternatively, the crisis might come from without, as when an outside power invaded the steppes. The crisis that precipitated the rise of the Xiongnu Empire came from without: the first emperor of newly unified China sent General Meng Tian (Meng T'ien) with a large army to conquer all "the territory south of the Yellow River" and then build walls and fortified towns to consolidate the gains. This became China's "first and massive conquest of nomadic territory."[28] The aggressive implications of China's advance into this region emerge from the fact that the Yellow River makes a great northerly loop, enclosing the Ordos region, an ecologically mixed zone, which had provided the Xiongnu with some of their best grazing land and an important base for attacking China.[29]

Militarization, the second phase of empire building, occurred about a decade later with the rise of Modun (Mo-Tun), the charismatic Xiongnu founder. As narrated by the Chinese historian Sima Qian (Ssu-ma Ch'ien), the story has a mythic air; yet it illustrates an important principle. Modun was the eldest son of a Xiongnu chieftain, or *chanyu* (*ch'an-yü*), who supposedly tried to get Modun killed to facilitate the succession of a younger son.[30] Modun planned his retaliation by carefully training the cavalrymen under his command. Preparing special whistling arrows, he ordered his men to shoot at whatever his whistling arrow struck. "Anyone who fails to shoot will be cut down!" On successive occasions, he shot at game, at one of his best horses, at his favorite wife, and at his father's finest horse. Not until he shot his father's horse were all his men well enough drilled that all of them did shoot and none had to be executed.

> Modun knew at last that they could be trusted. Accompanying his father, the Chanyu Touman (T'ou-man), on a hunting expedition, he shot a whistling arrow at this father and everyone of his followers aimed their arrows in the same direction and shot the Chanyu dead. Then Modun executed his stepmother, his younger brother, and all the high officials of the nation who refused to take orders from him, and set himself up as the new Chanyu.[31]

Modun had performed the most essential task for state formation on the steppes, that of molding his followers into a disciplined corps whose loyalty and obedience to him supplanted their tribal loyalties. Forming and maintaining such a retinue would remain the first prerequisite for transforming the military potential of nomadic society into a disciplined expression of state power from then on. Otherwise, the military potential of tribal society remained unorganized or undirected, in the way depicted by Sima Qian.

> The little boys start out by learning to ride sheep and shoot birds and rats with a bow and arrow, and when they get a little older they shoot foxes and hares, which are used for food. Thus all the young men are able to use a bow and act as armed cavalry in time of war. It is their custom to herd their flocks in times of peace and make their living by hunting, but in periods of crisis they take up arms and go off on plundering and marauding expeditions. This seems to be their inborn nature. For long-range weapons they use bows and arrows, and swords and spears at close range. If the battle is going well for them they will advance, but if not, they will retreat, for they do not consider it a disgrace to run away.[32]

Retreat was one thing, especially as a tactical maneuver to lure an enemy into a trap; lack of discipline was another. Having established command over his forces and having seized power, Modun embarked on a career of conquest. Soon, "the Xiongnu reached the peak of strength and size,

**Hunting with Falcons.** Horsemanship, hunting, and martial skills went together in the culture of the steppes. Hunters used falcons, as well as bows and arrows. This painting, bearing a later attribution to Ustad Mehmed Siyah Kalem (Master Mehmed the Black Pen, or the Draftsman), may have been produced somewhere between Herat and Tabriz in the fifteenth or sixteenth century. From Topkapı Palace Museum, Hazine 2160, f. 84a.

subjugating all of the other barbarian tribes of the north and turning south to confront China as an enemy nation."[33] The first phase of the transition from micropolity to macropolity, the crisis provoked by Chinese invasion, had precipitated the second phase, militarization, and that would lead in turn to the third phase, centralization.

Centralization amounted to a revolution, an abrupt shift from a decentralized, relatively egalitarian pattern to a centralized, hierarchical one that accentuated differences among "senior" and "junior" clans and concentrated power at the top. The key to the process was the rise of a supratribal leader of such stature that other tribal leaders would come together and elevate him to supreme rulership in a sacral investiture that recognized his rule as sanctioned by heaven.[34] The Xiongnu idea of a king-making divine power resembles both the Chinese idea of "heaven's mandate" and the later Turko-

Mongol concepts of a sky god, *tengri*, and of rulership by divine sanction; the fact that the ancient Iranians also believed in the ruler's divine charisma suggests that such ideas prevailed across Asia.[35] Less powerful than a Chinese emperor, however, the chanyu commanded in war and officially controlled relations with China but had to consult his tribal chiefs in internal affairs.[36] As yet, the extent of centralization was more limited than in either China or later Turko-Mongol empires.

The chanyu's duties spanned the cosmic and the mundane. Among them, Sima Qian includes the annual "reckoning . . . of the number of persons and animals" and law enforcement, as well as the chanyu's ritual duties and the sacrifices that he performed periodically at the Xiongnu sacred site, Longcheng (Lung-ch'eng), not far from modern Ulaan Bataar (Mongolia).[37] The idea of rulership by divine sanction turned the ruler's lineage into a charismatic one, in which every member shared attributes of sovereignty, though not actual rulership. Implicitly, succession could be contested, or it might be stabilized either brother to brother or father to son. The Xiongnu succession was orderly for two centuries after Modun, aside from a fifteen-year period of civil war—a remarkable record compared to the bloody succession struggles that became the norm for later Turko-Mongol dynasties.[38]

Once the authority of the supreme ruler—known to the Xiongnu as chanyu, later among Turks and Mongols as *kaghan*—had been recognized, assertion of centralized state power required him to expand his original power base beyond his own household, retinue, and tribe into a supratribal structure that could dominate the other tribes and provide enough benefits to retain their loyalty. In addition to his retinue or bodyguard, the ruler had to mold the manpower of the tribes into a permanently mobilized army. He needed to provide justice that transcended tribal dispute resolution. Military expansion was an essential part of the state-formation process, providing the tribute flows that enabled the ruler to reward loyal service and provide leadership positions for members of the dynasty and elite clans. Finally, state formation required creation of a governmental apparatus. Sima Qian identifies the top leadership as consisting of twenty-four chiefs of "ten thousand horsemen," identified by such titles as "the Wise Kings of the Left and Right, the left and right Lu-li kings, left and right generals, left and right household administrators, and left and right Ku-tu marquises." He adds that the highest offices were hereditary, being filled by members of three families who "constitute the aristocracy of the nation." Each of the twenty-four highest officials "in turn appoints his own 'chiefs of a thousand,' 'chiefs of a hundred,' and 'chiefs of ten,' as well as his subordinate kings, prime ministers, chief commandants, household administrators," and so forth.[39] The bilateral spatial organization in terms of left (eastern) and right (western) and the decimal organization of military forces would become enduring traits of later Turko-Mongol states.

Over time, Xiongnu principles of political science displayed their practical potentials in two major stages. In the first, recently united China confronted the steppe empire that Modun had created, reaching from Manchuria to Central Asia. Created by conquest, the Xiongnu state superstructure had to be maintained by the exaction of tributes. During their first period, the Xiongnu were strong enough to exact them not only from nomadic tribes and minor polities, like the city-states of the Tarim basin, whom they had taken under their rule and whose agrarian and mercantile production provided resource diversification for the Xiongnu economy, but also from China's Han dynasty. Following a crushing defeat of Emperor Han Gaozu (Han Kao-tsu, 206–194 B.C.E.) and the defection of numerous Han commanders, who coached the Xiongnu on how to get the most out of the Chinese, the emperor had to conclude a treaty of *heqin* (*ho-ch'in*), "peace through kinship relations," acknowledging China's inferiority and sending what amounted to an annual tribute.[40]

The *heqin* treaty (198 B.C.E.) was a response to the unprecedented threat that China faced in the Xiongnu, a massive, unconquerable, alien power. The Chinese rationale for the policy was to maneuver future Xiongnu rulers into dependency on China. The policy required sending Emperor Han Gaozu's eldest daughter to become Modun's legitimate consort, so that the Xiongnu heir would be the emperor's grandson and would accordingly owe him filial obligations. The marriage policy was to be accompanied by campaigns of "corruption" (supplying the Xiongnu with luxury goods) and "indoctrination" (sending scholars to explain proper conduct).

This and later treaties recognized a bipolar order with two "superpowers," the rulers of which were officially equal in status. Each of the two powers had its own tributary satellites. In fact, China was in a weaker position than the Xiongnu. No other "barbarian" ruler was treated as the titular equal of the Chinese emperor. China had to pay tribute; yet doing so did not stop raiding along the border or prevent demands for increases in the tribute. As soon as the Xiongnu won the tributes, moreover, they pressed for border markets. The tributes provided the chanyu prestige goods to distribute among his retainers and so helped maintain his position. The frontier markets enabled ordinary steppe dwellers to exchange their animal products for Chinese goods, while merchants moved back and forth between the agrarian and pastoral economies.[41] During the reign of Emperor Han Wendi (Wen-ti, 179–57 B.C.E.), Xiongnu power peaked. Modun stated in a letter that "all the people who draw the bow have now become one family." A letter from Emperor Wen conceded in 162 B.C.E. that "our two great nations, the Han and the Xiongnu, stand side by side."[42]

The transition to the second phase in Chinese-Xiongnu relations began thirty years later, when Chinese statesmen began to discuss abandoning the treaty system and adopting an aggressive strategy against the Xiongnu. By then, experience had shown that the costs of the treaty system outweighed the benefits. Violations of the peace continued. Often, the violators were the chanyu's subordinates or Chinese commanders who had defected. At times, rulers supposedly subordinate to the chanyu tried to set up their own heqin relations with China. China's tribute payments and the border trade might have been expected to reinforce the chanyu's authority by increasing his supply of goods, such as silks, with which to reward his retainers. However, the fact that the chanyu did not enjoy the same level of power and control over his subordinates that the Chinese emperor did kept that from happening. Realization that the treaty policy could not work, coupled with improved military capabilities in China, led it to change the policy.[43]

Although the first assault under the aggressive policy ended in defeat for China in 135 B.C.E., the policy assumed a scale and duration and produced results much larger than originally expected. The main reason for this outcome was the strategic realization that defeating the Xiongnu required cutting off "their right arm," that is, their ability to draw on the resources of their western tributaries, including the oasis city-states of the Tarim basin. By this time, the Han dynasty had consolidated its political control and strengthened its military by developing a regular cavalry, setting up horse-breeding programs, adopting improved weapons such as repeat-firing crossbows, and expanding its network of forts, roads, and supply stations. As the campaigns progressed, the Chinese integrated recaptured borderlands into their administrative system and demonstrated that they could stage surprise attacks deep in Xiongnu territory, daunting though it would always be for Chinese forces to sustain lengthy campaigns on the steppes.

After 119 B.C.E., the Chinese stopped paying tribute and expanded their goals from defeating the Xiongnu to destroying them. By 110 B.C.E., the Xiongnu had been forced beyond the Gobi Desert into the northern steppes and forest zones. There followed twenty years of Han campaigns to the west. The conflict had expanded into a total war. This conflict cut off the Xiongnu from their sacred site at Longcheng, which was essential for maintaining the chanyu's legitimacy, as well as from the tribute flows—both from China and from the western oases—that had maintained the chanyu's material power. In contrast, as Han China extended its reach westward, its resource base grew, and it began to recognize the potentials of long-distance trade on the silk routes of Inner Asia.[44]

The Xiongnu would continue an attenuated existence into the third century C.E. In 60 B.C.E., however, a series of succession wars began. Now, the Chinese demanded recognition of Chinese suzerainty as the condition for further treaties. In 54 B.C.E., the chanyu of a group of southern Xiongnu tribes accepted this condition. In 51 B.C.E., he even attended the Han court to pay homage to the emperor in person. He was handsomely rewarded for doing so, with thousands of pieces of silk, cash, and other goods. Subsequent steppe rulers never seriously objected to the well-rewarded sham of tributary relations with China.[45] The value of Chinese gifts to subsequent chanyus who visited the Han court mounted dramatically, and for a time these resources enabled the chanyu to maintain Xiongnu unity. Still, the Xiongnu slipped into dependency on China and tribal decentralization. By the second century C.E., one of their successor peoples, the Xianbi (Hsien-pi), had eclipsed them. The Xianbi were also the people who, around 265 C.E., adopted not the title chanyu but the title that later became most prestigious for a Turkic ruler, kaghan.[46] Another Xiongnu successor state was the kaghanate of the Rouran or Ruanruan (Jou-Jan or Juan-Juan), possibly the same people as the Avars of the European sources.[47] One of the Rourans' subject tribes was the first to bear the name *Türk* as its tribal name.

Based on the essential role of tribute payments in sustaining Xiongnu power, this period of Inner Asian state formation (209 B.C.E.–551 C.E.) has been characterized as one of "tribute empires."[48] Finding other, better ways to generate resources would remain a task for those who assumed command of the steppes later. Even in Xiongnu times, however, Chinese annalists found many traits worthy of notice and some worthy of emulation. For example, the Xiongnu had no permanent houses, dressed in animal skins, ate raw meat, drank blood, and—a theme persistently noted about Turkic and Mongol tribal societies—did not distinguish between men and women, that is, did not make inegalitarian distinctions in gender roles. Cultic practices, emphasizing Heaven, Earth, and Water (*Tengri, Yer, Sub*), took forms characteristic of the Inner Asian traditional religion.[49] The Chinese had to struggle to match the Xiongnu in equestrian skill; in weaponry, ranging from compound bows and arrowheads of bone and bronze to swords and maces; and in tactical tricks such as terrorizing enemies into surrender or feigning retreats to lure them into traps.

Xiongnu political culture established some of the most important and enduring themes. The Xiongnu ruling clan was the precursor of a series of charismatic Turko-Mongol ruling clans, all claiming rulership by heavenly mandate, an idea with counterparts across Asia. Elements of first lineal and then lateral succession portended later Turkic polities' practices and succession struggles. The story of Modun's rise to power provides an unparalleled example of the importance of retinue formation in an empire builder's rise, and the other offices and titles mentioned in the Chinese sources indicate the considerable institutional elaboration in this first steppe empire. Bilateral, left-right political and military organization anticipated later Turko-Mongol practice, as did military forces of ten thousand, subdivided along decimal lines.[50] Similarly, later nomadic empires' inability to maintain territorial unity was foretold in the Xiongnus' fragmentation into local "kingdoms," whose rulers did not always obey the chanyu's summons.

Most of the same traits reappeared among what seem to be the earliest Turkic inhabitants of western Eurasia. Their westward migration may have begun earlier but probably increased with the Xiongnus' defeat and expulsion from their homeland. Becoming known to Iranians, Byzantines, and Europeans by the name Hun or variants thereof, these westward migrants were probably elements of the Xiongnu, although documentary evidence to prove this is lacking. Displacing Iranians as masters of the steppes and thereby per-

**Family Scene from the Steppes.** Would a nomadic family on the steppes have looked like this? The man feeds his steppe horse, which looks rather like a donkey, while one child watches and two others cling to their mother. The scene evokes the elemental steppe existence, but could nomads' children have gone barefoot in the Inner Asian climate? No pictures evoke the steppe world more powerfully than those attributed to Mehmed Siyah Kalem, but fantasy and reality often mingle. From Topkapı Palace Museum, Hazine 2153, f. 23b.

manently dividing the Indo-European world, these migrants coalesced into the Hunnic confederation and began the Turkification of central and western Eurasia, even though Iranian city-states and merchants remained important there. Sometime around 370 C.E., the Huns crossed the Volga River, began to raid into eastern Europe and the Middle East, took control of Pannonia (roughly, present-day Hungary), and helped by their expansion to set in motion other migrations that shaped the populations of post-Roman Europe.[51] Under Attila (d. 453), the Huns became "for a few years more than a nuisance to the Romans, though at no time a real danger."[52] In part this may be a consequence of the fact that their style of warfare, derived from the steppe and dependent on expansive pasturage for their horses, could not be extended successfully much to the west of the Hungarian and Wallachian plains.[53] After Attila, the Huns fell apart, as had the Xiongnu, and as nomadic confederations typically did. Significantly, the Huns' language—at least the names that provide the surviving evidence about it—does contain Turkic, as well as other, elements.[54] Thus, a Turkic presence was formed as far west as the Caucasus and the steppes north of the Black Sea.[55]

## Pre-Islamic Turkic Carpets:
## The Period of Trade-Tribute Empires

Although there is earlier evidence of Turkic peoples, such as those whose large-wheeled wagons led the Chinese to dub them the "High Carts," the first state to bear the name Türk was founded in 552 C.E., opening the pre-Islamic period of Turkic state formation, which lasted until the tenth century.[56] In contrast to the earlier tribute empires, the states of this period have been described as "trade-tribute empires" because they not only sought to extract tributes from sedentary societies beyond their borders, as had the Xiongnu, but also engaged directly in trade or patronized merchants among their own subjects.[57] Turkic states in this category include the Türk Empires (first and second, 552–630, 682–745 C.E.) and their successors: in the east, the Uyghurs (744–840); in the west, the Khazars (630–965). The history of this period includes both continuities and changes that are significant in the patterning of the Turkic historical fabric.

Since this is the period when Turks first stepped clearly onto the stage of history, it is appropriate to note how they understood their origins, an inquiry that takes us from the realm of historical documentation to that of myth. Turkic and Mongol peoples have understood their origins in terms of a common mythic complex, combining references to "a Mountain, a Tree, a Cave, Water, and a Female Spirit" with "themes of enclosure and emergence." The widely known myth, preserved in Chinese sources, that attributes the origins of the sixth-century Türk tribe, the first bearers of that name, to a she-wolf is the first of numerous Turko-Mongol myths that combine the same thematic elements.[58]

In this myth, the Türks who founded the first Turkish empire, the Türk kaghanate, on the Orkhon River in 552 C.E. were a separate tribe of the Xiongnu, bearing the family name A-shih-na or Ashina. Enemies defeated and destroyed all the Ashina, except for a ten-year-old boy, whose feet they cut off. A she-wolf saved him, feeding him meat. He grew up and mated with her. Learning that the boy was still alive, the neighboring king again sent troops to destroy him. The she-wolf escaped to a mountain cave near Turfan in what is now Xinjiang province. Inside the cave was a large grassy plain surrounded by mountains. Hiding in those mountains, the wolf gave birth to ten boys, each of whom grew up, married a woman from outside, and had children. Each child took a family name, one of them taking the name A-shih-na. After several generations, they emerged from the cave and became subjects of the Rouran, working for them as ironsmiths.

What this tale lacks in historical plausibility, it more than makes up for in symbolic fecundity. The terseness of the narrative implies, too, that these symbols required no explanation. The wolf is the mythical ancestor of the Turks and Mongols. The wolf is also the form often taken by the tutelary spirit that guides the young shaman; and Turkic beliefs about shamans commonly ascribed to them the ability to shift into the shape of a wolf. An alternative interpretation suggests that identification with the wolf, the ancestral spirit of the ruling clan, may have had greatest salience for the ruler's bodyguard or retinue, who were known as *böri*, "wolf." Presumably recruited across tribal lines, they owed their highest loyalty to the ruler; and identification with the spirit of his mythical ancestor may have had more meaning for them than for ordinary Turkic tribesmen, for whom narratives of descent from their common tribal ancestors may have been more meaningful. This might also explain why some of the evidence on wolf symbolism is contradictory and why the wolf myth, preserved in Chinese sources, is weakly reflected in the Türks' own inscriptions.[59] Ironworking is another noteworthy motif, for shamanic societies ranked the smith second to the shaman, associating their functions closely with each other. Indeed, while premodern societies attached spiritual, as well as material, significance to all arts and crafts, metallurgy might well have seemed the most magically transformative. The more recent advent of ironworking, as opposed to bronzeworking, and its military significance must have inspired awe at the power of smiths—especially swordsmiths—to unleash and control the forces of nature.[60]

Also implied in the wolf narrative are long-lasting themes of Turkic political culture, starting with the ascription of sovereignty to a charismatic clan, now the Ashina, who are seen as stemming from earlier rulers, the Xiongnu. The linguistically non-Turkic name, A-shih-na, probably comes from one of the Iranian languages of Central Asia and means "blue," *kök* in Turkic, the color identified with the East, so that Kök Türk, another name for the Türk Empire, meant the "Turks of the East."[61] Sovereignty was further identified with possession of sacred sites. In the first Türk Empire, the kaghan and high dignitaries performed ancestral rites at the ancestral cavern, possibly an iron mine, located in mountains near the sacred refuge of the Turks in Mongolia, the Ötüken mountain forest.[62] However remote from the modern historians' thought world then, the Türk origin myths contained symbols of great resonance in Turkic political culture and have gained a new lease on life in twentieth-century nationalist imaginations.

The Türks' actual origins were more diffuse than the myth allowed. Aside from other, scattered references to Turks at earlier dates and far to the west, as well as Chinese notices of other Turks, probably splinter groups living outside the Türk Empire in its own day, signs of polyethnicity abound in the origins of the Türks. One sign is that the myth just recounted is only one of three Türk origin myths known in Chinese sources; one myth does not mention the she-wolf ancestor; and the origin myths of some other Turkic peoples mention entirely different ancestors, totemic or not.[63] The founders of the Türk Empire, Istemi and Bumın, both had non-Turkish names to go with their presumably non-Turkic clan name, A-shih-na or Ashina. The term *böri*, used to identify the ruler's retinue as "wolves," probably also derived from one of the Iranian languages. The earliest surviving Turkic texts, the eighth-century Orkhon inscriptions, carved on stone pillars set up near the river of the same name, include words not common to Turkic but found in unrelated Inner Asian languages.[64] Far from leading to a pure national essence, the search for Turkic origins leads to a multiethnic and multilingual steppe milieu.

Chinese sources trace the history of the Türks as far back as 439 C.E., when some 500 families, all bearing the surname A-shih-na, settled in the Rouran state, for which they made iron implements. When that state disintegrated, with a push from them to be sure, they took power in 552. At this point, "Türk" ceased to be merely a tribal name and became a political label; gradually, the name would be applied to various peoples who did not stem from the actual Türk tribe.[65] Within a decade, the Türk Empire had extended its power far to the west. Its cofounders, Bumın and Istemi, had become rulers of east and west, respectively. They first allied briefly with the Sassanians of Iran and then with the Byzantines, essentially at the behest of Sogdian silk merchants who wanted to trade directly with Byzantium. The Sogdians were an Indo-European people, historically settled in and around the oases of Bukhara and Samarkand, who for centuries played key roles in interregional trade and cultural exchange. In addition to exacting tributes as the Xiongnu had done, the Türk also sought to centralize control over Central Asian trade routes, and the collaboration of merchants like the Sogdians was instrumental to this end. The level of prosperity that resulted dazzled the celebrated Chinese pilgrim and translator of Buddhist texts, Xuanzang (Hsüen-tsang), when he visited the western Türk court in 628.[66]

The rise of the Türk Empire coincided with the unification of China, briefly under the Sui (581–618) and more durably under the Tang dynasty (618–907). Although the Sui, during their brief history, made the most they could of Türk succession conflicts, the Tang had a greater impact on the history of relations between China and the Türk. The Tang dynasty's family roots were in north China, which had been under foreign rule for centuries and had been much influenced by the cultures of the steppes. To cite one indicator that anyone versed in Turkic culture will recognize, yoghurt thinned with water (*ayran* in modern Turkish) had replaced tea as the drink of China's northern courts.[67] The eclecticism of musical tastes was indicated by the "Ninefold Divisions of Music" inherited form the Sui period, most of them defined by foreign origins. At least one Turkish actress is known to have performed at the imperial palace. At least one Tang poet waxed lyrical about the pleasures of snowy evenings in a felt tent.[68]

The second Tang emperor, Taizong (T'ai-tsung, 626–49), was a veritable Chinese kaghan, a great horseman and warrior, dynamic enough to murder his brothers and depose his father to get to the throne. Tactically, Taizong was ready to take the field personally against the eastern Türk kaghan, negotiate with him, or even challenge him to fight man to man, and then perform brotherhood ceremonies and horse sacrifices with him.[69] Strategically, he cultivated the western Türks while sowing discord between them and the eastern Türks, thus allying "with those who are far away so as to fight those who are close."[70] From the relations between Türk and Tang to those between the Turkish Republic and the European Union, participation in interregional diplomatic networks and the manifold exchanges that go with them has characterized Turkic states in every period.

Tough as he was, Taizong ruled in an era when the Türk preoccupied China's foreign policy. He understood that Chinese forces could not sustain long campaigns in the steppes. While waiting for the Turks' weaknesses to defeat them, he believed China had to pursue what he called "a policy of pacification through marriage." That required sending large diplomatic missions with costly gifts to accompany the Chinese princess brides.[71] When revolts did occur over the Türk succession and their Sogdian advisors' attempts to introduce regular taxation of nomads' flocks, depleted by harsh winters, the Tang intervened and captured the eastern kaghan. For the next fifty years (629–79), the Türk were subjects of the "heavenly kaghans" of the Tang.[72] Now the Tang embarked on conquests that surpassed those of the Qin and Han dynasties in China's first period of unity. Using the Türk forces, the Tang created a huge buffer zone including Manchuria, Mongolia, and East Turkistan, also defeating the western Türk Empire in 659. Tangible evidence of Tang interest in the west survives in the Buddhist temples and monasteries in the caves at Dunhuang. A major stop on both the silk routes and the routes by which Buddhism was transmitted from India to China, Dunhuang reached a high point in its artistic development under the early Tang.[73]

Yet fifty years later, the Turks successfully turned against the Tang, rebelled, and created a second Türk Empire. This might not have happened if Taizong had been succeeded by his Turkophile heir, Li Chengqian (Li Ch'eng-ch'ien). However, he died in exile for plotting against his father.[74] Taizong's successor instead was Gaozong (Kao-tsung, 649–83), a sickly emperor whose reign was dominated by Chinese bureaucrats hostile to military men. Looking back from the vantage point of the second Türk Empire, the Orkhon inscriptions analyzed how the descendants of Bumın Kaghan and Istemi Kaghan, who had "conquered all the peoples in the four quarters of the world," had brought ruin on themselves through conflicts that opposed not only individuals or tribes but also the elite (begler) and the common people (bodun).[75]

> [U]nwise kagans succeeded to the throne. . . . Their high officials, too, were unwise and bad. Since the lords (begler) and people (bodun) were not in accord, and the Chinese people were wily and deceitful . . . the Turkish people [let] their state . . . go to ruin. . . . Their sons worthy of becoming lords became slaves, and their daughters worthy of becoming ladies became servants to the Chinese people. The Turkish lords abandoned their Turkish titles. Those lords who were in China held the Chinese titles and obeyed the Chinese emperor and gave their services to him for fifty years.

Not for the last time had a Turkic nomadic elite succumbed to the temptation to imitate the airs and graces of a neighboring agrarian society. Rescue came in the person of Elterish (682–91), a descendant of the Ashina clan. His success in mobilizing the remnants of the Türk people and founding the second Türk kaghanate (682–745) is reflected in the name, derived from the Turkic "Kutlugh," the Fortunate or Heaven-favored, used for him in Chinese sources. For several decades the second empire flourished under

Tonyukuk Inscription, South and West Faces (Mongolia, c. 720–25 C.E.). The inscription recounts the deeds of the commander and statesman Tonyukuk in the second Türk Empire. The rubbing corresponds to the west (left) side of the pillar, the beginning of the inscription. The rubbing gives a clearer idea of the "runic" script. The inscription continues on a second pillar. Photo Talat Tekin; rubbing from S. E. Malov, *Pamyatniki Drevnetyurkskoi Pis'mennosti, Teksti i Issledovaniya* (Moscow: Akademiya Nauk SSSR, 1951), foldout plate following p. 56.

able rulers and their able field commander and statesman, Tonyukuk. The history of its relations with China alternates between the familiar mix of predatory raiding and exacting tributes, on the one hand, and campaigning to prop up the Tang at moments of greatest weakness, on the other hand. The combination shows that the motive was not to conquer the Tang but to profit from a united China from the safe distance of the Türks' ritual and political center in the Ötüken mountain. However, their state, too, was not invulnerable. The end came for the second Türk Empire with the poisoning of Bilge Kaghan in 734 and the resurgence of tribal rivalries, which led to its collapse and its replacement by the Uyghur state in 744.

The significance of the Türk Empire was great. For a comparatively long time by Inner Asian standards, it created a *Pax Turcica*, uniting lands stretching the length of the network of trade routes commonly known as the silk routes, from China to Byzantium, with a multiethnic society that served as a medium for transmission of both goods and ideas. Over all this diversity, the empire spread across Inner Asia a pan-Turkic cultural complex, with common traits in matters great and small, from the artifacts of everyday life to language and political culture. Politically, the Türk Empire "grew out of a tribal confederation." It had a core of "inner tribes" (the ruling clan and its allies, including "in-law" tribes), a second tier of tribes that joined freely (retaining their ruling houses), a third tier of tribes that joined under constraint (and whose ruling houses were usually replaced by state officials), and finally tribute-paying sedentary populations. Subject populations retaining their own kings included the Sogdians, with their major centers at Bukhara and Samarkand and farflung merchant colonies, willing collaborators with a nomadic state that possessed the military power to force open the Chinese markets.[76]

The Türk political system, with roots extending back to the Xiongnu, established norms for Turkic states for centuries. At the top, the kaghan ruled by heavenly mandate (*kut*), embodying and demonstrating heaven's favor through successful performance of his functions as ruler.[77] Prominent among these were ritual functions with shamanic overtones. The kaghan had to maintain control of Mount Ötüken and perform ancestral rites at the sacred sites there. Among the Türk, if not earlier among the Xiongnu, standards with set numbers of horse or yak tails, often together with flags and drums, served as symbols of rulership or office and were venerated with libations of kumis (fermented mare's milk) before battle. At his investiture ceremony, the kaghan was first wrapped in a felt rug and spun nine times, then mounted on a horse and made to ride, and then nearly strangled with a silk shawl. When he had almost lost consciousness, he would be asked to state how many years he would rule. The Arab geographer al-Istakhri, describing the survival of this ritual in the Türk successor state of the Khazars, reported that a kaghan would be killed when the number of years he stated had ended.

The kaghan had to come from the Ashina clan. His senior wife (*khatun*) had to come from the Ashete clan. Kaghan and khatun were seen not only as a royal couple but also as earthly counterparts of Tengri, the supreme divinity of the Türk pantheon, and Umay, the goddess of fertility. The kaghan's charisma extended to the entire royal clan. His—and their—blood could not be shed; when one of them was executed, it was by strangulation.

The kaghan's worldly functions were also indispensable. The kaghan, as one of the Orkhon inscriptions said of the Türk founders Istemi and Bumın, furnished the Turkish people with both state and laws (*törü*, corresponding to the *yasagh* or *yasa* of later Turkic and Mongol states).[78] The kaghan commanded, maintaining the unity of his empire and forcing enemies to pay tribute. Heroic in feasting and fighting, the kaghan also had to ensure the welfare of his retainers and subjects, dividing the spoils of war and redistributing tribute to feed and clothe them. The kaghan's practical success thus depended critically on his ability to mobilize and redistribute resources, whether through tribute or trade. Here appear early pressures for state dominance over the economy, a theme destined for a long history in Turkic statecraft.

The Türk Empire was both an administrative organization (*el*) and a tribal confederation (*bodun*), which combined Turkish tribes (*bod*) and clans (*ogush*). At the top, the *kaghan* wielded his power, guarding it, as if in emulation of the Xiongnu founder, by maintaining an armed retinue referred to as "wolves" (*böri*), a term linked in Chinese sources with the Türk origin myth. Although China and Tibet were also conceded to have kaghans, a foretaste of the claim to world empire (which the Mongols later asserted) appears in the Orkhon inscriptions' references to campaigning as far as "the cities of Shandong and the Ocean" in one direction and as far as "the Iron Gate and the (land of the) Täzik" (Tajiks, Iranians) in the other.[79] Below the *kaghan* in the power structure came the imperial governors (all from the Ashina clan) over the tribes and the indigenous tribal leaders (*beg*). According to Chinese sources, the ruling system had twenty-eight ranks, all hereditary.[80] The empire was bilaterally organized, as the Xiongnu and later Turkic political and military systems commonly would be; only here, the East-West bilateralism went to the extent of initially having two rulers (kaghan) who were brothers, Bumın (Tumen in Chinese sources, d. 553) in the East and Istemi (d. 576) in the West. By the late sixth century, the rulers of East and West had fallen out with each other over succession issues. Lateral, as opposed to lineal, succession might produce relative unity between brothers but was highly likely to produce conflict when the succession passed to cousins in the next generation. While awaiting their turn to rule, the Ashina princes governed different parts of the Türk Empire, which thus acquired numerous subdivisions in addition to the east-west bilateral division. Both this kind of appanage system and contested succession remained characteristic of states founded by Turkic nomads for centuries to come, helping to shape those states' typical trajectory of rapid rise and disintegration.

The Türk pattern of state formation would survive essentially through the Mongols; yet several factors add diversity to the political picture. One model did not prevail among all Turkic peoples of this period, many of whom continued to live in stateless tribal societies. Many elements of non-Turkic origin also became part of Türk statecraft. Important terms, for example, often came from non-Turkic languages, as in the cases of *khatun* for the ruler's wife and *beg* for "aristocrat," both terms of Sogdian origin and ever since in common use in Turkish. Practices, as well as terms, could be borrowed. The Sogdian merchants often bought slaves (*chakar*) and formed guards or even private armies to guard their homes while they were traveling; this may have been the model for slave military recruitment in later Islamic and especially Turkic societies.[81]

Türk society was stratified, divided between the *beg*s, the elite stratum consisting of the ruling clan and a hierarchy of other noble clans, and the *kara bodun*, or common people. Yet at the same time, the society was a unity in military terms. Every male was an *er*, "man" and implicitly "warrior"; every young man had to earn his "warrior name" (*er ati*) through prowess in battle or the hunt; and an elite male, too, was an *er bashi*, or commander of so many men.[82] Woman performed most of the productive labor, while men occupied themselves with their weapons and animals; given these gender roles, when captives were taken in war, they were almost all females, sometimes boys, but never adult males. The need for mobility and adaptability to extreme cold dictated many preferences, such as tastes for rich fabrics, furs, and richly made belts with straps to suspend useful objects. As had already been true in ancient times, the productive capacity and technological sophistication of such a society were not to be underestimated. It is no wonder that the skill required to produce steel swords over charcoal fires seemed supernatural. The same could be said for bow makers, who required great time and expertise to make the composite bows, which still set distance records exceeding those of European-style longbows "by humiliating margins."[83]

Türk religious life, not extensively documented, was based on an ancient complex of beliefs widespread in Inner Asia.[84] The term "shamanism," although conventional, is a misleading name for this belief system. Shamans,

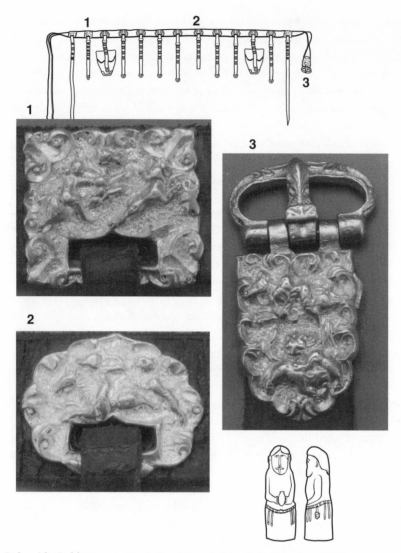

**Belt with Gold Mounts Depicting Mounted Archers Hunting** (Türk era, 552–745 C.E.). The outline drawings show the reconstruction of a belt excavated from a Türk era tomb in Butumuji, Suniteyouqi, Xilinguolemeng, eastern Inner Mongolia, with hanging straps and pouches for carrying things, as well as front and side views of a funerary effigy of a man wearing such a belt and holding a libation vessel. The photographs are closeups of gold mounts from the belt, depicting hunting scenes. Each gold mount is about 2.8–2.9 cm. in width. Photo Ding Xueyun; courtesy of Kong Qun, Inner Mongolia Museum, Hohehot, Inner Mongolia, China; graphics by Ron McLean, Digital Media Creation Services, Ohio State University.

male and female, served as religious specialists, who could communicate with the spirit world. They were called on, however, only for exceptional religious or medical needs, not for routine religious practice. Their ability, real or reputed, to divine the future or conjure up storms on the battlefield made their services especially significant for rulers. However, the heroic, ecstatic quest that transformed an individual from sickness and alienation through initiation into a shaman capable of performing such wonders little resembled his or her neighbors' usual religious observance.

That centered instead on the maintenance of life and health within the community and in relation to the ancestors and the cosmic forces. The most fundamental rites were offerings to the ancestors of the family and community.[85] The ancestral rites focused on the hearth (*ocak*), one of the most persistent and widely evoked symbols in Turkic cultures. At the hearth, offerings of food and drink were either cast into the fire or smeared on the mouth of wood or felt "idols" that represented the ancestors and were kept near the hearth. Ancestor figures, carved in stone and holding what appear to be libation vessels in their hands, were also common features of Turkic burial sites. Not only did the hearth fire symbolize familial continuity, but the hearth also possessed great spatial and cosmological significance. Dug out by the mother, it implied a gate opened to the ancestor's nether world. Centrally located in the round felt tent, it symbolized the center of the world. Through the smoke hole above, the hearth was on an axis with the cosmos. The sacred images of the Mountain, Tree, Cave, Water, and Female Spirit all became identified with the hearth through its cosmic orientation and through its opening into the nether world of the "grandmothers," the ancestral female spirits. The rites performed around the hearth helped to ensure *kut*, the life force that brought children to life, that fell through the smoke hole to bring good fortune to a family, or that conveyed the divine mandate to a ruler. Within such a spiritual frame of reference, as the Türk origin myths illustrate, the significant origin is not that of the universe or of humankind in general but of a specific family or kin group. The significant First Man is the progenitor, not of all humanity, but of one's own people. Such a narrative can serve, then, as a "confederative charter" on which to unite a people or build an empire. Later narratives of religious conversion combine in the figure of the First Man both the faith-bringer and the forefather of a new kinship or ethnic group.

The religious rites of a ruling dynasty would have been more elaborate but not different in kind. The identification of sovereignty with control of sacred sites—an enduring theme in Turkic political culture—elaborated on the symbolism of the hearth. For the Türk Empire, this meant particularly the Ötüken mountain, which had also been sacred for the Xiongnu and the Rouran.[86] Chinese sources mention Ötüken as the kaghan's constant place of residence, in contrast to his subjects' migratory habits, adding that each year the kaghan would "lead the nobles to the ancestral cave to offer sacrifices." If there was a difference in spiritual emphases between dynast and ordinary nomad, it took the form of the greater devotion to Tengri, the supreme deity, in the politicized state cult, with the kaghan as high priest.[87] Tengri had two messenger gods (*Yol tengri*), of which one brought *kut* to the individual while the other restored the state, in which emperor and empress (kagan and khatun) ruled as earthly counterparts of Tengri and Umay, divinities of sky and earth. Rulers may also have had greater need than ordinary folk for the services of *shamans*, especially to divine the future (or at least the rulers' preferences concerning future policy). For the nonelite, other spirits, especially ancestral ones, may have been more meaningful.[88]

In the long run, however, state formation in the steppes tended to be closely associated with conversion—first by the ruler—to one of the universal religions known among his subjects or in neighboring societies. In the Türk Empire, Zoroastrianism, Taoism, possibly Nestorian Christianity, and especially Buddhism were all known.[89] Taspar Kaghan (r. 572–81) converted to Buddhism, a politically neutral choice for a ruler with powerful Iranian and Chinese neighbors. He sponsored the building of monasteries and translation of Buddhist texts—a major development in the northerly spread of Buddhism. As was generally true in history, religion determined the development of writing systems, including both the Sogdian cursive used in the translation of the Buddhist texts and the "runic" writing used in the Orkhon inscriptions. Both scripts ultimately derived, like the Sogdian, from Aramaic, any resemblance to Scandinavian runes being incidental.

After the Türk Empire collapsed, various successor states appeared, as did a proliferation of Turkic tribes, which began to shift westward after 840. In the east, the major successor state and the only one to claim the title kaghan was that of the Uyghurs (744–840). Centered in what is now known as Mongolia, it controlled the sacred lands on the Orkhon River and Mount Ötüken. The Uyghur Empire was again a major power equal in status to Tang China. The Uyghurs continued the dual policy of supporting the Tang at critical moments, notably the series of rebellions that began with that of An Lushan (755–57), while extorting resources the rest of the time, particularly by supplying the Tang with horses in exchange for silk at extortionate rates.[90] Proof in the flesh of the Tang-Uyghur symbiosis, a series of Chinese princesses were again sent to become brides of the kaghans, including the first of the Tang emperors' own daughters to be married to foreign rulers.[91]

In many ways, the Uyghurs brought to the steppes a new degree of civilization, influenced more by Iranian peoples than by the Chinese. One sign of this development was the capital city, Ordubalik (Karabalghasun to the Mongols), built on the Orkhon River near where the Mongols later built Karakorum. For nomads, founding cities, although not unprecedented, was not natural. Cities created liabilities for warriors whose strategy depended on mobility. However, the volume of resources extorted from China meant that the Uyghurs "had too much wealth not to have a permanent fortified capital."[92] Sogdians in particular were ready to gather there to trade and offer their services as officials, architects, and builders. Whereas the traditional Inner Asian cults, Buddhism, and Nestorian Christianity were all practiced, the ruler and probably many other Uyghurs converted to Manicheism (762), a syncretic, dualistic religion founded by the Iranian prophet, Mani (216–76 C.E.). This was the only time a state ever adopted Manicheism as its official religion; the choice was another sign of Sogdian influence.[93] Following Türk precedent, the Uyghurs adopted the Aramaic-derived Sogdian script, which the Mongols and Manchus also later used.[94] Archeologists speak of a Turko-Sogdian cultural complex, one notable symbol of which was An Lushan (Rokhshan). Born to a Turkic father and a Sogdian mother, he became a Tang general but revolted against his Chinese master in 755.[95] Symbiosis could mean submergence: under this Uyghur state, the Indo-European Tokharians were gradually Turkified.

After the Kirghiz destroyed the Uyghur kaghanate (840), further population changes transformed the region ethnically from the Turkic heartland into that of the Mongols. The Turkic tribes migrated westward; and over the next several centuries, what has since been known as Mongolia became Mongol country. Because the Kirghiz remained centered on the Yenisei River to the north, the religiopolitical importance of Mount Ötüken faded into the past.[96] Kirghiz destruction of the Uyghurs also had economic consequences that show the importance of regional, as opposed to trans-Eurasian, trade. The horses that symbolize China's Tang dynasty, prominent motifs in its art but also practical necessities for controlling a huge empire, came from the steppes, as China's horses basically always did. Kirghiz disruption of the Uyghur supply system more than tripled the cost of horses to the Tang between 839 and 842, touching off a major crisis in China.[97] Proof that the relationship between the Uyghurs and the Tang was not only predatory but also protective, after the Uyghurs fell in 840, the Tang sank into internal revolt within a generation. In Turkistan, the Uyghur elite managed to retain the small kingdoms of Ganzhou (Kanchou, 840–1028) and Kocho (840–1209).[98] Of these, the latter in particular played an important part in transmitting the Uyghur cultural legacy to later peoples, especially the Mongols.

The expansion of Islamic rule into Central Asia began with the campaigns of Qutayba ibn Muslim (705–15) and the Muslim defeat of the Chinese at Talas in 751. As Central Asia began to become part of the Islamic world, Islam began to influence the indigenous populations, including both numerous Turkic peoples and three eastern Indo-European groupings: the Khwarazmians of Transoxania; the Sogdians around Bukhara, Samarkand, and Shash (now Tashkent); and the Tokharians in the east. The Iranian Samanid dynasty (819–1005), governing Transoxania for the Abbasid caliph who reigned over the Islamic empire from Baghdad, played a vanguard role in developing Islamo-Persian literary culture. This initiative ensured that Islamic high culture would appear to Inner Asian peoples through a largely Persian filter and that Persian would become an international prestige language from Iran into Central Asia and India. Simultaneously, however, the demography of Central Asia was becoming more Turkic. Turkic tribes had been migrating into Central Asia and the Black Sea region since Xiongnu times, supplanting or absorbing Iranian and other groups. Among Turkic peoples noted in this region after the Türk Empire were the Oghuz, an ethnonym already known from the east, here a confederation of twenty-odd clans or subtribes, among which the Kınık ranked first and the Kayı(gh) second. The later Seljuk ruling clan claimed descent from the Kınık; some Ottoman genealogies claim, perhaps fancifully, descent from the Kayı.[99]

Further west, the zone to the north of the Black and Caspian Seas also included important populations that were all or partly Turkic, as well as some Turkic states. Here the Islamic presence was as yet much weaker. At the collapse of the western Türk Empire in the eighth century, the most important contenders for power in the steppes north of the Black and Caspian Seas were the Khazars and the Bulghar union.[100] The main center for the Bulghars was on the middle Volga (Itil in Turkic), although one branch migrated into the Danubian basin where, Slavicized and Christianized, they gave their name to Bulgaria. The Khazars are of special interest for a number of reasons. In the West, they were the only ones to bear the title kaghan between the Türk and the Great Mongol Empire; their ruling house, possibly descended from the Ashina, had close connections with that of the Türks. The geopolitics of the region made them natural allies for the Byzantines against the Muslim caliphate; common interests led to at least one Byzantine-Khazar dynastic marriage.

The Khazar kaghan ruled over perhaps twenty subject peoples, speaking Turkic, Uralic, Slavic, Iranian, and Caucasian languages. The political system was a dual kaghanate, headed by a kaghan from the royal clan along with the actual ruler, who bore titles such as kaghan-beg or beg. The high kaghan had only a ritual role, assuring *kut*, the heavenly mandate, by his presence. His investiture consisted of the shamanic ceremonies noted in the case of the Türk kaghans, including the ritual strangulation; his blood, too, could not be shed, but he could order the death of any of his servants. This is enough to show that the Khazars shared elements of the Inner Asian religious and political culture of the Türk. Yet here, too, other religions became known. The royal clan and inner tribes adopted Judaism in the late eighth or early ninth century. Islam and Christianity were also known in Khazaria and may have been more widespread; some Khazar subjects also still followed the traditional Inner Asian cults.[101] For the ruling elite of a state with powerful Muslim and Christian neighbors, however, the appeal of Judaism as a universal religion without political entanglements is manifest, recalling the appeal of Buddhism and Manicheism to other Turkic rulers.

By the late tenth century, in any event, the Khazars were overwhelmed by the Rus' (proto-Russians) in alliance with Oghuz Turkic tribes. None of the other tribal unions in western Eurasia would succeed in forming a state until the Mongol conquest. Survivors of the Judaized Khazar elite may have contributed to the formation of Russian Jewry. The large array of Turkic and related tribal groupings noted in western Eurasia for the remainder of the pre-Mongol period included several groups of Bulghars in different places, such as those south of the Danube who converted to Orthodox Christianity in the ninth century and subsequently Slavicized; the Hungarians, whose language is Finno-Ugric rather than Altaic but whose ethnogenesis and culture were strongly influenced, prior to their migration into Hungary, by contacts with Turkic peoples; and finally the Bashkirs, Pechenegs, and Kuman-Kipchaks.

Lacking the incentives that rulers of empires had to convert to a universal religion, these peoples carried on many Türk traditions and spread them over a wide zone. Use of the title kaghan and some other elements of Türk political culture even spread to the Rus' principality.[102] Tenth-century Byzantine sources, speaking in cultural more than ethnic terms, acknowledged a wide zone of diffusion by referring to the Khazar lands as "Eastern *Tourkia*" and Hungary as "Western *Tourkia*."[103] The act of a Kuman chieftain on the eve of a battle in 1097 marvelously illustrates the vigor of Turkic culture on the eastern European steppe at that time. He "arose when it was midnight and rode away from his army. He began to howl like a wolf and a wolf answered him and many wolves began to howl," upon which he returned to camp predicting victory. The next day, he used the classic nomadic tactic of a feigned retreat to lure his Hungarian opponents into a trap, securing victory for himself and the Rus' prince with whom he was allied.[104] Clearly the myths and traditions of the pre-Islamic Turkic steppe culture were to prove durable and widespread motifs, long worked and reworked in the carpets of Turkic identity.

## Brides of the Kaghans

Between the carpet from Pazyryk (fourth century B.C.E.) and the next-earliest surviving carpets (thirteenth century C.E., from today's Turkey) stretches a lengthy period during which thousands of carpets must have been woven but have not survived. Textile fragments of other types suffice to show that stylistic norms observable in the Pazyryk finds persisted, continued to evolve, and eventually exerted their influence far afield. The prevalence of animals and birds shown with vigorously flexed bodies, the artistic vision that made those creatures shift at their extremities into the shapes of other species, and color choices unconstrained by nature—distinctive stylistic elements known since the Xiongnu period and earlier—reappeared, further elaborated, in Uyghur silks of the eleventh and twelfth centuries. Imitations of them turn up in Italian silks of the fourteenth century.[105] Still, one can only imagine what the textiles of this period might show had they survived in greater numbers.

The caravans that transported some of the finest textiles of Xiongnu, Türk, and Uyghur times would have accompanied diplomatic missions. Chinese rulers sent over seventy such missions to the Türk rulers between 545 and 742, and the Türk rulers sent over ninety in the opposite direction. Often, dynastic marriage was the purpose.[106] Some of the embassies brought the princess bride herself to her new life on the steppes. The costs of such a marriage might equal a year's revenue from one or more provinces, taking the necessary gift exchanges into account; yet that was less than the cost of border defenses during periods of active raiding from the steppes. Although the Turkic rugs that were surely woven in this period have not survived and little evidence survives about the women who wove them, song and story evoke the plight of high-born women caught up in the manifold exchanges across the frontier between China and the steppe world. For example, this song speaks for a Han dynasty princess married to a different steppe ruler to seal an alliance against the Xiongnu.

> My family married me, oh! Off to heaven's far side.
> Dispatched me to a foreign land, oh! As the Wusun king's bride.
> A yurt for a room, oh! A felt for a wall.
> Meat serves for my grain, oh! To drink? Kumiss is all.
> My homesick heart grieves, oh! To abide here so long.
> Were I but a yellow crane, oh! I'd take wing back home.[107]

It makes a good song. Is this what the princess sang, however, or what her Chinese relatives thought she ought to sing? Soul-baring revelations from a Chinese princess, who perhaps never had illusions about her chances of personal happiness in marriage, seem unlikely in this period. Available information suggests, in any event, that the changes awaiting her were not all for the worse. From Herodotus to modern anthropologists, observers have invariably noted that the status of women in a nomadic society was higher than in an agrarian one, such as China. If, as Chinese sources said, the Xiongnu did not make distinctions between men and women, there may have been a positive side to becoming the chanyu's bride. In the Türk Empire, important values attached to the idea of the kaghan and his khatun as a royal couple. At the Uyghur court, the khatun wielded power. Part of the original rationale for dynastic marriages between Han princesses and the Xiongnu chanyu had been to create bonds of filial loyalty and obligation between steppe rulers and the Chinese emperor. The practical outcomes never fully vindicated this argument; yet it was unassailable in Confucian logic and persistent in Chinese foreign policy. Perhaps that was because the policy did sometimes pay off.

The glimpses that Chinese historians offer into the lives of princess brides suggest such a conclusion. In the time of the Xiongnu founder Modun, *before* the Han founder Gaozu inaugurated the marriage policy by sending his oldest daughter to become Modun's consort, Modun had trapped Gaozu and his men during a battle. Emperor Gaozu escaped only by sending a gift-laden envoy to an unnamed consort of Modun. She then pleaded with Modun, who allowed Gaozu to escape. The same source does not record whether Gaozu's daughter, sent later to become Modun's bride, ever played a comparable role; perhaps she did.[108] In any event, the sending of Chinese princesses to marry the chanyu remained a fundamental principle of the *heqin* system of Chinese-Xiongnu relations for its duration. After the Han shifted to an aggressive policy against the Xiongnu, they contracted marriage alliances with rulers of other nomadic peoples.[109] In its last phase, sinicized members of the Xiongnu dynasty, with blood lines extending back to both Modun and the Han emperors, adopted the Han dynasty's original family name, Liu, and briefly set themselves up inside China in the early fourth century as the Later Han or Chao (Ch'ao) dynasty. At that, the original Confucian rationale did come to an ironic fulfillment.

Subsequently, the Tang emperors saw no choice, if they could not defeat the Turks, but to continue the diplomacy of marriage.[110] For the Tang, too, the policy produced payoffs at a price. In the upheavals touched off by the An Lushan rebellion in 755, the Tang grew desperately dependent on the Uyghurs for aid against the rebels and correspondingly unable to resist Uyghur demands and depredations. Women played critical roles in maintaining the Tang-Uyghur alliance at several critical moments. In 758, Princess Ningguo (Ning-kuo) was married to El-Etmish Bilge Kaghan (747–59). In 762, when the intrigues of An Lushan's son had nearly provoked the Uyghurs to attack the Tang rather than the rebels, news that the next Uyghur kaghan, Bögü (759–79), and his khatun were approaching saved the day. As the daughter of a Tang general, she was able to arrange a meeting between her father and her husband. The meeting saved the Tang from Uyghur attack.

Princess Ningguo (Ning-kuo), who had married El-Etmish Bilge Kaghan in 758, reportedly found herself facing a near fatal dilemma at his death in 759. According to Chinese sources, custom required that the kaghan's closest associates, both humans and horses, should be buried with him. Modern archeology does not find evidence of wholesale human sacrifice of this sort.[111] But why spoil a good story? In it, Ningguo escaped by convincing the Uyghur court that because she had no children, she should be excused from live burial. She would observe their customs by lamenting the deceased and slashing her face in mourning. In return, they would let her go home.[112] Princess Ningguo was the first of four Tang princesses married to Uyghur kaghans. Her great-grandniece, Princess Taihe (Tai-ho) made her bridal journey in 821. Widowed two years later, she neither committed suicide nor left the Uyghur capital at Karabalghasun, but remained there and only returned to China in 843, following the Uyghur collapse before the Kirghiz.[113] To go with the song about the princess who did not want to leave China, there ought to be a song about the princess-become-khatun who did not want to go back.

Compensating for the lack of evidence from the common women's world of carpet weaving, such stories about the brides of the kaghans offer sometimes dramatic insights into the human interactions that contributed to the historical formation of the Turkish peoples and polities. These dynastic marriages evoke a world of manifold exchanges—diplomatic, economic, cultural, even genetic, inasmuch as the Chinese princesses were expected to become the mothers of future kaghans. Such interactions create a picture of heterogeneity and intermixture in the formation of peoples and languages, much as in the borderless world of the carpet weaver's art. Shaped by these mixings and blendings, the Turkic peoples had nonetheless emerged, with their distinctive languages and cultures, and had begun the caravan journey through history that forms the vertical fibers in the carpets of Turkish identity.

The period surveyed in this chapter, from the prehistory of the Turkic peoples through the integration and disintegration of the Xiongnu, Türk, and Uyghur Empires, brings us to the first of two great boundary crossing points in their caravan journey, that of conversion to Islam. Thenceforth, Islamic motifs would become dominant in the fabric of social and political life—micropolity and macropolity. The second great boundary crossing would occur in the nineteenth and twentieth centuries with the Turks' integration into an emergent global constellation of modernity. Both transitions provoked profound changes, materially and culturally. Many cultural patternings seen among the Xiongnu and the pre-Islamic Turkic states are radically alien to the patternings of later periods. Yet both the warp and weft and the surface knottings of Turkic history also display major continuities. No longer transporting Chinese princess brides, the Turkic caravan would continue its way through history, crossing civilizational fault lines and border zones, always laden with brightly woven bundles but constantly leaving old ones behind and taking on new ones as it advanced.

# TWO

# Islam and Empire from the Seljuks through the Mongols

B etween the tenth and fourteenth centuries, most Turks converted to Islam, thus crossing the first great civilizational divide in their history. That permitted those who so wished to move freely into the Islamic heartlands of the Middle East. There, they quickly assumed leading roles in military and political affairs. As Central Asian peoples also began to convert to Islam, some of the most important stages in the creation of a Turko-Islamic culture occurred there. This northeastward advance of Islam continued for centuries. Mahmud al-Kashgari legitimized the Turks' political rise with a made-up *hadith*, or saying of the Prophet Muhammad. In the *hadith*, Muhammad attributes the following statement to God: "I have an army, which I call the Turks and have settled in the East. When I become angry at any people, I give them dominion over it."[1]

Still beyond Islamic frontiers initially, in the thirteenth century the Mongols reunited the steppe peoples into one state for the first time since the Türk Empire. The Mongols created "the largest contiguous land-based empire" in history, interlinking Eurasia permanently into one system.[2] Revitalizing steppe culture, the Mongol Empire left behind societies predominantly Turkic in ethnicity and Muslim in religion. By then, the old Turkic homeland, at the start of the trans-Asian migration routes, had become Mongolia, which remained outside the Islamic world. In contrast, the routes' western, Anatolian terminus was beginning to become a new Turkish homeland. However, many Turks, perhaps most, had not made the entire trip to Anatolia and probably knew or cared little that others had done so. Instead, all along the route, they had set up the metaphorical looms on which they would weave the fabric of the Turkish-Islamic cultures. European Latin writers began to refer to Anatolia as "Turchia" in the twelfth century. The Turks would not adopt that name for their new western home base until after World War I. But significantly, aside from the ancient Pazyryk carpet from Siberia, the earliest surviving carpets are Turkish ones from thirteenth-century Anatolia.[3]

Turkic and Mongol states of this period obviously had a great deal in common, culturally and historically. They have been characterized in several ways. They have been termed "military patronage states," in which a conquering nomadic elite acquires dominion over an ethnically different, agrarian populace and rules by force, but also protects the agrarian base from which state revenue derives.[4] Another characterization, offered for Inner Asia between 907 and 1259, is that of the "dual-administration" empire, whose control of both pastoralist and agrarian populations demands that rulers of nomadic origin acquire the necessary skills to administer populations of both types.[5] Both of these descriptions are applicable. To organize a discussion of this period, it will help to look westward at the Turks' movement into the Middle East and then eastward to Inner Asia under the Mongols, after first considering the profound consequences of conversion to Islam.

## Islam, Conversion, and Interfaith Relations

The Turkic peoples' adoption of Islam transformed their identity more decisively than any other change, before or since. Previously, the indigenous Inner Asian cults had formed the enduring foundation of their religious experience, although a series of other religions had also been adopted in different situations. Henceforth, one of the great world religions would become the foundation for most Turks by far. The significance of the change becomes apparent from basic attributes of Islamic faith. The dynamics of conversion and Islamic norms of interfaith relations are also extremely important topics for understanding the Turks' experiences in this period.

Islam means "submission [to the one God]," and a Muslim is "one who submits." Muslims see Islam as the religion of Abraham, whom the Kur'an identifies as both a Muslim ("one who submitted" to God, a monotheist) and as the ancestor of the Arabs. The Prophet Muhammad was born in 570 C.E., and his prophetic mission spanned the period from 610 until his death in 632 C.E. The revelations that came to him from 610 on were compiled after his death into the written text of the Kur'an. Although the Kur'an did not integrally incorporate earlier scriptures in the way that the Christian Bible incorporated the Hebrew Bible as the "Old Testament," the Kur'an includes many themes and personalities also found in the Bible and frequently mentions Jews and Christians. These similarities exist because all of God's prophets (*nabi*) and messengers (*rasul*) received the same revelation. Together, they form a series that includes a number of biblical figures, some nonbiblical ones, Jesus (a prophet, but no more than that), and finally Muhammad, the "seal" of the prophets, implying that he is the last and the validation of all before him.[6] The fact that the sacred history of Islam begins not with Muhammad but with Abraham or even Adam generated an understanding of relations among Islam, Christianity, and Judaism that proved profoundly important for later Islamic societies.

Accepting Islam meant, first, *tawhid*, or "affirming the oneness [of God]." It meant accepting certain beliefs, summarized in this oft-quoted verse:

> O believers, believe in God and His Messenger and the Book He
> has sent down and the Books which He sent down before. Who-
> ever disbelieves in God and His Angels and His Books, and His
> Messengers, and the Last Day, has surely gone astray into far error.
> (Kur'an, 4.136)

Believing made one a member of the worldwide community of Muslims, the *umma*. For the believers, certain practices were essential. The most basic are the "five pillars" of Islam: the profession of faith (*shahada*), prayer (*salat* in Arabic, *namaz* in Persian or Turkish), almsgiving (*zakat*), fasting (*sawm*) during Ramadan, and the pilgrimage (*hajj*). All of these act out equal participation in the community in different ways and with different frequencies. The obligatory prayer ritual occurs five times a day, although of course one can also pray at other times; the pilgrimage, occurring once a year, is obligatory once in a lifetime for every adult Muslim who is physically and financially capable of it. The fast occupies one month a year, during which rich and poor alike go without food and drink from dawn to dusk. The five pillars shaped Islamic societies in countless ways. Incidentally, for Turkish Muslims, the fivefold prayer helped Islamize the connection between carpet making and Turkic identity, inasmuch as the largest number produced were used as prayer rugs (*sajjada*). Struggle (*jihad*) is sometimes mentioned as a sixth pillar, with meanings ranging from the struggle for self-mastery to "holy war" to defend or advance Islam. In this period, the latter was more often referred to by the term *ghaza*. Originally referring to "raiding" of the sort bedouin tribes carried out among themselves, ghaza had long since been Islamized to refer to the struggle to defend or expand the frontiers of Islamic rule. Although often not in the terms of its formal legal definition, the ghaza would become a leitmotif in the Turks' reimagining of themselves in Islamic terms and in giving them a sense of common purpose that transcended tribal difference.

By the time large numbers of Turks began to convert to Islam, the dynamic set in motion by the Kur'anic revelation had resulted in the development of a whole civilization that went far beyond those basics. Questions of how to choose a new leader for the community after the death of the Prophet and how to understand that leader's role had given rise to a political split that evolved over time into sectarian differences, most notably between Sunni and Shi'i Muslims, of whom the former ultimately became the majority. For those who became Sunnis, seniority and experience were the most important qualifications for leadership; and maintenance of communal unity was a paramount value in its own right. For those who became Shi'is, direct descent from the Prophet in a specific charismatic line was the essential criterion in determining the leader. With time, what had started as a political difference gave rise to contrasting and at times antagonistic religious cultures.

Alongside the difference over leadership, Muslims also faced questions about how to live once Muhammad, who had been both Prophet and communal leader, was no longer present to tell them. This implied a need not only to record the revelations that had come to him as the Messenger of God but also to collect and preseve all other information about his sayings and acts in his human capacity. The former became the Kur'an; the latter became the *hadith*, or "reports," for which Sunnis and Shi'is developed distinctive sources and traditions of scholarship. Defining how Muslims should live implied the need to distill from these sources a system of religious law, the *shari'a*. With the study of the Kur'an, hadith, and jurisprudence, the disciplines of Islamic religious studies began to proliferate. With the rapid conquests of the decades immediately following Muhammad's death, the early Muslims also became masters of a large empire. Consequently, as they developed the Islamic religious sciences, they were exposed to the achievements of other, older civilizations; and many works from those sources began to be translated into Arabic, introducing new ideas, including the pre-Islamic Iranian tradition of kingship and statecraft. The civilization of Islam encountered by Turkic converts was, thus, already a highly developed one including heterogeneous elements, of which some were Islamic only by association. No doubt the perception of Islamic civilization as rich and dynamic helped attract Turkic converts.

What did it mean for them to convert? Answers to this question have long suffered from two exaggerations. One overestimates the extent to which Sunni Islam had yet fully developed. The other underestimates the Islamization of the early Turkic converts as "nominal" or "light," classifying everything nonstandard in Islamic terms as residues of "shamanism." Such arguments are wrong on both sides.

The creation of a widely accepted synthesis of Sunni Muslim belief, teaching, and practice was a project of roughly the twelfth to fifteenth centuries. Iranian religious scholars (*ulema*) played critical roles in this endeavor (Shi'i Islam would not become Iran's official religion until after 1500). Turkic converts began to move into Iran and assume important political roles there in the eleventh century, prior to the elaboration of this Sunni synthesis.[7] Paradoxically, the influence of the Iranian ulema would be compounded by multiple crises besetting the cities they inhabited. The crises included both urban growth, which had outstripped what Iran's agrarian economy could support, and the influx of converted but still nomadic Turks. Later, the conquests of still unconverted Mongols and the plague epidemics of the 1340s worsened things further. Such pressures forced many Iranian scholars to emigrate to Iraq, Anatolia, and India.

In the period through the fifteenth century, while Turkish warriors and dynasts were making their mark through the military expansion and political reintegration of the Islamic world from Anatolia to India, Iranian ulema were spreading the emerging Sunni synthesis and Persian (as well as Arabic) literary culture across the same domain. Hallmarks of this synthesis include the founding of *medrese*s as schools of higher Islamic learning, the rise of different schools of Islamic jurisprudence (which clashed, sometimes violently, until the eventual achievement of mutual accommodation among Sunni schools),[8] reproduction of Iranian-style models of religious leadership (such as the urban *shaykh al-Islam*, an office destined for a long history in the Ottoman Empire), the sufi brotherhoods that became organized from the twelfth century on, urban young men's associations known as the *futuwwa*, and the proliferation of pilgrimages, not only to Mecca, but also to the local shrines that began to define a new sacred microgeography.

Turkic converts entered the Middle East just as these constituents of a Sunni "international," not dependent for its maintenance on any government, were being put into place. The elaboration of this synthesis coincided with the Turks' formative experience of Islam; with time, the synthesis would become the official religion of the Ottoman Empire (1300–1922). Once fully developed, this Sunni synthesis was more than merely international. It provided Muslims with universal values and norms that made the forms of life recognizable everywhere Muslims lived and ideally made of the entire Muslim world one great reservoir of trust. Whether "international" or "universal," however, uniformity never overwhelmed diversity in religious activism. While the Sunni synthesis was still emerging, eye-catching proof of this fact appeared with the simultaneous spread of anarchical forms of radically renunciatory piety—wandering mystics (*dervishes*) known for their bizarre garb, or lack thereof, and their unconventional practices.[9] Openly ignoring or defying the Islamic law that the ulema propounded, such figures attracted larger followings and swayed many a convert.

Viewed from the vantage point of still unconverted Turks living beyond the frontiers of Islam, conversion was a dual process, involving both "the 'imposition' of Islamic norms in a new setting" and the assimilation of Islam "into indigenous modes of thought and action."[10] In the encounter between the old and new faiths, the new one could only prevail if it proved more persuasive than the old. The likelihood that the converts' understandings of their new faith would retain "unorthodox" elements from their old one could not be excluded. This had been true of earlier converts, held true for the Turks, and would also prove true of later converts. Yet, arguments that early Turkic conversions were only superficial or marked by residues of "shamanism" are misleading. In some sense, especially when the decision to convert was made by a ruler both for his subjects and himself, conversion could not be much more than nominal at first. Even when conversion occurred not by personal decision but by that of the ruler, as was often the case, the change must not be quickly dismissed as superficial. In a kinship society, an individual who deviated from the ancestral ways would have been dangerously unprotected. What could be more reassuring than for the entire society to make the same change at once, with its ruler in the lead?

The argument that any deviance in early Turkic Islam can be attributed to residues of shamanism misleads above all by treating shamanism as a black box with undefined contents. As already noted, "shamanism" is not satisfactory as a name for the indigenous Inner Asian religious cults. In these, the shaman was a religious specialist who performed certain functions, whereas the most common religious observances centered on ancestral rites that families performed around the hearth, without need for any shaman, or that rulers could perform in more elaborate style, perhaps with shamans as attending liturgical specialists. In addition, the traditional Inner Asian cults were not the only religions with which pre-Islamic Turks had experience; nor was syncretism—the mixing of elements from different religions—new to them. Finally, if conversion meant not only the imposition of a faith from outside but also its assimilation by the converts, the Muslims who impressed potential converts were as likely to be wild and woolly dervishes as learned ulema.

The process of conversion might be recorded in histories such as learned historians write. It might also be preserved in narrative forms that meant more to the people who lived through these events, narratives resembling the Turks' origin myths and oral epics about their legendary heroes. In such a case, the resulting narrative structure might be as implausible by the standards of learned historians as the idea that the Turks descended from a she-wolf.

However, if the narrative shared the same symbolic fecundity, it might offer powerful justification for the newly chosen faith. Implausible as academic
history, such a narrative would succeed as sacred history, as a record of what
was religiously meaningful to its audience.

Just such a sacred history survives, in Chaghatay Turkic, of the defini-
tive conversion of a Mongol successor state, the *ulus* of Jochi, or Golden
Horde, in the time of Özbek Khan (r. 1313–41).[11] His predecessor, Berke
Khan, had converted, but backsliding had followed. The account of Özbek's
conversion begins when four Muslim holy men decided to "[g]o and sum-
mon Özbek to Islam." They arrived outside his sacred precinct (*koru*, the
site reserved for ancestral rituals and burials) just as his "sorcerers and divin-
ers," Islamic usage to indicate shamans (*kam* in Turkic), were preparing for
a libation ceremony. Something spoiled the ceremony; the lack of clarity
on this point hints that details of pre-Islamic ritual were being forgotten by
the time the narrative was written down. The khan asked what was wrong.
The holy men answered that a Muslim might have come near. The khan
told them to go look. They did and found the four holy men outside the
royal preserve. The four asked to be taken into the khan's presence. As soon
as Özbek Khan saw them, God inclined him to show them favor. When he
asked who they were, the strangers told him and said that "we have come
by the command of God most high in order to make you a Muslim." The
khan's *shaykh*s (his shamans) cried out against them. But the khan said: "I
am a *padshah* [emperor]. . . . Whoever's religion may be true, I will be with
him. . . . [D]ebate with one another."

Debates on religion in the presence of a ruler have a long history in the
sources on both Muslims and Mongols, and many texts record what was
said. This account spares its audience anything as boring as what the debaters said, dismissing that as "turmoil and contention." The debate prov-
ing indecisive or meaningless to the audience, the contestants decided to
dig two oven pits. One contestant from each side should enter an oven.
"Whoever emerges without being burned, his religion will be true." When
the ovens were ready, one of the Muslim holy men begged to be allowed to
go in. This was Baba Tükles, so called "because all of his limbs were covered with body hair (*tük*)." Calling for armor, he donned the chain mail
"over his bare flesh." Everyone saw the awesome sight of his body hair standing straight and sticking out through the chain armor as he entered the oven,
reciting "the remembrance of God" as he went. The shamans, in contrast,
had to force one of their men into the fire, which incinerated him instantly.
Meanwhile, Baba Tükles's pious recitations continued from the other oven.
When it was opened, he asked why the hurry. His armor was red hot, but

**Baba Tükles and His Companions Might Have Looked Something Like These Men.** One art historian captioned this miniature "Three Dervishes from Turkistan." This and other works attributed to Mehmed Siyah Kalem do evoke the world of the steppes, both material and spiritual. These men suggest Baba Tükles's shagginess, but his garb would probably have been more bizarre. From Topkapı Palace Museum, Hazine 2160, f.85a.

"by the power of God most high not a hair of the Baba's body was burned." Seeing this, the khan and his people became Muslims once and for all.

Here, the hairy holy man convinces not by his words but by beating the shamans at their own wonder-working game. His "bare flesh" connects him with the socially deviant dervishes of the period. His astonishing body hair evokes the shaman's world of extraordinary traits and experiences.[12] His red-hot armor recalls the association between shamans and smiths. Symbolically most fertile are the resonances between the fire pit and the hearth fire of the ancestral rites. Having disrupted the shamans' libation ritual by his mere presence in the vicinity, he descended into and reemerged from the fire, whereas the shaman was reduced to ashes. His reemergence from the sealed pit reflects the emergence theme in Inner Asian origin myths. Although his verbal message made no impression, his intervention into the old rituals and appropriation of their symbols convinced khan and people alike.

Baba Tükles himself became assimilated into the narrative structures of Turkic myth, for he reemerged from the fire pit not just as bringer of Islam but as shaman, hero, ancestor, first man, and nation founder.[13] Also mentioned in conventional histories under the name Seyyid Ata and honored in a cult at the shrine containing his tomb, Baba Tükles was also presented in later tradition as the ancestor of Edigü Beg, a powerful commander and the founder of the Noghay horde after the breakup of the Golden Horde.[14] Özbek Khan, too, would later be cited posthumously as the forefather of the Özbeks, or Uzbeks. In an environment where the origins that required mythic narration were as much Islamic as Turkic, an Özbek Khan who brought Islam to his people *should* have been the ancestor of the Özbek Turks. What did it matter if they were only "born" as a people long after he died. The fact that Özbek Khan's own state, the Golden Horde, disintegrated less than twenty years after his death, probably amid the ravages of the plague, makes it all the more remarkable that his memory lived on as it did.[15]

Legendary accounts of the origins and Islamization of other Turkic peoples do not always include a direct counterpart to Baba Tükles. Sometimes the roles of ethnic progenitor and bringer of Islam are fused in one person. Islamized versions of the origins of the Oğuz Turks have the infant Oghuz refuse his mother's milk until she converts to Islam. Analogous motifs appear in accounts of several Turkic rulers and heroes.[16] In the seventeenth-century rendering of the Oghuz narrative, the Turks had been Muslims ever since the days of their ancestors Nuh and Yafes (the Kur'anic names for the biblical Noah and Japheth), until under Alınja Khan their prosperity caused them to forget God. Oghuz was his great-grandson. The infant Oghuz's refusal to nurse from his mother unless she converted was the first of the wonders by which he brought his people to Islam. They would then spread from Transoxania to Turkey and beyond. With them they took their tribal marks or brands (*tamga*), listed and depicted later in the same work, from which the distinctive *gül* motifs of the Turkish carpet-weaving tradition are thought to have derived.[17]

Sited at a point of contact between Islam and traditional Inner Asian religion, the Baba Tükles narrative implicitly brings up the question of interfaith relations. In Islamic law, the terms of interfaith relations depend on the religion of the non-Muslims in question and whether they are living under Islamic rule or not. These points proved important for the Turks, as they went from being non-Muslim polytheists (from the Muslim point of view) to being Muslims and even standard-bearers in the expansion of the lands under Islamic rule.

The Kur'an has much to say about other faiths, among which it draws a critical distinction. The Kur'an states, for example, that there shall be "no compulsion in religion" (2.256). As applied to non-Muslims, this statement is generally understood as limited to Jews and Christians. Both those faiths are mentioned in the Kur'an and have a recognized place in Islamic sacred history. As recipients of revealed scripture, their followers are *ahl al-kitab*, "people of the book." As Islamic law developed, it included provisions to accommodate Jews and Christians under Islamic rule as *ahl al-dhimma*, "people of the pact." From this derives *dhimmi* as a term for someone in that status. *Dhimmi* status conceded a measure of semiautonomy to the various religious communities on condition that they accept the subaltern position assigned for them in the law and pay a specific tax, the *jizya*. In an era when any state was assumed to have a religious identity, and law was thought of first and foremost as religious law, this was about as good a system for accommodating religious difference as could be devised. Peoples of the book living under Islamic rule could convert to Islam if they wanted to, but *dhimma* was a system for accommodation, not conversion. The survival of ancient Jewish and Christian communities in the Middle East attests to its benefits, as does the influx of Iberian Jews into Islamic lands after 1492.[18] For non-Muslims other than Jews and Christians, the situation was starker. De facto exceptions were made at times, but officially *dhimma* was not an option for them.

Whatever their religion, non-Muslims' status also differed in terms of whether they lived under Islamic rule or not. Islamic law, reflecting the vast Islamic expansion of the early centuries, assumed that the frontiers were expanding. In principle, when confronted with Muslim conquest, people of the book had the choice among conversion, *dhimma*, and the sword, whereas other non-Muslims had only the choice between conversion and the sword. In fact, real-life situations introduced variations into the application of these abstractions, such as the accommodation of Hindus under Muslim rule in India.

Historically, the Islamic borderlands were a zone of active defense that included episodic raiding (*ghaza*) into infidel territory. Islamic law forbade the enslavement of Muslims, but non-Muslims (other than *dhimmis* living peaceably under Islamic rule) were fair game. Prior to their conversion, the Turks' horsemanship and martial skills had made them prized catches in this kind of raiding as early as the ninth century. Many Central Asian Turks, as polytheists in Islamic terms, thus first experienced Islam from the wrong side of the firing line during raids by Muslim border warriors (*ghazis*). As Turks began to convert, they not only changed religion but also joined the other side in the border raiding and skirmishing. Al-Idrisi (1100–66) depicts a Transoxania where converted Turks raided and enslaved their unconverted brethren.[19]

Early Turkic Muslims, then, probably understood the ghaza not in Islamic legal scholars' terms but as a new name for the raiding unconverted Turkic tribesmen engaged in and for their old image of heroism. As Turkish Muslims moved further into the Middle East, they encountered other frontiers and different situations. Along the Iranian-Byzantine border in the eleventh century or in Anatolia and the Balkans in the thirteenth and fourteenth, Muslim border warriors confonted people of the book, mostly Christians. If civilizations sometimes clashed on those frontiers, syncretism and hybridization were more usual outcomes.

No transformation in the history of the Turks has been more profound in its consequences than Islamization. They had to live through this in terms that made sense to them at the time. The same point applied to their teachers, among whom not even the ulema, let alone the dervishes, yet knew all that later generations would see as correct Sunni Islam. Frontier life, encountered repeatedly on a series of frontiers, would profoundly affect the Turks' experience as Muslims; and the ghaza ideal would acquire lasting prestige among them. However, it did so as one more strand woven into histories and narratives thematically as heterogeneous as the earliest Türk origin myths or the account of the conversion of Özbek Khan. As the story of his meeting with Baba Tükles shows, the winning of converts depended primarily on teaching and example.

## The Formation of Turko-Islamic Peoples and Cultures

Viewed from a Middle Eastern vantage point, the Turkish influx into the Islamic world occurred in three stages. The first phase began in the ninth century, when unconverted Turkic nomads, captured in border raids, were used as slave-soldiers in Baghdad or elsewhere in the Middle East. Converted to Islam and assimilated culturally, they created no lasting Turkic presence in the Middle East. The second phase began in the tenth century, when a minor ruling clan from Transoxania, the Seljuks, converted to Islam and migrated into Iran to seek its fortune. So began the remarkable career of the Turks as empire builders in the Islamic Middle East. The Seljuks' tribal followers created a significant Turkic ethnic presence in the Middle East and no doubt also an oral Turkish-Islamic folk culture. Yet the Seljuk elite never created a Turkish-Islamic literary culture. That began to occur in the eleventh century in Transoxania where the Turkic Karakhanid dynasty and its subjects converted in mass. The Karakhanids' conversion marked a critical phase in the Islamization of Inner Asia. However, because they were sited north of the Amu Darya (Oxus River), this did not mark a new phase in the creation of a Turkish-Muslim presence *inside* the Middle East. The third phase in forming a Turkish presence inside the Middle East, that of creating a Turkish literary culture to go with the Turkish demographic presence, would have to wait nearly until the Ottomans' rise in the fourteenth century.

During the first phase of the Turks' entry into the Middle East, prisoners captured in the borderlands between Khurasan and Transoxania were brought into central Islamic lands, converted to Islam, and used as slave-soldiers.[20] The Turks' history thus intersected with that of the Abbasid caliphs, and earlier patterns of recruiting military forces that were either alien *or* servile were fused.[21] Muslims valued the steppe Turks' prowess in horsemanship and archery, memorably described by the Arabic essayist al-Jahiz (d. 868), and their fine appearance.[22]

The Abbasid caliphs began to use Turkic slave-soldiers early in the ninth century. In particular, al-Mu'tasim (833–42) created a retinue including regiments of Turkish slaves (*ghulam* or *mamluk*). Not subject to all the disabilities of chattel slavery, the ghulams were carefully trained to serve as agents of their powerful master, for whom their chief value lay in the unconditional loyalty they owed him. As stated in a verse quoted by Nizam al-Mulk, (1018–92), vezir to the Seljuk sultans and author of perhaps the best-known Islamic manual for princes,

One obedient slave is better
than three hundred sons;
for the latter desire their father's death,
the former his master's glory.[23]

Such thinking did not always pay off, but persistence in it turned slave recruitment into a key feature of Middle Eastern state formation for a thousand years. Unfortunately for the Abbasids, their slave-soldiers took only a few decades to traverse the distance from palace guard to regimental commander, unruly provincial governor, founder of a petty local dynasty, and even king maker in Baghdad. Forces intended to strengthen the Islamic caliphate had strengthened the centrifugal tendencies within it. Examples include the Tulunid dynasty in Egypt and Syria (868–905) and the Ikhshidids who followed them in Egypt (935–69).

There were also contestants for power who were of neither Turkic nor slave origin. The dynasty of governors most known for recruiting Turkic ghulams in this period was that of the Samanids (819–1005), Iranian governors of the Transoxanian frontier zone, who were also patrons of the nascent Perso-Islamic literary culture. So active were they in slave raiding and slave trading that by the late tenth century the market for slaves had become glutted and depressed. The Samanids acquired their own Turkic slave-soldiers and developed a slave-training system that Nizam al-Mulk declared exemplary. Perhaps the system worked too well; the Samanids were eclipsed by a dynasty that emerged from their slave-troops, the Ghaznavids, who founded an empire stretching from Khurasan to Central Asia and India.[24]

Many Turks thus first encountered Islam as the targets of slave raids conducted amid rhetorical flourishes about ghaza. Turkic tribesmen in the frontier zone lived by raiding the Muslims as much as Muslim border defenders lived by raiding them; in Arabic sources, the same verb, *ghaza*, applies in either case. Yet Islam gave a religious justification to this way of life—in addition to earthly booty, a promise of heavenly reward, a promise that probably helped win converts to Islam. The raiders' impact could be traumatic, especially on peoples whose religions, in this case the indigenous Inner Asian cults, made them ineligible for *dhimmi* status. In 893, for example, the Samanids took the town of Talas in what is now southern Kazakhstan, killing and capturing thousands, including the ruler's wife; some notables saved themselves by converting to Islam.

However much power they achieved, the local dynasties that were formed inside the Abbasid caliphate by Turkic slave-soldiers (ghulams) created no lasting Turkic presence there. Even slave states that lasted into the post-Abbasid period were not greatly different in this regard: neither the "slave-kings" (1206–90), from whom India's Delhi Sultanate emerged, nor Egypt's Mamluk sultanate (1249–1517) left Turkic societies behind.[25] To create an appreciable Turkish presence in the Middle East became the work of the Seljuks.

The Seljuks' origins lie clouded in the ethnogenesis of the Oghuz Turks, whose history of state formation began in the ninth century, prior to their conversion to Islam. The original Seljuk, a commander from the Kınık tribe of the Oghuz, converted to Islam in 985 at Jand on the Syr Darya (Jaxartes River). The biblical names of his four sons—Mîkâ'îl, Isrâ'îl, Mûsâ, and Yûnus (Jonah)—suggest previous acquaintance with either Khazar Judaism or Nestorian Christianity. Now, they and their followers "became part of the Islamicized, Turkic border population that warred with the 'pagans' in the steppe."[26] Pressured by tribal movements and political instability, they were "universally described as a bedraggled, sorry lot, driven by desperation and impending starvation to conquest."[27] Serving first one petty dynast and then another, under Mikail's sons Toghrul and Chaghrı, they migrated into Khurasan and began raiding the local populace.

Ghazis raiding infidels were one thing; Muslims preying on Muslims were quite another. Ghaznavid attempts to stop this led to battle at Dandankan (23 May 1040), a victory of Seljuk desperation over Ghaznavid exhaustion. The Seljuks became masters of Khurasan, expanding their power into Transoxania and across Iran. By 1055 Toghrul had expanded his control all the way to Baghdad, setting himself up as the champion of the Abbasid caliph, who honored him with the title *sultan*. Earlier rulers may have used this title, but the Seljuks seem to have been the first to inscribe it on their coins.[28]

The formation of the Great Seljuk Empire, which held together under Toghrul (1040–63), Alp Arslan (1063–72), and Malik Shah (1072–92), proved highly significant in both Islamic and Turkic terms. During the preceding century, signs of the Abbasid loss of control had included not only political decentralization but also, by some accounts, a proliferation of Shi'i movements and dynasties. Islamic historian Marshall Hodgson spoke of a "Shi'i century," from 946, when the Iranian Shi'i Buyids occupied Baghdad, to 1055, when the Seljuks took the city and rescued the Abbasid caliph from the Buyids. The idea that the Seljuks reversed a rising tide of Shi'i influence now seems inflated. The rise of Shi'i regimes in some places did not necessarily mean the wide spread of Shi'i allegiance among the populace. The Seljuks seem to have been sufficiently caught up in the religious controversies of Iran's nascent Sunni synthesis that their own religious position was not yet as clear-cut as the Sunni-Hanefi allegiance that has been retrospectively credited to them.[29] Yet they clearly immersed themselves in their new religious identity. It has been said that Muslim Turks "sank their national identity in Islam as the Arabs and Persians had never done."[30] The Seljuks launched a new period of Sunni Islamic reunification, integration under the Abbasid caliphate, and expansion against the Byzantines and the European crusaders. A century after Toghrul entered Baghdad, Shi'i power centers like the Egyptian-based Fatimid caliphate (1171) had been eliminated, and "prayers were [again] recited in the name of the Sunni caliph of Baghdad over all the lands of Islam from Central Asia into Africa."[31]

Not only reintegration and expansion but also a new stratification of power emerged, in which legitimacy and prestige belonged to the Abbasid caliph, but political power belonged to sultans or other synonymously titled rulers who acquired power by conquest and claimed legitimacy from him. As a late Seljuk sultan, Sanjar, wrote to the caliph's vezir in 1133, "[W]e have received from the lord of the world . . . the kingship of the world . . . we have a standard and a covenant."[32] This division of power continued on down the ladder in the *amir-a'yan* system, with the caliph theoretically at the top, then the various sultans or other autonomous rulers supposedly acting as his agents, then the commanders (*amir*) of their military forces, then the notables (*a'yan*) from the indigenous populace who mediated between conquerors and conquered, and lastly the subject populace.[33] Resembling this "amir-a'yan system," a somewhat similar "a'yan system" would later emerge in the Ottoman Empire.

The Seljuk sultanate was significant for Turkic, as well as Islamic, political culture. A new charismatic ruling clan, the Seljuks were the first such to emerge from the Oghuz Turks. The title sultan began to replace that of kaghan as the most prestigious title for a Muslim Turkic ruler, and Turkic ideas about rulership and its legitimization began to be interwoven with Islamic motifs. For example, the Seljuks adopted elements of Abbasid, Buyid, and Ghaznavid statecraft, including the creation of their own ghulam corps, or the assignment of *ikta's*—land grants or revenue grants, depending on the situation—as a way to compensate important functionaries.[34] In the long run, most Turkish dynasties did become identified with Sunni Islam and with the Hanefi school of jurisprudence, the one least restrictive of the ruler's discretion and the most accommodating to custom. The Seljuks benefited in far-reaching ways from Iranian religious and literary dynamism and from the crisis conditions that forced many Iranian scholars to emigrate in this period, spreading both Persian literary culture and the various constituents of the evolving Sunni synthesis, including the religious colleges (*medrese*) that provided the Islamic world with its institutions of higher learning.

Part of the excitement of Islamic high culture as the Seljuks encountered it was that it included heterogeneous elements, some of them pre-Islamic in origin. For example, the ideological resources that Islamic political thought offered the Seljuks included both genuinely Islamic themes, like sharia observance, and political-philosophical motifs with non-Islamic roots. Such was the old Iranian idea of the authoritarian monarch, who dispenses justice by his own unfettered judgment, or the "circle of justice," an idealized description of the reciprocal relationship between rulers and ruled.[35] Islamic civilization, in short, was already a synthesis of elements from different sources. This fact provided a basis for reciprocal interaction between Islamic and Turkic ideas, as became particularly apparent in the realm of political culture.

Clearly, the Seljuk Empire was a new kind of state in Turkic experience. A dynasty of nomadic origin had acquired power over an ethnically alien, agrarian society of ancient culture. The dynasty would have to employ experts from that society to administer it and would have to assimilate culturally to a significant extent. Emblematic of this shift, whereas the first Seljuk sultans bore Turkic zoonyms, or animal names, still redolent of traditional steppe culture—Toghrul, "gyrfalcon"; Alp Arslan, "hero lion"—the third bore a name that broadcast Seljuk political pretensions to all Muslims: Malik Shah, a name made out of two common nouns meaning "king" in Arabic and Persian, respectively. Toghrul had apparently divided rulership, east and west, with his brother Chaghrı, a familiar Turkic theme. The Syriac chronicler Bar Hebraeus noted another point evocative of steppe culture in speaking of Khâtôn, as he calls Toghrul's wife: "[A]ll the business of the kingdom was administered by her."[36] Of course, khatun ("lady") was not her name, but a title. Under Alp Arslan and Malik Shah, dual kingship vanished, and the administration was headed instead by the distinguished Iranian vezir, Nizam al-Mulk.

The dynasty's sedentarization and adoption of Irano-Islamic high culture could only alienate its original followers. To rise to power and turn against one's old supporters is a political game at once old and ever new; this would not be the last such occurrence. Not only founding medreses and hiring Iranian bureaucrats but also recruiting ghulams as a way to create a more reliable military force than their tribal supporters, the Seljuks began as early as 1048 to direct the tribes toward the Iranian-Byzantine and Caucasian frontiers. "Born on the eastern frontier against heathendom," their religious fervor was now "carried to the western frontier against Christendom." By now centuries old, the Islamic-Byzantine frontier zone, running from Tarsus to Erzurum, had long since ceased to be a site of active territorial expansion and become a place where many ghazis were really "knights of the prayer niche" (*fursan al-mihrab*). Yet cross-border raiding continued, and the border zone exerted a powerful attraction over Muslims who wished to escape the authority of rulers: ascetics, ghazis, even scholars, including the authors of major works on *jihad*. The Byzantines again pushed forward into this frontier zone between 950 and 1000.[37] On the Muslim side, however, the influx of Turks generated a new expansive dynamism, which led to the battle of Manzikert, or Malazgird (1071).

A truly decisive battle, Manzikert broke the Byzantine border defenses, opened Anatolia to Turkic in-migration, and so launched a new phase in the expansion of the frontiers of Islam. The Seljuks' tribal followers had done what earlier Muslims had failed for centuries to do. For the next several centuries, Anatolia would be a kind of "wild west," where the historic Turkic competition between micropolity and macropolity would continue, becoming reconfigured over time under the impact of Islamic culture and a new environment.

Political science, Seljuk style, thus introduced new elements into Turkic political culture; yet the Seljuks also failed to solve some of its old problems. Preserving the idea of the ruling clan's collective sovereignty, the Seljuks experienced both succession conflicts and territorial splits resulting from the assumption that each member of the ruling clan was entitled to rule a part of the dynastic patrimony. Another source of division was the appointment of *atabeg*s ("father-beys"), the young princes' tutors, who governed in the prince's name and could marry his mother and take over as governor if the prince died. A number of atabeg dynasties emerged as a result.[38] Gradually, the Seljuks lost control of the *ikta'* system, and the *ikta'*s, too, became hereditary. Malik Shah's death in 1092, a few months after Isma'ili Shi'i assassins

killed Nizam al-Mulk, ended Seljuk unity. In time the push toward political reintegration would resume, but lasting results would require solutions
to some of these problems in statecraft. Those lessons were learned painfully and anonymously, perhaps as scribes and soldiers who had served fallen
rulers rode off toward the horizon in search of a new master whose good
fortune (*dawla* in Arabic) was still on the rise.

Historians call the empire of Toghrul, Alp Arslan, and Malik Shah the
"Great Seljuk Empire," as opposed to the smaller Seljuk and *atabeg* states
into which it decomposed after 1092. One of those was the Seljuk State of
Rum, formed in Anatolia (to Arabs, *bilâd al-Rûm*, "the land of the Romans"
in the sense of Byzantines). Between 1071 and the Mongol conquest of the
Rum Seljuks (1243), perhaps a million Turks entered Anatolia, forming not
its largest ethnic group but the only one spread throughout that region.[39]
They were made up partly of "tribal groupings, but not entire tribes," as
well as other social groups, including bands of ghazis and dervishes.

Fragments of tribes, wandering dervishes, ghazi bands—this was a society in flux. A rebellious branch of the Seljuk dynasty, the sons of Kutlumush,
moved into Anatolia and rallied some of the tribesmen. One of Kutlumush's
sons, Suleyman, acquired control of Konya, made it the capital, and proclaimed himself sultan. Byzantine attempts to regain control ended at the
Battle of Myriokephalon in 1176, and the Seljuk sultanate of Rum reached
its height in the early thirteenth century. The Seljuks of Rum faced feuds
within the dynasty and rival Turkish statelets in Anatolia, even before the
Mongols invaded (1243) and reduced them all to tributary status. In particular, the Danişmend dynasty held parts of north-central Anatolia throughout the period.[40] Meanwhile, amid the migratory swarm that Turkified
Anatolia, the dispersion of learned men from the Persian-speaking east paradoxically made of the Seljuk court at Konya a new center for Perso-Islamic
court culture, as exemplified by the great mystical poet Jelaleddin Rumi
(1207–73).

A major reflection of the Anatolian Turkish culture of the time takes
the form of a prose epic on the exploits of Seyyid Battal Ghazi, whom Turkic
legend held to be the ancestor of the Danişmends.[41] Originally an Arab
commander who fought in ninth-century campaigns against the Byzantines,
Battal Ghazi became the stuff of legend first in Arabic and then, starting in
the late eleventh or early twelfth century, in Turkish. Resembling the Byzantine hero of the borderlands, Digenis Akritas, who is mentioned in the
*Battal-name* ("Battal-book"), Battal Ghazi and his mythic appropriation as
the progenitor of a Turkish dynasty show how the Turks tied themselves
into the syncretic warp and weft of life in the frontier world of Anatolia.[42]
Something of a sequel to the *Battal-name*, the *Danişmend-name* recounts the

exploits of the Danişmend ghazis. The exploits of its heroes and heroines interweave personal conversion, intermarriage, hybridity, and ghazi derring-do in the borderlands of Islam. Unconcerned about thematic consistency, the "Book of Dede Korkut," which acquired its present form after 1200, likewise works contemporary references and Islamic strands like the ghaza into a set of folktales recalling the Oghuz Turks' pre-Islamic heroics.[43]

In contrast to the starker terms on which the still unconverted Turks of Central Asia had first confronted Muslim frontier warriors, the Turks in Anatolia encountered a mostly Christian population, whose status as peoples of the book (*ahl al-kitab*) made them eligible to live under Islamic rule as *dhimmi*s. In Anatolia, for centuries after the battle of Manzikert, cultures and creeds coexisted as much as competed. Probably few places were not frontier zones at some point, and the defenders on both the Byzantine and Islamic sides of these frontiers came to know each other well. The long-term trend, however, was toward Islamization and Turkification.[44] Heroes as different as the Byzantines' Digenis Akritas, the "twice-born border warrior" (so called because he was the son of a Byzantine mother and a Christianized Arab commander), or two of Dede Korkut's heroes, Bamsı Beyrek and Kan Turalı, both of whom chose infidel brides, show that intermarriage was one of the most prominent themes in this environment.[45] Documenting the cultural symbiosis differently, twelfth-century coins of the Danişmends display their names and titles, such as amir and ghazi, in both Arabic and Greek letters.[46] If the Turks came to Anatolia as conquerors in 1071, the future Turkish people would be descendants of the conquered as much as of the conquerors.[47]

Between the 1240s and the 1340s, however, major crises disrupted both the macropolitics of Turkic state formation and the micropolitics of tribalism in this frontier environment. From 1243 on, repeated Mongol invasions and tribute exactions severely weakened the Seljuks of Rum—an oft-cited fact. In the 1340s, the Black Plague struck Byzantium and parts of Anatolia—a fact overlooked in historical writing on the Ottomans, possibly because the plague carried off literate eyewitnesses from their midst.[48] Henceforth, state formation would require coming to terms with a social landscape consisting to an unusual degree of ad hoc groupings that were in a state of ferment. A new round of statelets (*beyliks*) that formed in the Rum Seljuks' frontier zones became the dynamic elements in Anatolian politics. From one of these, the Ottoman Empire would emerge. The statelets competed for influence in an environment where popular social movements proliferated in response to distressed conditions. Fuad Köprülü characterized those of this period under four headings: *ghazi*s or *alp*s (an old Turkic term for warrior heroes), *akhi*s (the Turkish name for the town-based young men's associations known in Arabic as *futuwwa*), heterodox mystical *baba*s and their followers, and the "sisters of Rum" (*bacıyan-ı Rum*). About these women mystics or ghazis, tantalizingly little is known, although their mention in one source provides more evidence of the relative gender equality inherited from pre-Islamic Turkic societies. The amazon heroines in the tales of Dede Korkut and in the ghazi epics of this period—notably the infidel-born, "lion-like" Efromiya of the *Danişmendname*—reinforce that image.[49]

Anatolian counterparts of Baba Tükles, the "heterodox mystical babas" formed numerous, anarchistic movements of wandering dervishes, characterized by radical asceticism and socially deviant forms of renunciation, some of which—bizarrely accoutered states of seminakedness, consumption of alcohol or drugs, and deviant sex—were deliberately chosen to provoke censure from the pious, including the more respectable, organized *sufi* orders, which were also spreading in this period. Despite appearances to the contrary, the radical dervishes were often recruited from the well educated and socially prominent. Some of them accompanied the ghazi bands, while others helped to promote the spread of Islam wherever they wandered. Somewhat resembling Europe's itinerant monastic orders of the same period—the contemporaneity of similar impulses in different religious cultures is a recurrent theme—the wandering dervishes were most characteristic of Anatolia and Iran, thus of regions directly affected by Mongol expansion, and less characteristic of the Arab lands. Once a strong Ottoman state had emerged and become committed to strict Sunni Islam, the deviant movements would later be marginalized or shoehorned into formally organized dervish orders that respected state authority. The deviant movements left behind few documents of the sort historians typically study. However, new epics continued to be produced about both ghazis and dervishes, such as Umur Paşa, the seafaring ghazi bey of Aydın, or Sarı Saltuk, a heterodox, charismatic wonder-working hero of Turkification and Islamization west and north of the Black Sea. The production of such epics followed the advance of the Turkish ghazis and their dervish babas into southeastern Europe.[50]

Emerging from such a diffusely structured society, the Ottoman Empire would complete the third phase in the establishment of a Turkish presence in the Islamic Middle East by generating a Turko-Islamic high literary culture to accompany the demographic base. Most of the Ottomans' six-century history being discussed in the next chapter, it suffices here to note what bases existed for this Turko-Islamic literary culture in Anatolia on the eve of the Ottoman period. The heroic folk epics, which were ultimately recorded in writing, form part of this. During a revolt against the Mongols in 1277, when Mehmed Bey of Karaman briefly placed a pretender on the Rum Seljuk throne at Konya, the rebels—ignorant of Persian—ordered that "from that day forward, in the council, in the dervish lodge, in the court, in the assembly, in the square, no language but Turkish should be spoken."[51] Although that experiment ended with the revolt, a precedent had been set. Also active in the late thirteenth century was Yunus Emre, Anatolia's first memorable Turkish-language poet. Both he and Anatolia's great Persian-language poet, Jelaleddin Rumi, were men whose personal and literary lives were transformed by charismatic heterodox dervishes.[52] Rumi's Persian poetry has remained central to the rites of the Mevlevi dervish order, which flourished under the Ottoman Empire, and to Persian literature in general. The Turkish poetry of Yunus Emre and other folk poets has endured as the hymns of Turkey's Alevi religious minority and part of the literary patrimony of Turks everywhere. Little survives in writing from the fourteenth-century Ottomans; no doubt the bubonic plague is greatly to blame. Thereafter, they would create the most important of all Turkic literary cultures.

## A Karakhanid Postscript

During the same period in which the Turks entered the Middle East, the Karakhanid state in Transoxania established a lasting place for itself in the Turks' history by sponsoring the very first Turko-Islamic literary culture.[53] The Karakhanids claimed the title kaghan after the fall of the Uyghur kaghanate in 840, and their ruling house may have been descended from the charismatic Ashina clan. The state displayed many traits of traditional Turkic state formation, including a bilateral east-west division with kaghans in both places, as well as four subrulers beneath them. Each kaghan and subruler was known by a combination of an animal name with the appropriate title. The "lion black kaghan" (*arslan kara kaghan*) in the east outranked the "camel black kaghan" (*bughra kara kaghan*) in the west, for example. In 955, the Karakhanid ruler Satuq Bughra Khan converted to Islam; soon after, Arabic sources recorded the conversion of "two hundred thousand tents of the Turks" in 960. Thus, the Karakhanids became the first Muslim Turkish state beyond the Syr Darya. The world of Islam had begun to advance into Inner Asia.

The very first Turko-Islamic literary culture took shape under the Karakhanids. The most important of a number of works of Islamic content produced under their auspices is the *Wisdom of Royal Glory* (*Kutadgu Bilig*) of Yusuf Khass Hajib, dating from 1069. Like Nizam al-Mulk's Persian-language *Book of Government* (*Siyasat-nama*), this is a "mirror for princes" written by a high official, the privy chamberlain (*khass hâjib*). Unlike the Persian manuals for rulers, this is a work in Turkic and in verse, structured in terms of debates among four allegorical characters, of which three speak for ethical statecraft and life in society and one represents the opposing principle of sufi withdrawal. As he tames "the wild mustang" of "Turkish speech,"[54] the author meticulously equates themes of Turkic statecraft with Islamic values and philosophical principles, many of the latter deriving from pre-Islamic sources, especially Iranian or Greek. In particular, the "royal glory" of the title is conveyed by a word derived from the same term, *kut*, that was used in the earliest Turkic states to refer to the "mandate of heaven," an idea that this work equates with the *farr* claimed by pre-Islamic shahs of Iran and with the Arabic term *dawla*, originally meaning a turn of good fortune but coming by extension to mean dynasty or state.

Yusuf's Islamic intensity can be gauged from his articulation of the ghazi idea as seen in Inner Asian perspective.

> Crush the infidel foe with your armies, seeking strength and support from God. One who dies while fighting the infidel is not dead but alive. So direct all your weapons and troops against the infidel. Burn his house and hall, break his idol, and put a mosque and Muslim congregation in their place. Take captive his son and daughter, his male and female slaves. What wealth you take there, add to your own treasury. Open a way for Islam. Spread abroad the Sharî'ah. Thus you will gain a fair name and a good reward. But do not march against another Muslim, O king. His adversary is God alone. Muslims are brothers to one another: do not quarrel with your brother.[55]

Anomalous compared to the openness to other religions later expressed either in Anatolia or among the Mongols, this intense feeling signifies that for the Karakhanids, most of the infidels were idolaters who could not be accommodated under Islamic rule. Ironically, that usually meant fellow Turks who had still not converted. The larger purpose of the *Kutadgu Bilig*, which is to champion the life in society over that of solitude, affirms a major theme of Irano-Islamic political thought, that religion and state are twins. This idea would echo through the Ottoman centuries in the Persian-style doublet *din-ü-devlet*, religion and state.[56]

In part because Turkish Muslims identified with their new faith at the expense of their old life, in part because no Inner Asian Turkic dynasty achieved the continuity that the Ottomans did in the Middle East, the development of a Turkic-Islamic literary tradition would not become continuous in Central Asia until the fifteenth century. Another contributing factor was the continuing orality of Turkic culture for the illiterate majority. As stated in one of the prologues of the *Kutadgu Bilig*, actually written later, "every town and city, every court and palace, has called this book by a different name."[57]

The other most important work of Karakhanid literary culture is Mahmud al-Kashgari's Arabic work on Turkic lexicography. This work gives the impression that much of the sedentary, as opposed to nomadic, population was Iranian, although in advanced stages of Turkification.[58] Concomitant to the discontinuity in the development of the Turkic literary tradition, this ethnolinguistic Turkification coexisted with the continued prestige of Persian as the literary language in much of the eastern Islamic world. Whereas the Ottoman Empire in time would develop its own literary and official language in Ottoman Turkish, which assimilated large quantities of Arabic and Persian into a Turkish syntactical framework, Central Asia would remain a zone of extensive bilingualism, with literary production in Persian and in eastern forms of Turkic, even as the demography and folk culture of the region became increasingly Turkified. Perso-Turkish literary bilingualism among an increasingly Turkish-speaking population provides another illustration of how the Turkic peoples sank their "national" identity into Islam and its civilization. At the same time, in Inner Asia, Azerbayjan, and Anatolia, wherever Turks were present in large numbers and held political power, Turkification ensued. As Mahmud al-Kashgari put it,

> When I saw that God Most High had caused the Sun of Fortune to rise in the Zodiac of the Turks . . . placing in their hands the reigns of temporal authority, appointing them over all mankind, and directing them to the Right . . . [then I saw that] every man of reason must attach himself to them, or else expose himself to their falling arrows. And there is no better way to approach them than by speaking their own tongue, thereby bending their ear and inclining their heart.[59]

## The Mongol Empire and the Turks

In the East in the thirteenth century, the Mongols once again reorganized the steppe peoples into one state. The Mongols were paradoxically few in number—perhaps only 700,000. The masses caught up in this experience, and the human residues left behind in its wake, were largely Turkic. The Mongol experience ultimately completed the Islamization of most of the Turkic world. From that point forward, Islam remained the strongest source of solidarity among the Turks until the rise of modern nationalist movements.[60]

Although the Mongolian and Turkish languages may not be genetically related, the two people's cultural interrelationships have a long history. Some

Mongol tribes had been subjects of the Türk and Uyghur states. The collapse of the Uyghurs (840) led to a westward displacement of the Turks and opened the way for the Mongolization of Mongolia, which had obviously been a Turkic homeland before that. By the twelfth century, a Mongol nucleus had formed near the Onon and Kerulen Rivers, not far to the east from the Orkhon River, which was so important in Turkic history. The Mongols were unified by Khabul Kaghan (Qabul, 1130s). After him, the family fortunes fell very low but were restored by his great-grandson, Temüjin. Possessed of exceptional strategic and organizational abilities, he reunited the Mongol tribes into a new kind of tribal union.

In 1206, Temüjin was declared Chinggis Khan, a name often interpreted as meaning "oceanic," or all-embracing ruler, *chinggis* being cognate to the eastern Turkic *tengiz*, "sea." A nine-tailed white banner (*tuk*) was unfurled to honor the occasion.[61] He led his first campaign outside the steppes in 1209, when the Uyghur Turks became the first other people to submit to him. His first major victory occurred, however, in 1219 against the Iranian state of the Khwarazm Shah, following which parts of Khurasan and Afghanistan were also added to his domains. With these campaigns, the Mongols acquired not only huge territories but also access to the skills of sedentary peoples, including the sappers and military engineers who would enable them to take cities. An actual clash of civilizations, the Khwarazmian campaign was unprecedented in scale and ferocity. The Khwarazm shah's base at Urgench was destroyed. A river was diverted into the ruins. The population of whole cities was either destroyed or driven away to spread terror further on—and to encourage others to surrender without a fight.

When Chinggis Khan died in 1227, the Mongols were still an Inner Asian entity. His sons' and grandsons' conquests turned them into a pan-Eurasian phenomenon. The empire reached its height as a unified polity under Möngke (1251–59). Victorious from the Elbe to the China Sea, the Mongols extended their power over all China, much of peninsular Southeast Asia, the northern Islamic world, part of India, and half of Europe. In the armed conquests, civilizations clashed on an unprecedented scale. Yet in the aftermath, the Mongol Empire served as a "cultural clearing house" for most of Eurasia, permanently joining it for the first time into a single intercommunicating zone and thus facilitating "the emergence of a unified conceptualization of the world, with the geographies, histories and cultures of the parts coordinated with each other."[62] Identifying yet another mechanism in the tightening of Eurasian interlinkages, world historian William H. McNeill contrasts the "macroparasitism" of conquering Mongol armies with the "microparasitism" of disease-causing organisms, above all the bubonic plague bacillus, which spread with the Mongol forces, wreaking devastation from China to Europe between 1330 and 1350. The microparasites also devastated the macroparasites, ending the great age of the Mongols.[63]

In an adaptation of nomadic practice, Chinggis divided his vast conquests among immediate family members but also took measures to maintain the supreme ruler's control. Of his four sons, the oldest, Jochi, received the region extending from southern Siberia across the Kazakh steppe to the Rus' principalities. Chaghadai, the second son, received West Turkistan. Ögödei, the third son and political heir, received territory in Jungaria but later moved to central Mongolia. Tolui, the youngest, got the original Mongol homeland in eastern Mongolia. Significantly, neither of the richest lands falling under Mongol rule—China or Iran, both historic centers of agrarian empire—was apportioned. "These regions . . . were to be administered by the kaghan for the benefit of the Chinggisid lines at large."[64] China and later Iran were given out in shares, administered by an agency combining representatives of the imperial princes and the kaghan. Intense competition among the princes ensued, while from Karakorum the kaghan and his officials tried to hinder princely efforts to expand revenue entitlements into territorial claims inside China and Iran.

This competition led the fourth kaghan, Möngke (1251–59), to realign the territorial allotments in China and Iran while asserting the control of his line, the Toluids (descendants of Tolui), over both. Möngke did that by placing one of his brothers, Hülegü, in charge of Iran, and another, Khubilai (Qubilai), in charge of China, as his "right and left wings," thus establishing the Toluids as the most powerful Chinggisid line. At Möngke's death, the kaghanate passed to Khubilai (1260–94), who transferred its seat to Beijing, where he and his descendants ruled China as the Yuan dynasty. Henceforth, the descendants of Ögödei having been eclipsed in the struggle over Möngke's succession, there were four Chinggisid successor states, the Great Kaghanate of the Yuan in China, the *Ulus* of Jochi (later known as the Golden Horde), the *Ulus* of Chaghadai (including much of Central Asia), and the Ilkhanate based in Iran.[65] In keeping with Möngke's dispensation, the Iranian state retained the status of a "regional" or "subordinate" khanate under the great khan, which is what the term *il-khan* signifies. As the other lines turned against the Toluids, the close relation between China and Iran—the two Mongol states based in historic centers of empire—persisted, leading to cultural exchanges of even greater long-term importance than their political cooperation.

The Mongol invasion of the Middle East was the first time, apart from the Crusades, when non-Muslims ruled over Muslims in the historic core regions of Islam. The initial clash included such horrors as the sack of Baghdad (1258) and destruction of the Abbasid caliphate. In long-term perspective,

**Mounted Archer in Mongol Dress.** The Mongols seem to have seen no contra-
diction between military effectiveness and fine clothing. The robe that closes to
the right with three ties at the side and the elaborate headdress are Mongol traits.
The pen-and-ink drawing is inscribed Muhammad ibn Mahmud Shah al-Khayyam
at the bottom and Muhammad Khayyam at the left side; Ilkhanid Iran, early 1300s.
From Staatsbibliothek zu Berlin-Preussischer Kulturbesitz, Orientabteilung, Diez
A fol.72, S. 13; photo by Ellwardt.

however, Mongol empire building renewed the reintegrative political trend
that the Seljuks had begun. This fact gained in significance with the Islamization of the Ilkhanate and the Ulus'es of Chaghatay and Jochi, even though
the easternmost part of the Mongol world remained mostly non-Islamic
territory.

Many arguments have been advanced to explain the Mongols' rise. In
terms of political culture, Chinggis introduced to the steppe world a new
mode of statecraft, a new-model victory of macropolity over micropolity.[66]
Emerging out of a milieu where decentralized tribes with many chiefs coexisted with others having a khan and more centralized structure, Temüjin
created a new kind of centralization by forming a retinue on nontribal lines,
made up of retainers (*nökör*) who rallied to him singly or in groups from
Mongol tribes, from Uyghurs or other Turkic groups, and also from the

Muslim merchants of Central Asia.[67] The detribalization implied by joining one of the thirteen "wagon circles" (*küriyen*) that made up his retinue was voluntary before 1206 but acquired a forced character thereafter, as tribes were deliberately divided and mixed. In the grand army (*yeke cherig*) of the Great Mongol Empire (*Yeke Mongghol Ulus*), advancement would be based on merit, not kinship; however, people were no longer free to withdraw their allegiance. Temüjin, who ruled with the consent of his retainers, or *nökör*s, had grown into Chinggis, who ruled by consent of his commanders, or *noyan*s, the Mongol term corresponding to *beg* in Turkish.[68]

Detribalization in the sense of dispersing tribes had happened often in history; what was new was for a ruler to do it to his own people. In her study of the Mongols, Isenbike Togan concludes that Chinggis opposed not tribes as such but tribes that had acquired a more or less dynastic form of leadership, like the Kerait, Naiman, and Merkid. Chinggis built up his authority as "favored by Eternal Heaven" (Möngke Tengri) and as supreme arbiter of customary law (*yasagh, töre/törö*). He claimed all conquered peoples and lands, and he divided them among his descendants. Henceforth, his sons would be the charismatic "golden lineage" (*altan urugh*). Consent to their rule was acted out at the princely assemblies (*khuriltai, quriltai*), where each new kaghan was acclaimed; "election" is not the right word because succession depended on membership in the Golden Lineage and victory in the succession struggle.[69] What motivated political consent was above all the redistribution of the spoils of conquest. A critical part of Chinggis' new order was that he extended redistributive rights to all his retainers, not just to the leadership, as in the past. Prolific, as well as charismatic, Chinggis and his lineage founded peoples and empires: genetic research on sixteen populations from the Pacific to the Caspian Sea shows that nearly 8 percent of the men (0.5 percent of the male population of the world) carry nearly identical y-chromosomes with a pattern of variation suggesting descent from a single Mongol lineage—without doubt, the golden one of Chinggis Khan.[70]

The ability of the Mongols, starting with small numbers and the limited resources of the steppe, to create such an empire depended on organizational skill. When Chinggis Khan's empire was divided among his four eldest sons following his death in 1227, Ögödei became the new kaghan (r. 1229–41), retaining both control over foreign relations and significant influence in the internal affairs of the regional khanates through his right to name many officials, particularly the Mongol residents known as *darughachi* or *basqaq*.[71] As kaghan, Möngke (r. 1251–59) expanded his influence, as noted above, by placing his brothers Khubilai in charge of China and Hülegü in charge of what became the Iranian-based Ilkhanate, so using the traditional steppe motif of bilateral political organization to outflank the other khans' territories. The numerous wives and consorts of the rulers not only helped Chinggis and his sons pass on their y-chromosomes but also some of these women wielded great power. Among these, Sorqaghtani Beki (regent 1227–29) ranks foremost because of her political success in advancing the fortunes of her sons, Möngke (kaghan 1251–59), Khubilai (kaghan 1260–94 and founder of the Yuan dynasty), Hülegü (founder of the Ilkhanid dynasty), and Arigh Böke (Khubilai's rival for the kaghanate). The practice of leaving in place non-Mongol rulers who submitted peacefully helped to extend the reach of the Mongol cadres and also, like the Seljuks' reliance on Iranian officials, to secure administrative personnel skilled in governing sedentary societies.[72]

Patrimonial in nature, Mongol adminstration grew out of the ruler's household.[73] Closest to Chinggis and his successors stood functionaries whose titles, such as "cook" (ba'urchi), suggested that they were mere household servants. However, in a polity where government grew by expansion of the ruler's entourage, the man responsible for preparing the kaghan's food, protecting him from poisoning, and feasting his retainers was the logical person to acquire broad governmental responsibilities in provisioning. The ruler's stable master or personal secretary might see their roles expand analogously. Under Möngke, there was a central secretariat based in Mongolia, with a chief minister bearing titles like "chief judge" or "chief scribe" (yeke yarghuchi, yeke bichechi). The kaghan's capital, Karakorum, had developed to the point where it had a Muslim section, with the bazar; a Chinese section, where artisans and craftsmen worked; and a third section, with palaces to house the scribes, who produced official documents in Persian, Uyghur, Chinese, Tibetan, Tangut, and Mongolian. There were also regional secretariats for China, Turkistan, Iran, and apparently the Rus' principalities. Khubilai's orders to rulers of Annam and Korea made clear what was expected from dependent rulers: they had to pay court in person, register their populations, raise militia units, establish postal relay stations, and have a Mongol resident to take charge of affairs. Tributary rulers also had to send sons or younger brothers to the kaghan's court as hostages—another way to expand the ruler's household into a system of control for a complex empire.

Numerous examples show that the Mongol system of rule achieved high levels of efficiency and administrative capacity. The Mongols were thorough census takers. As early as 1206, Chinggis Khan ordered records to be kept in a "blue book" (kökö debter) on judicial decisions and on the apportionment of peoples and lands among members of the dynasty. In view of the later Ottoman use of the term defter for registers and ledgers, and especially considering the word's Greek etymology, Mongol usage of the term strikingly suggests the range and sophistication of the Turko-Mongol political culture. Under Möngke, all households of the empire were registered.

Following a system introduced in Central Asia by Mahmud Yalavach, an official of Khwarazmian origin, taxation came to include a poll tax on adult males (*qubchir*), an agricultural tax (*qalan*), commercial taxes (*tamgha*) and monopolies, and extraordinary levies (*taghar*).[74] Muslims especially resented the poll tax, likening it to the *jizya* that Muslim rulers collected from non-Muslim subjects. On the other hand, the Mongols exempted religious functionaries from census registration and taxation, thereby winning many of them as supporters and mobilizing their spiritual resources to bolster Mongol rule. Mongol taxation was designedly heavy and was gradually shifted from collection in kind to cash payment, a change that required expansion of the coinage.

The Mongols' ability to mobilize manpower provides one of the best indicators of their efficiency.[75] Starting with a mass levy of the "people who live in felt tents," Chinggis went on to conscript the soldiers of defeated armies and to impose service obligations on subject peoples. Effectiveness in mobilizing their nonnomadic subjects as infantry and technical specialists does much to explain the Mongols' speedy advance. Nomadic horsemen could be mobilized quickly, together with their families and herds. The Mongol army was "really . . . the Mongol people in one of its natural aspects."[76] For sedentary populations, mobilization was economically more disruptive; only a proportion of the men could be taken. Chinggis adopted the decimal system of organization, long used on the steppes, creating military units whose notional size ranged from ten to 10,000 although the larger units were never fully up to strength. The census also divided the population into decimal units, so that a *tümen* was both a military and a demographic unit of 10,000. Nonfighting, sedentary populations were subjected to labor duties, the most onerous being the maintenance of the postal relays. Their census records enabled the Mongols to locate and mobilize men with skills like metalworking or powdermaking. Thus enabled to locate 1,000 crews of Chinese catapult operators to join Hülegü's campaign to Iran in 1253, the Mongols proved as effective against the fortresses and walled cities as in steppe warfare.

Shifting the emphasis to the "symbiosis of *imperium* and *emporium*," Turkic scholar Omeljan Pritsak has seen, not warriors, but merchants collaborating with the charismatic clan as the primary catalysts in creating nomadic empires, which in this perspective appear as the extension of nomadic control over long-distance trade networks.[77] Extensive evidence on both goods and merchants substantiates the importance of trade in Mongol imperialism. Like the Tang horses, much of this evidence emphasizes exchanges, not between settled societies at the far ends of the silk routes, but between those societies and the steppe.

One of the key aspects of the Mongols' "dual administration," that is, their rule of both settled and nomadic populations, was the relationship they cultivated with merchants. Chinggis Khan's conquest of Khwarazm followed on a local official's misguided attack on a caravan that Chinggis had sent to ensure free movement of goods and merchants between East and West.[78] He had ordered his family members and military commanders to select Muslims from their retinues and entrust them with gold and silver ingots to trade in Khwarazm. This became normal practice thereafter; merchants operating on this basis became known as *ortogh*, from the Turkic word *ortak*, "partner." Most of these merchants were Turkic, either Uyghurs or West Turkistanis. Sometimes the basis of operation was a silent partnership of the type known as *mudaraba* in Arabic or *commenda* in Latin; sometimes the capital was loaned to the merchant. The merchants' influence reached its height under Chinggis' successors Ögödei (r. 1229–41) and Güyüg (1246–48). Ögödei habitually offered merchants 10 percent more than they asked. Some Mongol rulers offered more than that, presumably in order to attract goods to the new capital, Karakorum, near the Orkhon River, which could not be provisioned locally.[79] Merchants were also allowed to use the system of relay stations ( *jam*, or *yam*) as long as they did not interfere with military needs, and they received their keep en route. Merchants were thus virtually exempted from transportation and protection costs, the heaviest expenses of premodern long-distance trade, over unimaginably vast distances. An Italian merchant wrote that "the road you travel from Tana [on the Sea of Azov] to Cathay is perfectly safe, whether by day or by night."[80] A merchant could travel from the Crimea to China safely, almost without cost and without ever leaving Mongol territory.

Mongol patronage of the merchants extended to the point of creating major hardship for the subjects. The Chinese, for example, laid many extortionate practices at the Muslim merchants' door. For example, merchants known to be partners of the Mongol elites would falsely claim to have been robbed somewhere and force the populace to compensate them. Merchants also engaged in tax farming and usury at unbearable rates. The court became so deeply indebted to merchants that Möngke kaghan (r. 1251–59) had to introduce stringent measures, depriving the merchants of tablets of official authority ( *paizeh* in Persian, *paizi* [*p'ai-tzu*] in Chinese),[81] which ended their free use of post horses; ordering them registered on the census rolls; and subjecting them to taxation. Trade continued in commodities that would dominate intraregional trade for centuries—gems, textiles, and furs. Traveling bazars (*ordo bazar*) continued to follow the khan's mobile royal camp (*ordo*) in its movements. *Ortak* partnerships also continued, partly because the members of the dynasty had to invest their share of the booty to maintain their lifestyle. Aside from enabling the Mongol elite to enjoy the luxuries of the sedentary world while still living on the steppe, trade interests may have stimulated Mongol ideas of world domination, long-standing motifs in steppe culture that suddenly became tangible reality with the lightning conquests to the west.

Surprisingly for a people whose culture and history link them closely to the Turks, the Mongols, while known for their felt, had no tradition of loom weaving. Suddenly enriched with booty but still preferring a migratory life, they indulged in fine textiles, preferring the gold brocades of the Middle East to such an extent that the Arabic term *nasij* ("textile") passed into languages ranging from Italian to Chinese. Mongols became style setters, so much that "Tartary cloth" was popular in England. Mongol-style high women's headresses (*kökül*), probably deriving from the high headgear of the Scythians and those found in the ancient Turfan burials, inspired women's headdresses all over Eurasia, from the *kuku* of China to the conical headdresses known in France as *hennin*.[82] Mongol use of luxury goods extended to huge tents lined with costly fabrics, both Mongol-style round felt tents (*ger* in Mongolian) and Middle Eastern–style tents, and to other items of dress, including belts and shoes made of precious materials, as well as furs from the northern forests and no doubt also carpets woven by the peoples under Mongol rule.

The reasons for Mongol rulers' desire to promote the flow of goods toward their court were as much political as economic. Costly textiles displayed the court's magnificence and supplied the redistributive economics of retinue maintenance. Acceptance of the Mongols' court dress and their calendar became essential criteria of submission. An elaborate protocol developed, requiring not just the ruler but also all those present to don matching "robes of one color" (*jisün*), that is, robes cut from the same silk, gold-brocaded on a solid background.[83] At festivities lasting several days, the court might don robes of a different color each day. Marco Polo calculated that Khubilai had to have 156,000 *jisün* robes on hand just for the Mongols' thirteen seasonal festivals.[84] Seasonal festivals required specific colors. Different colors had different symbolic values. In a steppe tradition going back to the Scythians, the color gold symbolized imperial authority and legitimacy, an idea conveyed in references to Chinggis' descendants as the "golden lineage" and many analogous usages.

Recalling Middle Eastern robing ceremonies, including the gala robes (*khil'a*) that Islamic and pre-Islamic dynasties gave out, Mongol ceremonial elaborated such practices on unprecedented scale. Eventually, the Mongols acquired the ability to produce fine textiles in state workshops, forcing communities of artisans to migrate from Iran to Mongolia and China, and creating offices such as the Gold Brocade Office to oversee production of luxury goods for the Yuan court. In the patrimonial politics of retinue formation, the ruler's ability to provide food, drink, and clothing reciprocated his retainers' debt of unconditional loyalty. The most precious gift of clothing would be something the ruler had worn; the ancient water taboo of the steppes and the consequent reluctance to wash ensured that his sacred aura would indeed linger on it. To explain Mongol history with textile metaphors, the common tribesmen's felts and the courts' gold brocades would have to provide the inspiration, rather than carpets, although that might be different if carpets had survived from this period.

Mongol imperialism stimulated trans-Eurasian exchanges, not only in trade and material goods, but also in the realm of ideas. Examples have been documented in the writing of history, geography and cartography, language study and translation, astronomy, agriculture, culinary culture, medicine, pharmacology, and possibly printing. Although block printing dates back to the seventh century C.E. in East Asia, and printing from metal type dates back to the thirteenth century in Korea, the differences between printing in alphabetic and character scripts leave open the question of whether the advent of printing in East Asia only preceded that in Europe in time or directly stimulated it. Inasmuch as multilingual astrological calendars, referred to by Marco Polo as *tacuini* (from Arabic *taqwim*), were printed by the millions in China annually by the early 1300s, Europeans before Gutenberg may very well have seen examples of East Asian printing in alphabetic scripts; the astrologers who produced the calendars were not only Chinese but also Muslim and Christian, most often Nestorians. In their own time, the English philosopher Roger Bacon attributed the Mongols' success to "their wonderful works of science."[85] The Mongols, moreover, were not passive recipients of others' ideas. Rather, they analyzed with discrimination, ordering and patronizing exchanges and not hesitating to prefer foreigners and talented people of low rank over elites in an effort to mobilize all available resources, spiritual and material, to strengthen their empire. Just as geographical knowledge could strengthen their control of their far-flung lands or exchanges of crops could stimulate the agrarian zones under their rule, so astronomers and astrologers were valuable additions to the shamans on whom the Mongols, as conquerors ruling by heavenly mandate, relied in making decisions about the future. Not only did the Mongol Empire serve as Eurasia's "cultural clearing house" for over a century, but also Mongol values and priorities shaped the way it did so. The effects were felt far beyond Mongol borders. For example, in Yemen, which had far-reaching trading connections through the port of Aden, al-Malik al-Afdal Ibn Rasul (r. 1363–77), scion of a dynasty of Turkic origins, produced a multilingual "dictionary," defining terms in Arabic, Persian, Turkic, Greek, Armenian, and Mongolian. This was one remarkable work among many that reflected the priorities of the scribes who staffed Mongol chanceries and the intellectuals who carried out the far-flung cultural exchanges of the era.[86]

Mongol principles of political economy strike many notes resonant of the traditional steppe political culture. The ruler's heavenly mandate, the charismatic ruling clan, bloody succession struggles, dynastic law, the division of the territory among members of the dynasty, all these are now familiar themes. So is the identification of sovereignty with control of sacred sites, which appeared among the Mongols in various ways, including the symbolic importance attached to the site of Chinggis' original camp (ordo) in the Onon-Kerulen area or the treatment of royal burial sites as secret and inviolable sacred preserves (koruk). The dramatic encounter between Baba Tükles and Özbek Khan occurred in a koruk where an ancestral libation ritual was in progress. Mongol kaghans were literally elevated to office on felt mats, as had been their Türk precursors.[87] Ancestral rites and shamanic ceremonies were surely based on those inherited from earlier Inner Asian societies. The fact that in court libation ceremonies, the khan's daughter presented the cup to members of the imperial family before the heir apparent did, or that shamans might be either female or male, shows that Sorqaghtani Beki's political prominence was not the only sign of relative gender equality.[88]

At the same time there was much that was new in the Mongol experience. For political culture, two points seem particularly salient. First, tribal micropolitics could never be the same again after Chinggis. For example, the Kerait, a people of apparently mixed Turko-Mongol origin, were bested in the power struggle surrounding Chinggis's rise; their khanate was destroyed, although Chinggis's family took several of their daughters, including Sorqaghtani, as brides. Paradoxically, despite loss of their khanate, elements of the Kerait outlasted the Mongol Empire by centuries, as the Kirei among the Mongols, Kazakhs, Özbeks, and Bashkorts and as the Girays in the Crimea.[89] Other tribes were not so lucky. Whose lives were more changed— those who fled the Mongol advance or those caught up in it? In the Chinggisid period for the first time, Turkic neotribal entities began to appear that bore the names of their founding leaders. Examples include the Özbeg, Noghay, Chaghatay, Ottoman (Osmanlı), or Karamanlı—groupings found from Central Asia to western Anatolia.[90] After Chinggis created his retinue and dispersed the old tribes, the idea of taking on an identity based on that of the leader they served became a new model of social cohesion for survivors and later descendants who could not return to the old solidarities.

The advance of Islam into Inner Asia united the eastern Turko-Mongol world with that of the Turks in the Islamic Middle East. The religious policy

**Khan and Khatun Enthroned Side by Side, Ilkhanid Iran.** This miniature honors the Inner Asian tradition of viewing the khan and his khatun as a ruling couple but defies Islamic norms of gender segregation. Probably dating from about the time the Ilkhanids converted to Islam, the miniature gives an idea of how far they still had to go to assimilate the norms of their new faith and why their behavior shocked their pious Muslim subjects. The khatun and several ladies wear the high Mongol headdress (*kökül*). From Staatsbibliothek zu Berlin-Preussischer Kulturbesitz, Orientabteilung, Diez A fol.70, S. 22; photo by Ellwardt.

of the Mongols has been described as one of "situational tolerance" for other religions, including Nestorian Christianity and Buddhism, as long as they did not become sources of resistance.[91] The narrative of William of Rubruck, shows that the kind of debates among the three monotheistic religions that had long flourished in the Middle East also occurred in Karakorum in 1254–55, with the addition of Buddhists; and the debaters' statements were sometimes noted, instead of being dismissed, as in the Baba Tükles narrative.[92] In the long run, however, Islam prevailed in the Mongol lands west of Mongolia and China. As earlier among the Seljuks' nomadic followers, converts sometimes understood their new religion in unconventional terms. For example, one account of the Il-khan Öljeytü's conversion to Shi'i Islam has one of his amirs advise him as follows:

> In the religion of Islam, a person is a Shi'i who, in the Mongol *yasagh*, would consider the descendants (*urugh*) of Chingiz Khan to be his rightful successors after him; the school of the Sunnah is the one that regards an amir as worthy of his place.[93]

In other words, a person who thought just any commander was entitled to succeed Chinggis Khan should join the Sunnis, who believed that whoever was the most qualified man should be the successor (*khalifa*) of the Prophet as leader of the Muslim community. A person who thought only a member of the golden lineage was entitled to succeed Chinggis should join the Shi'is, who believed that the rightful leader (*imam*) of the Muslim community should be a descendant of the Prophet from a particular, charismatic lineage. Drawing such an analogy between Chinggisid and Prophetic descent would have horrified the ulema. Yet the account of the conversion of the Golden Horde under Özbek Khan reveals the profundity of the change wrought by conversion. For Turkic and Mongol converts, even where the new faith was not perfectly understood to start with, this was a transition of unprecedented significance in their historical journey.

## World Historical Ramifications: Bolad Chengxiang and Rashideddin

Between the tenth and fourteenth centuries, the Turks established their leading role in the late Abbasid amir-a'yan system; and the Mongols created their vast dual-administration empire, lastingly interlinking the separate histories of Eurasia. A "unified conceptualization of the world" emerged, a change symbolized by works such as Marco Polo's *Travels* or the prolific output of Rashideddin, the great scholar-statesman of Ilkhanid Iran.[94] One of the most important networks within this unification was the international civilization of Islam, the norms and values of which continued to spread even after the loss of Islamic political unity.[95] Thenceforth, the carpets of Turkic identity would incorporate the motifs of this Islamic international, as would the gold brocades prized by the Mongols. Together with circuits of exchange that overlapped the Mongol imperium but extended farther, the *Pax Mongolica* widened the scope of exchange for ideas and goods to cover most of Afro-Eurasia.[96]

Eurasian integration had its costs. Not only those of Mongol conquest and taxation, they also included the creation of what historian Emmanuel Leroy Ladurie called "the microbian common market,"[97] beginning with the permanent interlinkage of Asian and European disease pools by the plague epidemics that raged from China to England around the 1340s. William McNeill has argued that Mongol conquests in the Himalayan foothills between India, China, and Burma, where bubonic plague was endemic among burrowing rodents and their fleas, resulted in the Mongols' inadvertent transfer of the plague bacillus northward to the burrowing rodents of the Eurasian steppes.[98] The plague bacillus established new foci of infection in the rodent burrows of the northern steppes and spread overland along the caravan routes from China to the Crimea, whence it spread by sea in 1346, devastating most of Europe by 1350 and remaining chronic until modern times. Nor was the steppe world spared. The macropolitical integration of the Mongol era gave way to fragmentation, and the outflowing tides of nomads that had transformed the map of Inner Asia and the Middle East in the Seljuk and Mongol eras ended. Some places reverted to the micropolitics of tribal decentralization. The Mongol "world system," the Eurasia-wide system of interlinkages that had come into existence during the Mongol hegemony, had been shattered by 1350. Although Chinggisid lineage would remain the indispensable asset for dynasts in Inner Asia, elsewhere the Turkic fabric would have to be woven in new ways.

Destructive on some levels, the Mongol integration of Eurasia had produced extraordinary benefits on many others. Two well-documented individuals from opposite ends of the Mongol world illustrate the point: Bolad, a Mongol, and Rashideddin, an Iranian.[99] Bolad lived long enough (c. 1240–1313) to play major roles in both China and Iran, where he came into contact with Rashideddin (1247–1318), one of the great intellectuals of Ilkhanid Iran. Bolad's father had been a *ba'urchi* (cook, steward) to Chinggis Khan and thus an important figure in the kaghan's household. Not surprisingly, then, Bolad's father was also a commander of 100 in Chinggis' Personal Thousand, or palace guard. As a boy, Bolad showed a talent for languages and was tutored in Chinese along with Khubilai's eldest son. Proximity to power and Mongol–Chinese biculturalism launched Bolad on his first career in China. He springboarded from being a *ba'urchi* like his father to become Khubilai's director of Imperial Household Provisions. Bolad served, as well, in two of China's three most important governmental agencies, the Bureau of Military Affairs and the Censorate, which monitored civil and military officials. A true insider, he was honored with the Chinese title *chengxiang* (*ch'eng-hsiang*, "chancellor"). In 1284, Bolad was sent as an emissary (*elchi*) from the Great Khan to the Ilkhan of Iran, where he served for the rest of his life. Given the dependent relationship between the "regional khan" (*ilkhan*) in Iran and the kaghan in China, and the fact that China and Iran were the most productive parts of the Mongol Empire, Bolad's stay in Iran positioned him to play a major role in exchanges between the two countries. His acquaintance with Rashideddin ensured that this happened.

Rashideddin was born at Hamadan in Iran around 1247. His given name, Rashideddin, is distinctively a Muslim one. By birth, he was the son of a Jewish apothecary. He became a physcian, converted to Islam, and entered the service of the Ilkhan Geikhatu (r. 1291–95). Rashideddin's initial appointment was also that of a cook. He became prominent under Ghazan (r. 1295–1304), the Ilkhan who converted to Islam, as an advisor advocating reforms to restrain corruption and revive Iran's agrarian economy. He remained in high position until 1318, when a rival's intrigues led to his fall and execution. Rashideddin and Bolad frequently collaborated in policy matters, the result often being the introduction of Chinese models and their explanation in Persian in works by Rashideddin. Examples include the short-lived attempt to introduce paper money, which had long circulated in China, into Iran.

Rashideddin is remembered as an intellectual, as a writer, and above all as "the first scholar to try to treat in a systematic and comprehensive fashion the history of the known world," including the history of the "Franks" (Europeans), Jews, Indians, Chinese, and Mongols.[100] To produce his "Compendium of Histories" (*Jami' al-Tawarikh*), he worked with many collaborators. Bolad was the most important of them, requiring five or six assistants for his part alone. As a source on Inner Asia, the result was a work without precedent since Herodotus' account of the Scythians and without rival before the nineteenth century. Unparalleled as a source on steppe culture, the work contains information on the life of Chinggis Khan derived from Mongolian sources, since lost, information that only Bolad could have provided. He also helped Rashideddin compile a genealogical supplement, which contains information not found elsewhere. Rashideddin's ability to transcribe Chinese names and terms recognizably in Arabic script provides further evidence of how closely he worked with collaborators like "Pûlâd *chînksânk*" (Bolad chengxiang). Among Rashideddin's other works are four volumes of translations from Chinese into Persian, works that he could not have produced by himself, as well as works on agriculture and medicine that incorporate either translations from Chinese or extensive information on Chinese practice derived from Chinese sources. The account of Chinese medicine, including illustrations from the Chinese original, still survives. His influence was magnified by the fact that he built a suburb at Tabriz, the Rab'-i Rashidi ("Rashid's quarter"), and endowed it as a charitable foundation, one of its purposes being to produce additional manuscripts of his works in both Persian and Arabic. Plundered after his fall and death, Rashideddin's endowed institutions lasted long enough to ensure the diffusion of his major works.[101]

Here were two men, one a Mongol equally at home in Mongolian and Chinese culture and the other an Iranian Jewish convert to Islam, who not only lived in an empire that spanned Eurasia but also had the talent and good fortune to collaborate in realizing the possibilities for cultural exchange that it offered.

# THREE

# Islamic Empires from Temür
# to the "Gunpowder Era"

B etween about 1400 and 1800, another great age of indigenous empire building occurred across most of Asia. Although not all these empires proved equally durable, among Islamic states this period marks the culmination of the reintegration begun by the Seljuks. These empires have been variously characterized. Compared to the earlier "dual administration empires," states of the period 1260–1796 have been called "direct taxation" empires, in that they extracted all their resources from the territories they had conquered, without continuing the old steppe empires' pattern of exacting tributes from neighboring sedentary societies.[1] Much the same was true in the Middle East, where the Ottoman Empire has been described, with reference to its agrarian policy, as a "peasant empire." The great Islamic empires from the Seljuks on can also be referred to as "military patronage states," meaning that a conquering military takes control of ethnically different populations, providing the security that they need in order to produce the surplus that supports the state. From the mid-1400s on, the term "gunpowder empires" also becomes applicable. The suitability of that term has been challenged on grounds of the limited effectiveness of the artillery and gunpowder of the period.[2] Military technology aside, the term captures life in the Ottoman, Safavid, or Moghul Empires no better than "nuclear power" captures life in the United States after 1945. Still gunpowder weapons made a decisive difference, both in deciding battles where only one side had or used them effectively and in setting limits on imperial expansion.

The dialectic between imperial macropolitics and varying levels of decentralized micropolity also continued in this period, shifting the geographical sites of imperial state formation as it did. The spread of gunpowder weapons ended the invincibility of the mounted archer. The historic role of the steppe world as a source of nomadic invaders and empire builders never resumed. In the long run, Inner Asia was destined for division between China and Russia, a process completed by the end of the nineteenth century. On the expansive western steppe, the political decentralization that had been an affordable luxury when no imperial colossus loomed menacingly on the horizon, as China had always menaced Mongolia, became a recipe for disaster once the Russian Empire grew strong enough to expand at the expense of the steppe peoples. Meanwhile, the centers of Asian empire building shifted outward, with results on a grand scale. Three major Islamic empires emerged, all with Turkic roots to varying degrees: those of the Ottomans (1300–1922), Safavids (1501–1722), and Moghuls (1526–1858). Rounding out this last great age of indigenous imperial state formation in mainland Asia, two of China's greatest dynasties ruled in this period, the Ming (1368–1662) and Qing (1662–1912).

As these political changes occurred, the Turks' integration into the material and cultural circuits of the wider world continued, as indicated by the spread of gunpowder weapons. The development of cosmopolitan literary cultures in widely used languages—Ottoman and Chaghatay Turkic, as well as Persian—facilitated cultural integration at the regional level. So did the spread of far-flung "religious internationals" in the form of sufi orders. In commerce, important developments occurred in both trans-Eurasian east-west trade and regional north-south trade.[3] Although Europocentric narratives depict this period in terms of European overseas expansion, its impact on the major historical centers of civilization and state formation in Asia remained limited before 1800. From the Islamic Middle East to Japan, indigenous developmental dynamics prevailed.

The intensification of hemispheric and global interlinkages prepared the way for the second great transition in the Turkic peoples' history. The first had been their entry into Islamic civilization; the second would be their integration after 1800 into the global complex of modernity. Historians used to understand the history of the Islamic world in this period in terms of decline; some still do. In fact, no single linear trend extends without inflection across three or four centuries in the history of any civilization. Trends discernible over vast sweeps of space and time result from, and often also mask, divergent trends of smaller scale. Global trends are also at work. For example, although the demographic disaster caused across Eurasia by the Black Death of the 1340s produced long-lasting consequences, global evidence indicates population growth and rising prosperity in the sixteenth century and again in the late eighteenth and early nineteenth. In between, seventeenth-century evidence indicates socioeconomic and other crises in

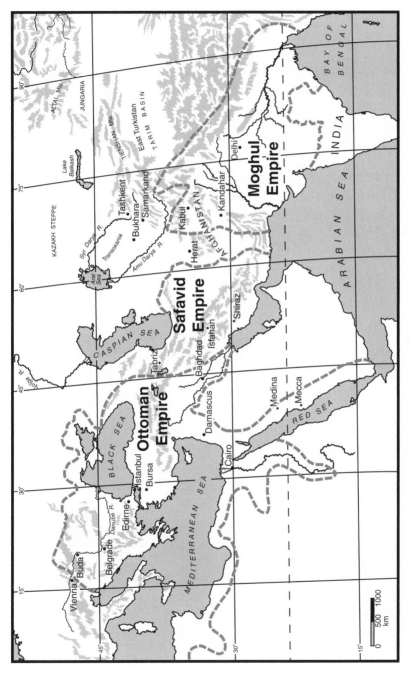

Map of the Ottoman, Safavid, and Moghul Empires, 1600. Map by Ron McLean, Digital Media Creation Services, Ohio State University.

95

many parts of the world, with climatological factors as likely unifying forces. At the start of the century, Moscow's "Time of Troubles" (1598–1613) and its sequels, which temporarily reversed Russian expansion at the expense of the steppe peoples, coincided in Ottoman lands with the Celali rebellions (1593–1610), which touched off the "great flight" that left much of the Anatolian countryside depopulated.[4] According to Voltaire, three things continually occupy people's minds: climate, government, and religion. Under preindustrial, agrarian conditions, if this was true in a land as richly blessed by nature as France, how much more so must it have been in the harsher climates of Inner Asia and the Middle East.

Better to understand the Turks' "gunpowder empires," we shall look first at Central Asia and then at the Middle East, with emphasis on the Ottoman Empire. In an increasingly integrated, competitive world, the trend of events signaled that the Turks' future destinies would depend heavily on whether they took charge of the processes of state formation or whether they persisted in decentralized forms of social and political life, by default leaving the initiative in macropolitical integration to others. Broadly speaking, the three empires spanning the lands from the Ottoman Balkans to Moghul India represented the former alternative, whereas the Turkic regions of Inner Asia represented the latter, with partition between Russia and China as the outcome. Yet in all zones of Turkic habitation, the micropolitics of kinship and voluntary association continued throughout this period. Valued by rulers and nomads alike, and surviving in significant numbers from the fifteenth century onward, carpets symbolize—and shed added light on—the commonalities of Turkic culture and the significance they assumed for the wider world.

## Lessons from the Carpet Weaver's Loom

The far-flung geographical dispersion of Turkic migrants and their cultural conservatism in retaining old motifs as they encountered new ideas affected the production of Turkic carpets in profound ways. It was probably no coincidence that the Türkmen (and thus Oghuz) tribe whose name is often associated with the typical, geometrical *gül* ("flower") medallions that typify these carpets was known as the Salghur, or Salur.[5] Scholars derive that name from the verb *salmak*, the meanings of which include "to let go, fling out, send forth shoots." As they migrated from Transoxania to Anatolia, the Salur lived up to that name. So did the other tribes descended from them, many of them also known for their weaving, such as the Yomud, Tekke, Ersarı, and Sarık. As far as they migrated, these tribes established design standards that spread even farther. By the fifteenth century, the same *gül* medallions had become such expected traits in carpet design that they were reproduced in rugs woven as far beyond the zones of Turkic migration as Spain. Carpet weaving also flourished in Iran, Syria, Egypt, and Timurid Central Asia; surviving Timurid carpets also show significant affinities with those from Anatolia.

Turkish or Turkish-looking carpets were prized and collected far beyond the places where they were produced. Distance and rarity increased their value. Carefully preserved in foreign collections as precious objects, several major carpet types, featuring the Turkic weavers' geometric *gül* medallions in distinctive configurations, became lastingly known by the names of European painters, such as Holbein and Lotto, who included them in their paintings, while the names by which the producers knew these carpets have been lost.

In addition to their old traditions of geometric design, carpet weavers also responded to new stimuli. For example, the curvilinear designs of brocaded silk textiles, although harder to produce on a carpet loom, provided one source of challenge and inspiration. The rise in the fifteenth and sixteenth centuries of the town of Uşak in Anatolia as one of the largest centers of commercial carpet production in history provided yet another stimulus, as did the work of professional artists in the palace workshops of Istanbul in creating designs. In the fifteenth century, in the zone between Tabriz and Istanbul, the interaction among these stimuli led to a revolution in carpet design, featuring elaborate curvilinear designs like those of the Uşak "star" and "medallion" carpets and often a much finer weave. A very fine Uşak star carpet appears on the cover of this book. In addition, court carpets, designed by palace artists and produced under strict controls, survive from the late sixteenth century on. These are distinguished by stylized flower and leaf forms, reflecting the premier importance of the arts of the book, especially calligraphy, in setting design standards for the arts under court patronage. The complexity of both the Uşak and the court carpets exceeded what ordinary weavers could achieve, except through radical simplification, sometimes with astonishing results. The best example of this fact provides a startling illustration of the proposition that technique and materials constrain the weaver's work, but her art knows no borders.

Among Turkish carpets, prayer rugs are the most common and best-known type.[6] Commonly, these have a niche motif corresponding to the *mihrab*, the niche in the mosque that points the direction toward Mecca. A well-known variation on this theme elaborates the niche into a triple arch supported by slender, paired columns, often with a hanging lamp suspended under the center arch. The design appears to have originated with a type of

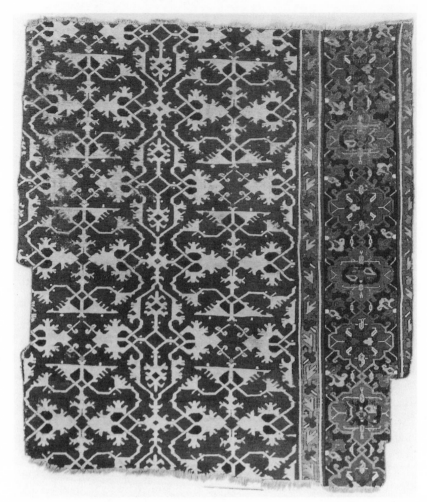

**Lotto Carpet.** Probably made in central Anatolia in the early 1600s, the surviving fragment of this carpet has the yellow lattice on a red ground that distinguishes Lotto carpets, so called after Lorenzo Lotto, who depicted such a carpet in a Venetian altarpiece painted in 1542. The Turkish names by which their makers originally knew the "painter carpets" have been lost. From the Textile Museum, Washington, D.C., R34.18.4; acquired by George Hewitt Myers in 1928.

Ottoman court carpet of the sixteenth century, a type emulated and reworked high and low, sometimes almost beyond recognition in village carpets. Many of these carpets survived in churches in eastern Europe. What makes this widespread appropriation of the design all the more remarkable is that neither the slender, paired columns nor the shape of the arches nor other ar-

chitectural details of the design correspond to anything in the history of
Ottoman architecture. Buildings with columns and arches like those that
inspired the carpet had been built, but faraway, in Muslim Spain, notably at
the Alhambra at Granada.

How did an architectural motif from Islamic Spain find its way into
Ottoman art a century after the collapse of Muslim rule in Iberia? That appears to have been the work of Sephardic Jewish refugees. Carpets were
sometimes used as the curtain (*parokhet*) before the Torah ark in synagogues,
and some surviving examples combine the Andalusian-inspired, paired-
columned arch with Hebrew inscriptions. Not only were Turkish carpets
appreciated in Europe, then, but also the Turks owed one of their best-loved
carpet designs to Sephardic refugees, who had brought it from their lost
Iberian homeland. The reworking of this design in the Ottoman world and
its widespread appropriation in synagogues, churches, and mosques speaks
of a Mediterranean cultural synthesis in which the Turkish weaving tradition was now embedded. Such cosmopolitanism not only typifies Ottoman
society and court culture but also should perhaps be borne in mind in con-
templating even something as quintessentially Turkish-looking as the motifs
of Turkish carpets.

## Central Asia After the Mongol Empire

The great premodern analyst of the rapid rise and decline of nomadic
dynasties was Ibn Khaldun, a son of the Arab world and North Africa,
not of Turkic Inner Asia. Although the leading traits of Turkic political
culture are not all found in his theory, the dynastic cycle that he theorized
also plagued Turkic states. The greatest question facing Turkic statesmen as
time went by was how to break this cycle. Ibn Khaldun saw a providential
solution in the *mamluk* system. Continually replenished with tribesmen from
the steppe who had the convert's zeal for Islam but had not lost their nomadic vigor, these military slaves could enable the states that employed them
to avoid succumbing to the debilitating influences of sedentary life, as nomadic dynasties normally had. After the Mongols destroyed the Abbasid
caliphate, wrote Ibn Khaldun, God rescued the Muslims by sending

> from this Turkish nation and from among its great and numerous
> tribes, rulers to defend them and utterly loyal helpers, who were
> brought from the House of War to the House of Islam under the
> rule of slavery, which hides in itself a divine blessing. . . . [T]hey
> enter the Muslim religion with the firm resolve of true believers

**Prayer Rug with Coupled Columns and Triple Arches.** Probably made in Istanbul in the second half of the sixteenth century, the carpet combines Spanish-derived architectural motifs with the flower and leaf motifs of Ottoman court art. Woven of wool and silk, it is an exceptionally fine and early example of its type. From the Metropolitan Museum of Art, New York, 22.100.51; Gift of James F. Ballard, 1922.

and yet with nomadic virtues . . . undefiled by the ways of civilized living. . . . Then [their masters] train them. . . . When the
masters know that they have reached the point [where] they are
ready to defend them, even to die for them . . . they use them in
the service of the state, [even] appoint them to high state offices. . . .
Islam rejoices in the benefit it gains through them, and the branches
of the kingdom flourish with the freshness of youth.[7]

This insight proved important for many of the post-Mongol successor
states. However, many other lessons also had to be learned, painfully and
anonymously, before long-lasting Turkish states would emerge. The record
of the greatest Turkic empire builders would continue to display a learning
curve in the dialectical oscillations between imperial centralization and tribal
or other kinds of decentralization. Some of these lessons were learned in
Inner Asia, yet the longevity record for Turkic states would be won in the
Middle East and environs by the Ottomans.

In Inner Asia, the Mongol imperium was replaced by political entities
ranging in scale from regional empires to tribal confederations. A commander
known as Temür the Lame (d. 1405)—Aksak Temür in Turkish, Timur-i
Lang in Persian, whence Tamerlane in English—created the most dynamic
of these Central Asian states out of the Chaghatay Ulus.[8] At the time, various groups, tribal and nontribal, that made up Chaghatay society had become autonomous under their own leaders. Born into the Barlas, a Turkified
Mongol tribe, Temür started out as a freebooter, attracted a following, and
achieved power by 1370. Unable to claim the high titles reserved for descendants of Chinggis Khan's golden lineage, Temür set up a Chinggisid
puppet. Becoming this man's son-in-law (küregen), Temür ruled with the
title amir.[9] A brilliant politician and commander, he conquered the capital
of the Golden Horde (Saray, 1391), Baghdad (1393), Delhi (1398), and defeated the Ottomans at Ankara (1402), bringing under direct rule primarily
territories that most resembled his home region. Nourished by conquest,
his state and army were an extension of Chinggis Khan's retinue system into
an era when the breakup of tribes and abandonment of nomadic life were
turning tribesmen into mere "troops." After his death, his lineage, too, took
on the aura of a charismatic ruling house. Although his sons and grandsons
could not match him militarily, they won fame in astronomy (Ulugh Beg,
r. 1447–49) and art patronage (especially Husayn Baykara, r. 1470–1506).

Temür's political machine had at its core his family and retinue, members of which commanded his garrisons and tümens, nominal units of 10,000.
Next came loyal tribes, like the Barlas and Jalayir; then two preexisting
nontribal military groups, the Qara'una and Qa'uchin; then soldiers drawn

from the nomadic population outside Transoxania; and finally men from the sedentary population serving in infantry or siege forces. Temür neutralized the tribes politically but avoided violent dispersal. Externalizing violence, he sought to keep peace internally and reactivate the Silk Road.[10]

Temür's military career was notable not only for conquests but also for creating a new kind of military machine and furthering the transition from regional styles of warfare to what has been called the "global arsenal."[11] Whereas the basis of earlier Mongol expansion had been the superiority of light cavalry, heavy cavalry had begun to gain the advantage by this period. Temür's campaigns against the Golden Horde marked the culmination of this process. His forces combined armored knights with steppe light cavalry. More commonly under his successors, the armored knights began to be assigned land grants (soyurghal) to maintain themselves and their large horses; these assignments further separated them from tribal society.[12] After his Indian campaign, Temür also had superheavy elephant cavalry, which he used against the Ottomans at Ankara (1402). Flame throwers, rockets, and various types of siege engines probably rounded out his arsenal.

In addition to his conquests, Temür has a reputation as a patron of Islamic religious scholars and mystics. The disappearance of Nestorian Christianity and of the traditional religion of the Turks and Mongols in Central Asia, identified with his reign, may have more to do with the magnetism of the sufis whom he patronized than with his military prowess or cruelty, although those on the receiving end of his campaigns had plenty to complain about, Muslim and non-Muslim alike.[13] Temür's successors made of their empire what has been called one of the first Renaissance monarchies. It "rested on and promoted a set of intellectual values and institutions," which "when linked to other such sets, eventually became a new world institution, the republic of letters."[14] Creating incentives for a "brain drain" toward Central Asia, the Timurids developed "a government uniquely intelligent and secular" and—to the extent that the policy derived from China—helped transmit the idea of meritocracy to the Ottoman state and Europe.[15] Taking a commercially motivated interest in diplomacy, the Timurids also sent embassies as far as Egypt and China. Cultural patronage reached its height under Husayn Baykara, who made Herat into a center of the arts, patronizing both the great Persian poet Jami and the founder of the Chaghatay Turkish literary language, Ali Shir Nava'i (1441–1501).

The fifteenth-century Timurid court thus became the center for literary production in eastern, Chaghatay Turkic, just as the Ottoman court lastingly did for literary production in western, Ottoman Turkish.[16] Whereas Ottoman literary culture was Persian-influenced, the Chaghatay realm remained a zone of Turkic-Persian bilingualism. The literary relationship between Persian and Chaghatay is symbolized by the fact that Ali Shir Nava'i, during a youthful phase as a Nakshibendi sufi, had the Persian poet Jami as his spiritual guide. Nava'i later wrote as a literary testament his "Judgment on the Two Languages" (*Muhakemat al-Lughateyn*), a vindication of Turkish over Persian.[17] The fact that the Timurids lost out in the power struggle that followed the death of Husayn Baykara and had to seek their fortunes in India did not help to sustain Chaghatay in competition with Persian. Still, Babur, founder of India's Timurid-Moghul dynasty, did write the memoirs that remain the best-known work in Chaghatay, which survived through the eighteenth century as the language of Turkic literary production for a region extending as far as the Volga and Kazan. Characteristic of the eastern Turkic world, this literary nonexclusivism reflects the Turks' greater tendency, compared to Arabs or Iranians, to invest their identity in Islam and its civilization, which they had first encountered in a Persian-speaking milieu, rather than quickly reasserting their distinctness.[18]

Before we consider post-Timurid Central Asia, a word may be in order about the phrase "republic of letters" as applied to the Timurids. A term first used in seventeenth-century Europe, the republic of letters "was a specialized differentiation of the basic information circuit," that is, the Eurasia-wide information exchange network formed in the Mongol period.[19] The republic of letters was "a new international nucleation of information, intelligence and criticism," centered in northwestern Europe but spreading— or having counterparts—in southern and eastern Europe, the Islamic world, India, and China. As world awareness widened, the republic of letters became the "precursor of the modern university world, with its research institutes, specialized journals, international conferences, scholarly correspondence, data banks, and information exchange." This vision of republics of letters in different cultures, "federating" through the exchange of information, rings true and goes far to restore balance to the literature on world history, which for too long emphasized material exchanges more than cultural ones. The interest taken in the Timurid Ulugh Beg's astronomical tables from China to Europe illustrates the point.[20]

The Timurid departure for India in 1519 left Inner Asia divided between nomadic states in the north and "the oasis states" of East and West Turkistan.[21] The macropolitics of empire building resumed in India under Babur, while in Central Asia the pendulum swung toward a new micropolitics of social and religious institutions.

The Golden Horde having splintered after Temür's conquest, old tribes had been so broken up that the name Tatar became common as a generic term for Turks of the western steppe. Chinggisid successor states formed, of which some, like the Özbek and Noghay, bore neotribal names based on the names of the leaders from whose retinues they had formed. Successor khanates to the Golden Horde included those of Kazan and Astrakhan, conquered by Tsar Ivan IV in the 1550s, and that of the Crimea, long under Ottoman overlordship until annexed by Russia in 1783. For many, to secede from state politics and regain the freedom of steppe life seems to have been a relatively free choice; in the Crimean khanate, the term for doing so was *kazak çıkmak*, roughly, "to go out as a kazak." The term implies independence from authority, adventure, lawlessness, and potentially the heroics that distinguished a man like Temür as a war leader. On the other side of the frontier, Russian subjects who tried to slip past government control in search of an unfettered life as cossacks (from the Turkish *kazak*) knew what this meant.[22] In his memoirs, even Babur referred to the many tough times on his road to power with the term *kazaklık*, roughly, *kazak* life.[23]

In Central Asia, the Timurids' successors were the Özbeks, or Uzbeks, a name once applied to the mass of the soldiers in the Ulus of Jochi and later connected with the personal name of one of its khans, Özbek (1312–41), probably a posthumous identification honoring him as the khan who definitively converted the Golden Horde to Islam.[24] Özbek is thus another neotribal name, as if these people were the retainers (*nöker*) or descendants of the long-dead Özbek Khan. Mixed fragments of Kipchak and Oghuz Turkic tribesmen brought the name into the region now known as Uzbekistan under Muhammad Shibani Khan (or Shaybani, r. 1468–1510), a descendant of Chinggis Khan through his eldest son, Jochi, and his son Shiban (or Shayban). Muhammad Shibani put an end to the Timurid state in Central Asia. Reportedly, he said of himself, "[T]hrough me the dying house of Chinggis flares up again. . . . [W]hen I breeze by . . . like the morning wind, the candle of Temür goes out as I pass."[25] Be that as it may, after him conflict among members of the ruling clan who held appanages, or land grants, based on the major oases led to divisions and frequent shifts in the distribution of power. Here, reassertion of traditional themes of Turkic political culture, particularly the collective sovereignty of the ruling clan, the parceling out of territories, and bloody succession struggles, stood in the way of unity.

In an involution of Chinggisid legitimism, the Uzbeks limited succession to the khanate to a line running from Chinggis Khan to his son Jochi, his son Shiban, and his descendant Ebulkhayr (r. 1428–68), khan of the region north and east of the Caspian. The Özbeks, or Uzbeks, properly speaking were the dynasty and its retainers. The retainers belonged to specific tribes who still defined their social positions in terms of their places in Chinggis Khan's army—right, left, and center. By now profoundly Islamized, the Özbeks perpetuated two bodies of law in symbiosis, the Islamic sharia and the Chinggisid yasa. In these terms, the Chinggisid model of statecraft survived into the late eighteenth century. A major factor in weakening it was the problem of sustaining the system of land grants without new conquests. Competitors of the Uzbeks, from the late fifteenth century on, Temür's descendants had also established their claims to a hereditary right to rule. The fatal deterrent to political integration in post-Timurid Central Asia was therefore the proliferation of both *khans* (descendants of Chinggis Khan) and *mirzas* (from Persian *amirzadeh*, "sons of the amir," meaning Amir Temür). One khan's or amir's inherited claims to rule were as good as any other's.[26]

Although it was not immediately obvious, the consequences of Inner Asia's post-Timurid pendulum swing from macropolity to micropolity would ultimately take the form of another *translatio imperii*, a "transfer of command" as momentous as the one that first made the Turko-Mongol peoples masters of the steppe world. When large-scale empire building resumed in Inner Asia, it would be the work of non-Turkic, non-Muslim powers: China in the East and Russia in the West. Russia and China moved toward the partition of the steppe world with the Treaty of Nerchinsk (1689), and the process was completed in the nineteenth century.[27] Most obviously attributable to the technological obsolescence of the mounted archer in the gunpowder era, the loss of empire-building initiative on the steppes had broader causes, including that "shared evolutionary progress in human organization" that raised the building of states and empires to a new, "critical threshold across Eurasia, if not the entire world" in this period.[28] In Inner Asia, one extreme consequence of this was that the ways of life of the steppe peoples and the empires that established control over them could come to be seen as inimical, making peace between them impossible. In East Turkistan, when that region was conquered (1757–60) and transformed into Xinjiang (Sinkiang, the "new province"), this danger was mitigated by the fact that the conquering power was a dynastic empire ruled by the ethnically Manchu Qing dynasty. The Qing saw themselves as ruling over "five nations under heaven"—Han Chinese, Manchu, Mongol, Tibetan, and Muslim. Not until 1884 did Xinjiang become just another Chinese province.[29]

Many Inner Asians of the pre-1800 period seemed to compensate for the weakening of their traditions of state formation by relying on religious institutions. By the time of the Qing conquest, the tradition of empire in East Turkistan had been so far lost and social life so far rearticulated around rival Nakshibendi sufi factions that the very name Uyghur had begun to seem un-Islamic and had fallen into disuse. Under Qing rule, Nakshibendi factions and reform efforts continued to provide foci for rebellion, among Chinese Muslims (Tungans) as well as Uyghurs.[30] Recent studies of Central Asia add vivid detail to a picture of landscapes transformed over the centuries into sacred geographies, densely mapped with shrines and places of visitation, or by local memories of a great heritage of Islamic learning, in Hanafi jurisprudence, for example. Not unique to any single region, such patterns measure the continued growth of what Hodgson called the "international civilization" of Islam.

Critically important, in Central Asia as elsewhere, were the charitable foundations (*evkaf*) established under Islamic law. Forces for continuity, often surviving, despite changes of regime, into the Soviet period, the foundations were important not only religiously but also socioeconomically, thanks to the revenue-producing properties deeded for their upkeep and to their roles in redistributing those revenues.[31] Finally, sufi orders, like the Yesevis or Nakshibendis, to name two that originated in Central Asia, did indeed become "internationals," which could be mapped in a way resembling airline route maps. An order's fraternities and foundations in far parts of the Islamic world, sharing the same rites and traditions, would take the place of airline hubs and terminals; likewise, the routes of communication followed by the order's adepts and the lines of spiritual filiation among their shaykhs would take the place of flight routes. Each order's map would be different, but the maps of different orders would converge at the greatest hubs of the sufi world.[32]

Tempting though it may be to attribute the weakening of state structures in post-Timurid Central Asia to decline of the overland trade, recent scholarship challenges that idea. The introduction of new world crops such as tobacco and cotton argues against agrarian decline in a region historically known for the productivity of its oases.[33] Furthermore, the idea that *imperium* and *emporium*, empire and market, declined together fails to distinguish between two types of trade: the long-distance trade that nourished empires and the regional trade that nourished local societies. Some scholars identify the former with the east-west trade in luxuries and the latter with the north-south trade in necessities.[34] Whether or not the assigned compass points are exact, this argument reaffirms that the trans-Eurasian Silk Road trade was never the whole economic story in Inner Asia. The seventeenth-century Indian merchant community in Astrakhan on the Volga estuary, exchanging Indian silks and cottons for European textiles and Russian leather and furs, not only proved the literal importance of north-south routes but also showed that not all the interregional trade went east and west.[35] Bukharan traders likewise controlled "the lucrative caravan between Siberia and Central Asia" for several centuries, a trade in which Muslim Russian subjects still had important interests in the nineteenth century.[36]

With the rise of the world market, Inner Asian economic history went through several phases. In the sixteenth century, the east-west trade again enjoyed relative prosperity. In the early seventeenth, worldwide depression struck the central land route a blow from which it never recovered; that stimulated the north-south trade, which outstripped the east-west trade in volume and value. After 1700, recovery of the world market further stimulated Inner Asia, so that on balance its trade increased from 1300 to 1800, while changing in composition. After 1800, growth in the world economy stimulated revival even in the east-west route, along which the products and technologies of the Industrial Revolution began to reach the region after 1850. After 1600, Inner Asia was a "taker" rather than a "maker" of change in the world economy; yet to say no more than that masks economic dynamism within the region. The major socioeconomic weakness of the region was probably demographic: before 1850 the Muslim birthrate in the Russian Empire was lower than the Russian, not higher, as it became under the Soviets.

The economic change of these centuries is more a matter of "portfolio rearrangement" than decline. At first, the transit trade in silk, porcelain, and rhubarb predominated. Of these, the only Central Asian product was rhubarb. Rhubarb roots, especially those of certain varieties from Xinjiang, were considered effective against many diseases and were the sole premodern drug effective against diarrhea, the leading killer of children. By the eighteenth century, Central Asian trade had shifted from transit to terminal, the dominant goods being those for local consumption. China supplied tea, textiles, clothing, drugs, paper, and porcelain and bought horses, camels, sheep, furs, swords, jade, ginseng, and other medicines.[37] Long-distance trade through Xinjiang was no less important in this period than earlier. Significantly, despite the European image of him as the epitome of a "Confucian" disdain for commerce, China's Qianlong emperor (r. 1736–95) acted vigorously to promote and balance exchanges between Xinjiang and central China and in the Asian trade.[38]

## Islam and Empire in the Middle East: The Ottomans

The last great outpouring of the steppe peoples during the Seljuk and Mongol periods left a large Turkish presence in the Middle East.[39] Overwhelmingly from the Oghuz Turks, the migrants were people whose tribes had been fragmented and who, now living in greater proximity to settled agrarian populations than had their steppe ancestors, were either shifting to seminomadism or denomadicizing for want of ample pasturage. In the post-Mongol period, these Middle Eastern Turks began to assert themselves on the micropolity-macropolity spectrum in distinctive ways. First, the most detribalized was a military dictatorship based on slave-soldiers, the Mamluk State (1250–1517), headquartered in Egypt but also controlling Syria. To the Byzantines, this was another "Turkey" (*Tourkia*). To Ibn Khaldun, this Mamluk State, where the sultans rose from among the Turkish military slaves, was the proof of how ongoing recruitment of slaves into the military elite could enable a state of nomadic origins to escape its characteristic cycle of rapid rise and collapse. In a second mode of state formation, religious movements regrouped individuals and fragments of tribes. The most dramatic example of this type became the Safavid State of Iran. A third form of political entity took the form of new tribal confederations, the most notable of which took the names of livestock, the Karakoyunlu and Akkoyunlu, the "Black Sheep" and "White Sheep" confederations.[40] More common was the fourth mode of regroupment, already noted for the post-Mongol period. These were neotribal groupings that took their names either from a place (Shamlu, meaning "from Syria," and Rumlu, "from Anatolia") or from the founding leader. The most dramatic example of this type combined truly diverse human elements to found what became the longest-lasting and one of the largest states in all Islamic history, the Ottoman Empire.

The Ottoman Empire left the most pronouncedly Turkish cultural and demographic imprint on the regional empires founded by Turkic dynasts in the gunpowder era. That fact alone justifies emphasizing the Ottomans, but appreciation of the widespread impact of Turkic political culture in this period also requires comparing "political science" as understood by the Ottomans, Safavids, and Timurid-Moghuls, the three empires that ruled the lands from Algeria and the Balkans to Bengal. Such a comparative discussion, below, will complement this examination of Ottoman history.

Ottoman history is conventionally divided into four periods: rise (1300–1453), florescence (1453–1600), crisis and readjustment (1600–1789), and reform (1789–1922). The first three of these periods contain yet another example of the dialectical shift from micropolity to macropolity and back to a new form of micropolity.

The first two Ottoman rulers, Osman (1300–24?) and Orhan (1324?–62), were ordinarily never referred to by any title grander than "commander" (*bey*). They ruled a frontier statelet (*beylik*), formed around 1300, in northwest Anatolia on the borders of what was left of Byzantine territory. Their followers took the neotribal name Osmanlı, derived from the name of the founder, from whose name the English term "Ottoman" also derived by a roundabout linguistic route. Whatever the tribal pedigree of Osman himself, whatever the surely diverse pedigrees of Turks and non-Turks who rallied to him, it was Osman's leadership and the benefits to be gained from riding and fighting with him that bound them together. Unsurprisingly, given the Turks' prior experience on the Khurasanian frontier or later in the syncretic frontier culture of the Anatolian borderlands between Byzantines and Seljuks, the Islamic idea of the *ghaza* reappeared here.

Many trees have been felled to publish arguments about the relative dosage of tribalism and ghazi enthusiasm among the early Ottomans.[41] Varied evidence indicates that ghaza had been prominent in the Turks' experience of Islam for centuries by this time. However, much of this evidence comes from epics and folktales, and it may prove fruitless to turn to the lawbooks to see whether Osman Bey and his supporters precisely followed the letter of Islamic law. Inasmuch as Islamic law provided for the accommodation of peoples of the book who accepted Islamic rule, the early Ottomans' unconcern about the religion of their subjects and collaborators is not startling. Many local Christians appear to have been happy to pass under the rule of an expanding polity with relatively light taxes. It is also true that Turks of this period continued to understand the Islamic terminology of *ghaza* and *ghazi* as synonyms for old Turkic ideas, such as *akın* ("raid") and *alp* ("warrior-hero"). If Ibn Khaldun is right that a tribe had to have a spirit of solidarity—*asabiyya* in his terms—to motivate them, then ghaza was one name for the animating spirit of the first Ottomans, and terms from the pre-Islamic Turkic past were others.

That raises the question of the relationship between the early Ottomans and tribalism or other principles of social cohesion. In terms of the Turks' Inner Asian heritage, the meaning of tribalism varied over time, as did understandings of motivational ideas like the ghaza. Osman Bey and his Turkish followers resembled Chinggis Khan and his retainers (*nöker*) far more than they resembled the historical tribes against which Chinggis turned his retinue. In fact, the Ottomans offer a perfect example of the neotribal formations of the post-Mongol era. To say rather that they were a "predatory confederacy," far from disproving this point, confirms it. The prominent place that Christians, mostly Greek, held among the retainers of the early Ottoman rulers reinforces the point that what united them was not common descent but being Osman Bey's followers (*Osmanlı*). However diverse the followers were in ethnicity and religion, riding and shooting with Osman Bey also necessarily meant becoming part of an emerging polity strongly imprinted with Turkish and Islamic elements.[42] Moreover, if "tribalism" remained a familiar model of social organization that Turks could try to recreate where its historical continuity had been broken, it was not the only available model in fourteenth-century Anatolia. Köprülü, as noted, mentioned four of these: ghazis or alps (treating the Arabic and Turkic words as synonyms), akhis, the "sisters of Rum" (*bacıyan-ı Rum*, women ghazis or mystics), and the "*abdals* of Rum" (*abdal* being a term for heterodox dervishes,

who later coalesced around the Bektashi sufi order). The Moroccan traveler Ibn Battuta relied on the akhis' hospitality in Anatolia in the 1330s and
left memorable descriptions of these brotherhoods.[43]

The early Ottomans thus operated in a religiously and ethnically mixed,
diffusely institutionalized social landscape where no government wielded far-
reaching power and where non-Muslims still accounted for a large part of the
population. The fact that Orhan Bey ruled in the very years of the Black Death
reinforces the picture of instability. Subsequent signs of a personnel shortage,
which increased willingness to take all comers, must have the same epide-
miological explanation here as all across Eurasia, and the shortage of written
sources probably testifies here, too, to the decimation of the literate few.[44]

The Ottomans, moreover, formed only one of several competing beyliks.
The story of a miraculous dream conveys how Osman Bey and his followers utilized Islamic and Turkic cultural resources to build bridges to other
social groups that they could not control. While the guest of a saintly dervish sheykh, Ede Balı, Osman reportedly dreamt that a moon rose out of
the sheykh's sash and set in his own chest. Then a tree sprang from Osman's
navel and spread its shade over mountains from which waters sprang. When
Osman Bey informed the sheykh of his dream, the latter interpreted it: "Son,
empire is yours, may it be a blessing to your descendants." Then he gave
Osman his daughter in marriage.[45] In the narrative, it is Sheykh Ede Balı,
one of the *abdals* of Rum,[46] who is the master of both great spiritual influence and large herds; it is he who takes Osman for his son-in-law. The
imperial title (*padişah*) that he predicts was only claimed by Ottoman rulers
several generations later.

Osman's dream has been often recounted, but one of its most significant features seems to have escaped notice so far: namely, that it combines
nearly all the elements—the Mountain, Tree, Cave, Water, Female Spirit,
and the themes of Enclosure and Emergence—that run through Turko-
Mongol origin myths, all the way back to the Türk myth of descent from
the she-wolf. The dream narrative combines these elements, but with a significant difference in its sequels, as compared to the earlier Turkic origin
narratives. In this, Osman is the progenitor, not of a new Turkic tribe or
people, but of an Islamic dynasty.

How the Ottomans grew over the next century is a story partly of raiding and conquest and partly of winning control over the society around them.
Militarily, the Ottomans took advantage of their location on the Sakarya
River, close to the Marmara littoral, to take Bursa (1326). They acquired a
permanent presence on the European side of the Dardanelles when they
gained control of Gallipoli (1354). After losing, then regaining, Gallipoli
(1366, 1377), they expanded rapidly, defeating both Serbs (Kosovo, 1389)

and Bulgarians (1394) to create a Balkan empire, reducing Byzantium to little more than a city-state. Reimplementing the bilateralism of Turkic military tradition, Bayezid I (1389–1402) expanded not only in Europe but also against the other beyliks in Anatolia. However, the beys he displaced fled to Temür and provoked him to invade. Temür defeated and captured Bayezid at Ankara (1402), attempted to restore the other beyliks, and divided Ottoman territory into three parts. It took until 1413 to restore Ottoman unity, following which the state cautiously resumed the expansion that culminated with Mehmed II's conquest of Byzantium in 1453.

The Ottomans could not have survived defeat by Temür had they not begun to develop institutions that distanced them from the norms of Osman Bey's retinue. In ways great and small, the Ottomans' awareness of Turkic and Perso-Islamic statecraft showed from the beginning. Orhan Bey already used an early form of the distinctive Ottoman imperial cipher, known as the *tughra*, a term derived from that used for the seal of the Oghuz khans. The Ottoman use of horsetail standards (*tugh*) as symbols of rank and sovereignty, numbering as many as nine for a sultan at war, evoked precedents going back to the Türk Empire.[47] To cite traits evocative of Perso-Islamic tradition, Osman Bey had already begun to strike coins in his own name, employ slaves and eunuchs, found charitable endowments, and issue written documents in Persian.[48]

A keynote of frontier culture, found in frontier epics Byzantine and Islamic, was that frontier warriors on either side had more in common with each other than with the societies of their respective hinterlands.[49] Soon such a gap developed between the Ottoman court and its frontier warriors. Under Murad I (1362–89), the first Ottoman ruler to take a royal title (*hünkar*), learned ulema and experienced administrators began to rally to the court, replacing the relative egalitarianism of the early retinue with accountability and revenue management. One result was the assertion according to the sharia that the sultan should receive one-fifth of the slaves captured in raids, as of other kinds of booty. Resented by the ghazis as a tax on booty that before would have been theirs, this "fifth" (*pencik*) of the captives gave Murad I the manpower to create a standing slave–infantry corps, which also became the sultan's new bodyguard. By this time, too, the Ottomans had developed a force of cavalry officers (*sipahi*) supported by *timars*, benefices consisting of revenue-collection rights over one or more villages.[50]

The name of the new infantry, *yeni cheri*, whence "Janissary," recalled Chinggis Khan's "grand army," *yeke cherig*. But whereas Chinggis built his army around his retinue, the Ottoman "new army" replaced the retinue of Osman and Orhan with an Ottoman version of the ghulam system. By the 1390s, the Ottomans had also found a way to make slave recruitment independent of the fortunes of war: periodic levies (*devşirme*) of boys from their own non-Muslim subjects.[51] The Battle of Ankara (1402) proved the value of the slave elite. The Ottomans' ability to survive and reunify the empire by 1413 has been attributed to the commitment of this slave elite, who would have lost its identity and high status without a powerful master. The Ottomans had begun to find their own ways to create and replenish elites devoted to the state.

Scholars have long debated the extent to which the Ottoman state owed more to Byzantine, Turkic, or Islamic precedent. The prominence of Christians and recent converts at all levels in early Ottoman society ensured that the Turks' roots in Anatolia's pre-Islamic history, growing ever since the Battle of Manzikert (1071), would continue to deepen. The fact that people of Inner Asian, nomadic origin had conquered lands of ancient agrarian civilization made it especially likely that the Ottomans would learn from the Byzantines in agrarian matters. The forms assumed by the Ottoman timar system, for example, strongly reflect Byzantine practice. The administrative laws (*kanunname*) that the Ottomans drew up for newly conquered provinces show their eclecticism in adopting fiscal and other arrangements to which local populations were accustomed.[52]

Yet the Ottomans could not emulate the early Mongols' religious impartiality. They started out with an Islamic identity, even if it was not yet as sharply defined as it would later become. As the empire expanded and ceased to be a mere frontier statelet, its survival depended on moving beyond neotribal retainership and creating the institutions to rule an Islamic state with a large interior. The people who could do this were not so much ghazis and heterodox dervishes, or foreigners and converts, as elites specially formed for the purpose and knowledgeable about the practice of the Ilkhanids, Seljuks, and earlier Islamic states. Champions of the ghazi tradition blamed the Çandarlı family, which dominated the administration for three generations, for changes in the Ottoman polity; but that was only to scapegoat one family. As the Seljuk clan had done when it entered the high politics of Iran, the Ottoman house had to part ways with its earliest retainers. As a result, ghazi culture for a time, and heterodox Islam at all times, became the sites of choice for mobilizing political opposition.

The Ottoman turn toward macropolity, begun by the reign of Murad I, was consummated by the conquest of Constantinople. Over time, the border raiders (*akıncıs*) were pushed off toward the Balkan frontiers. The imperial center appropriated the ghaza as one claim to legitimacy and set about modifying Turko-Islamic political culture to ensure state dominance. The creation of the standing infantry and cavalry was part of the process, but there was more. At the top, bloody throne struggles among multiple heirs continued through the sixteenth century, as prescribed in the dynastic laws attributed to Mehmed II. To prepare them for their future, young princes were assigned to provincial governorships. Yet the Ottomans very early abandoned the practice of dividing their territories among different heirs, as the nomadic Turkic states had. Challenged by Temür on this, Mehmed I answered that "the Ottoman sultans from the beginning have . . . refused to accept partnership in government."[53] In the succession struggle, the brother who won took all; those who lost had to be killed. Not for the Ottomans the territorial fragmentation or the proliferation of dynastic bloodlines that made political integration impossible for the descendants of Chinggis and Temür.

Murad I's appointment of the first *kadi asker*, or "judge of the army," showed, too, that ghazi egalitarianism was giving way to an official stratification into a military-administrative (*askeri*) ruling class and a subject class (*reaya*). This differentiation echoes the elites (*begler*) and common people (*kara bodun*) found already in the Türk period, with a critical difference: the Ottoman elite consisted of the sultan's slaves, not tribal or other leaders with independent power bases—something the Ottomans persistently avoided. Murad I's vezir Çandarlı Kara Halil gets credit or blame for organizing the treasury and introducing the system of land survey registers that the Ottomans used to control the timar system. In the same connection, the provincial military-administrative hierarchy headed by the governors general (*beylerbeyi*) and governors (*sancak beyi*) also took shape.[54] An Ottoman-Islamic imperial regime, with its sultan and administrative center, its "composite military" made up of Janissary infantry, provincial cavalry, and ghazi border defenders, had begun to emerge. Not by conquest alone did the Ottomans build their empire. They also knew the value of patronage, offering new subjects lighter taxes than they had under their old rulers and founding charitable endowments, for example, to support religious leaders, including popular babas, for whom a meeting hall might create the nucleus for spreading Islam and founding a town.[55]

The transition from ghazi retinue to military patronage state entered an entirely new phase with Mehmed II's conquest of Constantinople in 1453—an event of vast geostrategic and symbolic significance. Not only did ancient Turkic tradition link sovereignty to control of sacred sites; a saying of the Prophet Muhammad and memories of early Muslim campaigns also sanctified the goal of conquering this city. To Greek Christians, it was the Second Rome; to Slavs, Tsargrad. No longer merely ghazis, the Ottoman sultans now had universal claims to legitimacy. Even Pope Pius II wrote to the Conqueror that all it would take to make him "the greatest man of your time by universal consent" was "a little water with which you may be baptized."[56]

**Mehmed II, "The Conqueror"** (*Fatih*), **Ottoman Sultan, 1451–81.** Attributed to Şiblizade Ahmed, c. 1480, the miniature reflects both Timurid and Italian pictorial traditions, notably the Gentile Bellini portrait of 1480, now in the National Gallery in London. Reflecting the cosmopolitanism of Ottoman court culture in this period, the miniature also became a prototype for some later portraits of sultans. From Topkapı Palace Museum, Hazine 2153, f. 10a.

For the next century and a half, the empire experienced its most dynamic period of expansion. Mehmed II's annexation of Serbia (1460) and Bosnia (1463) in the west and his subjugation of the Akkoyunlu state in the east further consolidated the empire.[57] After defeating Safavid Iran, Selim I (1512–20) conquered the Mamluk state, so gaining Syria, Palestine,

Egypt, and suzerainty over the Islamic Holy Cities. Now the title "Servitor of the Two Holy Cities" made the Ottomans unique among all Muslim sovereigns. Süleyman the Magnificent (1520–66) extended Ottoman control over the rest of the Balkans, most of Hungary, the Black Sea littoral, Iraq, and the North African coastal region, except Morocco. Süleyman's siege of Vienna in 1529 and his fleet in the Indian Ocean, sent to aid Muslims as far away as the East Indies, indicate his strategic capabilities.

The empire reached the height of its power in the sixteenth century, but not all aspects of the imperial system reached highpoints then, or at any other single time. Now the charismatic clan whose conquests and claims to legitimacy held these many lands together, the House of Osman continued to evolve its own implementation of Turkic and Islamic traditions of rulership in ways that defy brief summary.[58] Now they were the ones whose blood could not be shed but who could order the death of their slave elite. The ruler's heavenly mandate (*kut*) was reexpressed in Irano-Islamic terms with titles such as "shadow of God on Earth" (*zill Allah fi'l-alem*) and "caliph of the face of the earth" (*halife-i ru-yi zemin*). Now it was the Ottoman sultan who claimed unique titles, perhaps most typically *padişah* but sometimes also *khakan* (corresponding to the earlier *kaghan*) and sometimes caesar (*kaysar*), titles that the Ottomans resisted conceding to other rulers.[59] Through the late sixteenth century, the princely governorate, contested succession, and the fratricide rule continued—brutal but effective means to ensure the succession of able sultans. By the early seventeenth century, the reconcentration of dynastic family life in the palace, the shift to succession on a basis of seniority, and the lapse of the fratricide rule opened a new period.

In the sixteenth century, the government was still a vastly extended imperial household, in which those who held power were in one sense or another the sultan's slaves.[60] The Ottoman adaptation of the ghulam system reached its highpoint between the conquest of Constantinople and the end of the sixteenth century. Then, the "slaves of the gate" (*kapıkulları*), recruited through the child levy, manned the Janissary infantry and the six palace cavalry regiments and also served in the provincial cavalry. The best of these slaves, educated in the palace school, served the sultan as pages and went on to the highest military-administrative posts. Wielders of as much power as the sultan chose to delegate to them, the slaves of the gate differed from ordinary slaves in many ways. However, the sultan's right to discipline, execute, and dispossess them at will, as he would not an ordinary subject, made their servility real. The principle of ruling-class servility, moreover, proved far-reaching and durable: until the 1830s, all members of the ruling class, very few of whom were literally recruited as slaves by then, became the sultans' official slaves in effect, the ulema forming the only de facto exception.

A "composite force" indeed, the Ottoman military included not only the Janissary infantry and palace cavalry but also the provincial cavalry; artillery and canon founders; ancillary land forces like the miners, sappers, and bombardiers; border raiders (akıncı) still led by famous old ghazi families; and the navy. Numerically most important, the provincial cavalry not only went on campaigns but also governed the provinces, where they were assigned *timars*, assignments combining revenue collection rights in a given locality and responsibilities for keeping order among the peasant households there. This form of fiscal decentralization was a necessary compromise for an incompletely monetized economy where not all revenues could be collected and disbursed from the capital. Organized in a hierarchy that extended upward to the provincial governor (beylerbeyi), the provincial cavalry merged administrative and military functions; incidentally, this hierarchy anticipated the supposedly French-inspired, four-echeloned local administrative system of the nineteenth century. However, the presence of judges (kadı) appointed from the ulema and provincial treasurers meant that provincial administration was not solely military in character. Nor was the timar system extended to all provinces. The Ottomans held parts of the Arab world and some outlying territories in various forms of tributary status.

Within the great patrimonial household of the state, the will to centralization expressed itself in many ways. The divan, or council, at the palace saw to policy and some judicial business. The sultan no longer presided in person after 1475 but had a grilled window from which he could listen unobserved. Only his decree could put any policy into effect. The divan included the grand vezir, in this period normally a slave of the gate; several other "vezirs of the dome" (that is, the domed hall where the divan met); and the two "judges of the army" (kazasker), assisted by the chancellor (nişancı) and treasurer (defterdar), heads of a nascent scribal bureaucracy that still numbered only a few-score clerks. Anyone who reads the entries in its registers of "important affairs" (umur-ı mühimme) cannot fail to note the divan's determination to micromanage local affairs and demand reports on implementation of each order.

This centralizing drive appeared equally in the ranking of religious functionaries—at least those performing the tasks most vital for the state—in a hierarchy at whose head Süleyman appointed the *sheykh al-Islam*, the chief consultant on religious law, with the judges and medrese professors below him. Heir to both the Turko-Mongol tradition of dynastic lawmaking and the Islamic sharia, both of which also recognized custom as a source of law, the Ottomans sought to hold this heterogeneous system together by giving judicial responsibility under all kinds of law to the religious judges (kadı), integrating the legal experts into the ruling class as official ulema, and relying on the jurisconsult at the top of the hierarchy to certify the religious legitimacy of state policy. Outdoing eastern Turko-Mongol states' attempts to balance Islamic and dynastic law, this Ottoman policy paradoxically gave the Islamic sharia the "highest degree of actual efficiency [effectiveness] which it had ever possessed in a society of high material civilization" after the Abbasid period while simultaneously maximizing the scope for dynastic law (*yasa*, *kanun*).[61]

The extent to which Ottoman economic policy combined elements of command economy with private initiative reinforces the impression of centralizing tendencies. One purpose of the sultans' tight discipline over their official slaves was, ideally, to protect the tax-paying subjects from fiscal abuse and exploitation. As of 1528, the state claimed ownership of 87 percent of the arable land, much of this divided into timars, each of which included a number of small peasant farms. In the towns and cities, craftsmen and small tradesmen were more or less grouped in guilds (*esnaf*), which the government dealt with through the judges (*kadı*) and the market inspectors (*muhtesib*) who worked under them, in the interest of protecting consumers and restraining competition. In contrast, merchants (*tüjjar*) in the long-distance trade, often with members of the ruling class investing with them in silent partnerships (*mudaraba*), might both enjoy greater freedom and take greater risks. They might, however, also be forced into ruinous contracts to provision Istanbul in essential foodstuffs, which the government, fearful of unrest in the capital, sold at fixed prices. The state intervened in the economy to regulate foreign trade by granting European states commercial "privileges" (*imtiyazat*, which Europeans referred to as "capitulations"). Government also intervened in the economy to develop certain types of production as state enterprises, to organize the provisioning for campaigns, and at times to purchase needed goods at below-market prices.[62] Already in this period, specie drain to pay for imports—not to Europe, but in other directions to pay for imported furs, porcelains, silks, and other textiles—caused concern. Requiring vast amounts of fur, muslin, and silk for ceremonial robes (*hil'at*) and for the turbans and fur-trimmed gowns proper to each rank, court etiquette aggravated the specie drain. Much silk and some furs were domestically produced. The finest cottons came from India, however, whereas the furs most valued all across Eurasia came from Siberia, where the mounting demands of Russian traders and tax collectors, particularly for sable, reduced Siberian peoples like the Yakuts—the most distant of the Ottomans' Turkic cousins—to subjection.[63]

In agrarian matters, the ecology and history of the Mediterranean world of the grain, the grape, and the olive shaped the Ottoman Empire as decisively as did its Turko-Mongol and its Islamic traditions. As a "peasant empire," the Ottoman state had more in common with the Roman and Byzantine Empires that had ruled the same lands than with the steppe empires of earlier Turkic history. In a system of divided rights to land, most of the arable land was technically classed as *miri* (from Arabic *amiri*, belonging to the amir, or ruler). Much of the miri land was administratively divided into timars, which were assigned to cavalry officers (*sipahi*) with the right to collect revenues and the duty to keep order. At the grassroots level, small farms prevailed. Over these, the heads of peasant households had permanent, legally protected use rights (*tasarruf*). Historian Halil İnalcık calls this the *çift-hane* system, equating it with Byzantine and Roman prototypes.[64] Combining the terms *çift*, referring to a yoke of oxen, and *hane*, house or household, the term *çift-hane* identifies the small family farm as the basic building block demographically, economically, and fiscally. Displaying easily as high a level of administrative capacity as had the Great Mongol Empire, the government periodically registered these households and their revenue sources. Apparently based on Ilkhanid prototypes, the survey registers provided the basis for the system of granting timars to cavalry officers. As long as they were regularly updated, the surveys also made it possible to reassign the cavalry officers as needed to raise their compensation and keep them from becoming too rooted or dominant in one place. The means of local administration and revenue collection changed in later centuries, but the goal of protecting the small family farm (*çiftlik*) persisted throughout the empire's history.

Between 1600 and 1800, the Ottomans went through a period of crisis and adjustment. Yet it was the only one of the Islamic empires of that time to survive with any significant degree of autonomy into the nineteenth century. Scholars used to define the period 1600–1800 as one of Ottoman decline, a view shaped by the Ottomans' military fortunes, assumptions about the world economy, and contemporary Ottoman and European thinkers' views on changes from the preceding period. More recent scholars have attacked this "declinism," opening new fronts of research and advancing economic reinterpretations comparable to the "portfolio rearrangement" noted for Central Asia.

In terms of the micropolity-macropolity dialectic, this period of Ottoman history resembles the late Abbasid or Seljuk period in that something resembling its *amir-a'yan* system reemerged. Without reference to the late Abbasids or Seljuks, Ottoman historians long spoke of an *a'yan* system in the seventeenth and eighteenth centuries, when imperial centralization had again yielded to decentralization. Within the old, officially imposed "class" structure, acknowledging only rulers and subjects, a new stratification appeared, with the sultan and his servile elites at the top and a lengthening list of intermediaries—great a'yans who resembled provincial warlords, smaller ones who were more leaders of the local populace, and other local religious or lay leaders—and finally the ordinary folk of the different religious communities. The decline, in one sense, of the center's ability directly to dominate the countryside amounted to the development, in another sense, of denser interlinkages between center and periphery. Seventeenth- and eighteenth-century conditions did not exactly reproduce those of the tenth through thirteenth centuries. Later, elements of this eighteenth-century a'yan system evolved into the "politics of notables" noted in the nineteenth century.

Ironically, the decentralizing trend began within the palace. Not only did the sultans evolve from warrior-patriarchs into sedentary monarchs, reigning more than ruling, but also the old discipline that maintained the ruling elite as slaves within one great household became harder to maintain. Süleyman had made a practice of marrying daughters of the imperial household to top-ranking "slaves of the gate," so making them imperial sons-in-law, as well as vezirs and commanders. Such individuals began to acquire their own ghulams, forming their own households and household-based factions inside the ruling class. Once the sultans began coming to the throne without the practical preparation of provincial governorship and the bloody succession struggle, they were less able to dominate their own households. The early seventeenth century witnessed an upsurge in political factionalism in the palace. Senior palace women acquired expanded influence, especially the sultan's mother, who became a key link in factional networks that included princesses married to powerful statesmen outside the palace. By 1656, this pattern no longer met the needs of the times. Then sultan-mother Turhan engineered the appointment, with exceptional powers, of the first of the Köprülü grand vezirs—a bid to use one elite household to control all others. The Köprülü family dominated politics and patronage for fifty years, although sultans episodically vied to reassert themselves as commanders and heads of the one great household. Patterns of appointment to high office wavered between periods of household dominance and episodes when appointees were drawn from the palace and its supporters.[65] With the failed second siege of Vienna (1683) and the territorial losses ratified at Karlowitz (1699), both the Köprülüs and the attempts to reassert palace control faltered.

The role of the households grew thereafter, not only in the center but also in the provinces. As complex changes in Ottoman financial administration led to a growth in the farming out of revenue collection rights, wealthy individuals began to acquire large power bases in the provinces. Eventually, even notables of reaya origin formed households and acquired high positions. Once provincial governorships had been combined with tax farms and big provincial tax farmers began to buy governorships, men of reaya origin could acquire the ruling elites' highest titles (bey and paşa).[66] The introduction of life-term tax farms (*malikane*, 1695), as well as a 1726 decree ending the appointment of district governors (*sancakbeys*) from the center and providing for provincial notables' appointment to those posts, made the local notables into the government's chief provincial interlocutors.[67] Especially in the wake of the catastrophic Ottoman-Russian war of 1768–74, some notables became warlords, dominating entire provinces. By 1808, one group of warlords, led by Bayraktar Mustafa Pasha, had grown strong enough to stage a coup, enthrone Mahmud II, and get his reluctant assent to a "deed of agreement" that ratifed their powers and implicitly limited his.[68] By then, popular sentiment had turned against the notables, but Mahmud still had to struggle to reassert central control.

Analogous changes had occurred in all branches of the Ottoman system. For example, the ulema hierarchy reached its highest point of elaboration in the early eighteenth century, with the top posts becoming the preserve of an intermarried oligarchy of elite families. Government in general had grown in size to the point that it could no longer fit within the palace, and a number of agencies sprang up around the city, the most important being the Sublime Porte (*Bab-ı Ali*), which contained the residence and offices of the grand vezir. As the state shifted from military expansion to a defensive posture, the scribal service, staffing the Sublime Porte and the Treasury, grew disproportionately in numbers and influence compared to other branches of the ruling class; and important household factions began to form in upper scribal echelons, too.[69]

Military history is critical in assessing the Ottoman response to the period of crisis and adjustment between 1600 and 1800. For much of this period, far from faltering, the Ottomans benefited from having already achieved some of the Europeans' most important post-1600 gains at earlier dates, including a large, disciplined, professional infantry corps; a sophisticated system of logistical support; and the centralized control of the revenue system needed to support them.[70] With time, the Ottoman provincial cavalry slid into technological obsolescence, and the government responded by reducing its numbers substantially by the late seventeenth century. The Janissaries also declined in discipline and effectiveness. Ottoman commanders relied increasingly on armed mercenaries recruited from the subject classes, the *sekban* infantry and the *sarija* cavalry. Although less disciplined than the old regular forces, the mercenaries were not sufficient in numbers in the seventeenth century to have caused the depredations between campaigns that have been blamed on them.[71] Later wars notwithstanding, Ottoman military policy had progressed beyond ghazi militancy, assimilating the concept of peaceful coexistence with Iran by the Peace of Amasya of 1555 and with the Habsburgs by the armistice of 1568. Even after the Treaty of Karlowitz (1699) forced the Ottomans to withdraw from north of the Danube, they won substantial victories against Russia, against Venice, and against Austria in the early eighteenth century. The state of Ottoman forces indicates, however, that they did not keep up with innovations in drill and in command and control, which transformed European armies, or with eighteenth-century improvements in artillery. A reckoning finally came, but not until after 1768, with the Ottoman-Russian wars that ended Ottoman control of the northern Black Sea littoral and the Crimea and, incidentally, left much of the Ottoman countryside under the control of great warlord households. Russian expansion had confronted the Ottomans with a huge enemy that had also become their neighbor. This and later crises left no doubt that the Ottomans would have to reorganize and strengthen their state and its forces in order to cope with a changing world.[72]

## Military-Patronage States Compared:
## Ottomans, Safavids, and Timurid-Moghuls

The Ottomans were exceptional not only in being the longest-lasting, and one of the largest, states of either Islamic or Turko-Mongol history. Among the dynasties of Turkish origin that were contemporary with them, they also left behind the most pronouncedly Turkish imprint, both demographically and culturally, even allowing for the cosmopolitan character of the Ottoman-Turkish court culture and language. These are reasons for emphasizing the Ottoman Empire. Yet it was contemporary with two other, major empires rooted in the Turko-Mongol tradition. To appreciate not just the Ottomans but also the overall significance of Turko-Islamic political culture for world history in this period therefore requires comparing the military-patronage states of the gunpowder era. The value of doing so can be illustrated by comparing the Ottomans, Safavids, and Moghuls selectively in terms of dynastic origins, state-society relations, imperial legitimization, and dominant patterns of change over time.

The commonalities among these states start with their Turkic dynastic origins, of which the Ottomans' have already been discussed. The Safavid family, which may have originated in Iranian Kurdistan, moved to Iranian Azerbaijan, where one of its members, Sheykh Safi, founded a sufi order in the 1250s.[73] In a milieu where various Sufi orders displayed Shi'i tendencies, the originally Sunni Safavid order split, and its Anatolian branch evolved into a militant ghazi movement that advanced millenarist claims on behalf of its leaders. The Safavid family intermarried with Turkic rulers and propagated its appeal in Azeri Turkic among Türkmen tribesmen in Azerbaijan and Anatolia. Although Sunni and Shi'i religious identities were not yet clearly differentiated, radical Safavid doctrine went beyond what any well-schooled Muslim could accept, whether Sunni or Shi'i. In a way commonly attributed to the influence of pre-Islamic Turkic religious ideas, the followers of the movement, known as "sufi ghazis" (*ghuzat-i sufiye*) or as "red-heads" (*kızılbash*) because of their red headdress, attributed divine status not only to the Prophet's son-in-law Ali, whom the Shi'is regard as the first imam, but also to the head of the Safavid order. Ismail I inherited leadership of the movement and transformed it into a state. He defeated his Akkoyunlu relatives in 1501; campaigned across Iran, Iraq, and Transoxania; and reunited Iran under himself as shah (r. 1501–24). That Ismail's propaganda was also effective in eastern Anatolia is clear from one of his Turkish poems: "[T]hose who gave their faith to the sons of the Shah were the akhis, the ghazis, and the abdals."[74] Surprisingly, Ismail also later established Shi'ism for the first time ever as Iran's official religion.

Unlike either Osman or Ismail, Babur, who founded India's Timurid-Moghul line, was a man with unassailable inherited claims to rule. He was a direct descendant of both Temür, on his father's side, and Chinggis Khan, on his mother's side. His foremost goal was to conquer an empire in Central Asia. His biggest problem in doing so was that too many others had the same idea. He ended by gaining a far more lucrative prize, northern India, ruling from Kabul to Delhi and Bihar (r. 1526–30). After him, his son Humayun (r. 1530–56) had to fight for decades to consolidate control of India.[75] Islamic conquests in India had begun a few decades after the death of the prophet Muhammad, Turkic dynasts had ruled parts of it since the tenth century, and now India was to experience one of its greatest episodes of imperial integration under the Timurid-Moghul rule.

All three empires resembled each other strongly in their organization of relations between state and society. All were land-based empires, created by conquest of adjoining territories; of the three, only the Ottomans developed appreciable naval capabilities. In each empire, a dynasty with Turkic roots ruled over ethnically different and internally diverse subject populations. The martial ethos was important for each dynasty, especially in its early period. Their rulers and elites all valued the title *ghazi*. All these states maintained the long-standing Turkic stratification between beys and commonfolk. Practices from the nomadic past that proved surprisingly durable, among both Ottomans and Moghuls, included the army's being accompanied on campaign by the administration and elements of the court, as well as by an *ordu bazar* of traders and craftsmen.[76] The ruling institutions of each state preserved attributes of an armed camp, one consequence of this being the wide spread and evolution of the term *ordu*. The term is still the word for "army" in Turkish. In the form "Urdu," it is the name for the Islamic, Arabic-script version of the language, originally spoken in the Delhi region, which is also known in its Hindu version as Hindi. All three states used familiar forms of land grants to sustain their elites, whether assigning provinces as governorates for members of the dynasty or grazing grounds for loyal tribes as earlier Turkic states had done, or by the more centrally controlled method of assigning revenues from specific districts to support members of the ruling elite (the Ottoman *timar* or the Moghul *jagir*). The system of decimal ranks survived, both in the Ottoman military and in a distinctive Moghul elaboration whereby each officer (*mansabdar*) had both a personal (*zat*) and a "trooper" (*suwar*) rank, the latter signifying the number of heavy cavalry-men he had to maintain.[77]

All three empires faced the problem that a state "conquered on horse-back" could not be "governed on horseback."[78] This forced them in time to shift their basis of support away from their original retainers. The early Ottomans did so by marginalizing their ghazi retinue and adopting the style of Islamic sultans who ruled over an agrarian empire. The Safavids did so by shifting from the charismatic millenarism that had sealed the loyalty of their *kizilkbash* sufi ghazis to "the legalistically and theologically rationalized Shi'ism of the Imami sect."[79] Along with this shift, the Safavids renewed the inclusive approach to the combination of Turkish military and Iranian bureaucracy that had ruled Iran since Seljuk times. Shah Tahmasp (1524–76) and Shah Abbas I (1587–1629) added to this a slave establishment, which they replenished with captives from the Caucasus and used as a counterweight to the *kizilbash*. Tahmasp also promoted the idea of *shah-savani*, a "love of the shah" as monarch, not sufi leader, as an appeal intended to unite Iranians across ethnic or tribal lines.[80] In the case of the Moghuls, the fact that a founder who aspired to an empire in Central Asia acquired one centered in North India—a performance that his son more or less had to repeat—makes the shifts in bases of support even more complicated, with a progressively lengthening list of additions: first Central Asian and Iranian Muslims (Turanis versus Iranis), then Indian Muslims, and eventually also Hindu leaders, starting with the Rajputs. The Moghuls differed in not using slavery as a means of elite recruitment, as both Ottomans and Safavids did.[81]

The three empires also resembled each other in their strategies of legitimization, even as their competition and the differences in the populations they ruled forced each to stake sometimes antithetical claims. In all three, elements of the sacralization of state authority, seen in all earlier

Turko-Mongol polities, reasserted themselves in Islamized terms, but always with elements that went beyond strictly Islamic bounds in some way. Of the three states, the Ottomans adhered most strictly to Sunni norms in elaborating their claims to legitimacy. Yet they condoned an extremely wide range of sufi orders, as long as they respected the sultan's authority. The resulting pattern somewhat resembles the Mongols' near impartiality in tolerating religions that would abide by their rule. Through their promulgation of *kanuns*, the Ottomans also asserted the legislative initiative of the state more strongly than did the other empires. Their dynasty, which started with nothing like Babur's claims to charismatic lineage, acquired not only an extensive list of Islamic claims and titles (starting with that of ghazi) but also a cross-culturally eclectic portfolio of legitimacy claims, including fabricated genealogies for certain uses, "caesarean" claims after conquering Constantinople, and Iranian-style titles. Over time, the Ottoman dynasty made itself the charismatic ruling lineage with the customary Turko-Mongol markers of that status (collective sovereignty, contested succession, blood taboo, treatment of their burial places as virtual shrines, and so on). Some scholars have seen in the Turko-Mongol, as opposed to Islamic, features of the Ottoman system a kind of "protosecularism" that could explain the strength of secularism in the modern Turkish republic. In the Eurasia-wide perspective of Turkic history, these elements appear rather as part of the bedrock of the Turkic tradition of state formation, going back to the pre-Islamic sacralization of state authority (ideas about *kut* or the Tengri cult). Part of the force of these ideas comes from the fact that they are not secular at all but originally sacred in terms of indigenous Inner Asian religion. After conversion to Islam, they survived, transcribed into a different register, that of ethnic rather than religious consciousness, but with vestiges of their numinous aura still clinging to them.

The Safavids' approach to legitimization, although quite different, also has more to it than the strictly Islamic. Their unique experience starts with the fact that the Safavid order, by the time Ismail inherited its leadership, had become identified with beliefs so extreme that they are difficult to reconcile with any kind of monotheism. In one of the poems he wrote in the Turkic language of his followers, Ismail asserted that

> Adam has donned new clothes: God has come! God has come!
> My name is Shah Ismail. I am God's mystery. I am the leader of
>     all these ghazis.
> My mother is Fatima, my father is Ali; and . . . I am the Pir of
>     the Twelve Imams.[82]

As had been true since Seljuk times, succeeding in the transition from the micropolitics of a tribal movement to the macropolitics of imperial state formation in the Islamic world required formulating an appeal that would pass inspection by the learned. For the Safavids, this fact set the terms in which the inevitable routinization of charismatic authority had to occur. Competition with rival Sunni polities, and especially the conflict that Ottoman reactions to Safavid propaganda in Anatolia generated, probably helped push the Safavid bid for a more respectable Islamic legitimization toward the Shi'a. In any event, Ismail converted Iran to the Shi'a at the point of the sword, importing Shi'i religious scholars from South Lebanon or Bahrain to create the necessary religious establishment, and thus added religious reinforcement to the Iranian sense of linguistic and cultural difference from neighboring Islamic lands. As the Ottoman-Safavid rivalry in religious ideology peaked and passed its acute phase, the sixteenth century witnessed an ongoing crystallization of "orthodox" religiosity on both sides. For the Safavids, this meant persistent efforts to suppress sufi movements and Sunnis, in addition to marginalizing—sometimes massacring—their *kızılbash* followers.[83]

More than either Safavids or Ottomans, the Timurid-Moghul dynasty of India set interests of state above narrowly defined interests of Islam in legitimizing their rule, especially under Akbar (r. 1556–1605). Muslim rulers of India confronted a dilemma for which there was no proper Islamic solution. Islam remained a minority religion in every region of India, and the nature of Hindu religion and social structure made it unlikely that this would ever change. Yet Hinduism was not among the monotheistic religions whose followers were eligible for accommodation as protected subject communities under Islamic law. A Muslim ruler in India had little choice but to stretch the law on that point and at least accommodate his Hindu subjects on payment of the *jizya*, the same tax paid by Jews and Christians for accommodation. Still, many issues would remain. Muslim rulers of India faced the insoluble problem of either embracing India's non-Muslim majority and thereby offending their strict Muslim followers, or else offending the non-Muslim majority in order to satisfy strict Muslims. The wealth, power, and public order that a strong central administration could generate in such a highly productive country, and the eclecticism of many Hindus (and some Muslims) in matters of religion and politics, offered great possibilities, if the state could formulate an effective policy.[84] For members of India's Rajput elite, for example, serving a great master was part of their ethos; the master's religion was not the issue. Akbar responded to the possibilities before him in the most far-reaching way, contracting marriage alliances with the Rajput elite and embarking on extensive religious experimentation.

He not only sponsored debates among spokesmen of different religions. He also took steps to restrict the power and wealth of the Muslim ulema, many of whom he thought corrupt. He abolished the *jizya*. He set himself up as the supreme arbiter in all matters of religion, formulated his own syncretic dispensation, and initiated members of the imperial elite as his disciples.

Akbar's successors modified his policy, and the long-term results are instructive. Jahangir's reign (1605–27) overlapped with the career of the influential Indian Islamic revivalist, Shaykh Ahmad Sirhindi, the "Renewer of the Second Millennium" of the Islamic era, which had just begun; Sirhindi's anti-Hindu sentiments had destabilizing implications.[85] With Shah Jahan (1628–58), state policy began to reflect strict Muslim reactions to the policies of Akbar and Jahangir. As the influence of Sirhindi and of the Nakshibendi dervish order spread, Islamic self-consciousness hardened in India; and Shah Jahan began to measure imperial policy more exactly against sharia law. Yet the sacral quality of the imperial house remained an important factor in cementing its retainers' loyalty as "sons of the emperor's household" (*khanazadgi*), whatever their religion.[86] In the succession struggle after Shah Jahan, the conflict over religious policy polarized around two of the contending princes, Dara Shukoh, exponent of Akbar's accommodative legacy, and Aurangzeb, champion of the Islamic revivalists. Dara lost and was executed on grounds of apostasy and idolatry. Aurangzeb (1658–1707), the last decisive Moghul emperor, set out to create a more strictly Islamic regime and to expand the empire's frontiers. Living to be nearly ninety, he enforced Islamic law and priorities in policy, he encouraged conversion to Islam, and he enacted discriminatory measures against Hindus, including destroying temples and reviving jizya collection.[87] His efforts to extend Moghul rule further into South India proved counterproductive, provoking intensified Hindu resistance. In the lengthy succession wars (1707–20) that followed his death, the structure of centralized empire shattered in India, almost at the same time that the Safavid dynasty fell in Iran, although the Moghul dynasty would continue an attenuated existence until 1858. Out of the Moghul aftermath emerged some of the clearest lessons in all the Turko-Mongol dynasties' history about the value of accommodative, rather than restrictive, policies in matters of religion.

The course of change over time in the history of the three empires under comparison, although obviously complex, displays further parallelisms. They used to be analyzed in terms of rise and decline, but for states with roots in the nomadic, tribal micropolitics of Inner Asia, the characteristic life cycle of nomadic polities, which generically rose and fell within a few generations after their foundation, might offer a more pertinent analogy. Over time, as Ibn Khaldun deduced from his study of nomadic state formation in North

Africa, this is a story of rags to riches and back again, as each new conquering host sweeps in to seize the urban centers, succumbs to luxury, and falls prey to the next wave. At a given time, the greatest weaknesses of these polities appears in the divisive tendencies of the appanage system, the practice of parceling out the provinces of the new empire among members of the ruling clan in the same way that they used to apportion their grazing grounds. Perhaps to a unique degree, the Ottomans drew from the experiences of past dynasties the lesson that such fragmentation must be avoided at all costs.

All three of the empires under comparison lasted longer than the few generations predictable by either Ibn Khaldun's theory or Inner Asian history, warning against facile acceptance of rise-and-decline models. Yet that still does not explain why the states lasted longer than that model would have predicted. Ibn Khaldun himself discerned one contributing factor in the way in which the practice of military slave recruitment could replenish the elites over time. The fact that the Moghuls differed from the Ottomans and Safavids in not relying on slave military recruitment signals, however, that other factors must have been at work. One repeatedly observable pattern is that favorite dirty trick of empire builders ever since Modun: consolidating their own power, then abandoning their original retinue and surrounding themselves with a new, dependent elite. Versions of this appear in all three empires, in the Ottomans' replacement of the neotribal retinue with a slave military-administrative elite and an official religious elite; in the Safavid transformation from charismatic shaykh with a following of Türkmen sufi-ghazi tribesmen to monarch over a Shi'i Iranian empire, with its corps of learned ulema; and in the Mughal widening of elite recruitment, even after Akbar, to include indigenous Indian elites of differing religions. Many other lessons, painfully learned from past experience, no doubt also contributed. As it happened, a partial translation of Ibn Khaldun into Ottoman Turkish made his theory of the life cycle of the state more widely known among the Ottoman elite of the eighteenth century at the same time that they were learning more about European states, some of which were even older than the Ottoman Empire. Fascinated with Ibn Khaldun's theory, Ottoman intellectuals began to manipulate it to argue that a polity, instead of declining, could regenerate and renew itself.[88]

The long-term rhythms of change that characterize these three Islamic empires also reflect major historical forces operating independently of their particular histories. In the seventeenth century, there are signs that the Ottoman and Safavid Empires were experiencing severe contractions—demographic, economic, perhaps fundamentally ecological—that may ultimately be explained in terms of a global "crisis of the seventeenth-century." If India

somehow escaped this, the fact remains that the Mughal regime never recovered from the succession crises of 1707–20. The Safavid dynasty likewise collapsed in 1722. The fact that the Ottoman Empire, two centuries
older than either of the other two, outlasted both of them may have been
another factor in prompting Ottoman speculations about Ibn Khaldun's
cyclical theory.

Whereas the longer lifespan of the Ottoman Empire (roughly 1300–
1922) surely differentiates it from the other empires, their developmental
patterns also paralleled one another in yet other ways. By the seventeenth
century, all three had developed grandiose imperial courts with a ceremonial so elaborate as to immobilize all but the most dynamic rulers.[89] This
was part of a long-term trend toward the "civilization of the military-
patronage state."[90] In the eighteenth-century Ottoman Empire, this manifested itself in the emergence of the scribal bureaucracy, previously quite
small, as a leading imperial elite, while the ulema likewise made great strides
in privilege and institutional consolidation. In Iran, the collapse of the
Safavid regime and the political instability of the rest of the century opened
the way for the Shi'i ulema to expand their claims at the expense of monarchs in ways that produced major consequences for modern Iran.[91] The
proliferation of such powerful vested interests appears to have been part
of a larger trend toward decentralization and the proliferation of powerful
households and household-based factions. This trend was observed in the
Ottoman Empire by 1600 and appeared in India, too.[92] By the time the
Ottomans embarked on their new turn toward centralization and reform
in the 1790s, they would be the only one of these dynasties still in a position to continue the evolution of the Turko-Islamic tradition of imperial
statecraft.

Ultimately, the comparison among the three great regional empires of
the early modern period reveals important continuities and discontinuities.
Some elements of the old legacy proved remarkably durable. The Moghuls,
for example, still fought bloody succession conflicts as late as 1720, long
after the Ottomans had abandoned this practice. In other respects, old traditions became meaningless and were abandoned over time. In his memoirs, Babur recounts a traditional Mongol ceremony where libations of kumis
were poured to the yak-tail standards and someone "said something in Mongolian." He also visited one of his Mongol uncles, who dressed him in Mongol finery, which he implies was as alien to him as the ritual words in
Mongolian. Although his Chinggisid descent was a critical political asset,
his cultural horizons were no longer where his roots were.[93] The old, un-
disciplined ways of tribal life on the steppe, already inexpedient for empire
builders by the time of the Seljuks, had become a positive liability. Babur

complains frequently in his memoirs of how "the Moghuls" plundered friend and foe.[94] Later Ottoman analysts would cite their Crimean Tatar auxiliaries' indiscipline as a factor in the failure of the second siege of Vienna (1683).[95] Many such moments, occurring over the centuries, propelled the evolution of both the macropolitics of empire and the micropolitics of small-scale communities across the Turkic world.


## Conclusion: Babur on Sovereignty

Between 1500 and 1800, the "global arsenal" of the gunpowder era ended the steppe warriors' military advantage. By the sixteenth century, the dialectic between tribal micropolity and empire building, just as it ground down the Inner Asian tribal formations and ejected many of their descendants onto the steppes as generic Tatars, had also created in Anatolia the basis of the modern, essentially detribalized Turkish ethnos.[96] The last great round of indigenous empire building had occurred all across Asia, not only among the Turks. Inner Asia proved unable to sustain this momentum, and the Chinggisid dynastic legacy reached exhaustion by the eighteenth century. Turkic and other indigenous peoples of Inner Asia would ultimately see the initiative in imperial-level state formation pass into alien hands, and they would pay dearly for that. To their south, the Ottomans, Safavids, and Timurid-Moghuls of India continued the legacy of empire building, writing a new chapter in the history of Islamic civilization as they did so. In the Ottoman Empire, with its remarkable trajectory from frontier micropolity to centralizing macropolity, to the decentralization of the a'yan system, and again toward centralization after 1800, the Turko-Islamic political tradition continued to develop long after the Safavids had collapsed and the Moghuls had lost control of India. The nineteenth century would bring the next great transformation, the integration of the Turkic world into the emergent global complex of modernity. Then the intricate patternings in the fabric of Turkic societies would begin to include standard motifs of global modernity alongside those distinctive of the Turko-Islamic heritage.

Although a premodern Islamic tradition of autobiographical writing existed, works that reveal much of the author's subjectivity are rare. In any culture, such revelations were perhaps even rarer among the many great sovereigns who ruled Eurasia in the sixteenth century, for whom a scrupulously maintained image of grandeur was indispensable. How much more significant it is, then, that one of the most extensive Islamic autobiographies was written in that period in Chaghatay Turkic by the founder of India's Timurid-Moghul dynasty, Babur (1483–1530). In the premodern Islamic world, "no other author . . . offers a comparable autobiographical memoir, a seemingly ingenuous first-person narrative enlivened by self-criticism as well as self-dramatization."[97] While recording his feelings and failures, Babur aimed to chronicle his career and leave to his heirs a manual on rulership. His work, therefore, also recorded for posterity his deep understanding of Turko-Islamic political culture, knowledge on which his success—sometimes his life—depended. He contrasted a ruler's downs and ups in terms of *kazaklık*, for someone of his lineage a time of throneless exile, and *istiklal*, a sovereign's "independence," or *mulkgirlik*, the "seizing of sovereignty."[98]

Babur experienced *kazaklık* repeatedly in his early attempts to carve out an empire in Central Asia. In 1502, having just lost control of Akhsi in the Ferghana valley, he was fleeing with a few of his horsemen, pursued by the enemy. One by one, his men were picked off or fell behind, until Babur was alone, pursued by two horsemen. Babur's empire was then no bigger than the back of his horse; yet he carried his inherited title to rule inside him. As the distance from Akhsi increased, his last two pursuers lost their nerve. Finally Babur confronted them, offering to reward them more than their "hearts could desire," whereupon they switched allegiance in a flash and promised to serve him wherever he went. The episode illustrates in elemental form the basic transaction of retinue formation, the exchange of service for reward. All parties knew that the service would not continue if the rewards did not.

Babur's appreciation of the potential to turn such a retinue into an empire emerges clearly from his reflections on the death of Husayn Baykara (d. 1506), Timurid ruler of Herat. Elsewhere, Babur criticized Husayn Baykara for lacking the martial vigor of their common ancestor, Temür, who had also started out as a *kazak* freebooter. Husayn Baykara had presided over a brilliant court, but that was not going to last.[99] Over many pages, Babur described Husayn Baykara's lineage, appearance, character, battles, dominions, wives, concubines, and numerous offspring. He praised Husayn Baykara for his Sunni beliefs, skill with sword and bow, and poetic talent. Yet he also criticized him for drinking, debauchery, and failing "to show royal resolve" in battle. Babur then recounted the different categories of court functionaries— commanders, treasurers, vezirs, ulema, poets, artists, musicians—and vividly characterized personalities in each category. Conspicuous among the commanders are tribal names illustrious in Timurid history, particularly Barlas (Temür's own tribe) and Jalayir. However, what made Sultan Husayn Mirza's time "marvelous" was that "Khurasan, especially the city of Herat, was filled with people of talent and extraordinary persons." Among throngs of lesser lights, Babur describes the preeminent painter, Bihzad, and the foremost poets

**Babur with Humayun and Courtiers.** The idealized portraiture gives no clue to which is the older man, but Moghul court etiquette would have placed Prince Humayun to the right of his father, Emperor Babur, that is, to the viewer's left. From the Late Shah Jahan Album, South Asian, Moghul, around 1650, Arthur M. Sackler Gallery, Smithsonian Institution, Washington, D.C., S1986.401.

of the day in both literary languages—Jami (Persian), and Ali Shir Nava'i
(Chaghatay), of whom the last also figured as a style setter. An era had ended,
ominously so, given the decision to enthrone two of the dead ruler's sons as
corulers in Herat. Babur concluded by quoting the Persian poet Sa'di: "Two
kings cannot fit into one clime." There could not be another great empire
in the eastern Turkic world without someone who had Babur's capacity for
*mulkgirlik*, the seizing of sovereignty.[100]

# FOUR

# The Turks in the Modern World
## *Reform and Imperialism*

The Turkic peoples' first great transition, their integration into the world of Islam, had depended on movement in two senses: some Turks had come to Islam by migrating into the old Islamic lands of the Middle East, whereas Islam had come to other Turks by spreading into the formerly non-Islamic lands of Inner Asia. In the Turks' second great transition, their absorption into the world of modernity, they did not have to go anywhere for modernity to come to them, although eventually a diasporic dispersion of global proportions occurred.

If adaptation to modernity did not require a migration in space, it required tremendous readjustment in other respects. The new reality that has enveloped the Turkic peoples during the last two centuries presented itself most conspicuously as a new force coming out of Europe, imperialism; but it was far more than that. Behind European imperialism, stood the much larger reality of modernity in all its manifestations, as it had emerged from the dual revolutions, economic and political, of the late eighteenth century and all that lay behind them. The nineteenth-century expansion and twentieth-century collapse of the Europocentric system of global domination defined two phases in the Turks' and other peoples' experience of modernity: a first phase of defensive efforts to modernize in order to fend off the looming imperialist menace, and a second, more self-confident phase, in which the European threat faded and the truly global nature of modernity became more apparent. Already in the first quarter of the twentieth century for the Turks of Turkey, not until its end for those of the former Soviet Union, the forces of modernity no longer appeared coupled with the threat of subordination to an outside power but increasingly presented themselves as what would

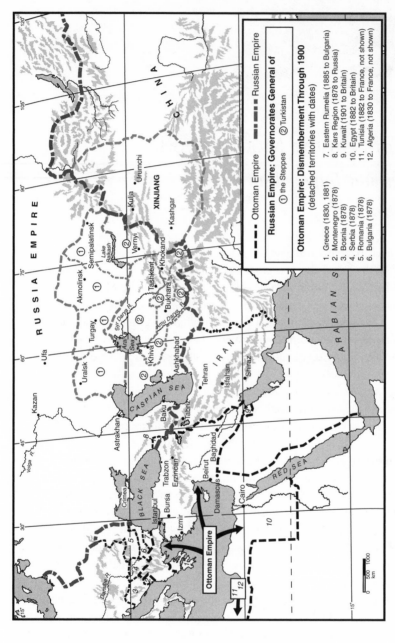

Map of the Turkic World, 1900. The map shows relevant parts of the Ottoman, Russian, and Chinese Empires. Some other regions inhabited by smaller Turkic populations are not shown or, in the case of Siberian peoples like the Sakhas (Yakuts in Russian), are far to the north and east, off the map. Map by Ron McLean, Digital Media Creation Services, Ohio State University.

The following labels appear on the map:

Legend:
– – – – Ottoman Empire
▪■▪■ Russian Empire

**Russian Empire: Governorates General of**
① the Steppes  ② Turkistan

**Ottoman Empire: Dismemberment Through 1900**
(detached territories with dates)

1. Greece (1830, 1881)
2. Montenegro (1878)
3. Bosnia (1878)
4. Serbia (1878)
5. Romania (1878)
6. Bulgaria (1878)
7. Eastern Rumelia (1885 to Bulgaria)
8. Kars Region (1878 to Russia)
9. Kuwait (1901 to Britain)
10. Egypt (1882 to Britain)
11. Tunisia (1882 to France, not shown)
12. Algeria (1830 to France, not shown)

RUSSIA EMPIRE
CHINA
XINJIANG
IRAN
ARABIANS
BLACK SEA
CASPIAN SEA
RED SEA
Aral Sea
Lake Balkash

Kazan, Ufa, Uralsk, Astrakhan, Turgay, Akmolinsk, Semipalatinsk, Vernyi, Kulja, Urumchi, Kashgar, Khokand, Tashkent, Bukhara, Khiva, Ashkhabad, Tehran, Isfahan, Shiraz, Tabriz, Baku, Trabzon, Erzincan, Baghdad, Beirut, Damascus, Cairo, Izmir, Bursa, Istanbul, Crimea

Syr Darya R., Amu Darya R., Volga R., Danube R.

Ottoman Empire

0 500 1000 km

eventually become known as globalization. It remains only to add that the recent artistic and philosophical postmodernism, however much a "halt of the caravans of modernity" for the avant-garde in highly developed countries, will probably "look more like yesterday's" than today's by the time most developing societies have leisure to ponder it.[1] Culture critic Edward Said made the same point by underscoring the irony that whereas "in the West, *post-modernism*" commands attention, in developing countries, intellectuals are still preoccupied "with *modernity* itself."[2]

The Turks' first great transition centered unambiguously on a change of religion, albeit with much variety in the way people lived out the consequences. Their second great transition was not as simple as a change of religion; it was more a process of entanglement in an incipiently global cultural fabric. This entanglement brought with it "new forms of organization of self and society, new forms of intellectual production, and new ways of imagining the world (and one's place within it)."[3] Henceforth, the fabric of Turkic identity not only would be woven in a new way but would also become enmeshed increasingly in this global fabric.

More than merely symbolic, changes in Turkish carpet production provide a microcosm of the Turks' nineteenth-century encounter with imperialism and modernity. In the main Ottoman centers of production in western Anatolia, Turkish carpets were objects of everyday familiarity; but like many other artifacts, they acquired added value when they were transported afar. This had always been true; however, steam engines, steamships, and railways vastly expanded the possibilities for such transport. Between the 1850s and 1914, Ottoman carpet exports grew seven- or eightfold in both volume and value, stimulated by rising middle-class demand in foreign markets and by the perception that these were unique, handmade artifacts from an exotic culture.[4] Such an expansion could not occur, however, without profound changes in production processes that aligned them more closely with evolving industrial practice. Most notably, with European chemical firms' development of synthetic dyes, these began from the 1860s on to eclipse the subtler but harder-to-produce colors of the old natural dyes, until the recipes for the latter began to be lost. Production began to shift, at least in part, from houses to workshops to factories, as carpet merchants and carpet firms, both Ottoman and foreign, grew in scale and began to intervene in production in more and more ways, including supplying "cartoons," or designs for the weavers to follow, and exerting pressure to drive down wages. To the historic carpet-weaving sites of western Anatolia, many new centers were added, and production became more widely dispersed. Particularly after the technical challenges in mechanizing the spinning of wool yarn were overcome at the end of the century, weaving and knotting remained almost the only parts of the production process that were hand-done.

Gender relations and other forms of production were affected as more labor was needed, although most of the weavers remained female, many of them young girls. Their depressed wages are testimony to the Ottomans' dependent integration into the world economy and to the disadvantaged terms on which they participated in international trade. In a multiethnic society, the expansion of the work force soon meant that many Turkish carpets were woven by non-Turks, often Armenians. Carpet weavers, concentrated in workshops or factories, became members of the emerging working class and took part in the wave of strikes that occurred in 1908 along with the Young Turk Revolution. Once so far enmeshed in the emerging global fabric of modernity, would the Turkish carpet-weaving tradition retain its identity? Would its artifacts retain their valued uses, their artistic distinction?

Creating turning points from which to look back on the changes that these textile images evoke, the consolidation of Soviet rule in Central Asia and the founding of the Turkish Republic, both events of the early 1920s, occurred some years after the conventional end of the nineteenth century in 1914; yet these dates were more meaningful to Turks than others that stood out to foreigners. To understand events of the century that led up to those turning points requires briefly defining the global complex of modernity and then considering the history of the Turks in Inner Eurasia and the Ottoman Empire.

## The Global Fabric of Modernity

Although the range of topics associated with the idea of modernity is vast, its simplest historical definition is as "an epoch turned toward the future," understood as a this-worldly future that can and probably will be better than the present or past.[5] The idea is clearly associated with that of progress in its modern meaning—not just the forward motion that the term originally signified but also qualitative improvement, achievable through reason, rationalization, and scientific experimentation—the application of human ingenuity. From these starting points follows the proliferation of phenomena that complicate the analysis of modernity: the cumulation and classification of knowledge, self-compounding innovation in science and technology, industrial production of goods, political revolution, the secular ideologies that have defined its programs, and the rise of myriad new forms of cultural expression.

Amid the phenomenological profusion of modernity, one of its most pervasive features is that ultimately no single value system, and especially no religion, dominates overall. Old religions and value systems persist and new ones emerge, but secularism wins adherents as a specific ideal or defining trait of many facets of modernity, even if reason has never vanquished faith, as some enthusiasts thought it would. If Islamic civilization historically included important features, such as philosophical and political ideas of pre-Islamic origins, that were reconcilable only by long custom with Islam, the accelerated innovation of modernity bursts the hoops of any single all-containing ideology—a profoundly disturbing fact for those who believe in the universality of their particular ideals. Where the Turks are concerned, this is the biggest difference between the transition into Islam and that into modernity; obviously, analogous statements can be made for other peoples and religions. However, this largely secular character of modernity gives many of its innovations a value-neutrality that may facilitate their modular adoption in other cultures and societies, even when those societies simultaneously feel threatened by the imperialist expansion of those who pioneered the innovations. If this kind of portability is one key attribute of modern innovation, another is that it achieved a self-compounding momentum, which has progressively accelerated change and shrunk distance, a process culminating in the revolution of globalization that ended the twentieth century.

If the phenomenology of modernity seems endless, there are axes along which its manifestations or their effects group themselves in patterns. In terms of its consequences for societies, modernity has had profound implications at all levels, from individuals, to families, voluntary associations, social classes, states and governments, and the world itself.[6] In western Europe specifically, the advent of modernity produced powerful forces to remold individuals from landlords and peasants into factory owners and workers, from subjects into citizens and even citizen-soldiers, and from believers into free thinkers in some cases. The economic and political revolutions that shaped new working and middle classes empowered the middle classes in particular, endowing them with new prosperity, a new sense of self, and a desire for new forms of self-expression. New forms of sociability arose to reconfigure human interactions. The economic map was redrawn by the emergence of the factory system, large firms, and the growing integration of world markets. Likewise, the political map was redrawn by the formation of nation-states in Europe and its overseas extensions and of colonial empires elsewhere.

Perhaps the most ironic of all the consequences of modernity has been the way in which the prestige of the nation-state idea prompted everywhere a reimagining of communities and spatialities in terms that the populations residing (or imprisoned) within their borders almost never fully matched. This reimagining had the positive consequence of generating new ideas of citizenship and political participation that provided the impetus for the creation of modern states. Alas, the same reimagining of ethnic homogeneity, extending uniformly to well-defended, linear frontiers, also had the negative consequence of generating murderous conflict in lands so prodigal in their ethnocultural diversity that the name of one exceptionally diverse region of the Ottoman Balkans, Macedonia, passed into Italian, French, and Spanish as the term for a mixed fruit salad.

Another axis, figuratively speaking, along which to consider the meaning of modernity is that of the different "routes to and through modernity" that different peoples followed.[7] First, the most fortunate of *European* societies could follow an internal route of endogenous change. Second, the *neo-European* societies, created mostly in the Americas and Australasia by European migration, responded to the same ideas but followed a route complicated externally by conflicts between colony and metropole and internally by those of race. For the other countries of the *colonial world* or those threatened with colonization, the third route to modernity passed through confrontation and conflict with colonizing powers or would-be colonizers, bearers of an exogenous modernity that they aimed to use as means of dominance, while the colonized had to try to adopt those same means selectively and turn them against their colonial masters. A fourth route was that of *externally induced modernization*, where a society threatened by Euro-American imperialism successfully imported features from the imperialist powers in order to defend itself from colonization.

These four routes exist at best as ideal types. The third and fourth routes may be hard to distinguish in the history of a given society. A number of Asian societies attempted externally induced defensive modernizations before falling to colonialism. Even Japan, the only nearly pure example of the fourth route, was subject in the second half of the nineteenth century to an unequal treaty regime, not unlike the longer-lasting one that Chinese historians regard as proof of their country's semicolonial subordination. Among Turkic peoples, the late Ottoman Empire was on the externally induced modernization route, like Japan only less securely so. The Ottomans progressively lost outlying provinces to separatist nationalisms in the Balkans or to European expansionism in Asia and Africa and always faced imperialist threats—whether diplomatic pressures or restrictions on their economic independence—that undermined their sovereignty. After 1923, the Turkish Republic had escaped the colonial threat and was unambiguously marching on the fourth route. For the Turkic societies of the Caucasus and Central Asia, colonialism arrived in Russian uniforms, later exchanged for Soviet, and lasted in a peculiar form until 1991. For the Turkic peoples of China's Xinjiang province, alien rule still continues, as indeed it does for some others, like smaller Turkic peoples inside post-Soviet Russia or like Azeris and other Turkic peoples inside Iran.

At the grassroots level, many people in peripheral parts of Europe, North Africa, the Middle East, or Central Asia never knew they were marching to modernity on the path here imagined for them. In the Ottoman lands, for example, Christian Arabs from Mount Lebanon, both men and women, began migrating in large numbers to the Americas after 1889, often return-ing after several years abroad.[8] Commonly known in Hispanic countries as "Turcos" because of the empire from which they came and as "A-Arabs" in the United States because of the ignorance of the host population, Leba-nese Christian migrants pioneered their own paths into modernity, first as itinerant peddlers in the Americas, then as social climbers after their return. As they did so, they experienced much of what Turkish emigrants would experience in large numbers in the 1960s. Both examples prove that gener-alizations about paths of cultural change risk underestimating individual experience, especially when it is a question of crossing supposed fault lines between civilizations.

In the era of imperialism, whether individually or collectively, peoples less advantageously sited in the world had to watch anxiously, trying to de-cide how to appropriate Europe's secrets for their own self-strengthening and how to protect themselves from colonial or semicolonial integration into the European-centered world system. In comparison to the progress of the most advanced European countries, they experienced the colonial version of the belatedness that had bedeviled many European countries, especially those that had to struggle for unification or independence, from Germany to Greece to Norway.[9] As peoples outside Europe and North America strove to become nation-states rather than colonies, most of them could not see the stirrings of crisis that would undermine European hegemony from within and bring on the interlinked crises that define the twentieth century (1914–91): World War I and the Bolshevik Revolution, the 1929 depression, World War II, decolonization, and the collapse of socialism. Even as that sequence ran its course, modern psychology revealed that the rational, patriotic citizen was also a creature of will and desire; old-time refinements of bourgeois manners and taste vanished into mass culture and mass consumerism, or even into mass murder and genocide; continued expansion in the scale of large firms made them into the imperialist powers of the postcolonial era; and nation-states the world over had to confront challenges, internally from increasingly discor-dant voices of their diverse citizens, and externally from the global disorder in which they interacted and competed but which they less and less could master.

By the end of the twentieth century, the citizens, classes, corporations, and nations that once seemed to structure modernity had become shattered fragments awash in a sea of globalization. Also awash in it were peoples of the world still struggling to obtain what modernity had promised, or perhaps, as in the case of the religiously motivated terrorists that emerge in countries around the world, lashing out against it as a threat.

## The Turks of Inner Eurasia in the Age of Imperialism

The experiences of the Turkic peoples in the era of imperialism display similarities arising partly from their common heritage and partly from the fact that they faced the same challenges of imperialism and modernization. At the same time, their starting points and their experiences of change also differed markedly. Although social structures defined in terms of kinship remained fundamental to their societies, some but not all Turks had become detribalized and had begun, as early as the sixteenth century, to meld into ethnic groups known as "Turks" in the Ottoman Empire and as "Tatars" in the Russian Empire.[10] With this change in social structure, it became only a question of time until the old political choices between the micropolitics of clan and tribe and the macropolitics of dynastic empire would need to be transformed into new ones of nation-state formation. Unfortunately, in the nineteenth-century world, colonization by foreign imperialist powers, threats of colonization, struggles to perpetuate old polities through partial modernization, and anticolonial nationalist resistance struggles had to come in between, complicating the transition from earlier sociopolitical forms to modern nationhood. To illustrate these points, this section will concentrate on Inner Asia, starting with the zones of Russian expansion and then turning to Chinese-ruled East Turkistan.

### Turkic Peoples in the Russian Empire

The situation of Turkic lands that passed under Russian rule differed according to the dates at which, and modes in which, Russian rule was established. The Russian conquest of the khanates of Kazan (1552) and Astrakhan (1556) under Ivan IV (1547–84) resembled the Spanish Christians' *reconquista* more nearly than Russia's later, colonial-style conquests, with the major difference that Muslim Turkic communities survived in a way that Iberian Muslims did not.[11] Catherine II (1762–96) connected the annexation of the Crimea (1783) to her dreams of reclaiming the Greek heritage and spreading Enlightenment to new lands. In Inner Asia, the Kazakh khanates passed under Russian protectorate around 1730 and were eliminated between 1820 and 1848. This phase resembled Russia's earlier advance into Siberia, the Russian counterpart to the United States' "winning of the West." The Caucasian conquests that annexed northern Azerbaijan from the 1790s on, leaving southern Azerbaijan lastingly as Iran's northwestern province, or the later campaigns that integrated Central Asia south of the Syr Darya (1864–84, with the most decisive campaigns in 1865–68) created a Russian counterpart to the French imperial presence in North Africa. Here, too, the new territories were treated as integral parts of the metropole, without any intervening sea in this case. Here, too, the conquered territories were simultaneously lands for

**Uzbek Woman Outside Her Yurt, 1905–15.** In this deliberately posed, ethnographic view, Sergei Mikahilovich Prokudin-Gorskii shows an Uzbek woman in indigenous costume standing in front of her yurt on a fine example of a Türkmen carpet with its characteristic *gül* motifs. A companion photograph shows the same scene with the woman facing forward. No mistake about it: the Russians are in control and the Uzbeks are subjects of both their rule and their scrutiny. From Library of Congress, Prokudin-Gorskii Collection, LC-DIG-prok-00006.

colonization and lands with an ancient civilization that had to be acknowledged, accommodated in some ways, and yet also subordinated as the material for ethnographers, orientalists, and colonial administrators.

In addition to those conquered in the era of imperialism, the Turkic peoples taken under Russian rule at earlier dates also played important roles in this period, often with repercussions felt in other Turkic lands. The Crimean Tatars, for example, experienced "one of the most heavy-handed policies of Russification anywhere in the empire," with the result that massive numbers of Crimeans—perhaps 1.8 million—emigrated to the Ottoman Empire between 1788 and 1922.[12] Notwithstanding, the remaining Crimean Tatar population produced one of the most influential thinkers and publicists of the entire Turkic world in Ismail Gaspıralı (Gasprinskii, 1851–1914), known for his long-running newspaper, *Tercüman* ("The Interpreter"); for his role in pioneering the "new method" (*usul-ı jadid*) to accelerate literacy acquisition; and for advocating unity among the Turks "in thought, word, and deed."[13]

Tatars of the Volga-Ural region assumed influential roles, notably in religion and commerce. In historical writing, against a backdrop of local particularism, the early nineteenth century witnessed the emergence of a sacred historiography promoting "Bulghar" identity, the term referring to the earliest Muslims of the Volga region. This self-concept reflects the enlarged horizon that the ulema of the region acquired under Russian rule, particularly after the creation of the Orenburg Muslim Spiritual Assembly (1788), which was headed by a mufti appointed by the tsar and which exercised responsibility in Islamic religious affairs for all the Muslims then under Russian rule except those of the Crimea.[14] The "Bulgharist" movement illustrates how cultural conservatives, whom others might dismiss as reactionaries or collaborationists, also strove to broaden their followers' sense of identity and solidarity in response to modern changes. A century latter, Yusuf Akçura (1876–1935), son of a Kazan Tatar family and educated in Istanbul and Paris, would become one of the most influential nationalist thinkers and leaders of his generation, both in Russia after 1905 and in Turkey after 1908.[15] These and many more such examples make clear that the nineteenth-century stages in the expansion of the Russian Empire do not tell the whole story of the Turkic peoples then under tsarist rule.

## Azerbaijan

For Azerbaijanis, Russian expansion is not the whole story in a different sense, for they were left divided between Russia and Iran. By the 1780s, not just Azerbaijan but the whole southern Caucasus had become the object of sustained Russian interest, and a state of war existed between Russia and Iran from 1804 to 1813.[16] Much of the resistance to the Russians came from the local khans who ruled the region. The Qajar dynasty, which had recently reunified Iran, sought to affirm Iran's control over its border regions, which historically extended as far north as Georgia and Daghestan. Still, the Russians prevailed. The Russo-Iranian treaties of Gulistan (1813) and Türkmanchai (1828) ratified Russia's conquests, establishing the present northwestern border of Iran and dividing the Azeri-inhabited territory into two equal parts, although the larger proportion of Azeri-speakers remained in Iran. Giving the Russians capitulatory rights in Iran, the treaties also opened Iranian markets to cheap foreign imports, shifting the Iranian-Russian trade balance heavily in Russia's favor, causing great distress among the merchants of Tabriz, and provoking the emergence from among them of the socio-religious protest movement of Babism, which seceded from Islam in 1848 and later gave rise to the Baha'i faith.[17]

The Russians also defeated the Ottomans in 1828–29. Parallel provisions of the Russo-Ottoman Treaty of Edirne (1829) and the Russo-Iranian Treaty of Türkmanchai (1828) provided for Armenian migration from the defeated states into Russian territory, migrations that the Russian military promoted with force so as to shift the population balance, especially in the former khanates of Revan and Nakhijevan, which the Russians combined into a single province of Armenia.[18] The migration of Armenians into the Caucasus increased after each of the later Russo-Ottoman wars. Whereas Shi'is predominated in Iranian Azerbijan, in Russian Azerbaijan, Sunnis initially formed a large proportion, declining by the 1860s to a minority of about one-third, presumably because of emigration to the Ottoman Empire. Still, the sectarian division of Azeri Muslims remained significant and later strengthened modernist demands for secularism in the region.[19]

The Russians kept Azerbaijan under Russian military rule until 1840, and the civil administration they introduced in 1841 still discriminated against Muslims and Turks while patronizing Armenians. In the Caucasus as elsewhere, Russian policy patronized the local elites, giving them the legal status of the Russian gentry in hopes of Russifying and assimilating them. In 1867, most of Russian Azerbaijan was combined into the governorates of Baku and Elizavetpol (Ganje). Although these were later abolished, the administrative consolidation helped to replace the particularism of the old khanates with a sense of wider commonality. So did economic changes that came with unification under Russian rule, starting with the common currency and consistent weights and measures.

Economic change accelerated rapidly with the oil rush that began around Baku in the 1870s, a development that further differentiated the Russian from the Iranian part of Azerbaijan. At its peak in 1901, Baku produced 70 million barrels of oil, more than the entire United States then produced. As early as 1905, overexploitation brought decline in Baku's importance on the world market. This boomtown on the Caspian had probably experienced a greater economic surge than any other part of the Turkic world in the nineteenth century, although the benefits went largely to non-Turks. The city acquired a non-Muslim majority (mostly Russians, secondarily Armenians). Non-Muslims were disproportionately prominent in business and administration, and European capitalists, notably Robert Nobel and the Paris Rothschilds, owned the largest oil firms. The Batum-Baku railroad, completed by the Rothschilds in 1883, brought Baku oil to western markets.

Azerbaijani Turks still considered Baku their city, however. In 1908, Turks managed to regain control of the City Council. As had happened earlier in the Volga region, a new Muslim bourgeoisie started to emerge, some of them distinguished by commercial capital, others by new kinds of intellectual capital. Often university-educated in Russia, Paris, or Istanbul, the latter became known via Russian as the "intelligentsia." Among Muslims, the term took on suspect meanings of "assimilators" or "renegades" and was not applied to people of Islamic learning.[20] These intellectuals played a leading role in promoting Azeri literary revival and secularism, especially because they saw the latter as a way to create a shared identity transcending Sunni-Shi'i difference. From Fath Ali Akhundzadä's (1812–76) writing of the first modern plays in Azeri in the 1850s to the rise of the Azeri press in 1875, these intellectuals explored the cultural space within which a modern Azeri culture could be created, and they debated competing orientations for the redefinition of collective identity—Iranian, Turkic, Islamic, pan-Turkic, and pan-Islamic. As elsewhere among Turkic populations of the Russian Empire, founding *jadidist* ("modernist") schools was a particular priority. Especially in the decade before World War I, the question of literary language also became a hot issue. Should all the Turks adopt a literary language based on Ottoman, as Ismail Gaspıralı thought; or should Azeris, Tatars, Kazakhs, and others develop their own literary idioms?[21] Azeri intellectuals of the north also reacted to changes in Russian politics, and both liberals and socialists had emerged among them by 1905.

The remainder of Russian Azerbaijan did not change nearly so fast as Baku but was profoundly affected by Russian rule, which it resisted in a series of peasant rebellions and a regular flow of young rebels (*gachag*), who took to the hills. Tensions mounted between Azeris and not only Russians but also Armenians, who were widely dispersed throughout the region. Like some other Christian minorities in Muslim-majority societies (the Maronite Christians, whom the French protected in Lebanon, for example), the Ar-

**"In Bukhara": Print Media Powers Cultural Change.** Published in Tiflis in a satirical newspaper, the cartoon presents an Azerbaijani view of how the mere appearance of a Jadidist newpaper publisher in Bukhara would cause panic among the cultural conservatives. The cartoon captures aspects of the innovative impact of Jadidist modernism. However, it implies an "old-new" antagonism that other sources do not confirm, as well as a certain orientalist stereotyping, as if something like this would only happen further east, not in the "western" Caucasus. From *Molla Nasreddin*, Tiflis, no. 15, 7 April 1907.

menians benefited from Russian favoritism, albeit inconsistently. They also had "a dynamic nationalist movement spearheaded by the Armenian Revolutionary Federation, the *Dashnaktsutiun*," at a time when the Azeri Muslims had nothing comparable, although the Dashnaks' "explosive mixture of nationalism and socialism" was as inimical to the tsarists as Dashnak territorial ambitions in eastern Anatolia were to the Ottomans.[22] In Azerbaijan, the 1905 Russian Revolution turned into intercommunal violence, starting in Baku, where much of the oil district was burned, and spreading, especially into Nagorno-Karabagh (see the map in chapter five). The violence marked a major stage in the Azeri intellectuals' assumption of communal leadership, including efforts to stop interethnic violence and restore peace. Russian Azerbaijan thus reacted to the global wave of disturbances in the years before World War I: the Russo-Japanese War and Russian Revolution of 1905, the Iranian Revolution of 1905–11, and the Young Turk Revolution of 1908, not to speak of far-off revolutions in China (1911) and Mexico (1910–20).

Iranian Azerbaijan contributed directly to the Iranian Revolution of 1905. Tabriz, indeed, became its "principal stronghold."[23] On both sides of the border, among those opposing the status quo, the sense of common Azeri identity gained strength, as it also did from efforts to organize migrants from the south, many of them low-paid workers, at Baku. Marking a major stage in mass political mobilization in Iran, the revolution engendered a proliferation of people's councils (*anjuman*), as well as paramilitary organizations, both republican-minded (*fida'iyan*) and Islamic (*mujahidin*). All these stood their test when Muhammad Ali Shah staged a counterrevolution in 1908, which provoked a civil war, prompting Tabriz constitutionalists to form a militia under Sattar Khan, who became an Azeri hero of the revolution. Pro-shah forces took Tabriz after a lengthy siege in 1909. Russia occupied the region from 1911 to 1915 as part of its role in repressing the Iranian Revolution, briefly reuniting Azerbaijan and facilitating the migration of both intellectuals and workers between north and south.

World War I came to the Caucasus with the Ottoman offensive of 1914, which the Russians halted at Sarıkamış (January 1915) and reversed, advancing as far into Anatolia as Erzerum, Trabzon, and Erzincan by 1916. The Ottomans also briefly held Tabriz in January 1915, but the Russians quickly reoccupied the city. Russian troops and Armenian irregulars controlled much of eastern Anatolia until 1917. Civilian and military casualties were extremely high on both the Ottoman and Russian sides of the front, a fact compounded in the Caucasus by the anti-Turkish, anti-Muslim impact of Russian rule. In the Russian Duma, representative Muhammad Jafar rose to denounce the "horrible things . . . perpetrated on the utterly helpless" in the rear of the Caucasian Front.

> The extortion, robbery, and murder of Muslims have become a matter of everyday occurrence. Wholesale expulsions of the male population, violation of the unprotected women . . . ruined and devastated villages, an impoverished, hungry, terror-stricken and unprovided-for population—this is the situation of the Muslims in the region.[24]

Because Russian Azerbaijan remained beyond the combat zone for most of the war, and because Muslims were exempt from conscription and many oil workers were deferred, World War I at first affected that region relatively little, although prices of oil and consumer goods rose. The 1917 Revolution, however, brought into the open a number of political parties, most with earlier roots.[25] The *Musavat* (Equality) Party supported secular Turkic nationalism and an autonomous republic of Azerbaijan. The conservative *Ittihad* (Unity) supported unity of all Russian Muslims in "one organization that would represent them religiously." Migrants from Iran, including oil workers and labor militants, supported the socialist *Ädälät* (Justice) Party. Russian Azeri socialists backed the *Himmät* (Endeavor) Party, which became the leading socialist party. The end of tsarist occupation in Iranian Azerbaijan created a new sense of freedom there, too, leading to the emergence of Shaykh Muhammad Khiabani's Democratic Party of Azerbaijan, which made autonomist demands on Tehran.

Early in 1918, Transcaucasia briefly separated from Russia, forming the Transcaucasian Federation of Georgia, Armenia, and Azerbaijan. This fell apart in May, however, and never controlled Baku, where the Bolsheviks took over in March 1918 by bombarding the Muslim quarters and forcing Muslim forces to withdraw, after which the Armenian Dashnaks looted the Muslim quarters, killing many and forcing thousands of Turks to flee. Six months later, the tables were turned, as Muslim forces retook the city and plundered the Armenians. Still the memory of the March 1918 takeover caused the Azerbaijani Turks to see Soviet rule as Russian-Armenian rule.[26] After the Transcaucasian Federation collapsed, Azerbaijani nationalists outside Baku formed the Azerbaijan Democratic Republic (*Azerbaijan Khalg Jumhuriyeti*, 1918–20), the first republic in the Muslim world.[27] It was initially overshadowed by a final push by the Ottomans, who nearly took all of Azerbaijan, north and south, including Baku, before withdrawing from the war in October 1918. The fledgling republic then had to contend with British forces coming from Iraq in 1918 to intervene in the civil war that followed the Bolshevik Revolution in Russia, and it was only briefly independent and unoccupied between the British withdrawal (1919) and the final Soviet conquest of Baku (1920).

While the republic lasted, nationalists embarked on a vigorous cultural program, founding Baku University (1919) and making Azerbaijani Turkic the language of instruction. Some 3,000 former Ottoman soldiers and teachers also entered the Azeri republic's service, helping to consolidate it.[28] Gradually, however, the Azerbaijan Communist Party (founded 1920) undermined the republic's coalition governments from within while the Red Army advanced from without. Contrary to later Soviet claims of voluntary unification with Russia, the parliament had been given an ultimatum to surrender, with guarantees of Azerbaijan's "independence and territorial integrity," which were later ignored.[29] With territorial disputes with its neighbors still unresolved, Russian Azerbaijan thus passed under Communist rule. An independent Soviet state until 1922, it became the site for a shining moment of revolutionary enthusiasm, the Baku Congress of the Peoples of the East (September 1920), which brought together representatives from thirty-eight countries, mostly from Turkey and Iran and mostly nationalists rather than communists.[30]

Also in 1920, Iranian Azerbaijan—Iran's most rebellious province— revolted against Tehran.[31] Unhappiness with the Tehran regime was at a peak in reaction to the Anglo-Iranian agreement of 1919, which threatened to turn Iran into a British semidependency. Responding to widespread protests, the Iranian parliament refused to ratify the treaty, but the British proceeded as if it were in force. The Caspian province of Gilan, adjoining Iranian Azerbaijan, had been in revolt since 1917 under Kuchuk Khan, who declared an Iranian Soviet Socialist Republic after Red Army troops landed there in 1920. Amid these tensions, the democrats of Iranian Azerbaijan, led by Muhammad Khiabani, probably aimed at nothing more radical than autonomy within Iran. However, they renamed their province Azadistan (Land of Freedom) and formed a "national" government, a term implying more than autonomy. When it could, the Tehran government reasserted its control in Tabriz and killed Khiabani. Azerbaijan and other peripheral regions of Iran would continue to reassert their difference whenever central control weakened.

*West Turkistan*

The Russian conquest of Inner Asia, came in two phases. First, between 1730 and 1848, the Russians took most of what is now Kazakhstan. Later, between 1864 and 1884, they expanded further south and took what are now Turkmenistan, Uzbekistan, Kyrgyzstan, and Tajikistan.[32]

After 1730, the Kazaks (or Kazakhs in the Russianized form of the name), a group of nomadic tribes sharing common Turkic speech but divided into several disunited hordes, confronted Russia, which was then expanding into Siberia. Kazakh khans began to seek patronage relations with the Russian tsar, chiefly to strengthen them in conflicts on the steppes. By the time of Catherine II (1762–96), however, Russian peasants and military forces were beginning to colonize Kazakh territory. Volga Tatar traders, under Russian rule since the conquest of Kazan (1552), spread out into Central Asia, benefiting Russian commercial and political interests there. During the last century before the conquest of Central Asia in the 1860s, Russian officials used the Tatar elites, both mercantile and religious, as proxies in Kazakhstan. Conventional scholarship overestimates the tardiness of the Kazakhs' Islamization and the role of Tatar ulema, post-1800, as their Islamizers. Prior to that date, the Kazakhs' appropriation of Islam was already apparent from the elaboration of Islamic themes in Kazakh oral epics, the importance of Islamic rites to Kazakh nomads, and the history of "sacred" lineages of *kozha*s (from the Persian term *khwaja*), who claimed prophetic descent and played an important political role under certain khans.[33] Nonetheless, it appears that the Kazakh khans' creation of a formal Islamic establishment does date to the nineteenth century and that the ulema of the Volga region played a prominent part in it, even as Kazakh ulema were also trained and employed. From the Russian point of view, the process was also conducive to the extension of Russian control over the Kazakh hordes, which were completely subdued by 1848.

Between 1864 and 1884, the Russians extended their conquests to the south. From west to east, they took the territory of the nomadic Türkmen tribes between the Caspian and the Amu Darya, the Khanate of Khiva, the Emirate of Bukhara, and the Khanate of Khokand. In 1865 the Russians took the city of Tashkent. In 1868 they defeated the emir of Bukhara, taking part of his territory, including Samarkand, and leaving him the rest as a protectorate. In 1873, the same thing happened to the khan of Khiva. In 1876, the Khanate of Khokand was defeated and annexed. The Russians defeated the Türkmens at the Battle of Göktepe in 1881. The Russians rounded off their conquests in 1884 by taking Merv, near the Afghan border, touching off exaggerated British apprehensions—a fit of Mervousness, someone called it—about the defense of India and the extent of Russian ambitions in that direction. The southern border was definitively settled by Anglo-Russian negotiation in 1895, and the region was organized into a Governorate-General of Turkistan, with its capital at Tashkent, including the two protectorates, Bukhara and Khiva. Separately, Kazakhstan was divided into four districts, of which sometimes all four, sometimes only the eastern two, were governed by the Governorate-General of the Steppe.

Russian rule brought law and order in place of warfare and raiding, but at the price of alien domination. Economic development came at the price of colonial economic relations: cotton was pushed to the point of monoculture, and a region historically famed for the diversity of its produce became dependent on wheat imports from Russia. Russian and Ukrainian settlers began to move into Kazakhstan and into Semireche, the easternmost region of Turkistan, seizing nomads' grazing grounds and blocking their seasonal migrations, with disastrous consequences for their survival. Urban migrants shifted the demographics of some cities and took over Russian trade with Central Asia. Russian radicals were also exiled to Central Asia; after 1917, their skill, organization, and access to military means would ironically play a decisive role in preserving Russian control of the region and thwarting the nationalist hopes of unarmed and politically less experienced Mus-

**Said Alim Khan, Last Emir of Bukhara (r. 1911–20).** The emir wears a brilliant blue silk robe heavily embroidered with floral designs. The sword and decorations do not dispel the impression that the heroic age is long past. From Library of Congress, Prokudin-Gorskii Collection, LC-DIG-prok-01886.

lims. Meanwhile, in the late imperial period, telegraph and railroad lines began to reach into Central Asia. The rail link to the rest of the empire, completed in 1906, materially embodied the difference between Central Asia's incorporation into the Russian Empire and the more tenuous maritime links that tied other colonies to their dominant European powers.

World War I started to affect Central Asia in 1916, when Muslims began to be drafted for labor behind the lines. This led to uprisings, directed against both the government and the agricultural settlers. Considerable loss of life resulted, among both Russians and especially Muslims. The Kyrgyz, who had attacked settlers particularly violently, suffered the harshest repression, and many of them fled to Xinjiang, with further loss of life during the winter. Events were soon overtaken by the revolutions of February and October 1917. The latter was followed by a dramatic declaration of 20 November

1917, signed by V. Ulyanov (Lenin) and J. Dzhugashvili (Stalin), addressed to the Muslims of the Russian Empire, and proclaiming: "From now on your beliefs and customs, your national and cultural institutions are being declared free and inviolable. Arrange your national life freely and without hindrance. This is your right."[34]

Only a few days before, however, when the Third Congress of Central Asian Muslims, meeting in Tashkent, had offered its collaboration to the Turkistan Council of People's Commissars, the latter rejected the proposal because the "attitude of the native population" toward the revolution was "uncertain" and because that population lacked "proletarian organizations," which the Bolsheviks would welcome.[35] This would not be the last time declarations of comradely solidarity from the center were neutralized by colonial exclusivism in Central Asia. A Soviet nationality policy would be worked out over the next few years, however; and for a time, some room to debate self-determination would remain. Rebuffed at Tashkent, the Muslim leaders tried again in Khokand, forming a "People's Council" (*Khalq Shurasi*, using the Kur'anic term *shura*, "consultation," to translate "soviet") and declaring Turkistan "autonomous in union with the Federal Democratic Republic of Russia." The Tashkent Bolsheviks had the means to exert force, however, and the Khokand nationalists did not; the result was their defeat in February 1918. The Alash Orda movement among the Kazakhs experienced a similar fate by 1920.

Up to that point, Lenin, Stalin, and other top Bolshevik leaders were still willing to negotiate with Muslim leaders like the Bashkir, Zeki Velidi (later prominent under the surname Togan as a historian in Turkey). The Fifth Regional Communist Party Congress in Tashkent in 1920 even passed a resolution in favor of a unified Turkic Soviet Republic within revolutionary Russia. Moscow answered that there could be no unified Turkic republic, asserted its military and political control, and organized two ASSRs (Autonomous Socialist Soviet Republics), roughly overlapping the Kazakh region and the old Turkistan governorate; the Turkistan ASSR would be subdivided along ethnic lines in 1924. The old protectorates of Bukhara and Khiva, briefly turned into the Soviet Republics of Bukhara and Khorezm in 1920, were also eliminated in the national delimitation of 1924.

Not merely victims of tsarist expansionism, Inner Asia's Turkic peoples also took steps to create modern Turkic cultures during the nineteenth century. The way they did so resembles the corresponding efforts in the Ottoman Empire or in other Turkic centers under Russian rule, but usually with a significant time lag and with other differences resulting from conquest during the era of imperialism. In Inner Asia, the early nineteenth century witnessed, if anything, a new florescence of traditional forms of cultural production, based in the Kur'anic primary schools (*mekteb*) and seminaries for higher religious studies (*medrese*). As elsewhere in the Islamic world, this cultural complex accorded primacy to oral transmission of knowledge, with written texts serving essentially as mnemonic aids. Literacy remained an elite trait. At the same time, the Central Asian cultural milieu continued to display its characteristic Turko-Iranian bilingualism. As recent studies of musical performance traditions have shown, appreciable elements of this cultural complex still survive.[36]

By the last decades of the nineteenth century, as already seen in examples from the Crimea, Volga region, and Azerbaijan, Turkic intellectuals in Russian Central Asia had begun to explore new realms. Integrally associated with the rise of the modern print media and new literary genres, this transformation required educational reform, which produced a new reading public with a new, desacralized concept of literacy. The florescence of the print media thus required not only newspapers, followed by novels and modern-style theater, but also new schools with improved methods of teaching to shape a new and larger reading public. In Central Asia, the entire modernist intellectual movement took its name from the "new method" (*usul-i jadid*) of teaching the Arabic alphabet, pioneered among Crimean Tatars by Ismail Gaspıralı in the 1880s. From this, progressive Turkic intellectuals of the Russian Empire came to be known as Jadidists (*jadidchilar*, "new-ists") or just Jadids, and cultural conservatives came to be known by default as *kadimchilar*, "old-ists."

The new instructional methods had been pioneered in the 1860s in the Ottoman Empire. They assumed added importance in the Russian realm, however, because Muslim schools operated in a quite different context there. Whereas the Ottoman Islamic authorities, who enjoyed considerable political power, vigilantly watched over the empire's Muslim schools, the Russian Empire relegated minority schooling to the concerned community, thus leaving scope for the Muslim schools to become sites of cultural experimentation. The Ottomans had their own imperial regime to provide leadership in diverse fields of reformist policy, but the Turks under Russian rule could only exercise independent initiative in matters outside the sphere of state interest. For Muslims under Russian rule, unlike their Ottoman cousins, education was such a sphere.[37]

The tsarist police did, however, watch the Jadidists as presumed separatists or as collaborators in a supposed Ottoman-backed pan-Islamic movement. In fact, the Ottoman government, although rightfully interested in promoting Muslim unity, was too heedful of Russian military power to promote it in provocative ways. The Jadids are better understood in their immediate cultural context as a "modern response to 'modernity,'" which sought to reconfigure the entire world, including Islam."[38] Flourishing between about 1900 and the early years of Bolshevik rule, the Central Asian Jadids, although they might satirize cultural conservatives, never attacked Islam, which advanced Ottoman intellectuals did attack by that time. Far from advocating separation from the Russian Empire, they joined Ismail Gaspıralı in seeking fuller participation in the Russian sphere to gain its advantages. Jadidists did attack the Turkic commercial bourgeoisie, enriched by economic integration into the Russian Empire: the intellectual wing of the Muslim middle class attacked its commercial wing for its mindless materialism. Jadidist intellectuals used the new print media to explain the outside world to their compatriots. In doing so, the Jadids implicitly transformed Islam from the all-encompassing cultural reality into one realm in the world of knowledge. To the extent that "progress" was best exemplified by societies outside the Islamic world, this modern, universal knowledge empowered them to critique and admonish their own communities about their backwardness and the necessity to achieve the advantages of modernity.

Through their works, the Jadids imaginatively opened a new world of Turkic modernity and furnished it with new ideas. Through their schools, book shops, reading rooms, and theatrical performances, they created new forms of sociability. Their new schools helped train the elite of the future. By revisioning the future of their society, they called for transformations in the lives of women and children. By 1900, Tatar women, from communities long under Russian rule, had ceased veiling, and those of them who went to Central Asia became symbols and agents of changes that the Jadids advocated there.[39] The Jadids also began to refashion collective identity concepts at the national or protonational level.

In Central Asia, the category "Turk" had historically had significance as a designation of collective identity only in contrast to the symbiotic category "Tajik" (Iranian). The Turkic proverb, "There is no Turk without an Iranian, just as their is no hat without a head" (*Tatsız Turk bolmas, bashsız börk bolmas*), recorded by Mahmud al-Kashgari in the eleventh century, still expressed the dichotomous nature of these two categories. Neither "Turk" nor "Tajik" constituted a unified category except as contrasted to the other.[40] Each community presented an internally variegated panorama, and for most of their members the more salient identifiers had historically been tribal or local, or perhaps based on class or religious affiliation. The Central Asian Jadids offered instead a new cultural-nationalist vision that pointed toward collective identities of larger scale, although their ideas about the largest relevant collective identities oscillated among Muslims of Turkistan, Muslims of the Russian Empire, or Muslims in general. Writing textbooks, newspaper articles, and literary works, they began to elaborate the modern literary languages of the eastern Turkic world. Having previously sought to create a modern Muslim voice in their own societies and to achieve Muslim participation in the mainstream of life in the Russian Empire, after 1917 they transformed themselves into Muslim Communists and played a political role during the few years when scope was allowed for national communism. The 1924 subdivision of Turkistan into the "autonomous republics" that appeared on the maps of the Soviet Union was thus not solely a matter of "divide and rule" by the Soviets but rather had origins in pre-1917 Jadidist thought about "new ways of imagining the world and Central Asia's place within it."[41]

The ancient symbiosis of Turkic and Iranian in Central Asia may have given unique dimensions to the redefinition of collective identities in that region, but such redefinition was at the top of the intellectuals' agendas everywhere in forms responding to local conditions. The earlier rise of "Bulgharist" historiography, promoting an enlarged sense of collective identity for Muslims of the Volga region, shows that religious conservatives also sought broader bases for social solidarity. Redefining collective identities was not uniquely the work of modernist intellectuals, but defining the place of Turkic Muslims in the modern world was their task. In Azerbaijan, for example, Ali Huseinzade offered the slogan "Turkicization, Islamization, Europeanization" (*Türkleshtirmek, Islamlashtirmak, Avrupalilashtirmak*). This closely resembles the formulation proposed by the Ottoman-Turkish nationalist Ziya Gökalp: "Turkicization, Islamization, Modernization" (*Türkleşmek, Islamlaşmak, Muasırlaşmak*).[42] These formulations precisely define the task of reinvisioning Turkish and Islamic identities in the world of modernity as it then existed.

*East Turkistan*

With the division of Central Asia between Russia and China, the historic Turkic territories of the Tarım basin and vicinity passed under Chinese rule in 1759 as Xinjiang, the "new province"—a province larger than Alaska and three times the size of France.[43] Far from being motivated by sinocentrism, the ethnically Manchu Qing emperors made Xinjiang a family possession of the dynasty rather than integrating Xinjiang into the Chinese provinces. The shaved forehead and queue that Han Chinese men were required to wear as a sign of submission to the Qing likewise were not enforced on East Turkistanis. The Qing left considerable autonomy to the indigenous Turkish-speaking Muslims and forbade Chinese immigration. The result was a large measure of peace and contentment until after 1810. Then uprisings began, led by successors of the seventeenth-century *khwajas* (here, Nakshibendi Sufi sheykhs) with support from the khanate of Khokand to the west. In Xinjiang, relations between the Muslims and the Chinese and Manchus began to break down. In 1835, China had to conclude a treaty with Khokand that infringed Chinese sovereignty in Xinjiang and granted Khokand extensive rights. Thereafter, some Chinese statesmen suggested strategic retreat from the region, whereas others advocated colonization by Han Chinese and an increased military presence. The latter option appealed increasingly to the Qing regime as its ability to control the region's Muslim population diminished.

As a result, the Khoja jihad flared from 1847 on. After the revolt of the Chinese Muslims (Tungan) in Gansu and Xinjiang provinces in the 1860s, Qing control of Xinjiang collapsed. The Russians occupied the Ili valley, and a Khokandi army under Muhammad Yakub Beg (1820–77) invaded. Yakub established himself as ruler of a Muslim state, Yettishahr, or "Seven Cities" (Kashgar, Khotan, Yarkand, Yangihisar, Aksu, Kucha, and Korla, 1867–77). In a context of Russo-British rivalry over the "Great Game in Asia," Yakub attracted considerable international attention, including some from the Ottomans, receiving honors from them and minting coins in the name of their sultan, Abdülaziz (1861–76). That did not save him from defeat by the Chinese, after which Xinjiang was integrated into the normal system of provincial government in 1884, albeit with a menacing growth of Russian interests and influence.

With the Chinese revolution of 1911, Xinjiang became a province of the Republic of China. Xinjiang felt the effects of World War I and revolution, with the influx of Kyrgyz and Kazakh refugees from Russian territory, and again in 1920 when anti-Bolshevik White forces retreated from Russia into Xinjiang. The ferment of the times stimulated the growth of nationalism among Muslim Turks of Xinjiang, who in the 1920s revived the long-extinct term "Uyghur" for their collective name. Developing a new sense of Uyghur identity, and working out its accommodation with Chinese and other local claims, would remain a task for the future.

## The Ottoman Empire

While the Turkic peoples of Inner Eurasia and the Caucasus faced incorporation into empires ruled by non-Muslims and elaborated their responses to modernity in those contexts, the Turks of the Ottoman Empire responded to similar threats by trying to defend and modernize an Islamic state that ruled over non-Muslims. This is the biggest point of contrast between the nineteenth-century experiences of the Turks in Central Asia and in the Ottoman zone. Eventually, emerging consciousness of this difference helped stimulate the growth of Turkish nationalism in the Ottoman realm. However, nineteenth-century Ottoman experience also presents other intriguing similarities with, and differences from, that of the Turkic peoples further east. In contrast to Turkic Central Asia's history of political fragmentation prior to the Russian conquest, the most obvious difference is that the Ottomans had inherited by far the strongest and largest state still standing anywhere in the Islamic world.

Ironically, however, the Ottoman Empire had come to be "imperial" in two senses. On one hand, it was a multinational empire, in which a cosmopolitan imperial elite ruled over heterogeneous peoples of the Balkans, Middle East, and parts of North Africa. In contrast to the Turk-Tajik difference among the almost entirely Muslim population of Central Asia, the most salient differences within the Ottoman realm had historically been those among religious communities in a population that only acquired a strong Muslim majority after 1878.[44] In this period, the word "imperialism" also applied to the Ottoman Empire in the sense that it was threatened by European expansionism, as seen in the seizure of outlying territories (for example, Algeria, 1830; Cyprus, 1878; Tunisia, 1881; Egypt, 1882), in the economic semidependency represented by the transformation of the old capitulatory trading privileges into free trade treaties, in the later imposition of international controls on Ottoman government finance, and in endless diplomatic interference in Ottoman affairs. The Ottomans' sense of belatedness, the sense of a need to catch up with others who had become dangerously more advanced, was profoundly conditioned in this period by the spread of separatist nationalism among their own subjects, starting in the Balkans, and by European imperialism in their Afro-Asian domains.

As much as in their comparative success in maintaining independent statehood, the Ottomans also differed from their Central Asian cousins in an important cultural sense. The Ottoman state had patronized and promoted a sustained tradition of literary production in a way that there had, for centuries, been no major state to do in Central Asia. Before the advent of modern print media, literary production depended primarily on the patronage of rulers; and long-lasting, powerful dynasties had more patronage to dispense than others. As a result, the Ottomans maintained an officially sponsored literary culture, in contrast to the characteristic Turkic-Persian bilingualism of Central Asia, from which in time Tajik and not one but several modern Turkic literary languages emerged. The Ottomans' preferred mode of expression was not plain Turkish but Ottoman Turkish, syntactically Turkish but profusely embellished with Arabic and Persian words and expressions. The need to adapt this literary language to modern purposes would eventually lead to the emergence of a single modern Turkish language for the Turkish Republic. To make that change required a long-term cultural revolution that spanned a century and more, whereas the political revolutions and crises that transformed empire into republic occurred as shorter-term phenomena at various points along the way. In short, understanding what was revolutionary about the Ottoman and republican Turkish engagement with modernity requires considering multiple dynamics of change that occurred on different time scales, creating their most profound effects when their trends converged at critical turning points.

For the Ottomans, the need for new ways to defend the empire became unmistakable with a series of crises in the last decades of the eighteenth century. The Ottoman-Russian War of 1768–74 definitively established Russia as the empire's most dangerous enemy; ended the Ottoman monopoly of the Black Sea and Ottoman suzerainty over the Crimea, which Russia soon annexed as a result; and raised doubts among Muslims everywhere about the sultans' ability to defend Islam. The Napoleonic invasion of Egypt in 1798 showed that the danger was not limited to the European peripheries of the empire. Partly because of these defeats and other crises like the Greek Revolution of the 1820s, the Ottomans also faced persistent, severe economic stress through the 1830s.[45] All together, these troubles precipitated a major shift of long-term trends in Ottoman history. During the previous two centuries, the Ottoman "old regime" had become increasingly decentralized, and vested interests had proliferated. Provincial magnates and warlords had become so powerful that they finally provoked demands for reassertion of the sultan's authority, demands voiced not only in Istanbul but also in at least some provincial centers, such as Mosul in Iraq.[46]

The reassertion of central initiative and defensive modernization began under Sultan Selim III (1789–1807) and became permanently established under Mahmud II (1808–39). Ottomans saw military reform as their foremost need. Following on earlier initiatives, Selim attempted to reform existing forces and to found a new infantry corps as the centerpiece of his "New Order" (Nizam-ı Cedid).[47] A better military required better revenue collection, which required more efficient government overall. Selim's financial reforms included a special treasury (Irad-ı Cedid) to finance his corps. Mahmud II's abolition of the Janissaries (1826) and his attempt to found a modern army opened a period of dynamic, sustained reform, including an ambitious initiative to replace tax farming with direct tax collection and centralize receipts and disbursements in the state treasury (1838). Simultaneously, Mahmud introduced official salaries to replace the perquisites and revenue-collection rights on which most members of the ruling class had hitherto depended for their compensation. If tax collectors were to turn over their receipts to the treasury, they would have to have salaries. However, the government needed the benefits of fiscal centralization before it could meet its new salary obligations. In the event, inadequate preparation and opposition from vested interests thwarted fiscal centralization. Tax farming survived, but so did the salary system—limpingly.

Failure in fiscal centralization was fraught with consequences for the later empire, as was its tightening integration into the European-dominated world economy, symbolized by the adoption of free trade with the Ottoman-British commercial treaty of 1838. It also preserved the legal and other privileges of the earlier "capitulations," as Europeans called them, or "privileges" (*imtiyazat*), as Ottomans had called them. The Ottoman government had historically granted these privileges to European governments to regulate their subjects' trade and legal status within the empire. The adoption of free trade under the 1838 treaty with Great Britain and later treaties with other powers also required sacrificing the state enterprises—free traders denounced them as "monopolies"—on which the Ottomans had previously relied in their efforts at industrialization. This was not an insignificant sacrifice: the most innovative economic policy initiative of the early Turkish Republic would again emphasize industrialization through the creation of state enterprises.

Other centralizing reforms proved more successful than the effort at fiscal centralization. Demarcating the past from the Ottoman reform era, Selim's New Order represented the first attempt to overhaul and rationalize the government comprehensively.[48] With his diplomatic appointments of 1793, the Ottomans also adopted permanent, reciprocal diplomatic representation, instead of the occasional, temporary embassies that they had previously sent abroad to exchange treaty ratifications or the like. The Greek Revolution led to replacing the Greek translators of the Imperial Divan with the Translation Office of the Sublime Porte (1821), which became the nursery for westernizing civil officials and writers. Diplomatic representation, interrupted since Selim's fall, was revived for good in 1833. Already by 1820, Mahmud had regained control over provincial centers in Anatolia and parts of the lower Balkans. Some of the formerly dominant local families were forced to move to Istanbul and join the bureaucracy; meanwhile, the revitalized sultanate continued to implement a "politics of notables," in which tractable local notables retained major roles as intermediaries between the state and the local populace.[49] The chief exception was Egypt, where Muhammad Ali Paşa (r. 1805–49) won power after the expulsion of the French and became the biggest warlord, indeed an empire builder. He eventually turned on the sultanate and nearly destroyed it twice in the 1830s.[50]

In the 1830s, Mahmud enacted measures to turn the old scribal corps into a civil bureaucracy. He founded new schools to train civil and military elites; these also became the foundation for what would later develop as a system of state-sponsored public schools. Mahmud began reorganizing the central government into ministries; created a standardized table of civil, military, and religious ranks; abandoned the old system of annual reappointment; introduced salaries; and abolished some of the legal disabilities of officials, who had previously been in the status of slaves of the sultan. Proclaimed shortly after Mahmud's death, the Gülhane Decree (1839), critical in improving officials' status, extended its guarantees of rights and due process not just to the elites but equally to the subjects of all religions. At the end of his reign Mahmud even abolished the grand vezirate (1838), merging the successor post of prime minister with that of interior minister. The grand vezirate was restored in 1839 after Mahmud's death, but the change illustrates the lengths to which he would go to concentrate power in his own hands.[51]

The age of decentralization had ended. A new age had begun, characterized by strong sultans during some reigns and consistently by new elites, civil and military. Ironically, despite Selim's and Mahmud's desire to replace the old provincial households with new, more educated elites loyal to the sultan, members of these elites would in time shift their loyalties to abstract ideals of state and nation, a change from which patriotic movements of political opposition later emerged.[52] In the centuries-long transition from tribe and clan to empire and nation, the creation of new elites with, ideally, depersonalized, professional loyalties was as momentous a change as had been the creation of detribalized retinues personally loyal to their ruler.

After Mahmud II's death in 1839, there would not be such decisive leadership from the palace again for nearly four decades. Reform continued, much along the lines he and Selim III had traced, so much so that the period from 1839 through the 1870s is remembered as the *Tanzimat,* "the reforms," par excellence. What was different about this period is that leadership now came out of the civil bureaucratic elite. Given the initial military goals of reform, not to mention the Turko-Mongol tradition of military statecraft, the civil-bureaucratic hegemony of the Tanzimat may seem paradoxical. However, a crisis like the clash between the central Ottoman government and Muhammad Ali Paşa of Egypt, which had menacingly overshadowed Mahmud's last days, showed that the empire could no longer count on defending its interests militarily without international support. The men who could negotiate that support were not soldiers but rather the French-speaking diplomats of the new civil-official elite. The Tanzimat proved a very important period for the technical modernization of the Ottoman military.[53] Still, it was a time of civil-bureaucracy hegemony, symbolized by three diplomats who rose to become grand vezir: Mustafa Reşid Paşa

(1800–58), Keçecizade Fuad Paşa (1815–69), and Mehmed Emin Âli Paşa (1815–71). Mustafa Reşid had guided the empire through the Egyptian crisis, concluded the free-trade treaty of 1838, and drafted the Gülhane reform decree of 1839. For the rest of their careers, first he, and then Fuad and Âli in tandem, elaborated the reforms of the Tanzimat.

The Tanzimat produced an impact so widely ramified as to defy summary; however a number of themes stand out. One urgent goal was to reconsolidate the goodwill of the empire's heterogeneous population in the face of the rising tide of separatist Balkan nationalisms. Building on the traditional discourse about the ruler's justice and on the promises of the Gülhane Decree, the Tanzimat statesmen elaborated a new policy of equality among Ottoman subjects, regardless of religion. They redefined Ottomanism (Osmanlılık), theretofore the identity of only the ruling elite, as a new imperial supranationalism intended to counteract the appeal of separatism and hold all the empire's subjects together. European governments would continually accuse the Ottoman government of not observing the egalitarian policy, especially whenever conflict broke out in provinces where separatist movements were gaining strength. However, the Ottoman government reiterated and expanded its egalitarian promises, for example, in the Reform Decree (Hatt-ı Hümayun) of 1856 and in the constitution of 1876 and also began to recruit non-Muslims into civil officialdom in a way unprecedented since the earliest period.

One important point that European critics and most modern scholars failed to grasp was the destabilizing consequences of declaring equality among different religious communities in what was still officially an Islamic state, in which Islamic law, the şeriat (sharia) was in principle the basic legal system. As a system of religious law, concerned first and foremost with the believer's relationship with God and only secondarily with civil and penal matters, the şeriat, like other systems of religious law, had no legal standard by which to measure equality between believer and unbeliever. Only a secular legal system could do that. The şeriat did have something that some other religious legal systems do not, namely, principles for accommodating believers in certain other religions, specifically Jews and Christians, as semiautonomous communities living under the rule of the Islamic state. However, accommodating religious difference under Islamic rule and proclaiming equality without regard to religion are not the same.

The Gülhane Decree of 1839 had promised new laws to implement its egalitarian promises. The effort to produce them would launch the Ottomans into uncharted territory where incompatible legal systems, Islamic, on the one hand, and secular, on the other, would coexist and compete, generating confusion and conflict, until the issue could eventually be resolved in favor of one or the other. If egalitarian Ottomanism formed one theme of the Tanzimat, legal dualism and a rapid expansion of secular legislation at the expense of the şeriat formed another. The expanding volume of legislation became something measurable with a yardstick when, toward the end of the Tanzimat, the government began to publish the volumes of secular laws, the *Düstur*, in ever-lengthening series that continue to the present day. In this way, the Turko-Mongol tradition of state law acquired new vitality in the definition of Ottoman modernity. From this point dates the modern contrast between a political culture that idealizes the rule of law yet condones arbitrary and despotic actions by those in power—a paradox with deep historical roots.[54]

The swelling tide of legislation formed one dimension of what must have seemed to Ottomans like the advent of "big government," and this forms another theme of the Tanzimat. Centralization meant not only concentrating power at the center but also asserting that power throughout the empire. Although the effects of the Tanzimat were hardly limited to provincial administration, some of its biggest impacts were in that field. An early indication of what was coming occurred in the mid-1840s, when the government surveyed taxpayers and revenue sources in Anatolia and the Balkans south of the Danube. Intended to lay the basis for a new fiscal administration, this survey left some 17,000 registers in the Ottoman archives, probably the most thorough such survey in all of Ottoman history and proof that the Ottomans were then able to carry out a large-scale administrative program comparable in scale to these noted in earlier periods in this and other Turko-Mongol states.

The Tanzimat was also the period when the Ottoman government finally parted ways with the old Islamic and Turkic practices of combining military and administrative functions in the provinces and began to create a provincial administration staffed by civil officials. Qualitatively, the increased importance of the diplomatic role and, quantitatively, this expansion into provincial administration made the civil officials into the premier elite of the nineteenth century. What had in 1790 been a scribal corps with perhaps only a couple of thousand members, almost all employed in Istanbul, had expanded by 1890 into a civil bureaucracy with 35,000 or more career officials, most of whom surely served in the provinces.[55] As the government expanded its role in fields like education, trade, agriculture, public works, and public health, it also created innumerable councils (*meclis*), which in many cases brought together not only officials but also heads of the religious communities and local notables. Important factors in the survival of the "politics of notables" on a reduced scale into the era of centralization, these councils further expanded the scope of government and provided growing numbers of the populace with administrative experience.

The weak link of the Tanzimat was finance. The failure of the effort to centralize revenue collection and disbursement, just at the point when free-trade treaties began to be signed with European governments, started a downward spiral in government finance. Although the long-simmering monetary crisis of preceding decades ended with the launching of a new, bimetallic coinage in 1844, the government also had to issue paper money in 1840, which depreciated seriously from the time of the Crimean War onward and was only retired in 1862; later issues of paper money (1876–79, 1914–22) again resulted from war conditions and depreciated even more.[56] The rapaciousness of Ottoman tax collectors was an ever handy theme for anti-Ottoman nationalists, and Ottoman taxation certainly had inequities and inconsistencies; yet some evidence suggests that the Tanzimat reforms may have been underfinanced from the beginning.[57] European-style banks were established in the empire from the 1840s on and engaged in lending to the state, which also began to contract foreign loans during the Crimean War. In the wake of the international financial crisis of 1873, the government had, in 1875–76, to suspend service on its debts, then amounting to more than 200 million pounds sterling. That led to the establishment of the Ottoman Public Debt Administration (1881), which took control of six of the government's most important revenues to service the debt. Ultimately head-quartered uphill from the grand vezir's offices at the Sublime Porte and in a taller, finer building, the Public Debt Administration symbolized the economic semidependency of the Ottoman state. However, as illustrated by examples such as the growth of carpet exports and the economic stimuli resulting from railroad building, first in the Balkans and then from the 1890s on in the Asian provinces, the Ottoman economy experienced significant forms of growth and change despite the restraints placed on it.[58]

Egalitarianism, a rising tide of secular legislation, and countless policy initiatives enacted by officials with diplomatic experience in Europe—all added up to rapid westernization. To Ottoman reformists, this was essential to overcome backwardness. Yet rapid westernization caused great uneasiness among Muslims, partly because the will behind the Tanzimat reforms was no longer that of the sultan, who had the legitimate right to issue laws and decrees, but that of bureaucrats who prepared decrees for the sultan to sign. For non-Muslims, too, there were doubts, motivated both by the siren song of nationalism and by concern to see that old communal privileges were not lost in the name of the new Ottoman egalitarianism. Sociologist Niyazi Berkes characterized the cultural conflicts that ensued in terms of cultural bifurcation. In fact, the dualism between old and new, east and west, over-lay a complexity of divergent trends and proliferating differences.[59]

The Tanzimat was also the period when "intelligentsia" and "ruling elite" ceased to be virtually identical among Ottoman Muslims. The obvious reason for this was the advent of privately owned Ottoman Turkish print media in 1860, just when educational reform had begun to produce a significant widening of the reading public. Analogous developments occurred at different dates for subject communities, starting in the late eighteenth century in the Balkans and in the late nineteenth century for the Arabs. Among Ottoman Turks, too, this change also had less obvious causes that went further back. Mahmud II (d. 1839) was the last sultan who personally produced poetry in the old style, a fact that must have had major implications for palace patronage of traditional forms of literary production. Writers were going to have to find a new audience. In a time of rapid social change and spreading literacy, they would have to find a new language to address that audience. The government, too, faced the need to articulate its policies in simpler language in order for them to be widely implemented. Ottoman Turkish was an enormously rich and expressive language; however, its amalgam of Turkish, Arabic, and Persian completely lacked a "national" character and was unsuitable for mass communications.

A revolutionary transformation in language and communication got under way as Ottoman intellectuals inside and outside government began to struggle with this issue. If the need for such a change can be traced as far back as the death of Mahmud II, in some senses the issue has never yet been fully resolved. The Ottoman cultural revolution has thus occurred on a scale far longer and vaster than the revolutions and crises that have marked the obvious turning points in Ottoman and Turkish political history. Emerging from 1860 on, the privately owned Ottoman print media became the arena for the exploration, not just of Ottoman issues, but also of the new world of global modernity. For that reason, the print media also became the prime arena for political protest and oppositional politics. Governmental efforts at censorship and control, while persistent, proved ultimately ineffective, as opposition intellectuals went into exile and found ways to publish beyond the sultan's reach. Growing out of the longer-term cultural transformation, these political opposition movements also led over time to the more dramatic political revolutions and crises that later occurred in the foreground of shorter-term political events.

Thus, as other peoples under Ottoman rule began to acquire their modern cultural history and increasingly their separatist nationalisms, the Ottoman intelligentsia, too, reshaped Ottoman culture and produced a new kind of ideological opposition in the Young Ottoman movement of the 1860s and 1870s.[60] Drawing selectively on aspects of Islamic legal thought, they mounted a moderate-conservative critique of the Tanzimat's reckless westernization, proposed criteria to test the compatibility of Western borrowings with Islamic tradition, and offered their own visions of the society of the future, with constitutional monarchy and Ottoman nationalism as central themes. Most influential among this group, Namık Kemal (1840–88) added intellectual content and emotional fire to the ideal of Ottoman identity.

In the 1870s, the conditions that had made the Tanzimat a distinct period changed. Reformist policy would continue to show strong continuities; literary culture, too, continued to develop in such a way that the label "Tanzimat" is applied to late Ottoman literature without fine distinctions of chronology. Politically, however, the ground shifted irrevocably between the death of the last leading Tanzimat statesman in 1871 and the accession of Abdülhamid II (1876–1909), following the deposition of two other sultans earlier in 1876. At the time, the Ottoman Empire had come closer to extinction than at any time since the depths of the Egyptian crisis of 1839–41. Famine had ravaged Anatolia for three years, and provincial rebellion racked the Balkans. The disastrous Russo-Turkish War (1877–78) ensued. It ended with so much loss of Balkan territory and such large-scale refugee movements that the population remaining under Ottoman rule acquired a decisive Muslim majority for the first time. In the midst of all this, reformists gained enough influence to secure the adoption of a constitution in 1876; as in 1839, their hand had been strengthened by the need to play for diplomatic support from abroad.[61] However, Abdülhamid was about to show that he was the first sultan since Mahmud II capable of wielding autocratic power. In one of the most decisive reigns in Ottoman history, Abdülhamid supported the constitution long enough to gain power and then, with the Russian army at the gates of Istanbul, used the emergency powers that the constitution gave him to suspend the new parliament, suppress or coopt the Young Ottomans and other constitutionalists, and rule as if the constitution had never existed. So ended the Ottomans' First Constitutional Period (1876–78).

Once again centralization meant rule from the palace. The secretariat at Abdülhamid's new Yıldız Palace became the most dreaded power center of the empire, while the Sublime Porte, the grand vezirs' headquarters, which had been the power center during the Tanzimat, became a backwater. Abdülhamid left behind a contradictory legacy. To some, he was a bloodthirsty tyrant who massacred rebellious subject peoples, suppressed constitutionalism, and instituted a regime of internal espionage and censorship that left no one secure. A paranoid, he never forgot the two depositions in 1876 that brought him to the throne, became increasingly reluctant to leave the palace, feared his own military forces, and relied on modern technologies—

photography, the railroad, the telegraph—to control and inform himself about a huge empire he never visited.

To others, however, Abdülhamid was a reformer and the legitimate ruler of the largest and most independent Muslim state.[62] Among the reasons for his positive image, the railroad age came to the Ottoman Empire during his reign, with important stimuli to the economy. Another overlooked fact is that Abdülhamid probably carried out one of the largest building programs of any Islamic ruler in history.[63] His buildings were less likely to be the mosques and palaces of early sultans and more likely to be schools, government buildings, train stations, docks, and bazaars in distinctive styles that left an imprint still recognizable throughout his farflung dominions. Under Abdülhamid, the scope of educational reform expanded, producing the

**Heroes of Modern Science, the Imperial Military Medical School, Istanbul.** The sixth class poses amid elaborately displayed medical specimens. Living a regimen that combined scientific modernity, military discipline, and enforced religious and political conformism within the confined environment of a residential college, these men's heads must have been about to burst. This medical school became a hotbed of political opposition against Abdülhamid II. From Library of Congress, Abdülhamid Albums, LD-USZ62–77267.

rudiments of an empire-wide system. Even under censorship, the print media and the volume of knowledge about the world that they conveyed to Ottoman readers expanded vastly. Somewhat as in the Russian Empire, the fact that many political issues were beyond the realm of discussion left the field open for debates on social and cultural issues. Abdülhamid's censors often let these pass, even when their implications for politics might be far from oblique. The best example is the women's novels that began to be published about 1890, bluntly depicting life inside patriarchal households, each in essence a microcosm of the patrimonial sultanate. Abdülhamid persecuted his political opponents but patronized writers who "only" dealt with social and cultural issues like those.[64]

If thinking about Ottoman egalitarianism had focused on non-Muslims during the Tanzimat, after the Russo-Turkish War Abdülhamid implicitly shifted emphasis to employing and mobilizing the support of Muslims from outlying parts of the empire, from Albania to the Arab world; among non-Muslims, he cultivated Arab Christians and Jews. The shift corresponded to the advent of a Muslim majority in the general population. Whether this change contributed to his positive or negative image obviously depended on each observer's point of view. One reason that Muslims tended to view Abdülhamid positively was that he had legitimate claims to the power he wielded, claims that the Tanzimat statesmen had lacked. European fears that he sought to promote a "pan-Islamic" foreign policy greatly overestimated Ottoman resources and aggressiveness. Abdülhamid was keenly conscious of his role as caliph of the Muslims and was devoted to defending the interests of Muslims everywhere. However, he also showed a sense of measure in his Islamic policy and an awareness of the paramount need to protect the Ottoman state. Tellingly, there was not another Ottoman-Russian war between 1878 and 1914. He also restrained Muslim resentments of Europe from assuming destructive forms.[65]

After the suppression of the constitutionalists, Abdülhamid enjoyed a decade without major opposition from the Ottoman intelligentsia. In 1889, however, an organized opposition began to reemerge within the Military Medical School, a self-conscious bastion of scientific modernity. Opposition grew slowly among both military and civil elites. Some opponents were arrested or fled to Paris, where they formed the Committee of Union and Progress (CUP, *ittihad ve Terakki Cemiyeti*) and began to be known in French as *Jeunes Turcs*, "Young Turks." Scattered across the map, with divergent bids for leadership and subject to the sultan's alternating attempts at repression and cooptation, the Young Turks faced many difficulties. In time, trends turned in their favor. Japan defeated Russia in the Russo-Japanese War of 1904–5, Russia and Iran both experienced revolutions in 1905, and rising prices caused worsening hardship and unrest among the Ottoman military and civil officialdom, even as they learned of these stirring developments abroad. In 1907, a new attempt was made to unite the opposition both inside and outside the empire. Macedonia, a hotspot of ethnic conflict in the Ottoman Balkans about which rumors of Anglo-Russian partition plans had begun to circulate, became the launching point for revolution when Young Turk officers took to the hills with their troops and demanded restoration of the constitution. Unable to suppress them this time, the sultan gave in (23 July 1908). Once again a constitutional monarch, Abdülhamid remained on the throne until an attempt at a rightist coup provided a pretext to depose him (April 1909).

The Young Turks had shown that they were not just a movement of ideas, like the Young Ottomans of the 1860s and 1870s.[66] Significantly, their supporters included many of the military elite, as well as the civil-bureaucratic intelligentsia; many of the officers commanded troops. The Young Turks also showed an awareness of the need to mobilize support and organize for action. In ideas and political principles, particularly as concerned their demand for constitutional, parliamentary government, they continued along the lines the Young Ottomans had traced. However, their awareness of contemporary European thought was much wider and more diverse, taking in emergent fields like sociology and psychology. Intellectually, their biggest point of difference with the Young Ottomans was that they had largely abandoned the earlier movement's Islamic reference points in favor of a militant secularism resembling French anticlericalism. Despite what the contrast between the names "Young Ottomans" (1860s and 1870s) and "Young Turks" (1889–1918) might seem to imply, the Young Turks were also Ottoman nationalists, whose vested interests were tied up in maintaining the empire as long as possible. For Turkic peoples everywhere, the onset of modernity created crises of collective identity just as it changed ideas of individual and class identity. Awareness of Turkish identity—both that of Ottoman Turks and that of the wider Turkic world—was growing in this period but still in company with Islamism and Ottomanism. If individual self-awareness moved in the direction of Turkishness, the political interest of ruling an empire still weighed on the side of Ottomanism. In the Arab provinces, too, despite stirrings and suspected stirrings of Arab nationalism, the situation was comparable.[67]

The Young Turk Revolution unleashed the greatest outburst of reformist energy that the empire had seen but also provided the pretext for a series of international crises that brought the empire to its end. The restoration of the constitution was greeted with joy, intercommunal fraternization, and eagerness to enjoy the new freedoms of speech and the press. Still relatively junior officers and bureaucrats in a society that associated leadership with age, the CUP operated as a secret society from behind the scenes, at first leaving the sultan and his old grand vezir in place and allowing multiple parties to form and compete in elections. The first contested elections in the Ottoman lands—today considered an essential indicator of democracy— thus occurred before the collapse of the empire. Measures were also quickly introduced to pardon political prisoners and exiles, abolish the system of spies and reformers, and "reorganize" the bureaucracy to get rid of informers and reduce overstaffing, which Abdülhamid had used as a way to make more people beholden to himself so that he could control them. Tens of thousands of men were removed from government payrolls. In 1909, an attempted counterrevolution, backed by certain religious conservatives and suppressed by military resistance again coming from Macedonia, provided the pretext to depose Abdülhamid. Thereafter, reforms continued in quick succession. Constitutional changes of 1909 completed the transition into a constitutional monarchy and made the cabinet responsible to the parliament. An unprecedentedly comprehensive attempt was made to draw up regulations for all government agencies. The 1913 law on provincial administration, the first new law of that type since 1871, later became the basis for local administration under the Turkish Republic. Ambitious efforts were undertaken to promote a "national economy" and the formation of a Turkish middle class. A new law made military service obligatory for all male Ottoman subjects, regardless of religion. Secularizing measures included reductions in the authority of the religious hierarchy and the 1917 Law of Family Rights, which contained provisions for Christians, Jews, and Muslims.[68] For the Ottoman state to enact one law of family status for all these religious communities, each of which had historically regulated such matters under its own religious law, was a radically secularizing measure indeed.

Internationally, however, the Young Turks faced an unrelenting series of crises. In 1908, in reaction to the revolution, Austria-Hungary annexed Bosnia, which it had occupied since 1876; and Bulgaria proclaimed its independence. The Italian occupation of Tripolitania (now Libya), the only part of Ottoman North Africa not already occupied by a European power, precipitated the Italo-Turkish War of 1911–12. Worse came with the First and Second Balkan Wars of 1912–13, in which Edirne, the Ottomans' second capital, was lost but regained. Most of the rest of the Ottoman Balkans was lost for good, including regions, like Macedonia, Albania, and parts of Thrace, that had been under Ottoman rule for over five centuries. The Ottoman frontier in Europe ended up where that of the Turkish Republic still remains.

The Balkan Wars provoked the Unionists, who had hitherto operated from behind the scenes, to intervene directly, stage an armed coup at the Sublime Porte, and set up a dictatorship that ruled until 1918. This CUP government concluded the secret alliance with Germany (2 August 1914) that brought the Ottomans into the war on the side of the Central Powers. That fateful miscalculation resulted from fear of the diplomatic isolation that the Ottomans had endured in the Balkan Wars and from the Germans' willingness to negotiate with the Ottomans on an equal footing—something that European governments were still not often willing to do with non-European ones. The Germans also were willing to provide armaments and financial assistance, which the Ottomans desperately needed. Unfortunately, the Ottomans were unaware that German plans required violating Belgian neutrality in order to invade France, and that would expand the war by bringing Britain into it.

Ottoman forces scored some successes in the war, defeating the British and Australian attack on the Dardanelles and capturing an entire British-Indian army in Iraq (1915–16). From 1916 on, however, the war turned against the Ottomans on all fronts. In the Caucasus, the Ottoman offensive of 1914 ended in defeat with heavy casualties, leaving eastern Anatolia open to Russian counterattack, which caused tremendous devastation until the Bolshevik Revolution and Russian withdrawal from the war turned the tide again in 1917. In all, the Ottomans mobilized 2.85 million men for the war, of whom up to 800,000 were killed or died of disease, 400,000 were wounded, and 250,000 were taken prisoner, mostly in Russian or British custody.[69]

Even as conditions worsened, most Ottoman subjects remained loyal. However, some Ottoman Armenians, like others from the Russian-ruled Caucasus, fought with the Russians in Armenian volunteer units in Anatolia; a former member of the Ottoman parliament commanded one such unit. Armenian guerrilla bands appeared in several places, and armed rebellions occurred in the Anatolian city of Van and elsewhere. While the impact of the war produced disproportionately Turkish casualties on the Russian side of the front lines, on the Ottoman side the Armenians suffered disproportionately, especially after the Ottoman government decided in 1915 to deport most of the Armenians to Syria. The Ottomans had a security problem in eastern Anatolia; but this response to it was disproportional and could not have been carried out humanely, least of all in a resource-strapped empire and in a region ill equipped with transport facilities, where armed tribesmen preyed on the sedentary population even in peacetime.[70] Scholars still debate whether the scale and severity of the deportations was intentionally decided by the CUP government in Istanbul or whether a secret, inner group, the "Special Organization" (*Teşkilat-ı Mahsusa*), abetted the depredations of predatory elements in the region. The result was Armenian fatalities numbering from the hundreds of thousands to over a million, depending on the estimate. Even after that, the front lines in eastern Anatolia and the Caucasus moved back and forth as the Russians advanced into eastern Anatolia until 1917 and the Ottomans regained lost ground from then until 1918. Additional large numbers of Muslims or Christians could find themselves trapped on the wrong side of the lines at some point. Vast numbers died in a region where war made agricultural production impossible for several years in a row. Between 1914 and 1923, war and civil war, famine and epidemic, caused population losses of 20 percent for Anatolia as a whole, with the highest percentages of Muslim, as well as non-Muslim, fatalities in the eastern provinces.

In the Arab provinces, the war generated similar worries and reactions, although with less reason and smaller consequences. As governor of Syria, Cemal Paşa terrorized the populace by executing prominent individuals on charges of subversion and by deporting several thousand Syrian families to Anatolia. In Syria, the threat of Arab nationalist uprising was more imagined than real.[71] The actual Arab revolt came at the far periphery of Ottoman control and was launched under quite different circumstances by the sharif of Mecca, a prestigious, semiautonomous, and politically ambitious ruler under the protection of the Ottoman sultanate. Sharif Husayn revolted in 1917 after an exchange of letters with the British in Egypt, containing ill-defined promises about Arab independence. The advance toward Palestine and Syria of Sharif Husayn's forces, in coordination with the British forces coming from Egypt, was part of the bad military news for the Ottomans in the last years of the war. Unfortunately, the reward that Sharif Husayn and his supporters reaped in the postwar peace settlement disappointed their hopes in ways that have had lasting political consequences for the Arab lands.

When the Ottoman government signed an armistice at the end of October 1918, it marked the end of both the Young Turk regime and, practically speaking, the Ottoman Empire. The sultan's government would survive for several more years in Istanbul, but the city was under foreign occupation from 1920 on. The Entente powers had begun making plans to carve up the empire as early as 1915. By the time the war ended, they had made more promises to one another, the Zionists, and the Arabs than could be reconciled at the Paris Peace Conference, a fact with consequences still felt in the Middle East.[72]

The Treaty of Sèvres (1920), drawn up as the death warrant for the Ottoman Empire in all its parts, assumed that the Turkish people were as dead as the empire. The treaty not only disposed of all the non-Turkish parts of the former empire but also gave away most of Anatolia, leaving only part of the center and north otherwise unassigned. For the Turks of the former Ottoman Empire, survival in the modern world of nation-states would re-quire a revision of the peace terms. Hopeless as this task may have seemed, with the founding of the Turkish Republic, they became the only defeated people of World War I who managed to force a revision of the peace terms that had been imposed on them. They did so through a combined political and military effort.

Politically, the task was to show that the Turkish-Muslim heartland of the empire was indeed that and wanted to stay united and independent. To do this, CUP branches in provincial centers founded "defense of national rights" societies; societies also formed under other names. The societies organized congresses to prove their representative character. Among many such congresses, particularly important ones were held in 1919 at Erzurum and Sivas, the latter forming a representative committee that moved to Ankara and formed the nucleus of a national government, creating its Grand Na-tional Assembly (April 1920) after the occupation of Istanbul deprived the Ottoman parliament there of any freedom of action.

The success of the political effort depended on that of the military struggle engaged after Greece, which had entered World War I only at the last minute, attempted to occupy parts of western Anatolia that had been promised to it at the peace conference. The Ottoman army, though depleted, was still intact, with its strongest forces in eastern Anatolia. The commanders sabotaged the Istanbul government's efforts to demobilize. When one of the most successful generals of World War I, Mustafa Kemal Paşa, was sent to Anatolia in 1919 on such a mission, he instead worked to unite the different commands and resistance organizations.[73] He called for the Sivas congress and went to Ankara as president of the national com-mittee that emerged out of it. The Turkish Independence War (1921–22) then took the form of campaigns led by Ismet Paşa and Mustafa Kemal (later known by the surnames Inönü and Atatürk, respectively) to defeat the Greeks.

By 1922, France and Italy had become suspicious of British and Greek aims and were ready to renounce the territories that had been promised them in Anatolia, and the allied forces were soon ready to abandon the occupa-tion of Istanbul as well. By adroit maneuvers, the protogovernment in An-kara abolished the defenseless remnants of the Ottoman government in Istanbul and prevailed against opposition elements in Anatolia. Recogniz-ing that the dictated terms of the Treaty of Sèvres had become inoperable in the Turkish heartland, albeit not in the other formerly Ottoman lands, the Entente powers invited the Turks to renegotiate.[74] The Treaty of Lausanne (1923) recognized the Turkish Republic within its present borders, excepting only the district of Hatay (Alexandretta), which Turkey acquired from French-ruled Syria in 1939.

Whereas in the eastern Turkic world, the advent of the post–World War I order meant the defeat of Turkic nationalists, to the west the Turkish nationalists succeeded in creating a new republic, one of the few independent developing countries outside Europe and the Americas in the interwar period. The Turks of Turkey had scored a great success in escaping the imperialist threat and achieving a place for themselves in the modern world as a nation-state. As in Central Asia, this had not been the work of political activists alone, and the obvious political and military turning points—such as the 1908 Revolution and the national struggle of 1919–23—had not been the only essential struggles. Behind them stood a slower-moving, broader-based cultural transformation in which even figures who were not politically active or progressive had played important roles. Young Ottomans like Namık Kemal (1840–88) and Young Turks like Ahmed Rıza (1859–1930) championed the great themes of constitutional, parliamentary government. While promoting those talismanic symbols of modernity, such thinkers opened a whole new, modernist worldview.[75] At the same time, many thinkers who did not espouse constitutionalist ideals made other contributions to the new culture of modernity. At odds with the constitutionalists, Ahmed Midhat (1844–1912) promoted progressive ideas on social and cultural questions, notably gender relations.[76] Sultan Abdülhamid's Islamic policy itself can be interpreted as a project in the construction of an Islamic modernity.[77] The many Turks from Central Asia who came to Istanbul offered a totally different perspective, that of Muslim Turks living under non-Muslim rule, to their Ottoman cousins, Muslim Turks ruling over non-Muslim minorities. The resulting stimulus to debate over issues of collective identity is best symbolized by Yusuf Akçura (1876–1935), whose work Üç Tarz-ı Siyaset ("Three Types of Polity," 1904) has been referred to as the "Communist Manifesto of Turkism," that is, the "first coherent statement of Pan-Turkist political aims."[78] From the 1860s on, female writers also explored the relationship among gender, modernity, Islam, and Ottomanism, as symbolized by the many who wrote for Ottoman women's magazines and by the pioneer woman novelist, Fatma Aliye (1862–1936).[79] As these women's writings show, it was not possible to talk about women's lives without exposing the patriarchal social order to unprecedented scrutiny. In a patrimonial sultanate, that scrutiny implied demands for change that could easily expand from social into political.

## Conclusion

F or the Turkic world in general, the nineteenth century had brought en
    counters with imperialism, a sense of backwardness, and the manifold
challenges of adapting, responding, and elaborating new cultures of modernity. The differences between Central Asia and the Ottoman Empire had
proven significant in important respects: absorption into the Russian Empire in the east and struggles to revitalize the embattled Ottoman Empire
and remain independent in the west; multiple literary languages that emerged
in the eastern world of Turk-Tajik symbiosis and struggles to turn Ottoman
Turkish into a medium for mass communications in the west; collective
identity debates differentiated in part by the relevant non-Turkish "others"—
Russians and Irano-Muslim Tajiks in the east and non-Muslim religious communities (and later non-Turkish ethnic groups) in the west.

The commonalities in the Turkic world were also still legion, a fact
evidenced in countless points great and small. This was the last period in
which, not just Turks, but Muslims in general, could still communicate with
each other without using European languages.[80] It is a remarkable coincidence, if nothing more, that the Ottoman Ahmed Midhat called his newspaper *Tercüman-i Hakikat*, "The Interpreter of Truth" (1878–1922), while
the Crimean Tatar Ismail Gaspıralı called his *Tercüman*, the "Interpreter" or
"Translator" (1883–1915); but then, in this period newspaper titles often
referred more to conveying ideas than to reporting events.[81] By another
remarkable coincidence, one of the first modern Ottoman schoolbooks was
Ahmed Midhat's *Hoca-i Evvel* ("First Teacher," 1868), while pioneering
*usul-ı jadid* textbooks included Ismail Gaspıralı's *Hoca-i Sıbyan* ("Teacher of
Children," 1884) and Said Aziz Khoja's *Ustad-i Avvval* ("First Master,"
1902).[82] Attitudes toward the outside world, too, were sometimes articu-
lated in nearly the same words. The Ottoman intellectual Hoca Tahsin Efendi
is remembered for a catchy couplet from the 1860s: "Go to Paris, young sir,
if you've got any wits; / If you've not come to Paris, you've not entered the
world." In 1911, Mirza Siraj Rahim of Bukhara wrote of his own travels to
Europe: "Whoever comes into this world and does not see Paris might as
well not have been born."[83] The Azeri intellectual Ali Huseinzade expressed
his view of Turkish identity through the slogan "Turkicization, Islamization, Europeanization"; inspired by this, Ziya Gökalp, leading Turkish
nationalist theoretician, wrote a book on "Turkicization, Islamization,
Modernization."[84]

Such parallels—surely replicable in the thousands—show how much
the weaving of the new fabric of Turkish modernity still had in common as
a task for Turks both east and west. As their means of communication and

travel improved, intellectuals from all over the Turkic world also became increasingly conscious of their common identity. Dreams of pan-Turkic unity began to coexist and compete with regionally or locally defined senses of ethnic identity, on the one hand, and with universal ideals of Islamic community, on the other. As the twentieth century opened, intellectuals in exile from the Russian Empire assumed vanguard roles in promoting this pan-Turkic awareness.[85] Fulfillment of such dreams would, however, prove elusive, especially for the duration of Soviet rule over most of the eastern Turkic world.

# FIVE

# The Turks and Modernity
*Republican and Communist*

For world historians, the twentieth century is defined chronologically by the multiphased terminal crisis of a Eurocentric system of global domination, whose origins go back at least to the end of the fifteenth century but which became truly global only in the nineteenth. That is why modernity manifested itself to non-European societies in the nineteenth century most pointedly through the menace of imperialism. Some world historians believe in a "long twentieth century" (1850–1991), in which multiplying crises around the world after about 1850 signified the mounting of resistance in countries adversely affected by the circumstances of their integration into the world system. India's Great Mutiny (1857), China's Taiping Rebellion (T'ai-p'ing, 1850–64), the Balkan crises of the period, and the struggles against imperialism in North Africa are evidence for this point of view. So would be the pre–World War I wave of revolutions including the Iranian and Russian ones of 1905, that of the Young Turks in 1908, and the Chinese one in 1911. Other scholars argue for a "short twentieth century," defined by an interlinked series of crises running from 1914 to 1991: World War I (1914–18), the Bolshevik Revolution (1917), the Great Depression (1929), World War II (1939–45 for Europe), decolonization (from 1947 on, peaking around 1960), the Cold War (1945–mid-1980s), and the collapse of communism in eastern Europe and the Soviet Union (1989–91). Prefacing these with the anticipatory tremors of the late 1800s, advocates of the long twentieth century take much the same view of the crises of 1914–91.

Among the twentieth-century crises, the Bolshevik Revolution has special relevance for the Turks. Arguably, the Soviet combination of internationalist ideology and a distinctive approach to nationality issues inside

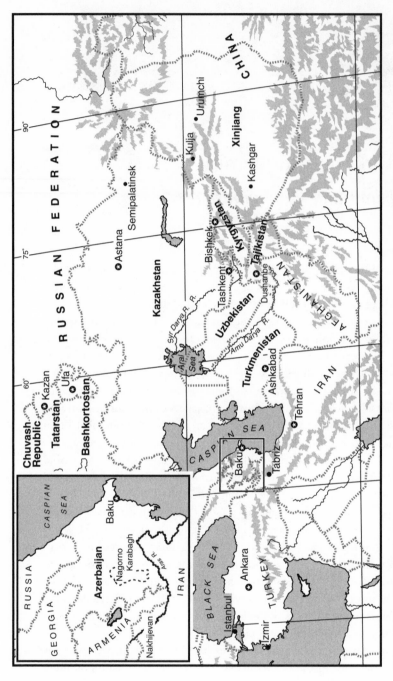

Map of The Turkic World, 2000. The map, which spans the region from the Turkish Republic to China's Xinjiang Province, illustrates sites mentioned in the text. As in the map in chapter 4, some of the smaller and more remote populations cannot be shown for reasons of scale. Map by Ron McLean, Digital Media Creation Services, Ohio State University.

the Soviet Union, reinforced with the repressive power of the state, explains why the multinational empire of the tsars did not break up when they fell, whereas the other multinational empires that fought in World War I, Austria-Hungary and the Ottoman Empire, did both collapse. Arguably, too, the weakening of the distinctively Soviet combination of the carrot and the stick did much to explain why the breakup averted in 1917 occurred in 1991. If the Bolshevik Revolution opened the twentieth century, the Soviet collapse closed it. As much as the Turkic peoples suffered from 1917, few peoples benefited more from 1991.

Space, as well as time, is at issue in large-scale historical conceptualizations, and an alternate route to conceptualizing the twentieth century emphasizes shifts in spatial terms. From the political and economic revolutions of the late eighteenth century until decolonization and the Soviet collapse, the world was spatially reconfigured in profoundly different ways. The eighteenth-century world had been one of cosmopolitanisms and local particularisms. After the French Revolution, the world began to reconfigure into nation-states and would-be nation-states, ultimately almost 200 of them. While exceptional circumstances enabled the Russian Empire to postpone that fate, multinational empires like it or that of the Ottomans gradually became obsolete, as did political landscapes as diffusely organized as Central Asia on the eve of Russian conquest. The prodigality of difference that either region harbored was now supposed to reconfigure into nation-states, whose leaders would remold the old micropolitics of kinship, regional or religious particularisms, and hybrid identities to create border-to-border uniformity of patriotic citizens. This formation of citizens and the creation of a sense of shared national identity showed the smiling face of nationalism. However, the positive aspect of nationalism was never all there was to it.[1] Countries that started out disunited, whose lands were claimed by competing nationalist movements, or which could not retain enough autonomy to chart their own course toward modernity had to struggle for unification, liberation, or both, demonstrating the warlike face of nationalism. In lands taken under foreign rule or threatened by it, the spatial reconfiguration and the idealized outcome of national independence would be separated by lengthy struggles to construct a new national culture of modernity and combat imperialism. In multiethnic or multicultural societies, trying to achieve the illusory goal of border-to-border uniformity could lead not only to benign forms of social engineering, such as public education, but also to massacres and "ethnic cleansing."

Success in struggles for unification, or against foreign rule or the threat of it, required mobilizing the whole people, not just the elites. The usual result was a unitary national mobilization behind the leaders of the struggle, often depending on high-pressured tactics to activate an unready populace and pre-empt rival attempts at mobilization. Turkey's national liberation struggle and the first phase of the republic's history formed an archetypical case of this kind. Contemporaneous Central Asian attempts to achieve some kind of Turkic national communist unification might have done likewise, had Soviet power not overwhelmed them. Usually in developing countries, the unitary mass mobilization has held together for about a generation after victory in the national struggle, until dissatisfaction with its leadership mounts, and old internal differences resurface. In Turkey, this began to happen with the transition to multiparty politics after 1945, and the pace accelerated from the 1960s on. For the world in general, the 1960s were a watershed when, partly because of surging demographic growth and an exceptionally large cohort of young adults, old political alliances of Left and Right began to fragment and differences of gender, race, ethnicity, religion, and class began to gain salience anew. Powered by technological innovation, particularly in transportation and communications, the pace of change accelerated and distances seemed to shrink.

These changes together precipitated another spatial reconfiguration. Even though nation-states continued to proliferate into the early 1990s, a new global pattern—more like the eighteenth-century one of cosmopolitanism versus particularism than like the nation-state pattern—began to emerge in the new form of today's omnipresent tension between the forces of globalization, on the one hand, and those of identity and difference, on the other. The term "globalization" has been commonly used in incompatible senses. In some discussions, globalization is equated with the promotion worldwide of a single set of values and practices identified with democracy, free enterprise, and the West. Analyses that depict a "clash of civilizations," in which some have succeeded while others "went wrong," represent this point of view. In other discussions, globalization is defined open-endedly to include *all* the networking processes and technologies that are transforming the world.

After centuries of gradually accelerating development, the growth of globally interconnective processes intensified at the end of the twentieth century, pushing space-time compression to the point where the global and the local could be experienced everywhere at once. Some of the globalizing forces are cultural in nature—religious activism, for example. Others are fundamentally material, such as the consumer democratization that makes certain products in demand globally. Still other globalizing forces are part of both realms at once: the internet, bringing together both computer systems and information, may be the best example. To the extent that a particular subsystem of globalization is perceived as projecting a specific cultural identity, it tends to provoke resistance. The hostility provoked across much of the world by attempts to project Euro-American values as universal demonstrates the point. This explains the interactive-conflictive, protagonist-antagonist relationship between globalization and the localism of identity politics. To the extent that subsystems of globalization are—or come to be perceived as—neutral in value content, they gain readier acceptance. Euro-American concepts of what is universal in human rights provoke resistance in cultures where those standards appear alien rather than universal. However, in sports, enthusiasts willingly adopt arbitrary rules in order to compete internationally, even globally, oblivious to where the rules were written but keen to play and win. More significantly, all who conform to the standards and protocols that make electronic communication possible can do so, asserting their identity and their values globally, if they wish.

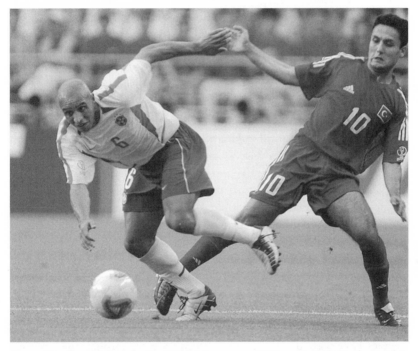

**Sports Heroism, Turkey in the World Cup, 2002.** Yıldıray Baştürk (Turkey, right) and Roberto Carlos (Brazil) struggle for control of the ball in the semifinal game at Saitama, Japan. Turkey lost to Brazil (0-1), then defeated South Korea (3–2) to finish third in the World Cup, a remarkable achievement. Yıldıray is a second-generation German Turk who normally plays for Bayern Leverkusen. He is one of several players with dual nationality who chose to play for Turkey rather than Germany in the World Cup, an irrevocable choice under International Football Federation rules. Photo by İhlas Haber Agency, courtesy of Turgay Sakarya, *Türkiye Gazetesi*.

Amid the flux of globalization as understood inclusively, what had before seemed the building blocks of modernity—including business firms and markets, nation-states and alliance systems, international organizations and movements—remain powerful actors. However, instead of defining global order, they are caught up in a global disorder defined by countercurrents of globalism (in the inclusive sense) and localism. These countercurrents did not cause each other, but each provokes and intensifies the other.[2] One consequence of space-time compression has been that particular identities can hurdle local boundaries and become deterritorialized. In the case of the Turks, this began to occur on a significant scale with the Turkish worker migration to Europe in the 1960s. Since then, diasporic Turkish communities have spread out across the world, giving the Turks a truly global presence, while fragments of Turkish culture—bits of Sufi music and certain foods—have also become part of global fusions.

Within the spatial and temporal frames that distinguished it, several major themes characterized the twentieth century. First was the tightening of global interconnectedness, which transformed the Turkic peoples' encounter with modernity from a struggle against European (or Soviet) imperialism into an effort to find and shape their place in global modernity. A second theme was that of identity and difference, as groups defined by all the axes of difference—race, ethnicity, religion, class, gender, and disadvantage or personal preference—defended and asserted their identity in a shrinking world. Third, these changes were accompanied by the rise of the mass society, in both qualitative and quantitative senses. Politically, the fall of imperial and monarchical regimes opened the way for the rise of mass-based polities, ranging from democratic to dictatorial, in which sovereignty belonged to the people, in word if not always in deed. Demographically, unprecedented growth in human numbers more than tripled world population, with most of the increase in developing countries, including the Turkish Republic and the Turkic lands of Inner Asia. The fourth great theme can be symbolized at the global level in terms of technology versus nature, as human beings have expanded their ability to manipulate, but also to degrade or even obliterate, their natural habitat. As in most developing countries, the Turkic peoples have particularly experienced this problem through the environmental degradation that accompanied runaway population growth and exploitation of the natural environment, which assumed grotesque proportions under Soviet rule.

To illustrate these observations with the historical experience of the Turkic peoples, this chapter will examine their twentieth-century history, first in the Caucasus and Inner Asia, then in Turkey, and finally in the Turkish diaspora.

## The Eastern Turkic World

A s the engagement with modernity that began in the nineteenth century continued and intensified, the development of Turkic societies in the twentieth century continued to display both significant parallelisms and large differences, particularly in their degrees of independence. For the Turkic peoples of Inner Eurasia, the dominant fact of twentieth-century life was foreign rule. Still, differences between the histories of the Soviet Union and China, compounded by the diversity of Turkic peoples, are such that their experiences can only be discussed selectively here.

### Turkic Nationalisms and Soviet Nationality Policy

By 1900, Turkish intellectuals were increasingly conscious of their common identity. Although pan-Turkism coexisted with smaller-scaled concepts of regional or local identity, as well as with an even larger-scaled concept of Islamic community, the growing awareness of common identity naturally appealed to Turks' imaginations. It was, however, particularly significant for those of the Russian Empire. After the Russian conquest of Central Asia, more than half of all Turks lived under Russian rule. Ninety percent of the Muslims in the Russian Empire spoke Turkic languages, and they confronted Great Russian chauvinism and pan-Slavism. It was not surprising, then, either that the intellectual fathers of pan-Turkism, like Yusuf Akçura and Ismail Gaspıralı, came from the Russian Empire or that their ideas gained a hearing amid the geopolitical uncertainties of Ottoman and tsarist collapse.[3] Circumstances seemed to favor pan-Turkist enthusiasm at several times during the twentieth century. One occurred in the wave of revolutionary enthusiasm touched off by the Russian and Young Turk revolutions of 1905 and 1908. Another occurred in the first few years immediately following the Bolshevik Revolution of 1917. A third occurred in 1941 when the possibility that the Nazi invasion might destroy the Soviet Union awakened fleeting hopes. Not until the Soviet collapse (1991) did real possibilities emerge for Turks everywhere to take advantage of all the modern possibilities for communicating and interacting with one another. The ways in which they did so, examples of which are noted in this chapter, showed that the pan-Turkic dreams of the past were by then caught up in the contending currents of globalization and identity politics that defined the new era.[4]

As long as the Soviet Union lasted, not only did it make pan-Turkism an impossibly dangerous pursuit for its citizens, but also the Turkish Republic, with such a large and dangerous neighbor, had to prioritize its national interests over visions of wider solidarity among Turks. The appeal of such visions was obviously not limited to Turks under Soviet rule, then. For those who were, however, they formed one side of a story whose other side consisted of Soviet nationality policy. That was a reality impossible to ignore.

Assuming power just as the other multinational empires were collapsing, the Bolsheviks were well aware of the power of nationalism and of the challenges that ethnocultural differences posed to new rulers of the former tsars' empire.[5] While some argued that the victory of the proletariat made national self-determination irrelevant, Lenin and Stalin were more sensitive to the non-Russian peoples' historical distrust of Russian imperialism. Class analysis indicated, too, that the Bolsheviks should act to prevent the nationalist alliance between middle class and workers that made nationalism irresistible in other countries. What in 1924 became the Soviet Union would therefore retain a kind of self-determination. This was intended to prevent cross-class nationalist alliances among the peoples under Soviet rule while the workers and peasants of the various nationalities passed through the unavoidable nationalist phase on their path to socialist internationalism. For the time being, then, a distinction needed to be drawn between the nationalism of the oppressors, like the former Russian Empire, and that of the oppressed. Stalin's Georgian ethnicity and Lenin's youthful years in Kazan influenced the positions they took.

To implement these concepts was a challenge. For Stalin, Soviet nationalities had to be "national in form, socialist in content." The resulting political organization was an ethnically based federalism that has been likened to a communal apartment, a familiar feature of Soviet housing. Different nationalities had separate rooms; communists were in control throughout, but all the nations had supposedly equal rights. Later Soviet terminology used different words for "international" in the sense of relations with non-Soviet states (*mezhdunarodnyi*) and relations among the nationalities inside the Soviet Union (*internatsionalnyi*). For the constituent republics of the USSR (Union of Soviet Socialist Republics), the only "international" relations were of the latter kind, specifically, relations with their Russian "elder brother." To promote socialism among all these nations required promoting their respective languages and cultures. In Soviet terms, achieving equality of "form" among nationalities would reveal the superficiality of national difference and the underlying "content" of common class interests, awakening common sympathies that would eventually lead to socialist fusion. Paradoxically, then, the surest path to unity in content was diversity in form.

Organizing diversity in form required a vast effort at ethnolinguistic classification and geographical partition. The results bore a paradoxical relationship to the desires and characteristics of the people affected. The Soviet Union came to be configured into fifteen Soviet Socialist Republics (SSRs), including Russia as the Federative Republic (RSFSR). Like a set of nesting dolls, the SSRs had inside them Autonomous Soviet Socialist Republics (ASSRs) for smaller nationalities or, smaller still, autonomous districts (*oblast*). In the 1920s, national institutions of one kind or another were created by the thousands, down to the grassroots levels, although many of these were later eliminated. The obvious winners in nationality policy were the "titular nationalities" of the fifteen SSRs. Yet many members of even those nationalities lived in diaspora communities elsewhere, and the republics were never inhabited only by their titular nationalities. The development of different literary languages for different nationalities was likewise encouraged and taken under "scientific" direction from the center. Furthermore, the policy of "nativization" (*korenizatsiya*, literally "taking root) defined a major role for nationality in politics. Representatives of each ethnic group were to be recruited preferentially to run its affairs, even though for years this normally meant serving as deputies under Russian chiefs. In this, the Soviet Union became the first country in the world to establish affirmative action programs of a kind for national minorities, doing so on a scale that no other country has yet matched.[6] While eventually giving Turks and others powerful positions, *korenizatsiya* (*milliylashtirish* in Uzbek) would also subordinate processes of elite formation—which loom so large in Turkic political history—to the priorities of the Soviet state. This had high long-term costs and created unexpected linkages between Soviet politics and modern recreations of the old micropolitics of clan and retinue.

This project to build a utopian, supranational "imagined community" for the Soviet Union. abounded in paradoxes. What was formally structured as a federation of sovereign nations was at the same time a centralized, invasive, and extremely violent state.[7] Whereas Jadidist intellectuals had debated issues of unity and diversity among the Muslims of the Russian Empire, the Soviets decided for diversity, mobilizing ethnographers and linguists in a "scientific" effort to define differences among peoples who did not yet see themselves as distinct or cohesive nationalities. Particularly where issues of Islam and gender relations were concerned, the policies were counterproductive, stigmatizing as backward and dirty those practices that a given people regarded as part of their culture and indirectly revalorizing those traits for eventual reassertion as markers of "national" identity.[8] Soviet scientific analysis of the historical Turko-Persian bilingualism of Central Asian literary and musical culture found it necessary, too, to sort out what "belonged" to the Turkic nationalities or to the Tajiks, to set up conservatories to teach the partitioned musical culture, to reduce performance traditions historically transmitted from master to student to written notation, and to form choruses to perform polyphonic renditions of monophonic song cycles—all in the name of nationality and modernity.[9] From the 1930s on, moreover, Soviet citizens were required to carry internal passports that assigned to each person an unchangeable nationality. Soviet citizens, many of whom lived outside their "national" territories, therefore carried their nationality with them wherever they went, and assimilation became virtually impossible. While making nationality ineradicable, Soviet policy nonetheless criminalized political expressions of nationalism to such a point that baseless accusations could produce fatal consequences. Great numbers of Turkic intellectuals learned this the hard way in the 1920s, long before the purges of the late 1930s swept through the entire Soviet intelligentsia.

Geography and history introduced large variations into the experience of specific Turkic nationalities. Among twenty ethnic groups accused of disloyalty during World War II, the Crimean Tatars, who had their own Crimean ASSR for a time after 1921, were abruptly deported in 1944, mostly to Uzbekistan or Siberia. Their right to return was not recognized until 1989, and their attempt to recreate a national presence in the Crimea unfolded in the post-Soviet period.[10] Less fortunate still, the Meskhetian Turks were deported from their villages in Soviet Georgia in 1944, perhaps in preparation for an invasion of Turkey that Stalin never got around to. They were dispersed and never allowed to return.[11] Among Turkic peoples inside the Russian Republic, the Chuvash, Tatars, and Bashkirs were more fortunate in that their ASSRs survived; their post-Soviet development continues as contiguous ethnic republics within the Russian Federation. Numerous small Turkic nationalities, extending to the Yakuts in the far Siberian east (or Sakhas, as they call themselves), occupied analogous positions.[12] Highest among Turkic peoples in the Soviet hierarchy of nationalities were the titular ones of the five Turkic SSRs (the Azerbaijan, Turkmen, Uzbek, Kyrgyz, and Kazakh Republics). The remainder of this section will focus on them. Its division between Iran and the Soviet Union again places Azerbaijan in a separate category.

## Azerbaijan

Although twentieth-century events have confirmed the north-south division of Azerbaijan, there were moments of interaction. These probably did a lot to distinguish Iranian Azerbaijan as Iran's most rebellious, radical province. Further north, despite the official Soviet view that the Red Army's entry into Azerbaijan in April 1920 was a "shining example" of the Russian people's "fraternal assistance" to the "toilers of Azerbaijan," the proclamation of an independent Soviet Republic of Azerbaijan was an act of force. Azerbaijani

Communists were placed in conspicuous positions, but the Communist Party leadership was primarily Russian and Armenian. As long as the Soviet system lasted, it set the terms for the engagement with modernity here.[13]

Initially, communists had no support outside Baku. The Red Army had to fight to gain control of Ganje and other places, and armed resistance continued until 1924. Over 100,000 Azeris are thought to have died in purges between 1920 and 1925.[14] Nationalization of the economy began with the publishing and oil industries. In industrial production, 1913 levels would not be regained until the 1930s. In agriculture, as in tsarist times, the government continued to demand cotton at the expense of food production, promoting colonial-style integration into the Soviet economy.

The Soviet republics of Azerbaijan, Armenia, and Georgia corresponded to the imperial viceroyalty of Transcaucasia. Lenin demanded their economic integration in 1921, and they were combined into the Transcaucasian Soviet Federated Socialist Republic (TSFSR) from 1922 to 1936.[15] The TSFSR controlled the economies of the three republics and channeled resources, particularly oil, to the USSR. The party and security agencies served as organs of control and employed disproportionately fewer members of the local population than did those of Georgia and Armenia.

Yet Soviet nationality policy aimed to improve on chauvinistic, Russifying policies of the pre-1917 period. The decision of the Twelfth Party Congress (1923) to grant nationalities under Soviet rule rights to develop their own cultures and languages and to "train and employ native cadres in their republics" in a policy of "nativization" (korenizatsiya) sprang from certain perceptions: that it served Bolshevik ends better to promote millät, separate "national" identities, over ummät, Muslim solidarity, and that the intelligentsia would have to be mobilized as the "surrogate" proletariat of the Muslim nationalities.[16] The tendency of those Turkic intellectuals who promoted distinct literary languages, rather than the common one advocated by Ismail Gaspıralı, was approved and officially promoted. The Arabic script was replaced in 1922 by the Latin script, and then in 1940 by a modified Cyrillic script, deemed more "progressive" and more conducive to learning Russian. Education was closely controlled and pushed in the direction of technical training. The push for secularism—a policy that some Azeri intellectuals had already espoused as an antidote to Sunni-Shi'i sectarianism—began with the "attack" (hujum) of 1927, a campaign for the emancipation of Muslim women, soon followed by mosque closings and attacks on religious leaders. Not only were the same cultural policies applied in other Soviet republics at the same time, but also the parallelisms in content and timing between these policies and those freely enacted by the Turkish Republic are remarkable enough to suggest more than coincidence.

Soviet decisions about territorial issues showed how efficiently the nationality policy served the purpose of dividing and ruling. The Nakhijevan ASSR, although officially classed as part of the Azerbaijan SSR, was completely cut off from it by the region Zangezur, which was assigned to the Armenian SSR, so extending Armenia southward all the way to the Iranian border and separating Nakhijevan from Azerbaijan. Further east, inside the Azerbaijan SSR, Karabagh was gerrymandered to create the autonomous district of Nagorno-Karabagh, with an Armenian majority to whom political and cultural concessions were made. During the 1920s, Armenians migrated out of Nakhijevan, as did Azeris out of Zangezur, but Nagorno-Karabagh retained a mixed population.[17] Seventy years later, the Soviet collapse would unleash violent conflict over Armenian demands to take Nagorno-Karabagh from Azerbaijan.

Terror, in recurrent waves from 1920 to 1941, reinforced state policy. In the 1920s, opponents of communism and Soviet rule were crushed. In the late 1920s and 1930s, for all Turkic peoples in the USSR, old leaders, including national Communists like Nariman Narimanov, a Marxist who had believed that revolution would liberate Azerbaijan from Russian imperialism, were eliminated.[18] Anticommunism and widespread opposition to the collectivization of Stalin's first Five-Year Plan brought terror to the countryside in the 1920s and 1930s. Villages that resisted were destroyed, man, woman, and child. Soviet forces pursued and wiped out those who fled into Iran.[19] The impact of Soviet rule intensified in the 1930s. From 1933 through 1953, Stalin's man in Azerbaijan was the party first secretary, Mir Jäfär Baghirov, who had risen through the secret police.

With the adoption of the Soviet constitution of 1936, the TSFSR was abolished; each of its three republics became part of the USSR; and its union and autonomous republics received constitutions of their own, including verbal guarantees of freedoms, autonomy, and the right to secede. The practical effect of this reorganization was to leave each republic with vertical links to the center but no horizontal links. Assuming disproportionate scale in Azerbaijan and other Muslim republics, the "great purge" of 1937–38 wiped out over 100,000, not only old Bolsheviks, but also the entire party elite and most of the intelligentsia. Anyone could be denounced as a "saboteur," "enemy of the people," and "fascist lackey." Those who were liquidated were replaced by others molded by the Soviet system.[20] Such were the conditions under Soviet nationality policy and *korenizatsiya* on the eve of World War II.

Between the two world wars, the fate of Iranian Azerbaijan diverged from that of the north even more sharply. In Iran, a man on horseback, Colonel Reza Khan, emerged in the early 1920s, suppressing rebellions among many of the peoples under Iranian rule, including the Azeris in 1922. By 1925, he had become powerful enough to set himself up as Reza Shah Pahlavi, founder of a new dynasty. In contrast to Soviet nationality policy, he was a centralizer and assimilator, who restricted Azeri cultural expression and divided the region into two provinces in 1937. Under his rule, the many Iranian Azeris who had spent time in the North came under suspicion as Communist sympathizers—a self-fulfilling prophecy in some cases.[21]

World War II brought new hardships but for a time permitted greater contact between Azeris north and south of the Soviet-Iranian border. Invading the Soviet Union, Germany aimed to take the Caucasus and Baku's oil. Although German forces never reached Azerbaijan, the Red Army used Central Asians and Caucasians as cannon fodder, conscripting them in proportions perhaps three times as high as the general Soviet population. Many fought bravely, sometimes as partisans behind enemy lines. Like other non-Russians in the Red Army, large numbers also surrendered or were captured by the Germans, who formed many such captives into units to fight the Soviets. Several hundred thousand Muslims and Caucasians fought against the Soviets in these units as of 1943.

To Allied strategists, the German invasion of the Soviet Union added new strategic value to Iran as the best remaining route to send supplies to their Soviet ally. The result was the British-Russian invasion of Iran (August 1941), the abdication and exile of Reza Shah, the succession of Muhammad Reza Shah (r. 1941–79), and the conclusion of a tripartite British, Iranian, and Soviet treaty (1942).[22] Iran was occupied by British, U.S., and Soviet troops, many of whom were Soviet Azeris. By the end of the war, cultural exchanges between North and South Azerbaijan had been renewed, and there was talk of a Greater Azerbaijan. With the revival of party politics in Iran following the overthrow of Reza Shah, a new leftist party, known as *Tudeh* (Masses), also emerged, with Azerbaijan as one of its centers. With Soviet encouragement, the stage was set to revive autonomist tendencies in Iranian Azerbaijan and in the adjoining Kurdish region of Iran, as well.

The issue of whether the Azeris were a nationality or not provoked a split with the Tudeh Party, and Sayyid Jafar Pishevari in 1945 spearheaded a breakaway movement to form a Democratic Party of Azerbaijan. At the same time, Stalin announced that Soviet troops would remain in Iran longer than previously announced, until six months after the defeat of Japan. The Democrats seized power in Tabriz in November, denying separatist ambitions but proclaiming extensive autonomist demands. Surviving for a year, the autonomous government in Tabriz accomplished significant reforms, including a virtual cultural revolution to reverse Reza Shah's assimilationist policies; but both the Tabriz government and the Soviets overplayed their hands. In March 1946, instead of withdrawing their forces, the Soviets sent in more, in what proved to be one of the opening gambits of the Cold War. This provoked a vivid international reaction, which led, in this case, to Soviet withdrawal in May. Pishevari was still influential enough to negotiate autonomist concessions from Tehran. However, in Azerbaijan discontent was mounting over the anti-Islamic and pro-Soviet implications of his policies, economic hardship, and his Soviet-style reactions to opposition. By the time the Iranian army entered Tabriz in December, the populace welcomed it with fleeting enthusiasm. Pishevari and perhaps 15,000 others fled to the Soviet Union. Astonishingly, Tehran prevailed against Moscow, probably because Stalin prized eastern Europe more than Iran and Azerbaijan.

In Soviet Azerbaijan, the period from war's end to Stalin's death in 1952 brought a return to central control and Russian dominance. Thereafter, the remaining decades of Soviet rule displayed a number of important features, many of them paralleled in Central Asia. In Azerbaijan, de-Stalinization meant the fall of Stalin's man, Mir Jäfär Baghirov. The cultural elite grew more assertive. Writers who had died in the purges were selectively rehabilitated; traditional literary texts, like the collection of tales, *Dede Korkut*, were reinterpreted and relegitimized as folklore; and historians worked to recover Azerbaijan's identity. Azerbaijani Turkish was declared the official language, and Azerbaijan stiffly resisted Soviet efforts to dilute the teaching of it in the schools.[23]

Demographic trends supported cultural ones, contributing significantly to political and economic change. In these decades, Soviet Azerbaijan acquired an urban majority. Azerbaijani Turks believed (probably rightly) that they had become a majority in Baku, and their majority in Azerbaijan as a whole had increased from two-thirds to over three-quarters. As in Turkey, the twentieth century was when the Turks completed their "conquest" of first the countryside and then the largest city—changes launched in ethnic conflict but due more in the long run to explosive demographic growth. Inside the Soviet Union, differential growth rates among Slavs and Muslims made the "sons of Temür" increasingly visible in the Soviet military, where they were harassed and mistreated.

The shifting ethnic balance in Azerbaijan affected the complexion of its Communist Party, which had an Azerbaijani Turkish majority from the 1960s on. Heydar Aliyev's long career as party secretary illustrates how Moscow became increasingly dependent on indigenous apparatchiks who had mastered the art of satisfying both Moscow and their local clienteles. After Aliyev's fall in 1987, he was accused of "mafia" or "clan" politics.[24] Similar charges about party bosses in Central Asia show that modern versions of the old

Turkish micropolitics of kinship and retinue formation, and the exchanges of goods and favors that sustained the retainers' loyalties, had been recreated inside the communal apartment of Soviet nationality policy. In a 1990 article on Azerbaijani politics, a Moscow magazine dissected the situation in Central Asia and the Caucasus precisely: "[V]estiges of a feudal system adapted themselves with astonishing harmony to the Stalinist model of socialism, and the power has not simply been put in the hands of bureaucracy, but the bureaucracy itself has become enmeshed with the networks of family and kinship bonds."[25]

Resembling their counterparts in other Soviet republics, those in power in Soviet Azerbaijan did their part to worsen the consequences of demographic growth and technological change by steadily demanding increased production of cotton and grapes. As the centers of Soviet oil production shifted after 1945 to the Volga basin and later Siberia, Azerbaijan went into relative economic decline and became increasingly a supplier of agricultural commodities to the Soviet economy, with accompanying growth in the use of chemical pesticides and fertilizers.[26] Irrigation was expanded to the point that shrinkage of the Caspian Sea had already been noted with alarm before 1980—a change vitally affecting other republics that shared the Caspian coastline as well. In Azerbaijan, as in Central Asia and other parts of the socialist world, policies that jeopardized the environment and public health helped turn politics from red to green in the last years of Soviet rule.

Bringing these and other abuses into view, Gorbachev's policies of restructuring (*perestroika*) and openness (*glasnost*) produced little positive impact in Azerbaijan, partly because of personal antipathies among Aliyev, Gorbachev, and others.[27] Here, as elsewhere, those policies helped unleash the nationalist demons that Soviet nationality policy, combined with Soviet repression, had kept bottled up since the 1920s. To some observers, what ensued was a "decolonization" comparable to the breakup of other colonial empires.[28] For Azerbaijan, change began in 1987 with the fall of Heydar Aliyev.

Upon Aliyev's fall, Armenians advanced the first of recent demands for the annexation of Nagorno-Karabagh to the Armenian SSR. When violence broke out in 1988, refugees began fleeing to reach the "right" side of the lines, and in January 1990 Armenia annexed Nagorno-Karabagh. As Azeri refugees from Armenia and Nagorno-Karabagh flooded into Baku, the Azeri party headquarters became the meeting point for protests, aimed as much at Moscow and its local henchmen as at Armenia. As the Communist Party demonstrated its unreadiness to cope with a crisis so far beyond normal routine, the first Azerbaijani political organizations outside the party began to organize, coalescing in 1989 into the Azerbaijan People's Front (APF), which demanded civil rights, sovereignty within the USSR, return of the land to the peasants, and protection of the environment. Religious demands were notably absent, although the Soviets would opportunistically allege Islamic radicalism when it suited their purposes. The political spectrum did, however, include "gray wolves" (*boz gurd* in Azeri), a spillover from the ultranationalist and pan-Turkist wing of rightist politics in Turkey.[29] In adopting the gray wolf as their emblem, modern-day Turkish nationalists harken back to ancient myth, although the symbol was largely forgotten for centuries until modern scholars rediscovered it.

Violence against the regime began in a number of towns, becoming more serious with the start of Armenian terrorist operations in Azerbaijan and other parts of the Caucasus in 1989.[30] In January 1990, heavy street fighting between ethnic groups broke out in Baku. In stark contrast to its lenient treatment of Baltic separatists at about the same time, Moscow ordered Soviet troops to the Caucasus, where agents of the KGB (the Soviet secret police) blew up the power stations in Baku, causing a blackout. In the midst of that, the Red Army entered the city for the first time since 1920, firing on unarmed civilians during a four-day rampage officially announced as a "security operation to constrain hooliganism and Islamic extremism."[31] The scope of conflict over Karabagh expanded with the Soviet collapse and the declaration of independence in 1991 both by Azerbaijan and by the Armenian leadership of Nagorno-Karabagh. In the southern part of the latter, Armenian armed forces started ethnic-cleansing operations, and the governments of Baku, Yerevan, and Moscow did nothing effective to stop it.[32]

Independence had come to Soviet Azerbaijan with neither the people nor the government prepared for it. The leadership—former Soviet apparatchiks turned heads of state—could not cope effectively with basic governance, let alone the Karabagh crisis. Exciting developments occurred, including new relationships with Turkey and other countries, as well as cultural innovations such as the adoption of the Latin alphabet in 1993, Azerbaijan's fourth change of script. The government's unreadiness was well illustrated, however, by the fact that it had a minister of defense but no real army.[33] Better prepared and supported by sympathizers in Russia and other countries, Armenian forces had freedom of action in southwestern Azerbaijan. When Armenian and Russian forces destroyed Khojali in 1992, thus completing the ethnic cleansing of Nagorno-Karabagh, it led to the fall of Azerbaijan's government and later brought the Popular Front to power. A competitive presidential election occurred in 1992, but President Abulfaz Elchibäy, one of the founders of the Popular Front, was unable to keep order or cope effectively with Karabagh. The upshot was the reemergence of Heydar Aliyev as president in 1993. He introduced a democratic constitution but also reinstated the authoritarianism and intolerance of criticism to which seventy years of Soviet rule had habituated his people.

By then, the Karabagh front had virtually collapsed, 750,000 Azeris had become refugees, and another 300,000 or more, mostly Armenians, had fled Azerbaijan. A Russian-brokered cease-fire in 1994 has been much violated since, with much negotiation but no final agreement.[34] Economically, the best hope for Azerbaijan was its still unexploited Caspian oil and gas resources. They might now be marketed on the world market, but only if problems about existing pipelines and alternate routes for new ones could be solved. Politically, recycled Communists like Aliyev appealed to Azerbaijan's "silent majority" more than did the intellectuals of the Popular Front, as the former offered the less unsettling prospect of gradual change and a newly cultivated image of benevolent populism. In the first dynastic power transfer in the ex-Soviet states, before dying in December, Heydar Aliyev arranged the election of his son, Ilham, as president in October 2003.

Azerbaijan was still divided and likely to remain so. Since its brief flourish of autonomism at the end of World War II, Iran's most rebellious region has experienced two more periods of centralizing, assimilationist policy. Muhammad Reza Shah severely restricted cultural expression. The reforms of the vaunted shah-people revolution of the 1960s contained no reference to Iran's minorities, and its Literacy Corps consisted entirely of Persian-speaking military personnel. With the oil boom of the 1970s and rapid population growth, Iran's Azeris moved increasingly to Tehran, where they reportedly numbered 1.5 to 2 million.[35] As with the Kurds in Turkey, then, their concentration in their historic home region was attenuated. When the 1979 revolution overthrew the shah's regime and led to the formation of the Iranian Islamic Republic, Tabriz again became a major center of activism, and hopes for freer cultural expression and local self-government rebounded. Ayatollah Kazim Shariatmadari emerged as not just the region's most prestigious Shi'i religious authority but also a national figure, opposed to Khomeini's view that the religious leadership should seize state power and not confine itself to teaching and upholding religious law. As Azeris joined other Iranian minorities in advocating federalism, the new Tehran government asserted its control, and Shariatmadari was placed under house arrest. Many Azeris subsequently achieved high positions in the Islamic Republic. Iranian Azerbaijan's incorporation into a centralizing Islamic Republic and the former Soviet Republic of Azerbaijan's independence under secularist leadership have since accentuated differences between the two regions.

### Soviet Central Asia

In Central Asia, efforts to create a unified Turkic Republic and a Communist Party of the Turkic peoples had been squelched by 1920. The political geography was updated, with a Turkistan Autonomous Soviet Socialist Republic (TASSR, 1918) and a separate Kazakh entity, initially referred to as the Kirgiz Autonomous Soviet Socialist Republic (1920), replacing the old governorates general,[36] and with Soviet Republics of Bukhara and Khorezmia, which replaced the old protectorates of Bukhara and Khiva in 1920. Leaders of the Muslim population began to rally to the Communist Party, which in the interests of "nativization" (*korenizatsiya*) overlooked the issue of their social class. Many of these people were Jadids, for whom national liberation, not communism, was the goal. Until 1924, Moscow policy encouraged them to believe that they could reach that goal as national Communists.

However, not all Central Asian Muslims who rallied to the Communists were intellectuals. For example, among the Kazakhs, who had been much battered in the civil war preceding the establishment of Bolshevik control, the surviving clans, villages, and *auls* (migratory groups) reconstituted themselves as soviets and tried to carry on as before.[37] For want of better alternatives, early Soviet authority might be represented on the steppes by Kazakh "white-beards" (*aksakal*), who were illiterate and had never heard of Marxism. Decades later, the party had still failed to undermine indigenous religious and clan authority. Although some other Turkic nationalities emerged through processes of detribalization, the modern Kazakhs emerged instead through expansion and adaptation, under the weight of Soviet power, of structural forms evolved out of their historical nomadic micropolitics.

While the Bolsheviks at first seemed undecided about whether Turkistan should become one unit or be subdivided and would listen for a time to proposals like those of Zeki Velidi (Togan) for a single Turkic republic, by 1924 Moscow had decided on a national delimitation of Turkistan. With the demarcation of 1924, the five republics of Central Asia emerged, although some were only in preliminary form. The Turkmen and Uzbek SSRs were set up at this point; the Kirgiz (in today's terms, Kazakh) ASSR had the members of that ethnic group living in the former Turkestan ASSR added to it; the Kara-Kyrgyz (now Kyrgyz) and Tajiks initially received only autonomous regions. Whereas Central Asia had historically been characterized by two literary languages—Chaghatay Turkic and Persian—and extensive bilingualism, from the 1920s on there were four Turkic states and one Iranian (Tajik) one, each with a "national" cultural policy intended to elaborate its language into a distinct literary language.

The Turkic and Tajik Muslims of Central Asia thus found themselves caught up in "the most extravagant celebration of ethnic diversity that any state had ever financed"—a dictatorship of the proletariat that was also a Tower of Babel centrally directed from Moscow.[38] Among the Turkic peoples, partisans of linguistic differentiation had appeared before the revolution. In that sense, the Soviets did not create but magnified these divisions. To some observers, the survival of these republics as independent nations in the post-Soviet era offers further proof that the national distinctions were meaningful to the people concerned. To other observers, this survival resembles the "hardening" of colonies into nations, a phenomenon observed globally after decolonization. As in Azerbaijan, their preindependence leaders—recapitulating the decolonization experiences of Asia and Africa—showed a remarkable instinct to cling to power after independence and a deeply vested interest in holding "their" territories together, despite the fact that they were no more ethnically or linguistically homogeneous than most nations.

Perhaps even more than in the nineteenth century, then, Central Asians encountered modernity in a Russian—now a Soviet—guise. Between 1924 and 1936 each of the five Central Asian republics became one of the USSR's fifteen union republics. After the adoption of the USSR's 1936 "Stalin" and 1977 "Brezhnev" constitutions, each republic also received its own constitution, which guaranteed nominal sovereignty and the right to secede but also asserted the primacy of the Soviet government. Moreover, for each republic, the Communist Party of the Soviet Union was the "pivot," and one of its "advance platoons" was the Communist Party of that republic.[39] As in Azerbaijan, high positions in the republican governments usually went to Uzbeks, Tajiks, and so on. However, "number one" always had a "number two," usually a Russian or Ukrainian. An elaborate doubling of institutions further reinforced Soviet control. Every republic had its Communist Party, Academy of Sciences, or Union of Writers; at the top, each of these had its all-union counterpart for the entire USSR.

Central Asia's advance into the modern world in the 1920s and 1930s proved considerable and paralleled that of the Turkish Republic in some ways; yet Soviet rule also entailed terrible costs and constraints. Literacy advanced rapidly among the school-age population, as well as among adults who benefited from literacy campaigns. Education was expanded along the Soviet model, from compulsory elementary schools to universities. In an age of strongman leaders and personality cults, all students learned that the universal genius, Lenin, was their benefactor. The volume of publication, limited before 1924, expanded rapidly in a "linguistic-cultural revolution" that replaced Persian with Tajik and Chaghatay Turkic with Uzbek, Kazakh, Kyrgyz, Turkmen, and Karakalpak.[40]

Socioeconomic transformations accompanied those in politics and culture. Islamic religious endowments (*evkaf*), which were extensive and had
historically played a major role in Central Asian society, were confiscated.
Only a few mosques and medreses were allowed to remain open. Here, too,
1927 witnessed the "attack" (*hujum*) on Islamic norms in veiling and gender
relations.[41] The first Five-Year Plan followed: industry and natural resources
were nationalized, and agriculture was collectivized, whatever the cost. In
Kazakhstan, where Stalin intended collectivization to end nomadism and
the old social order, the number of Kazakh households fell by over half in
the 1930s. The destruction of the Kazakh herd was even greater.[42] Although
"nativization" replaced the tsarist separation of Russians and "natives" with
a theoretical equality, permitting considerable upward mobility, Soviet policy
maintained the primacy of the Russian "Big Brother"—a potent image in
Turko-Islamic thinking about hierarchies of gender and age. By such means,
twentieth-century mass mobilization came to Central Asia in highly controlled forms.

Opening the age of the mass society in the quantitative sense as well,
the early Soviet decades were also when the twentieth-century demographic
explosion in Central Asia began. Starting about the same time as in other
developing regions, this increase was at least partly the result of tsarist policy,
which had established law and order in place of endemic warfare, and later
Soviet improvements in public health. Although the collectivization drive
set back population growth seriously, the population of the region nonetheless grew from 14 million in 1926 to 49 million in 1989. In-migration
from Russia and Ukraine accounted for part of the increase, especially in
Kazakhstan and in major cities like Tashkent. Primarily, however, the increase resulted from high birthrates among Muslims.

As throughout the Soviet world, modernizing achievements came at a
price that proved unjustifiable and unsustainable past a certain point. In a
supposedly classless society, the Communists' total power created a new
privileged class of bureaucrats, whose main interest was to perpetuate their
position. As long as the Soviet system lasted, it limited Central Asia's engagement with modernity in other ways as well. In the Soviet distinction
between "international" in the sense of relations with non-Soviet states
(*mezhdunarodnyi*) and relations among the peoples of the Soviet Union
(*internatsionalnyi*), Central Asians' experience of the wider world was limited to the latter. The long-term goal of this experience, moreover, was
supposed to be a reduction of difference into the Russified identity of the
idealized "soviet man" (*sovetskiy chelovek* in Russian, *sovet kishisi* in Uzbek).[43]
Heirs to literary traditions centuries older than the Russians', the peoples of
Central Asia were to accept without criticism the Russian people and cul-

ture as models for emulation. Russian was the principal official language for each republic and the "international" language. Russian place names replaced some of the indigenous ones in Central Asia; the script was changed from Arabic to Latin to Cyrillic, and undigested Russian words invaded the languages. After many of the region's modern writers disappeared in the purges, their names could not even be mentioned.

During World War II, Central Asia was far from the front lines. Yet roughly 40 percent of both the population and the grain-producing land of the Soviet Union had fallen to the Germans by 1941, creating pressures everywhere. Demands on Central Asian agriculture increased markedly at a time when hundreds of thousands of the region's able-bodied men had been mobilized to fight, when Moscow could not provide materiel or assistance to the region's collective farms at accustomed levels, when large numbers of evacuees poured in from other regions, and when indigenous women, old men, and boys had to try to maintain production. After 1941, agricultural production fell and did not recover for a decade.[44]

In the post-Stalin period, even as the Soviet Union postured as defender of the former colonial peoples of the Third World, its colonial-style economic exploitation of Central Asia assumed devastatingly unsustainable forms. In Uzbekistan, Turkmenistan, Tajikistan, and parts of Kazakhstan, monoculture in cotton—"white gold" (*ok oltin* in Uzbek)—was pushed to unsustainable limits, with overuse of chemical fertilizers and pesticides, expansion of irrigation beyond the capacity of the natural water sources, and substitution of cheap local labor, including that of schoolchildren, for mechanization. Before the war, in Kazakhstan and Kyrgyzstan, forced sedentarization of nomads and collectivization of their herds had provoked resistance and repression. The resulting loss of life had reduced the Kazakhs by the late 1930s to less than a third of the population in their own republic. This depopulation invited Slavic settlers and helped prepare the way for the misbegotten "virgin lands" campaign of the Nikita Khrushchev era. Predictably, the attempt to farm semiarid lands better suited to pastoral nomadism led to erosion and desertification. Soviet disregard for the environment did not stop there. Semipalatinsk in Kazakhstan was used as the site for 468 Soviet nuclear tests in four decades, and toxic wastes were dumped in the region. The indigenous Communist elites betrayed their peoples' interests to keep the favor of their Soviet bosses.

Like their Azerbaijani cousins, the peoples of Central Asia had had plenty of opportunity to learn the importance of conformity in the 1920s and 1930s, when surviving Jadids and political leaders of the pre-1924 national Communist phase were liquidated.[45] Soviet nationality policy meant, however, that such people were usually replaced by members of their own nationality.

By the post-Stalin period, growing numbers of Central Asians had profited from the free education of the Soviet era and had entered the professions and academia. They had a fine sense of their limits and possibilities amid the contradictions of cultural policies that criminalized "bourgeois nationalism" in the name of classless Soviet "internationalism," yet obsessively assigned every Soviet citizen a "nationality" and promoted education and publication in the languages of the various republics.[46]

The Kyrgyz writer Chingiz Aitmatov (b. 1928) memorably exemplifies such intellectuals. Son of a party member purged in 1938, he was protected by his clan until he could make his way into the Soviet educational system and become a writer. His novel *The White Ship* (1970; *Belyi Parokhod* in Russian, *Ak Keme* in Kyrgyz) portrays the marginal existence of an abandoned boy and his grandfather, still dependent on the remains of the old social structures and beliefs. They are surrounded by petty people whose only thought is to wrest whatever they can from their immediate situation. These people cut and sell the ancient trees in the forest they are supposed to guard. They kill and eat the Horned Mother Deer, the mythical ancestor of their clan and bringer of fertility and plenty, when she unexpectedly reappears there after a long absence. With great pathos, the story evokes surviving elements of traditional Kyrgyz culture and social norms and their tragic corruption by contemporary power relations. Soviet critics required Aitmatov to change the tragic ending of his story to realign it with "life-affirming" socialist realism.[47] The original version remains precisely accurate for both the Soviet and post-Soviet periods.

The corruption portrayed in Aitmatov's *White Ship* ultimately became a major factor in the demise of Soviet rule. After Mikhail Gorbachev came to power in Moscow (1985), his policies of "openness" and "restructuring" helped disclose that the leaders on whom Moscow relied to control Inner Asia were a major part of what needed to be "restructured," and that the process could not be carried out without major, unpredictable consequences. Such leaders were the Soviet equivalent of a common colonial phenomenon: local elites who create a privileged niche for themselves by collaborating with the outside power to dominate and despoil their country. However, such problems were larger in scale in Central Asia than elsewhere in the Soviet Union, partly because the Soviet government had committed even graver faults there than elsewhere through predatory exploitation of the region and disregard for the safety and well-being of its populace.

Moscow's men in Central Asia included Sharaf Rashidov, who headed the Uzbek Communist Party from 1959 to 1983. Put in place partly as a matter of "nativization," leaders like Rashidov knew how to give Moscow exactly what it wanted—more cotton than demanded, some of which existed only on paper—without regard to environmental or public-health costs. While at it, Rashidov lined his pockets and those of his cronies, including strategically coopted Russians, as well as Uzbeks. Consequently, many Uzbeks still see him as a hero.

Another showplace of "international" cooperation was Kazakhstan. Although Kazakhs had lost majority status in the population there, Dinmukhamed Kunaev presided as party first secretary from 1964 to 1986. He, too, built a large network of people who owed their power only to him and who in most cases were, not merely Kazakhs, but also members of the Greater Horde, just like Kunaev. Socialism was supposed to have swept away such "remnants of feudalism" long ago. But the micropolitics of family, clan, and clientage had renewed itself inside the macropolitics of the Soviet neo-empire that launched Kazakhstan into modernity by using it, among other things, as a nuclear test site and toxic waste dump. Independence, if anything, enlarged the scale for this kind of politics. Rising to party first secretary in 1989 and president since 1991, Nursultan Nazarbayev created an even grander network of family, clan, and clients, vastly enriched by the new economics of privatization and the inducements that foreign firms provide to get oil and mineral concessions.[48]

By the 1980s, Gorbachev's efforts to reinvigorate the idea of a "single culture of the Soviet people, socialist in content, diverse in its national forms, internationalist in spirit" faltered against the fact that nationalism had acquired meaningful content to Soviet citizens in a way that socialist internationalism had not.[49] For seventy years, the carrot of Soviet-style "internationalism" and the stick of Soviet repression had squelched demands for independence while promoting nationalism in other ways. This combination had prevented the breakup of the multinational empire, which otherwise would probably have collapsed after World War I, along with Austria-Hungary and the Ottoman Empire. With repression now eased, "openness" and "restructuring" were about to launch the Soviet Union, too, into a new world of identity politics. Moscow found itself faced with the choice between "nativized" elites, who were corrupt but loyal to Soviet "internationalism," and alternative leaders in the republics, who were nationalists and not loyal to the Soviet Union. Moscow's efforts to purge discredited officials emboldened alternative leadership candidates to accuse Russia of colonial domination and of destroying the environment and people's health.

By 1990, events in the small Baltic republics—Latvia, Lithuania, and Estonia—had begun to set the pace for change elsewhere in the Soviet Union. In the five Central Asian republics, preparatory steps had begun in 1989–90, when each republic's legislature had declared its language the official one. In 1990, Turkmenistan, Tajikistan, and Kazakhstan also proclaimed their sovereignty. In March 1991, when a referendum was held on whether to preserve the Soviet Union, all five Central Asian republics overwhelmingly voted to preserve it. If this seems paradoxical, it follows from the fact that large numbers of people who owed their positions to the Soviet Union and Soviet nationality policy were still in leadership positions and did not hesitate to use government power to influence the vote. Kazakhstan had added reasons: a 3,000-mile border with Russia, a substantial Russian population in its northern districts, and an economy highly integrated with that of Russia.[50] What decided the issue, however, was the Moscow coup of 19 August 1991, which toppled Gorbachev and brought Boris Yeltsin to power. All five Central Asian republics had declared their independence by the end of 1991.

The Soviet republics of Central Asia were the last to declare their independence. All of them also joined the post-Soviet Commonwealth of Independent States (CIS). Prominent Communists continue to fill the bureaucracy and the parliaments (not all the political parties even changed their names). Mistreatment of those who attempt to form opposition parties persists. Personality cults at times have reached pathological extremes, notably in Turkmenistan, where President Saparmurad Niyazov assumed a new name to express his greatness—Türkmenbashy, "chief of the Türkmens." With this, he likened himself to the first president of the Turkish Republic, Mustafa Kemal. The latter, however, had no surname at all until a new law required Turks to adopt them, and he also had achievements to warrant calling him "father Turk" (Atatürk).[51] After its independence, Tajikistan, with a much weaker sense of national cohesion than the Turkic republics, sank into civil war. As a result, when Islamists with aid from Afghanistan seemed about to prevail in 1992, the Tajik Communist Party came back to power as the most experienced option and called in CIS troops, most of them Russian, to keep order and police the border with Afghanistan, as they had when it was the southern border of the Soviet Union.[52]

Authoritarianism has thus survived in Central Asia, although the regimes no longer have to obey Moscow. Communism and atheism are gone, and recycled Communists do have to change in order to lead in new circumstances. Kazakh President Nursultan Nazarbayev, a former Communist functionary who until recently had still opposed doing anything to antagonize the Russians, summed things up in 1994: "The world has changed. People are seeking their identities."[53] Nor was significant change limited to identity politics. Between 1992 and 1996, all the republics adopted new constitutions that guaranteed human rights and political freedoms. Such standards set goals for the future, perhaps; they certainly did not govern present realities. Uzbeks searching for their identities soon discovered that the government had taken charge of the search, promoting a new nationalism based on the Uzbeks' "golden heritage" (*oltin meros*), with Temür as its foremost hero, and recycling Soviet-era systems to maintain state control over Islam and keep religion depoliticized.[54] In economics, too, the change from central control by Moscow to a locally controlled market economy occurred in form, even if significant economic improvement also remained a goal for the future. International relations have been another arena of major change, as the Central Asian republics have begun to conduct their own foreign relations, join international bodies like the United Nations, and set up diplomatic relations with numerous countries, including Turkey, Iran, the Arab countries, and Israel. Relations with Russia remain especially important because so much of the new republics' intellectual and governmental life is Russian-derived, and Russian continues to serve as a common language. The sudden emergence of a number of Turkic states, however, creates possibilities that could not have been imagined for over a century. For the Turkish Republic, the change—no longer being the only Turkish nation in the world—has been exhilarating. A number of Turkic summits have occurred, business ventures have been launched; and young Central Asians have been brought to Turkey to study in Turkish universities. Uzbekistan, Turkmenistan, and Azerbaijan have all adopted the Latin alphabet, although with differences from the model used in Turkey.

Economic interests in many ways reinforce the diplomatic ones. Like Azerbaijan, the region has rich reserves of oil and natural gas, which were comparatively little developed in the tsarist and Soviet periods. Kazakhstan—by far the largest of the Turkic republics, two-thirds the size of the United States—has an exceptionally rich endowment in oil and minerals. Major oil companies have been eager to gain access to them, and complex negotiations have ensued over how best to build international pipelines to bring Central Asia's oil and gas to ports from which they could be shipped. As of December 2001, U.S. oil companies were talking of investing $200 billion in oil and gas production in the Caspian basin over five to ten years, and competing pipeline proposals for routes through Turkey, Iran, China, Russia, and eastern Europe—a range of choices with dizzying political implications—were under discussion.[55] In addition to its oil and mineral resources, the region also has an important agricultural economy and a degree of industrial development far beyond that of most "postcolonial" lands. In an era of increasing economic integration around the world, economic cooperation among the Central Asian states has been another concern, one sign of this being the economic union formed among Uzbekistan, Kazakhstan, and Kyrgyzstan in 1994. The most serious socioeconomic problems of the region

are those that combine the demographics of the mass society with the ecological impacts of Soviet technology and development policy. As a result,
the peoples of Central Asia face all the problems of an abused, overburdened
ecosystem—including a badly shrunken and polluted Aral Sea, whose tributary rivers no longer reach it because of excessive irrigation in the republics
through which they pass—and a population that has yet to emerge from the
twentieth-century population explosion, which has begun to abate in other
developing countries.[56]

### Xinjiang

China's 1911 revolution made Xinjiang a province of the Chinese Republic. From 1912 until 1943, Xinjiang had three Chinese governors, whose
relatively long tenures were marked by problems arising from Muslim separatism and from the province's greater proximity to the Soviet Union than
to China proper. Nearly independent at times from China but dependent
on the Soviets, Governor Yang Zengxin (Yang Tseng-hsin, 1912–28) nonetheless managed to avert the fate of Mongolia, which became a virtual protectorate of the USSR in 1924. He could not avert the growth of Muslim
Turkic nationalism, however. Influenced by Jadidist intellectuals further west,
the Uyghurs founded new schools, brought in Uzbek and Tatar teachers,
founded newspapers, and sent thousands of students for higher education in
Soviet Central Asia. Searching for a common identity, the cultural elite
revived the long-extinct name of Uyghur and set to work to reformulate a
sense of identity.[57] In a "First Revolution" in 1933, Uyghurs under Khoja
Niyaz at Kashgar rebelled, demanding independence or autonomy. Governor Sheng Shicai (Sheng Shih-ts'ai, 1933–43) quelled this "revolution" but
permitted Uyghur language and culture to flourish, at least until 1941. Then,
expecting a German defeat of the USSR, he switched from pro-Soviet to
pro-German, patched up his relations with the Chinese Nationalist government, and began to repress non-Chinese minorities. In a "Second Revolution" of 1944, both the Uyghurs and the Kazakhs of Xinjiang's Ili region
declared autonomy at Kulja. The Chinese Nationalists never fully suppressed
this uprising, and coalition governments headed by Muslims were formed
under Masud Sabri in 1947 and Burhan Shahidi in 1948.

China did not fully regain control until the Communists defeated the
Nationalists in China's Civil War, setting up a Provisional People's Government in Urumchi (December 1949). The subsequent reorganization resembled the Soviet one of the 1920s in recognizing local ethnic difference
while maintaining central control. The entire region became the Xinjiang
Uyghur Autonomous Region, which contained autonomous districts for

both the Kazakhs at Ili and the Kyrgyz at Artush. In Soviet style, members of the local population nominally held the highest positions, with Chinese as doubles. Uyghur intellectuals were strictly controlled.[58] Thereafter, much as Moscow did, the Beijing government allowed the local population personal equality and cultural self-expression. However, the script used for writing Uyghur was officially changed from Arabic to Cyrillic in 1956, to Latin in 1960, and back to a modified Arabic script in 1978, with predictable consequences for literacy. The government also imposed Marxist economics and collectivization and denied democratic freedoms. When Mao Zedong's efforts to revolutionize China reached their most extreme pitch in the Cultural Revolution (1966–76), the people of Xinjiang lived their equivalent of the Soviet terror of the 1930s, and organized Islam was placed under restrictions comparable to Soviet religious restrictions. From 1987 on, Uyghurs also felt the impact of China's population control policy, although the number of children allowed per couple, set at one for Han Chinese, was set at three for rural Uyghur couples and two for urban ones, limits still incompatible with Uyghur kinship norms.

Over time, the Chinese language gained in importance as a medium of communication, much as Russian did across the Soviet border, and bilingualism became essential for the upwardly mobile. The central government also promoted Chinese immigration. The westward extension of the railway in 1962, from China proper to Urumchi, proved especially important in promoting industrial and agricultural growth in Xinjiang, a region important to China for its resources and the geopolitical significance of its borders. As Chinese immigration increased, the Uyghurs (47 percent of the total) no longer formed a majority of the population of Xinjiang by the 1990 census, a situation recalling the Kazakh's pre-1997 loss of majority status in Kazakhstan. Adding the local Kazakh minority to the Uyghurs produced a Turkic-speaking majority (55 percent) for Xinjiang, but the major centers of political or economic power usually had heavy Chinese majorities.[59]

This suggests that Xinjiang will remain under Chinese rule, unlike the former Soviet Turkic republics. Sensing as much at the time, Uyghur peasants joked that the Chinese government used to say, "only socialism could save China," but now said, "only China could save socialism."[60] Indeed, most Uyghurs realized that independence was highly unlikely. The fact that one of the leaders of the student protests on Tienanmen Square in Beijing in May 1989 was an Uyghur, Urkesh Döulat (Wuerkaixi to the Chinese), filled Uyghurs with pride in their "only hero" but also betrayed their ambivalence about the Chinese state. Offered a choice of several labels for self-identification in a survey around 1990, Uyghur merchants, who often have economic ties outside their home region, most often chose a term identifying them as citizens of the People's Republic (*Junggoluk*, a Turkic term derived from the Chinese name for China, Zhongguo), whereas peasants most often chose "Muslim." Only intellectuals preferred the nationalistic choices, "Turk" first and "Uyghur" second.[61]

Throughout the century, Uyghur nationalists, including exiles, never gave up on their cause. As the century ended, Islamic revivalism and Turkic nationalism were both at work, and some Islamic militants from Xinjiang even went to fight with 'Usama bin Ladin in Afghanistan. By then, some Uyghurs feared that Chinese repression of religious activism, widespread but especially severe in Xinjiang, would turn what had been "a small ethnic-based movement into a more volatile religious one."[62] If Uyghur identity still seems mobile and ill defined, one reason is that only since the 1980s has intellectual life become free enough for many Uyghurs to learn about the great figures of their past, like Mahmud al-Kashgari, the eleventh-century author of the vast encyclopedic dictionary of eastern Turkic. Another reason is the historical lack of ethnocultural exclusivism reflected in continuing cultivation of the same kind of bilingual tradition of music and song as in the former Soviet republics.[63]

Throughout the twentieth century, foreign rule conditioned the Inner Asian Turkic peoples' experience of modernity, with often catastrophic impacts on their societies, cultures, and even natural environments. In Xinjiang, foreign rule persists. Today, for the former Soviet republics as well as for Xinjiang, the tightening of global integration—in economic, cultural, technological, and other forms—defines the new reality that surrounds their interaction with modernity and intensifies their determination to assert their distinct identities. In Inner Asia, some have reacted violently against this newly reconfigured encounter with global modernity, such as those who went to fight in Afghanistan or tried to launch movements against the highly secularized, corrupt regimes in their homelands. Others reacted far more peacefully. In a region where the idea lives on that one's social identity depends on knowing one's ancestry to the seventh generation,[64] the people interweave new threads with old in the fabric of their lives. Kin-based micro-politics is far from the only example of this phenomenon.

In the case of the musical culture historically common to both Xinjiang and the former Soviet republics, recent studies show that however much has been lost to the cultural manipulations of the Soviet and Chinese governments and however loudly new music blasts from speakers today, the complex of instrumental and vocal music that makes up the *maqam* music of Central Asia survives and evolves. Its historical Irano-Turkic bilingualism persists, projecting the Turk-Tajik cultural symbiosis into the twenty-first century, as do the historical forms of sociability—wedding feasts (*toy, ash*), circumcision celebrations (*sunnat*), memorial assemblies (*maraka*), and gatherings of private social circles (*gap, majlis*)—where people historically enjoyed this music with food, drink, and conviviality. Members of these societies, scattered in diaspora communities around the world, attempt to recreate these social and cultural forms, finding new followings in "alternative music" circles and contributing to cultural globalization as they do so.[65]

## The Turkish Republic

Emerging miraculously from the wreckage of the Ottoman Empire and achieving victory in its National Struggle, the Turkish Republic stood alone, from its foundation in 1923 until the Soviet collapse in 1991, as the only independent Turkish state. Until the post-1945 collapse of European colonialism, it was one of very few independent, modernizing nations anywhere in Afro-Eurasia. Between 1923 and 1945, Turkey's development invites comparison with that of Japan. If Japan accomplished more economically, the Turks learned from late Ottoman history, made more astute political choices than the Japanese did in the 1930s, and escaped Japan's fate in World War II. Since 1945, the number of developing countries with which Turkey can be compared has increased several-fold. Given Turkey's geography and history, many Turks are more interested in comparing and aligning themselves with Europe. Statistical indicators show, as well, that if Turkey does not fully match the highest European standards in democracy and development, its performance ranks it high among democratizing, developing countries anywhere in the world.

The Young Turk Revolution of 1908 brought to power the combination of late-Ottoman military and civil official elites who dominated Turkish politics until 1950. This revolution established parliamentary government as the norm for the Turkish polity. The Young Turk period also included contested elections, which would not happen again in a sustained way before 1950. In this sense, Turkey's National Struggle (1919–22) was a struggle over the national—as opposed to multinational—character and independence of a state, rather than over the political form of its government. That had already been decided in 1908, both the constitutional sultanate (through 1922) and the presidential republic (from 1923 on) being compatible with the parliamentary, constitutional model of government. From the late Ottoman Empire, the Turkish Republic also inherited many governmental institutions, large amounts of legislation, schools for training civil and military elites, and generations of leaders trained in those schools. From even further back in time, the republic inherited a long tradition of thinking about state authority and statecraft. These ideas came from disparate sources and conflicted at points in ways that the new republic would have to sort out as it took the lead in weaving the new fabric of Turkish modernity.

Chronologically, the history of the Turkish Republic can be analyzed in terms of three successive "republics," differentiated by their constitutions. Some scholars question the significance of this terminology; certainly, other chronological divisions merit consideration. Here the "three republics" periodization serves only as a device to organize discussion.

### The "First" Republic

In describing the National Struggle (*Milli Mücadele*) and the events that followed, the terminology used in Turkey at the time varies but on balance implies that it was more a matter of reform (*inkilap*) than of revolution (*ihtilal*).[66] Later leftists, using the new Turkish, would shift the emphasis by referring to a National Liberation Struggle (*Milli Kurtuluş Savaşı*). Chronologically, the creation of the nation-state occurred in two phases. First the National Struggle (1919–22) and the international recognition of the Turkish Republic by the Treaty of Lausanne (1923) constitute the political, military, and diplomatic phase of creating the new state and securing its independence. Then Turkey's socioeconomic and cultural transformation occurred under the republic's first president, Mustafa Kemal, who acquired the surname Atatürk in 1935 and remained in power from 1923 to 1938. By then, the wars that define the terminal crisis of the Ottoman Empire (1908–23) had ended. Whether by reform or revolution, another phase in the long-term transformation of late Ottoman and Turkish society had begun.

In the 1920s, the Turkish Republic experienced revolutionary changes in its cultural life. Generated from within, not enforced from without, Turkey's republican reforms show enough parallels in form and timing to suggest that analogous visions of modernity drove change here and in the Soviet republics. In comparative perspective, it seems highly exceptional that something as drastic as a cultural revolution could occur in a country that had not first undergone a social revolution. As in the Soviet case, however, "social revolution" is usually understood in terms of a class conflict designed to overthrow the supporters of an old political regime that must also be changed. In the late Ottoman Empire, the lines of sociopolitical conflict had been drawn chiefly in terms of ethnicity, not class. The collapse of the empire had turned most of those ethnic conflicts from domestic into foreign policy issues, reducing their urgency in the process. Its leaders proclaimed Turkey a classless society, and they set themselves up as the elite to mobilize the people for the march toward modernity.

The cultural transformations of the 1920s form climactic events in the foreground of a longer-term cultural revolution with roots in the preceding period. For most Ottomans, cultural change had been a matter of vacillation and dividedness of mind, and preserving the Ottoman Empire had remained the essential task. The empire once gone, secularist-nationalists whose minds were *not* divided came to power and, under the leadership of Mustafa Kemal, set out to change once and for all what had been a multinational, Islamic empire into a modern, secular, Western-oriented republic. The determination to end the "cultural bifurcation" or "cultural dualism" of the late Ottoman period is what made the cultural changes of the 1920s so sharp.[67] As in the Soviet Union or China, total victory in the cultural revolution ultimately proved elusive. Under Turkey's "First Republic," this only began to become apparent. Certainly through 1950, Turkey experienced a unison-voiced mass mobilization. Even after voices suppressed in that process again made themselves audible, Kemalist secularism remained firmly imprinted on some of the most important bastions of power. It also had a wide enough following that secularism remains one of the most influential "belief systems" in the country, and many Turks who are privately religious practice secularism in public.[68]

The socioeconomic and cultural transformations of the 1920s and 1930s depended on the concentration of sufficient power in the central government, a process that had already started before the conclusion of the independence struggle.[69] Victory gave Mustafa Kemal immense prestige and, with that, political influence. Henceforth he was officially Gazi Mustafa Kemal. The historical term for a "warrior for Islam," *ghazi* in Arabic, now designated the victor in the national independence struggle, secularist though he was. He prepared the transition from sultanate to republic carefully, abolishing the office of sultan in 1922 but leaving the otherwise empty title of caliph, declaring the republic on 29 October 1923 and then abolishing the caliphate in 1924. Having a politically heterogeneous Grand National Assembly (*Büyük Millet Meclisi*) to deal with in Ankara, he dissolved it in 1923, personally vetted the candidates for the new election, and reorganized his followers as the People's Party, including all the members of the new assembly and all the former Defense of National Rights societies. The new assembly elected Mustafa Kemal president of the republic, declared Ankara the new capital, and adopted a new constitution in 1924. For more than twenty years, the Turkish Republic would remain a single-party state. Experiments with opposition parties occurred twice (1924–26 and 1930). In both cases, emergencies soon provided occasions to terminate the attempts.

Opposition provided the regime with other occasions to strengthen its hold on power.[70] The transition from Islamic sultanate to Turkish nation-state, and the lack of recognition of Kurdish nationalist aims in the Treaty of Lausanne, had politicized Turkish-Kurdish difference in a way that had not occurred under the Islamic Ottoman Empire. One result was Kurdish rebellion in eastern Anatolia. The fact that the leader of the rebellion of 1925–26 was a Nakşibendi shaykh, Şeyh Said, was not surprising. Sufi orders were the only organizations that crosscut tribal lines in Kurdish society, and religious appeals figured prominently in the revolt. Ankara seized the opportunity to portray the revolt in terms of reactionaries versus progressives. The government responded not only militarily but also by strengthening security legislation and activating "independence tribunals" east and west.

The scope of these security measures expanded greatly in 1926 when a plot to assassinate Mustafa Kemal, discovered in Izmir, became the pretext for the independence tribunals to try the surviving Unionists and other public figures. Many were convicted, and some were executed in what expanded into a purge of prominent figures from the national struggle who had questioned Mustafa Kemal's leadership.[71] The next year, Mustafa Kemal set his personal stamp on these events in an astounding thirty-six-hour speech at the Republican People's Party Congress. Purportedly a history of the past eight years, this was mostly a defense of the purge that had just occurred. Soon officially published in English, French, German, and Turkish, and thereafter the foundational text in the republic's historiography, this speech is the first of many signs of Mustafa Kemal's consciousness of the importance of "history" for determining which versions of the nation's past were to be recorded and for shaping Turkey's future.[72]

No text or act could better exemplify how the long-term transformation in Ottoman and Turkish culture and the near-term process of founding the republic converged in the 1920s. But this was only one sign of republican aspirations to redirect Turkish society and culture. The process began with the dismantling of everything that had made Islam an official part of the Ottoman state and bureaucracy.[73] In 1924, the headship of the Ottoman religious hierarchy, the post of *Şeyhülislam*, was abolished, and Directorates for Religious Affairs and Religious Foundations (*Evkaf*) were set up to bring them under government control. Institutional and legal dualities that had existed since the Tanzimat because of the late Ottoman combination of Islamic and westernizing policies were eliminated. The role of Islamic religious law, already restricted almost totally to family law under the Young Turks, was further restricted with the adoption of the Swiss civil code and Italian penal code in 1926; Islamic religious courts had been abolished in 1924. In education, the dual tracks of secular and religious schools were combined and completely secularized with the Unification of Education Law of March 1924. At the same time, the medreses were closed and replaced by a religious studies faculty (*ilahiyat*) at Istanbul University. These measures resemble the attack (*hujum*) on Islam launched in the Soviet republics in 1927.

The goal was not to separate religion and state but to do something more radical, to subordinate religion to the state. The effort to do so, consequently, did not stop with dismantling the official bastions of Islam that had existed in the Ottoman Empire. In 1925, the most important popular religious movements, the sufi orders (*tarikat*s), were suppressed, a measure that some religious reformers also thought was needed but that had the main effect of driving the orders underground. In the 1930s, there were even efforts to nationalize Islam, for example, by giving the call to prayer in Turkish rather than Arabic.

From the mid-1920s on, the scope of social and cultural reform broadened out in other ways intended to mobilize the populace into active citizenship and bring Turkey into line with modern, European norms. In 1925, Turkish men were told to stop wearing fezes and start wearing European hats. Islamic veiling was never forbidden, but elite women set an example in modern, national dress. The Western calendar and clock were adopted in 1926 (in Ottoman timekeeping, the day began at sunset). Metric weights and measures were adopted in 1931. Beyond clothing, changes in the status of women included the introduction of coeducation in 1927, voting rights in 1934–35, and entry into electoral politics soon after. The war-battered demographics and gender ratios of the early republic magnified the significance of these changes. Starting in 1932, the Republican People's Party also set out to mobilize the common people by creating People's Houses as adult education centers with cultural and sporting activities.[74] The success of these centers was mostly limited to the local elites, but they created a precedent for a more ambitious effort at rural education, the Village Institutes (1937–50).

The most revolutionary cultural measure of all occurred in 1928: the adoption of the Latin alphabet in place of the Arabic alphabet. One impetus may have been that the Soviet Turkic republics had already done this, the Azeris as early as 1922.[75] However, the main motive was to make the Ottoman-Islamic thought world inaccessible to the children of the republic. In addition, although the Arabic letters well represented the sounds of the Arabic and Persian languages, they worked far less well for Turkish. Nationalists demanded excluding Arabic and Persian elements to make the language more purely Turkish, and a slightly modified Latin alphabet worked far better for the new language. The alphabet change was followed in 1932 by the founding of a Turkish Language Society (ultimately known as the *Türk Dil Kurumu*), which was soon taken over by purists intent on replacing Arabic and Persian words with "pure" Turkish words found in the various Turkic dialects and languages, old and new. A historical society, now known as the Turkish Historical Society (*Türk Tarih Kurumu*), had been founded in 1931.

In the intensely nationalistic climate of the 1930s, language and history became the stuff of fantastical theories magnifying the importance of Turks and Turkish in the development of the world's civilizations and languages. By identifying the ancient Anatolian civilization of the Hittites as proto-Turkish, these theories also gave the Turks deeper roots in a country that they had only entered in numbers after the Battle of Manzikert (1071 C.E.). Whatever may be said about the substantive merits of Turkish theorizings of the 1930s, they were another sign of the country's growing synchronization with the modern world. Countries all across the political spectrum produced analogous ideas, sometimes with far more harmful consequences than occurred in Turkey. In other periods, too, ethnic pride movements have played central roles in constructing new identity concepts.

The historical theories of the 1930s were abandoned over time, but the language revolution truly lived up to that name, creating a situation in which the language has never stopped changing, until, not only Ottoman, but even early republican Turkish, is so foreign to students that Atatürk's speeches have to be "translated." In beginning decisively but never fully reaching resolution, the language revolution became a "catastrophic success."[76] As long as each new generation has trouble reading what the last one wrote, it will be difficult to create a national literary culture for future generations to appreciate with pride. Although some had also hoped that the reform would strengthen the mutual intelligibility of Turkish and the Turkic languages of Central Asia, this hope foundered for want of free communication between these linguistic communities before the 1990s.

By the 1930s, the Turkish Republic, like many other countries, was moving in a more authoritarian direction, with its tight integration of party and state. However, the regime's response to the depression of 1929 was far more constructive than has been commonly realized. The republican leadership, which had shown a lack of original economic ideas in the 1920s, showed a new capacity to innovate in the 1930s. The critical innovation was the policy of "statism" (*étatisme* in French, *devletçilik* in Turkish), implemented in 1932. The policy had precedents in the Young Turks' "national economy" policy; it also borrowed from then recent European and U.S. economic policy and perhaps especially from Stalin's first Five-Year Plan. It included centralized planning, five-year development plans, import-substitution industrialization behind high protective barriers, and creation of a public sector in which the state would lead in developing major industries. Unlike the Soviet model, the state took responsibility for production only in key sectors of the economy, leaving others in private hands. Turkish statism led to roughly a doubling of public investment in the 1930s, mostly concentrated in transportation and communication but with increased emphasis on industry and human services from 1936 on. As a share of gross domestic product, manufacturing increased from 8.4 percent in 1927–29 to 13.4 percent in 1937–39. Industrialization was only beginning. Agriculture still accounted for nearly 60 percent of Turkey's economic growth in the 1930s, stimulated partly by state investment in roads and railroads and partly by the distribution of surplus government land for cultivation.[77]

Whatever its shortfalls, the impact of Turkey's statist policy on the populace was far more benign than that of Stalinist economic policy in the same period. The dividends of the Turkish statism policy may also have been political, as well as economic. Among comparable independent developing countries, Turkey weathered the political stresses of the depression years uniquely well. Aside from Japan, with its turn toward militarism, most of the other independent developing countries of the 1930s were in Latin America. The large Latin American countries all had political leaders whose political ideas—roughly, nineteenth-century political liberalism, with its emphasis on constitutional government and individual initiative—were little different from Atatürk's. Like their counterparts in Europe and North America, such men characteristically had no effective response to the 1929 depression or the social distress it created. The result in Argentina and Brazil was a regime crisis that toppled the old leaders and brought populist strongmen to power. Mexico escaped that fate by adopting policies similar to Turkey's only slightly later. Conceivably, Turkey's statist economics helped it not only to respond to the depression but also to avert a regime crisis that could have been fatal to the fledgling republic.

In longer-term perspective, it is also significant that essentially the same policy package known in Turkey as statism was adopted by developing countries around the world, in increasing numbers from the post-1945 decolonization on. The idea of industrializing by producing substitutes for formerly imported products became standard policy all around the developing world until the turn toward privatization and export-led growth in the 1980s. This is not to say that other countries learned these policies directly from Turkey, although nearby countries may have. Rather, the other countries, like Mexico, may have borrowed from the same models. The fact remains that Turkey's vanguard role in inventing this policy provides perhaps the best measure of its exceptional developmental achievements in the interwar period.

It has been worthwhile to emphasize Turkey's experience under Atatürk for several reasons. Although the myth that grew up around him makes it hard to assess his impact accurately, he was extraordinary in many ways. What became the Turkish Republic suffered graver demographic losses than any other belligerent in World War I, a conflict whose cost in lives lowered the quality of postwar leadership in many lands. Rising as a military commander amid such carnage, Mustafa Kemal almost miraculously provided Turkey with charismatic leadership. He also had the vision to use his personal charisma for realistic goals. Setting aside his uniform and regularly appearing in civilian dress as president, he maintained the principle of civilian control of the military, even if the single-party republic did not live up to those ideals fully. If Turkey in the 1930s was less democratic than it had been in the early Young Turk years, it never became as authoritarian as the European dictatorships whose examples confronted it. In contrast to fascist-style militarism or expansionism, one of Atatürk's most universally accepted principles, a major lesson learned from the Ottoman past, was and remains "peace at home and peace abroad." Atatürk eventually formulated his political ideas in terms of six principles, or "arrows of republicanism"—republicanism, nationalism, laicism, statism, populism, and reformism. However, these never became a tightly elaborated, restrictive ideology. Parts of his life and legacy are controversial, and radical Islamists, especially in other countries, vilify him for his secularism. However, the most telling measure of Atatürk's stature is that, of all the strongman leaders of the 1930s, he is the only one anywhere in the world whom a large proportion of his countrymen still revere.

Atatürk's death in 1938 and the outbreak of World War II defined the context for the last phase of single-party politics . Atatürk was succeeded as president by İsmet İnönü (1884–1973), who had served as his lieutenant in the independence struggle and as prime minister from 1925 to 1937.[78] A figure of immense prestige, İnönü presided over the transition to multiparty politics (1939–50) and helped guide the course of Turkish politics for the rest of his long life. Important earlier initiatives continued, notably the Village Institutes, designed to promote literacy and rural development based on local initiative—the early republic's truest experiment in its much-vaunted "populism," in reality an elitist strategy for mobilization from the top.[79] Through 1945, however, the foremost goal—shaped by memories of World War I—was to keep out of the war. In this, Turkey succeeded, declaring war on Germany only at the last minute to qualify as a founding member of the United Nations (UN). Neutrality had its costs, creating pressures that brought an end to single-party rule by the Republican People's Party in 1950.

Neutrality in the war required mobilization to defend Turkey's neutrality if necessary. With the drafting of large numbers of men and requisitioning of farm animals, the gross domestic product (GDP) fell nearly 40 percent during the war. Unwise economic policies, including forced

**Gazi Mustafa Kemal, Hero of the National Struggle, President of the Republic.**
Dating from before the alphabet reform of 1928 and signed in Arabic script "Gazi
M. Kemal," the photograph shows the man who would later become known as
Atatürk in his prime and conveys an idea of the intensity and charisma that magne-
tized contemporaries. From Gazi Mustafa Kemal, *Nutuk* (Ankara: Türk Tayyare
Cemiyeti, 1927), frontispiece; photographer unidentified.

sale of agricultural goods at low prices and a capital levy that discriminated
against minorities, worsened matters. Yet Turkey amassed foreign exchange; and some commercial and agricultural interests profited from
wartime inflation and goods shortages. By 1945, both commercial and
landowning interests had tired of single-party rule and demanded change.
As in the history of Ottoman reform, domestic policy also proved highly
sensitive to international changes. After 1945, the defeat of the Axis, the
triumph of the democratic powers, and Turkey's adhesion to the UN all
pointed toward democratization. When the Soviet Union pressured Turkey

with demands for changes in its eastern border and in the status of the straits flowing past Istanbul from the Aegean to the Black Sea, and when the United States supported Turkey in resisting the Soviets, the combination of domestic and international forces for democratization in Turkey reached critical mass. The most important result was the founding of a new Democrat Party (*Demokrat Parti*), followed by other small parties. The Democrats won the elections of May 1950. At that, single-party rule ended, and multiparty politics resumed for good.[80] After this rare triumph of democratization in the early Cold War years, Turkey confirmed its pro-Western stance by fighting in the Korean War and joining the North Atlantic Treaty Organization (NATO) in 1952.

With Adnan Menderes as prime minister, the Democrat Party ruled Turkey for a decade (1950–60).[81] It did not chart a radically new course. Unfamiliar with multiparty politics, the Democrats reacted tensely to the Republican People's Party opposition, especially the prestigious İnönü. With rapid population growth and faster urbanization, the commercial-agrarian interests that backed the Democrat Party made government more responsive to voters and established closer links between Ankara and the countryside. The Democrats relaxed some secularizing policies. Conservative rural voters liked that; yet the Democrats did not abandon secularism.

Economically, too, the Democrats shifted emphasis more than changed policy. Their policies favored private enterprise, agriculture, and consumers. Although Turkey was officially committed to import-substitution industrialization, some of the most important changes still came in agriculture. Until the late 1950s, land supply still exceeded demand. The İnönü government had used a 1946 land reform law mainly to distribute state land and communal pastures, policies that Menderes continued. Increasingly, however, agricultural growth depended on mechanization, chiefly tractors. Smallholders who could not afford them benefited by making crop-sharing deals with tractor owners. As rural-to-urban migration accelerated, land distribution and mechanization boosted productivity to compensate for the population shift.

Benefiting at first from foreign exchange acquired during World War II and a boom during the Korean War, the Democrats opted for consumer-oriented policies, including liberalization of imports, which sparked inflation. The Democrats remained popular at the polls through 1954. By 1957, however, inflation and Democrat intolerance of opposition had eroded voter support. Menderes's problems worsened when growing foreign debt forced him to accept a World Bank stabilization program in 1958. Inflation hit salaried officials and the military severely. Seeing themselves as guardians of the republic and seeing İnönü—their revered former commander—reviled as head of the opposition party, a group of military commanders overthrew Menderes in a coup on 27 May 1960.

Political scientists regard Turkey's 1960 coup as differing significantly from military coups occurring in many developing countries at the time. Unlike poorly institutionalized postcolonial regimes where military intervention in politics reflects lack of consensus about governmental norms, the Turkish Republic was a strongly consolidated state. Identifying with Atatürk, Turkish officers were well versed in democratic norms—including civilian control of the military—which their experience in NATO reinforced. However, Atatürk also charged the military to defend the republic. When the commanders thought civilian government faltered, they would act to correct its course, as they did in 1960 and twice later.

Although later revisions of the constitution would expand the military high command's autonomy in relation to the government to a point that brings civilian control into question,[82] the 1960 coup makers quickly showed that they did not mean to rule permanently. They banned all political parties but also appointed a group of professors to write a new constitution that introduced checks and balances not found in the 1924 constitution. The 1961 constitution expanded the role of the judiciary, added a second legislative house (the Senate, in addition to the Grand National Assembly), strengthened the presidency, and guaranteed many freedoms, giving autonomy to universities and the media and the right to strike to unions.

## The "Second" Republic

In force until 1980, the 1961 constitution solved some problems but gave rise to others. In the 1960s, demographic growth—especially the youth of much of the population—gave mass political mobilization new meanings. Even faster urbanization transformed the largest cities. If the Ottomans conquered Istanbul in 1453, this time the Turks did, as rural-to-urban migrants began transforming a cosmopolitan former capital into a Turkish supermetropolis. Favorable economic trends made these political problems more bearable. With economic planning entrusted to a State Planning Organization created in 1960, the GDP grew at an annual average rate of 6.4 percent, more than keeping up with population. From 1962 on, Turkish workers also migrated to Germany, and their wage remittances injected hard currency into the economy. Yet Turkey, too, lived through its share of the worldwide youth radicalism of the 1960s, as the unitary political mobilization of the Atatürk years faded into the past.

The two major parties of the period were the Republican People's Party (RPP), repositioned as a "left-of-center" social democratic party, and the Justice

Party (JP), successor of the now-abolished Democrats. The Justice Party under Süleyman Demirel ruled from 1965 until 1971. Turkey's political troubles came not from the centrist parties but from new, extremist groups not committed to the constitution. By 1970, the far Right had divided into a secular ultra-nationalist National Action Party and a religious National Order (later National Salvation) Party. The Left had produced a Confederation of Revolutionary Workers' Unions and a Turkish Workers' Party. Leftist and rightist groups also formed among university students. Rapid social and economic change fueled political extremism, which could be more freely expressed under the 1961 constitution. Violence in the universities, whose new autonomy prevented an effective police response, proved especially frightening.

Mounting violence led the military to intervene again in March 1971. This time, without suspending the constitution or civilian rule, they installed civilian governments and forced them to take their advice. The Workers' Party was abolished, constitutional amendments limited freedoms, and martial law was declared in some provinces. Having tried to correct the course of politics, the army again withdrew from politics in 1973.

The restoration of civilian rule could not compensate, however, for the consequences of the global economic downturn sparked by the OPEC (Organization of Petroleum Exporting Countries) oil price increase of the same year. As a populous developing country that had a weak currency and depended on imports to meet its energy needs, Turkey was in the worst possible position. Developed countries also went into recession, and the consequent drop in remittances from the half-million Turks working in Europe worsened Turkey's plight. In 1978, the surge in Turkey's foreign debt forced it to accept an International Monetary Fund (IMF) stabilization program. OPEC's 1979 oil price increase caused further contraction, and inflation reached double digits.

Extremist activism made Turkey's politics less stable in the 1970s than in the 1960s. A large majority of Turks still voted for one of the large parties, either the center-left RPP or the center-right JP. Governments, however, usually combined one of these with smaller, extreme parties. Such coalitions magnified the small parties' influence, enabling them to demand concessions. Politics polarized, and ministers "colonized" their ministries by filling them with like-minded officials. This practice jeopardized the ability of the police to keep order.

As post-1960s trends in identity politics compounded economic stress, law and order became harder to maintain. In the late 1970s violence broke out along several lines of cleavage: students versus workers, Sunni Muslims versus the Alevi minority, and the military versus the Kurds. Of these, the Alevis were differentiated as followers of Turkey's historical folk Islam; they

posed no separatist threat. Mostly Sunni Muslims, the Kurds were ethnically different as speakers of languages related to Persian; historically living
in southeastern Turkey and adjacent parts of Iran, Iraq, and Syria, they did
pose a separatist threat. Islamic revivalism created tensions throughout Turkish
society, jeopardizing the Alevi minority and angering secularists, notably the
military elite. As order declined, prominent figures began to be assassinated.

## The "Third" Republic

In 1980, the military intervened in politics a third time, more decisively than
in 1971 and with wide support. They mounted security operations to halt
political violence. They kept an economic stabilization program started by
Turgut Özal, head of the State Planning Organization before the coup. With
IMF traits like devaluation, rises in subsidized prices, public sector cuts, and
restrictions on labor, this program had a truly far-reaching goal: to replace
protectionist import-substitution, pursued since Atatürk, with a promarket
orientation. The generals meant to restore democracy, but under a new
constitution crafted to solve problems faced since 1961; they also banned
old parties and many politicians.

The new constitution of 1982 prescribed a strong president who could
appoint the prime minister, dismiss parliament, and declare a state of emergency. It expanded the autonomy and power of the military, giving the
recommendations of the National Security Council priority even over those
of the civilian cabinet.[83] It restored a single-chamber parliament on the
grounds that two chambers were not needed; limited the rights granted in
1961, chiefly by forbidding their use to undermine the constitution; and—
to limit small party influence—denied parliamentary representation to any
party receiving under 10 percent of the vote. Elections resumed with all
new parties in 1983. The winner was neither of two parties the military
preferred but the Motherland Party of Turgut Özal, the technocrat in charge
of the economic program, which had restored growth in per capita GDP
and even achieved double-digit export growth.

Having pioneered import-substitution and public sector expansion in
the 1930s, Turkey became one of the most successful developing countries
in shifting to export-led growth in the 1980s. The new policy had its shortfalls. It widened inequality. It also did little to shrink either the public sector
or inflation. Yet the extent of change became clear from the fact that while
agromineral products had made up more than 90 percent of Turkey's exports
in the early 1960s, by 1990 manufactures accounted for over 75 percent.
Between those dates, too, the value of Turkey's exports had grown thirty
times over, to about $12 billion, and their destinations had become more

diverse. Compared to the countries of the Middle East in the mid-1990s, Turkey was one of the few where per capita incomes were higher than ever before.

Prime Minister Özal dominated Turkish politics through the 1980s and served as president from 1989 until he died in 1993. The significance of those years for Turkey goes far beyond his economic policies. He combined economic liberalism with a pro-Islamic attitude. He facilitated the founding of private radio and television stations, permitting a diversity of perspectives that had not been possible as long as the media were state controlled. Under Özal, educational opportunity expanded vastly. Private universities were founded. Special secondary schools known as Anatolian lycées, which combined mathematics and science with foreign language education, were greatly increased in numbers, for the first time allowing large numbers of Turks from nonelite backgrounds to be educated in an international language. Government lycées for training mosque functionaries, the *imam-hatip* (prayer leader-preacher) schools, also expanded greatly. Many of their students were girls. Although they could not aspire to become mosque functionaries, religious families found the *imam-hatip* schools reassuring, and that greatly increased the number of girls from such families who received at least a secondary education. Özal also permitted greater cultural freedom for the Kurds. Under Özal, Turkey applied for membership in the European Union in 1987. Individuals were also allowed to petition the European Commission on Human Rights. Unlike most other Turkish politicians, Özal was a policymaker with vision. With him, moreover, the children of the segment of society that had been on the receiving end of the early Republican reforms—business oriented, Anatolian rooted, religiously committed, and now largely urbanized—came to power for the first time.[84] No longer peripheralized, such interests would henceforth assume a central role in charting Turkey's future.

In the 1990s, Turkey benefited greatly as the Russian and Soviet threat receded, but Turkish politics faced difficulties of adjustment to changing circumstances, both domestic and international. Disunity and lack of new ideas for the post–Cold War era virtually killed the left half of the political spectrum. That left the field to the Right. However, most politicians lacked interest in anything beyond deal-making, and the ruling coalitions had only short-term, tactical goals.[85]

Amid so much contestation, Turkish voters' choices among the parties shifted, while the ground shifted under everyone's feet—literally so in the 1999 earthquakes. Turkey acquired its first woman prime minister, Tansu Çiller, in 1993. Yet soon after this triumph for secularism, the Islamist party, then known as the Prosperity Party, won 21 percent of the vote in 1995, electing mayors in Istanbul and Ankara. Party leader Necmettin Erbakan and Çiller made a surprising power-sharing deal in 1996: he, Turkey's first Islamist prime minister, and she, its first woman prime minister, would each hold that office for two years in rotation. The Prosperity Party had outshown its rivals in grassroots organizing, largely by women, and in providing effective services where it gained power. Yet Islamists in power made blunders that reignited secularist opposition. Particularly, Erbakan's diplomatic ventures to Iran and Libya exposed the naiveté of his vision of Islamic brotherhood. The military reacted by turning the February 1997 National Security Council meeting into a veiled coup and presenting demands for secularist policies. Erbakan soon resigned; his party was abolished, reappearing next as the Virtue Party. More coalitions followed, often made up of strange political bedfellows. Among other signs of changing times, the Republican People's Party—Atatürk's own—emerged from the 1999 election with less than 10 percent of the vote and for the first time had no representation in the assembly.

No clear trend emerged until the November 2002 elections, which the Justice and Development Party won with 34 percent of the vote. Organizationally, this was the latest reincarnation of the repeatedly abolished Islamist parties. However, the party had new leadership and had repositioned itself, essentially taking up the Özal legacy and proclaiming itself a "conservative democratic" party. A winning strategy, this enabled Justice and Development to form Turkey's first noncoalition government in fifteen years.[86]

All these changes resulted from the interaction of three factors: secularism, Islam, and external relations, particularly with Europe. The triad remarkably resembles the three issues that Ziya Gökalp saw, nearly a century ago, as defining Turkey's place in the world: Turkishness, Islam, and modernity. Issues of many kinds complicated Turkish politics in the 1990s. Scandals, revealing links between top politicians and organized crime, implied that Turkey was not totally free of the mafia-like corruption seen in Central Asia. Military guardianship of secularism came under new scrutiny, as the political weight of religiously committed segments of the middle class grew. The 1999 earthquakes in the Marmara region shook the prestige of state institutions that failed to respond effectively. On a more positive note, the emergence of five new post-Soviet Turkic republics thrilled Turks everywhere. In 1998, after fourteen years of separatist Kurdish rebellion in southeastern Turkey, the government captured Kurdish leader Abdullah Öcalan, tried him, and imprisoned him. Economically, despite slow progress in privatization and inflation control, Turkey's GDP grew an average of 4 to 5 percent a year from 1980 to 1998. At $200 billion, Turkey's 1999 GDP exceeded Russia's.

No barometer of Turkey's fortunes was more sensitive than its relations with the European Union (EU). After Turkey became an associate member in 1963 and applied for membership in 1987, a Turkey-EU Customs Union was approved in 1996. In 1997, when the EU began "enlargement talks," Turkey was left out. Yet in 1999, Turkey was finally invited to become an official candidate. A successful response to this invitation would require far-reaching changes, of which most Turks knew little until the EU issued its "partnership" criteria in November 2000. These required reforms in human rights, cultural freedoms, abolishment of the death penalty, tightened civilian control over the military, and a comprehensive settlement of the Cyprus problem, all within set time frames.

It would be tempting to identify admission to the European Union as another of the great transitions in Turkic history, were it not that EU membership would amount more precisely to one more step in Turkey's transition into modernity. Much of the business and intellectual elite and the center parties seemed ready for this step. Some ultranationalists and other ideologues, and some of the bureaucratic elites, would have trouble with it. Having greatly expanded their powers as guardians of the Atatürk legacy, the military high command would have as much difficulty accepting effective civilian control as the civilian agencies of government would have in making the control effective. By the time the Justice and Development Party won its majority in 2002, its leaders also advocated meeting the EU accession criteria as a way to safeguard democracy and make Turkey freer for people like them. If the European Union could include Germany, with its center-right Christian Democrat Party, why not also Turkey, with its center-right Muslim counterpart, the Justice and Development Party of Prime Minister Recep Tayyıp Erdoğan? Admission to the European Union would fulfill dreams that Ottoman thinkers and statesmen began to dream more than two centuries ago. The fact that a moderate Islamic party has adopted such a position suggests that the radical secularism of the early republic might not be Turkey's only route into modernity after all. Might other Muslim countries also notice this model for balancing the competing claims of national identity, Islam, and modernity in the new era of globalization and identity politics?

## The Turkish Diaspora

For a historically migratory people, new patterns of migration cannot be surprising in the world of space-time compression. Turkey itself, long a country of emigration, has again become a country of immigration, much

**Akmerkez Shopping Center and Towers, Istanbul.** Symbolic of ultramodernity in Istanbul today, Akmerkez offers consumers world-class goods from both international and Turkish firms. Of the towers surmounting the multistoried complex, two house offices, and the tallest tower is residential. Symbolizing Turkey's transition to export-led growth, many such developments display the success of a century of effort to develop modern commerce and industry. Akmerkez is the winner of five international awards, including those for best shopping center in Europe and best in the world. Photo courtesy of Akmerkez.

of it from other parts of the Turkic world and from Muslim populations of the Balkans. Starting in the 1960s, however, a new emigration pattern developed, that of Turkish workers to Europe, especially Germany. Other Turkic countries have joined in this migration to a degree. Data from the 1990s indicate that 11,290 Kazakh nationals and smaller numbers of Azeris, Kazakhs, and Turkmens live in Germany, for example.[87] However, the migration of Turks from Turkey to Europe, especially Germany, has been vastly larger. See table 5.1.

The migration documented in these figures reflects a stage in global reconfiguration since the 1960s. Push factors inside Turkey that helped launch this migration included accelerating urban-to-rural migration. Pull factors were decisive, however: Europe needed workers. In Germany, especially, the sealing of the East-West border by the Berlin Wall (1961) ended the migration from East Germany that had sustained the West German labor market and thus increased the need for workers from other sources.

Among German labor recruitment contracts with eight Mediterranean countries, the contract with Turkey dates exactly from 1961. Expanding and contracting with the recessions of 1966 and 1973, the number of Turkish workers in Germany rose from 6,700 in 1961 to roughly 600,000 in 1973. The Netherlands, Belgium, Switzerland, Austria, France, and Sweden also concluded agreements with Turkey for labor recruitment. In Germany

Table 5.1. Turks in Ten European Countries (in Thousands)

|             | 1973  | 1984    | 1995    | 1998    |
|-------------|-------|---------|---------|---------|
| Germany     | 615.8 | 1,552.3 | 1,965.6 | 2,110.2 |
| France      | 33.8  | 144.8   | 254.0   | 197.7   |
| Netherlands | 30.1  | 154.2   | 252.5   | 102.0   |
| Austria     | 30.5  | 75.0    | 150.0   | na      |
| Belgium     | 14.0  | 63.6    | 90.4    | 70.7    |
| Switzerland | 19.7  | 48.5    | 76.7    | 79.5    |
| Britain     | 2.0   | 28.5    | 65.0    | 63.0    |
| Sweden      | 5.1   | 20.9    | 36.0    | 17.4    |
| Denmark     | 6.3   | 17.2    | 34.7    | 38.1    |
| Norway      | —     | 3.1     | 5.6     | 3.2     |
| TOTAL       | 757.3 | 2,108.1 | 2,930.5 | 2,681.8 |

SOURCE: Talip Küçükcan, *Politics of Ethnicity, Identity and Religion: Turkish Muslims in Britain* (London: Ashgate, 1999), p. 59; SOPEMI, *Trends in International Migration: Continuous Reporting System on Migration* (Paris, 2000), 44, table 1.6.

and Switzerland, the migrants were officially classed as "guest-workers" (*Gastarbeiter*), a concept that assumes temporary employment and rotational replacement. In France, a former colonial power experienced in dealing with Muslims, Turkish migrants were termed *immigrés,* as were the more numerous North Africans.[88]

The end of the global economic expansion of 1945–73 led to a closing of frontiers to Turkish migrant workers. Yet ultimately, this did not reduce the number of Turks in Europe. German workers had insisted from the beginning that guest-workers be integrated into the wage structure so as not to depress wages; employers developed vested interests in retaining workers; and the 1965 law on foreigners' status in Germany, although seeming to exclude permanent settlement, had less drastic effects in application, which was delegated to the local authorities. In the 1970s, some 400,000 Turkish workers did return to Turkey, but others took advantage of the right of family reunion to have their families join them in Germany. As a result, between 1974 and 1988, the number of Turks in Germany nearly doubled, acquiring a normalized sex ratio and a much younger age profile than the German population because of the larger numbers of children per family. By 1987, 21 percent of ethnic Germans were under twenty-one, compared to 42 percent of the Turks in Germany.

By then, the shift in manufacturing toward outsourcing production had made importing workers a thing of the past. The collapse of socialism and German reunification also produced major social impacts.[89] Still, in Germany in 1997, migrants from Turkey numbered over 2 million, about 30 percent of all the foreign population of the country. In all, 3.3 million migrants from Turkey then lived in Europe. Turkish migrants elsewhere included Turkish workers, generally all male and numbering about 250,000 in the early 1990s, employed in Arab countries like Kuwait and Libya, in addition to diasporic communities further afield in the United States, Canada, and Australia.[90] By 2000, some diaspora Turks were second- and third-generation residents of their host countries.

Differences in the policies of the host governments created significant differences in the situations of the Turkish diasporas. For example, few "centralized, representative umbrella organizations" developed among Turks in Germany, in contrast to the situation in Sweden and the Netherlands, of which the latter gives officially recognized minorities representation in parliament.[91] Such differences aside, the situations of Turks in Europe present important commonalities. Many of these cluster around issues of hybridity and marginality among people who are inescapably regarded as "other" in Europe and yet have also changed enough to stick out on return visits to Turkey as *almancı,* roughly "Germanish," so called wherever they live in Europe.

Furthermore, all the forms of difference in contemporary Turkey proliferate in the Turkish diaspora as well—Turks and Kurds, workers and
intellectuals, Islamists and leftists, Sunnis and Alevis. This is especially true
for groups that can operate more openly in Europe than in Turkey. Examples include the Gray Wolves (*Bozkurt*), which originated as the youth
movement of the far-right National Action Party in Turkey, where they
played a significant role in the political violence of the years preceding the
1980 military intervention. The eclecticism with which Turkish migrants'
children combined and discarded badges and emblems in sometimes im-
compatible combinations magnified the visibility of such symbols in Europe.[92]
Equally part of the radical landscape were the militant nationalist supporters
of the Kurdish Workers Party (PKK), which the German government
cracked down on as a terrorist organization. Numbering perhaps only 1,500
followers, Germany's most radical Islamic group was that of Metin Kaplan,
the "caliph of Cologne," who proclaimed an "Islamic-Turkish state in exile." A German court convicted him in 2000 of operating a terrorist organization and having a rival "caliph" murdered. Some of Kaplan's followers
later turned up among the fourteen Turks detained as fighters with Al-Qa'ida
militants in Afghanistan.[93]

Especially since 1980, however, most European Turks' concerns have
less to do with politics in Turkey and more to do with their situation in
Europe. In Germany, recessions in the early 1980s and after German unification in 1991 created new problems, heightened by the rise in violence
against foreigners.[94] One result was a rekindling of Islamic concern, overwhelmingly channeled not into fundamentalist groups, which attracted perhaps 1 percent of Muslims in Germany, but rather into groups focusing on
adaptation to life in Europe. For such groups, the key religious issues in
Germany were gaining recognition for Islam as an established religion, per-
mission for ritual slaughter of animals, religious instruction for Muslim children in German schools, and official support for mosque construction.
Nonreligious demands shared by all groups included voting rights at local
levels and recognition of dual citizenship.

In Germany, the concept of the nation as a community of shared descent and of citizenship as a right of blood (*jus sanguinis*) acquired by descent has greatly impeded the integration of foreigners. Not until the late
1990s was place of birth (*jus solis*) recognized as an entitlement, under limited circumstances, to citizenship for persons not German by descent.[95] Such
restrictions have been keenly sensed by people who are regarded in Germany as foreign and in Turkey as Germanized. Moreover, full assimilation
in Europe, if attainable at all, would require the sacrifice of much that they
value about their own heritage. Such issues are especially hard to escape for

women. Women's observance of Turkish and especially Islamic norms in dress and deportment clashes with European lifestyles. Muslim girls' head scarves are controversial in French schools for the same reason as in Turkey, whose official laicism models that of France. Increasingly, Turks of the second and third generation in Europe discuss such issues in the language of the country where they reside. So do those who debate the writings of influential Turkish Islamic thinkers, such as Ali Bulaç, imaginatively constructing a "postmodern" identity for themselves as Turkish Muslims in Europe.[96] As stated by a specialist on Turkish migrants, "the categories by which Turks in Germany are labeled and perceived are now in flux, unwound and respun in complex ways on the loom of German and European unification."[97]

## Conclusion: The Turks in the Fabric of Modernity

In the nineteenth and twentieth centuries, the Turkic peoples went through the second great transformation in their history: their absorption into an emerging global pattern, identified first with European imperialism and later with global modernity. Their first great transformation, their entry into Islamic civilization a thousand years earlier, had profoundly altered not only their religious beliefs but also their cultures in general. The same happened again in modernity, perhaps in an even more far-reaching way, in that their particular paths into modernity, those of colonial rule or—in the Ottoman case—of defensive modernization in the face of imperialist threats, raised the risk that important aspects of their heritage would be deformed or lost. The Soviet attack on Islam provides the most acute example. Yet the ruling elite of the early Turkish Republic undertook comparable measures to transform its populace. In Turkey, the social forces associated with the broader, deeper current of change, which sought to combine the legacies of the Turks' first and second transformations in an Islamic accommodation with modernity, had to struggle for decades to reassert themselves within the republican framework. Coinciding almost exactly with the span of time that defines the twentieth century, from the Bolshevik Revolution to the collapse of the Soviet Union, the difference in the dates of independence for the Turkish Republic and for its Central Asian cousins is all too long on the scale of a single century. In the longer sweep of history, the differences in the dates of these historical milestones may seem less significant, although the impact of Soviet rule on politics, culture, and the environment will long persist.

# CONCLUSION

# The Turkic Caravan in Retrospect

Images of carpets and caravans have provided insight in these pages into the ways Turks have projected their identity across time and space and have revealed how quickly questions of unity and diversity arise in discussions of Turkic identity. Those questions bring to light the contrast between how much the Turkic peoples have in common linguistically and how diverse they are in other ways. Now that borders have become more open and communications freer, the Turks themselves are discovering this contrast in startling new ways. Among visitors from Turkey encountering the Uyghurs of Xinjiang for the first time, for example, some of the visitors excitedly exclaim: "Here are our roots!" Despite the obvious linguistic affinity, however, others are equally likely to protest: "These people have nothing to do with us." Without missing a beat, one of the naysayers may then turn to tell a friend about a new recording of Tuvan throat singing, surely one of the most atypical art forms for a Turkic people.[1] However counterintuitive it may seem that people who share a family of closely related languages can differ in other respects to the point of not always recognizing a common identity, exceptions can be found to almost any other generalizations about Turks. This paradox derives in large part from the role that migration across Eurasia, and constant interaction with other peoples and cultures along the way, have played in Turkic history. The conclusion of this study therefore invites reflection anew on unity and diversity among Turkic peoples. Although historical in nature, this reflection occurs from the vantage point of a new age in which some see a clash of civilizations while others see an interactive dynamic between localizing and globalizing processes of integration that no single power or ideology can dominate.

The range of the Turks' diversity has narrowed as time has passed, more so under some headings than others. Among axes of differentiation that figure prominently in discussions of Turkic origins, the one that has changed least in the aggregate is diversity of physical type. In genetic makeup, the Turkic peoples have mixed both relevant categories, European and East Asian, from the beginning. Variations across space and time are wide; yet the aggregate picture cannot vary beyond the mixing and remixing of two categories that were already in contact to start with. What is not to be found anywhere is the racial purity that used to appear in pan-Turkist writings. Turkic communities were "polyethnic and political in character" from the beginning.[2] However, although the variety of genetic types available for mixing could not vary beyond a certain range, the bearers of those genes brought different cultures with them; and this fact has greatly heightened Turkic diversity in a way that genetic data alone cannot convey. Specific examples are sometimes startling. Today, the genetic makeup of the Uyghurs mixes European and East Asian almost half and half, and even that of the Yakuts (Sakhas) of Siberia has a small yet measurable European element.[3] The early Kirghiz of the upper Yenisei River, who appear in seventh-century Chinese sources as pale, blond, and green-eyed, later migrated westward, tangled with the Kalmuks, and acquired predominantly Mongoloid features. The Kirghiz became "oriental," in short, by migrating westward.[4] In Anatolia, the early Turkish literary evidence reveals how much intermarriage and conversion contributed to the formation of the modern Turkish people, who are just as much descendants of the non-Muslim, non-Turkish peoples who inhabited the region before the Battle of Manzikert (1071) as of the Turks who migrated in from the east thereafter. Whole books can be and are written about the modern Turks' roots, not in Inner Asia, but in Anatolia. In a much-quoted phrase, "we are both the conquerors and the conquered."[5]

In religion, the variability of pre-Islamic times has yielded to an increasingly uniform Islamization that includes all but small, peripheral groups. In that sense, Islam has became the next most decisive constituent of Turkic identity after language. Prior to Islamization, while the indigenous Inner Asian cults served as the bedrock of their religiosity, Turks adopted any and all of the other religions known in their environment at some point. By comparison, Islam appears as a major unifier. More than that, it made Turks members of an Islamic "international" and endowed them with universal standards in law and ethics rooted in the Abrahamic scriptural tradition. Naturally, the Turks' experience of Islam ranged across the wide spectrum that any great religious tradition offers its adherents. At a time when Sunni Islam itself had not fully developed, the earliest Muslim Turks often understood their new religion in terms of their old. The development of what appears in hindsight as the prevalent Turkic combination of Sunni Islam and the Hanefi school of law occurred only gradually. Until modern times, moreover, the mysticism of the sufi orders remained the preferred channel of religious experience for many, perhaps most Turkic Muslims. In modern times, this form of religiosity came under the kind of challenges that led the early Turkish Republic to close the sufi meeting halls. Since then, the stricter impulses now identified with the Islamic resurgence have gained ground dramatically. Still, religious diversity within Islam remains strong and significant, as, for example, between Sunnis and Alevis in Turkey today or among different factions and traditions of the Nakşibendi sufi order over a region that stretches from the Balkans to Xinjiang.[6] Overwhelmingly, for religiously committed Turks today, their religious life is part of their engagement with modernity, not a way of striking out against it.[7]

Yusuf Akçura (1876–1935), one of the greatest Turkish minds of his time, listed extreme tolerance in religion as one of the traits that the Turks carried with them as they moved across Eurasia. Voluminous evidence supports this observation, pointing out that attitudes toward religious diversity are also a salient issue in discussing the religious commitments of the Turks. For pre-Islamic times, the lack of doctrinal definition or systemic boundedness in the indigenous Inner Asian cults left great latitude for mixing and matching among belief systems. The coexistence of "shamanism" with organized religions continued in Inner and East Asia into modern times, culminating in post-Soviet Siberia in a would-be neoshamanist resurgence among the Sakhas (or Yakuts) and others seeking to reinvent their tradition.[8] Much earlier, in the Mongol Empire, the lack of closure in the traditional cults led to a permissive religious policy by which Mongol rulers aimed to mobilize all the empire's spiritual resources, just as they mobilized all its material resources.

Creating a distinct patterning in the history of Islam among the Turks, something of this attitude persisted after their conversion. Presumably operating in a plague-ravaged environment, the earliest Ottomans certainly took an anything-goes approach to recruiting followers. Later, the Ottoman, Safavid, and Moghul Empires, although necessarily approaching questions of interfaith relations via Islamic legal norms, stretched those norms in the Moghul case to accommodate Hindus. The Ottomans observed the Islamic prescriptions on accommodating Jewish and Christian subjects in general while violating them in detail through the *devşirme*, the levy of Christian boys, who were, however, assimilated into the ruling elite. All of these empires also went beyond the limits of Islamic law in some way, suggesting that something of the pre-Islamic religious eclecticism lingered on. The earliest Safavid shahs advanced heretical claims to near divinity; the Moghul emperor Akbar made up his own syncretic religion. Responding to other traditions of the peoples they ruled, Ottomans and Moghuls both advanced claims to legitimization defined in other than exclusively Islamic terms. Promoting lawmaking on the ruler's authority, the Ottomans perpetuated the Turko-Mongol tradition of dynastic law while also acting to harmonize it with Islamic law. Such points have important implications for the political dimensions of the Turkic tradition. Across time, for all the Turks' warlike potential, their openness about cultures and belief systems has also facilitated the kind of passage across supposed civilizational fault lines that appeared in the collaboration between Bolad Chengxiang and Rashideddin in Ilkhanid Iran, as well as the late Ottoman and republican adaptation to global modernity.

Modes of ecological adaptation, and the socioeocnomic systems that go with them, define another major axis of change for the Turkic peoples. Pastoral nomadism was clearly prevalent among the earliest Turkic societies. Yet even then, in settings like the oasis towns of the Tarim basin, they acquired experience of town life and agriculture. Linguists' efforts to reconstruct proto-Turkic show that even in prehistoric times, aspects of agriculture and crafts like metallurgy were known. Over the centuries, although the list of possible lifestyles—pastoral, agrarian, and urban—has remained basically stable, their relative importance has shifted radically. From the Seljuk through the Mongol periods, urbanization and sedentarization increased. Even where they did not, the Mongol impact on the preexisting tribal structures, and the disruption of old unities by such lengthy migrations as those that brought Turks into Anatolia, started processes of detribalization that had profound implications for the future. On the one hand, there occurred numerous attempts to create neotribal solidarities, as in the earliest phase of Ottoman history. On the other hand, the longer-term trend for some significant Turkic populations—by no means all—pointed toward the loss of tribal identity and the incipient formation of generic identities as Turks or Tatars, identities on which modern efforts at nation building could be based.

By the sixteenth century, the spread of gunpowder weapons and rising levels of political and economic organization across most of Eurasia had essentially eliminated the prossibilities for major state formation on the steppes. Once a large Russian Empire had risen on the other side of the steppe world from China, and once the possibilities for state formation in Inner Asia had been lost to the extent apparent in the early misadventures of the Moghul founder Babur, it was only a question of time until the steppe world would be divided among outside powers. If *mulkgirlik*, the siezing of sovereignty, was the great game in Asia, as Babur thought, then the new master players would be the Chinese and the Russians, and the losers would be the steppe peoples.

The game might have been over for the Turkic peoples had they not already expanded into the Islamic heartlands of the Middle East (also into India in the Timurid-Moghul case), adapting there to new ecological and cultural settings. In a sense, what was lost in Inner Asia was recovered in major historical centers of agrarian civilization, as Turkic dynasts expanded the frontiers of Islamic rule and opened the last great age of indigenous empire building across the vastness of the Ottoman, Safavid, and Moghul realms. The Ottomans not only did that but also, as they projected the Turko-Islamic tradition of state formation into modern times, created the bases for what is now the flagship country of the Turkic world. With the development of a modern managerial and technocratic class, Turkey has also moved beyond being an agrarian country to become a significant industrial producer and exporter. Together with its geographical location, Turkey's adaptation to modernity makes its integration into Europe a topic for active consideration, not just among Turkish intellectuals who have discussed the idea for over two centuries, but also within the European Union.

If Turkic diversity has not changed much in terms of human types, has narrowed in religious terms, and has shifted in terms of ecological adaptation as nomadism has lost ground to agrarian and urban life, political culture is clearly the area of greatest diversity, particularly as forms of political integration have evolved over time. Over the millennia, it has been argued, a progression has occurred from tributary empires like the Xiongnu, which depended on resources extracted from other societies; to trade-tribute empires like the Türk, Uyghur, and Khazar, which added resource extraction from commerce to tribute flows; to dual administration empires like the Seljuks or Mongols, which ruled both nomadic and agrarian peoples. The dual administration empires began to develop the capacity to rule while extracting resources from the populations within their borders, although exaction of tributes from external sources persisted among the early Mongols. The Ottoman Empire and its contemporaries represent another phase, that of direct taxation empires, which generated all their revenues internally, without tribute flows from outside. In that phase, the Turkic tradition of state formation was transformed in contact with the ancient agrarian civilizations of the Middle East and India.[9] For the formation of the modern Turkish people, naturalization into the Mediterranean agrarian world has surely been as decisive as has the genetic and cultural inheritance from the peoples who inhabited those lands in Byzantine and earlier times. In the most recent phase of all, the ideal form for political integration has been the nation-state, although the terms of the Turkic peoples' integration into the modern world complicated realization of that ideal everywhere, introducing the seventy-year gap between independence for Turkey and independence for the Turkic countries of the former Soviet Union.

A tremendous learning process has occurred in the evolution of political forms. The long-term trend has also clearly rewarded the macropolitics of state formation far more than the micropolitics of decentralization, although elements of those have survived or reemerged in significant ways. So great have been the changes that some of what is recorded about the earliest Turkic polities now seems not only antique but even antic. If an early kaghan's accession rites included shamanic details such as nearly strangling him, then asking how many years he would rule, and by some reports later killing him if he outlasted that span, then surely political culture is the realm where things have changed beyond recognition. Vocal about his distaste for the customs and behavior of his Mongol relatives, the Moghul founder Babur was obviously not the last Turkic ruler who was less interested in seeking his roots than in exploring new horizons and opportunities.

The long chronology of dynastic states provides a span across which to measure some of the refinements that replaced the antic with the efficient. The idea of the charismatic ruling lineage and its collective right to sovereignty lasted until the Ottomans' fall in 1922. The idea of contested succession remained a lasting source of crises for Turkic dynasties, into the eighteenth century among the Moghuls. Lateral succession, which permitted brothers to succeed one another by order of birth, provided an alternative but not greater stability unless ways could be found to prevent the rise of collateral dynastic lines. The lessons of not allowing the dynastic lands to be divided, nomad style, had been learned by the Ottomans from early times; Central Asia paid the price for not learning that lesson. For all the states under comparison, elite recruitment was an everlasting problem. For the dynastic states, the essential challenges were to escape dependency on tribal forces that could not be disciplined and to create a retinue that would obey the ruler instead. Historical solutions to this problem range from Xiongnu founder Modun's unique approach to disciplining his retainers, to the problematic use of slave-soldiers in the Islamic world, and—the most successful solution to that problem—the Ottoman slave–military elite. From the Seljuk period on, direct rule over centers of agrarian civilization required also developing a thoroughly institutionalized system of governance, focusing on a highly elaborated imperial household that would serve as the source of honor and preferment and the core around which specialized elites and governmental agencies would grow. Continuing the elaboration of the Islamo-Turkic tradition of state formation into the modern period, the Ottomans modernized their governmental institutions, successfully in many ways, even though their goal of saving the multinational empire was an impossible one. The benefits of late Ottoman defensive modernization were then reaped in the Turkish Republic.

This kind of gallop through the centuries can no more than hint at the rich development of "political science" among Turkic rulers across the centuries. It also risks implying teleology: that the observed outcome was somehow the "goal" of all that went before. To dispel that impression and to add more nuance to the assessment of change over time, it will be worthwhile to discuss a few major themes further: the sacral quality of the state, militarism, and the formation of modern elites and citizens.

Yusuf Akçura's summary of the Turks' customs implicitly underscored the match between their nomadic heritage and their culture: they were attached, he said, not to particular territories, but to their language and culture. From this fact springs a lasting feature of Turkic state formation, a distinctive calculus of the relationship among state, people, and territory. Akçura's warlike nomads formed a political and military, as well as a social and economic, unit when they migrated. They were an armed camp (*ordu*) on the move. They also had to take their political organization with them. The state existed, not at a fixed site, but in the realm of ideas and practices. To withstand the centrifugal dispersion of tribal micropolitics, the state had to be concentrated at a commanding center. Tribal micropolitics implied horizontal dispersion and equality; macropolitical state formation implied vertical stratification and command. The state was defined not by fixed borders but by its center. The ruler further consolidated his legitimacy through control of his dynasty's sacred sites. The idea that the kaghan ruled by heavenly mandate ideally reinforced this state-centrism. His position also had practical requirements: he needed retainers and functionaries loyal to him rather than to the tribes, and he needed great prestige and vast resources so that he could make it worthwhile for tribal leaders to accept, rather than resist, his authority.[10]

Such patterns survived and metamorphosed as the Turks moved across the great thresholds in their history. Islamic political culture, or certainly its Iranian-influenced political philosophical tradition, translated the sacralization of the state into Islamic terms. The Ottoman Empire ruled over diverse peoples and over lands so numerous that they were hard to remember; yet the dynasty's continuity held it all together. The elites of that empire were defined, not by an ethnic identity, but by membership in a cosmopolitan ruling class distinguished by the imprint of Ottoman court culture. In the late Ottoman period, as separatist nationalism began to undermine the empire, responding to that challenge reinforced the transcendence of the state in particular ways. Although the sultans tried to create new, highly trained elites to serve them, the new thought world that these elites discovered in school led them to transfer their loyalty from the person of the sultan to the state as they idealized it. The mismatch between their identity as a cosmopolitan ruling class and the cross-class ethnic solidarity posited by nationalism, as well as the increasingly dubious future of the multinational empire, made it difficult for them to envision how to configure state, ethnicity, and territory in the way that the idea of the nation-state implied. Who were the people? What were the territories? In contrast, pure abstraction made the ideal of the state clear.

By routes such as these, the sacralization of the state survived the great transitions marked by both Islamization and modernity; it persists even today. To most analysts, the state-centrism of Turkish political culture is part of the secularism of modern Turkey, a reason for that secularism, or a sign that there was a protosecularism already present in the Turko-Mongol tradition. One of the more unconventional arguments of this study is that it only looks secular because it is not Islamic. In fact the "semidivinization" of the state has persisted because it has never lost vestiges of the numinous aura that it had in pre-Islamic times. These may not be recognized as such because they survive in a realm of ethnic rather than religious consciousness, but the force with which they persist transcends the natural order of things. The ideal of the state not only has an "aura," but unlike the rulers of Turkic history's charismatic lineages, it is immortal; it has an "afterlife."[11] In the metaphorical carpet of Turkish identity, it has become the most persistent *gül* (flower-like motif) or *damgha* (seal, brand). Like such a carpet motif, this ideal of the state does not exist in just one configuration but has a recognizable range of manifestations.

Many examples can be cited to illustrate the point. The comparison with Anglo-American polities offers an illuminating paradox. In the contemporary United States, for example, most people do not idealize the state or speak reverentially of it; yet they expect the state to treat them well. In Turkey, in contrast, one hears even phrases like *devlet ana* and *devlet baba* ("mother state" and "father state"), but most Turks complain that the government does not treat them very well. Obviously, this is a case where the paradox is between the two polities, not in the relations observed inside either one of them. The weak development of civil society, a subject of obsessive concern in Turkey today, goes with the pattern observed here. Some of the most interesting social-science research on Turkey demonstrates the extent to which Turks have displayed "state-ness," emulated the forms of state institutions, or engaged in state-revering behavior in situations where state initiative was not actively or directly at work. Revelations of scandal in high places do not unsettle this pattern. Certainly not, for as Yusuf Akçura pointed out long ago, the Turks regarded their rulers' powers as limited by law yet also as very extensive. Authoritarian leadership and leadership bound by law cannot easily be kept in equilibrium, as Turko-Mongol history illustrates at many points. In its modern form, this tension appears in the coexistence of military and bureaucratic elites who shifted their loyalty in late Ottoman times from the person of the sultan to their own ideal of the state, on the one hand, and the flood of new legislation issued to carry out the reforms, on the other hand. Now that there are no more sultans, the result has been a tension between one ideal of the state as protected by elite guardians and another ideal of the "law-state" (hukuk devleti; compare German Rechtsstaat) as the alternative to tyranny.[12] Even if, as has been argued, it is not even clear that state and society are separate spheres today, the sacralization of state authority does not rule out controversy over vital constitutional issues.[13]

If it is possible, then, to speak of an "ethnosacralization" of state power, the image of the early Turkic tribe as migratory armed camp raises the question of militarism, which obviously has a powerful role in any such concept. For modern descendants of the mounted archers of the steppes—"sons of Temür," as they were referred to in the Soviet army—it is not surprising that the military has an important place in society or that its power is not only feared but also revered. Yet this has not always been the case to the same degree, and the particular political role that the military has acquired in the Turkish Republic may be more a modern construction than a legacy from the past. The military potential of nomadic steppe societies is obvious. The great periods of conquest under the Mongols, Temür, or the Ottomans are also beyond dispute. Still, this was never all there was to the history of Turkic peoples.

In the history of particular dynasties, militarism was not a constant. Babur's nostalgic reverie on the court of Husayn Baykara, cited at the end of chapter three, evokes the rapid transition of Timur's actual sons away from world conquest toward art patronage. The history of the Ottoman Empire, too, displays major long-term shifts in the prominence of the military. By the sixteenth century the Ottomans were concluding peace treaties with neighboring states. After 1520, the Ottomans avoided wars of religion of the sort that plagued Europe. By the eighteenth century, a "civilianization" of government began to occur, as the members of the scribal service gained in prominence and began to rise to the highest positions. In the nineteenth century, when this scribal service was transformed into a more modern type of civil officialdom, its responsibilities were expanded to include local administration, whereas in early Ottoman times cavalry officers on provincial service had been the nearest equivalent. From the Russo-Ottoman wars of the late eighteenth century on, the Ottoman Empire could not count on being able to defend its interests militarily without outside assistance. Of the existing military institutions, the Janissaries had become an obstacle to military effectiveness. Although persistent efforts were made to modernize the Ottoman military and its officer corps, effective defense also required diplomacy, and that had a great deal to do with making civil officials the dominant figures of the Tanzimat (1839–71). Abdülhamid II subsequently took power back into his own hands and continued modernizing the military, but he also made sure that it was not in a position to endanger his rule.

Military forces and institutions certainly did not dominate Ottoman politics and institutions in the reform era, then, at least not after the abolition of the Janissaries (1826). They became active in opposition politics from 1889 on, but their role in state politics dates from 1908 and after. The military elite's political role today reflects its elaboration of the mission, entrusted to it by Atatürk, as guardian of the constitution; the late-Ottoman shift of elite loyalties, from the person of the sultan to the elites' ideal of the state, obviously underlies this position. This sounds a bit like an army without a master, which was presumably not the case in the time of Modun, Chinggis Khan, Temür, Süleyman the Magnificent, or Atatürk himself, who set the precedent for civilian control of the military in the Turkish Republic. The Turks' tradition in state formation shows a very significant capacity to learn and adapt; and the question of Turkey's admission to the European Union once again defines a crossroads at which the question of the military's role will be reevaluated.

This discussion of political culture, as it approaches modern times, has emphasized the Ottoman Empire and Turkish Republic, as if neglecting the broader vision of earlier chapters. To a great degree, this results from the loss of continuity in state formation in other Turkic lands in the same period. For the post-Soviet Turkic republics, it is too early to draw long-term conclusions. However, there is at least one significant interpretive question that sheds light on broader issues of political culture in the Turkic world. Under Soviet rule, patterns evocative of the old micopolitics of kinship, badly battered as the old society had been by Stalin's purges and collectivization, reappeared within the workings of Soviet nationality policy and became the inner reality of a corrupt politics of clan and "mafia."

A traffic accident at the town of Susurluk in 1996 revealed that Turkey has not completely escaped such problems; however, the aftermath disclosed certain differences. A truck crashed into a car in which four bodies were found, those of a member of parliament, Istanbul's former deputy chief of police, a mafia figure with ultrarightist nationalist ties, and a prostitute with false identity papers.[14] Only the member of parliament survived. He was badly injured and was hospitalized for months, during which his memory of the event changed. A member of the ruling party, he was also a member of a pro-Turkey Kurdish tribe in the southeast, from which several hundred of his relatives came to visit him in the hospital. The episode rightly became a *cause célebre* in Turkey, confirming the cynics' worst suspicions. Those suspicions were completely framed, however, by the conditions of the Turkish Republic.

Surely very few people in Turkey could make knowledgeable comparisons between the Susurluk incident and conditions in the post-Soviet Turkic republics. This was a country where the detribalization of the Turkish population, although still not complete, had been under way for five or six centuries. Ties among kin, old schoolmates, and professional or interest groups are still very important, but efforts to remold the populace as citizens of a modern state also have a long history. The country has never been colonized. As a result, neither elite formation nor the education of the populace has been constrained or limited by the goals of alien rulers. In addition, the organizational structures and the regulatory and procedural apparatus of a modern polity have long been in place in a way that far exceeds the average for postcolonial countries, even if it does not match the standards of the most highly developed nations.

The post-Soviet Turkic republics vary greatly among themselves. One such axis of difference, relevant to this discussion, is the extent to which social structures rooted in the old tribal micropolitics have been replaced by the creation of a generic ethnicity; on this axis, the Tatars and Kazakhs, for example, would occupy significantly different positions. Yet all these peoples share the experience of alien rule, during which their developmental processes were subordinated to tsarist and later Soviet priorities. In the Soviet period, elite formation was governed by the nationality and indigenization policies, and efforts to create the "Soviet man" had to start with people whose level of readiness varied between that of the Baku intelligentsia at one extreme and that of herders on the Kazakh or Kyrgyz steppes at the other. When "clan" and "mafia" resurfaced in the late Soviet and post-Soviet periods in these republics, they did so not as occasional scandals but as the politics of hastily decolonized countries that did not have the historically established and independently developed structures of law and government that Turkey has. In the Turkic republics, as in many other postcolonial countries, whether or not the apparent strength of social structures with origins in a now remote past can really compensate for the weakness of a sense of national community is an open question.

Political culture thus constitutes one variable that displays extremely wide variations, not only across time, but also across space. In addition to the vast evolution in patterns of state formation over time, the contrast between decentralized micropolitics and state-forming macropolitics has presented itself anew in every period. Generalities about the Turks' historical vocation of empire building have to be measured today against the elaboration of the state in Turkey, on the one hand, and the consequences of the Inner Asian Turks' loss—centuries ago—of initiative in state building, on the other hand. Today, the best proof that the Turkic peoples have a vocation for state building would be democracy and development in all their states.

## Weaving the Fabric of Modernity

Like many others of the traditional Turkish arts and crafts, the rug weaving that has often served in these pages as a metaphor for the elaboration of Turkic identity went through a near death and rebirth that more than merely symbolize the impact of the modern world. As recently as the 1960s, a visitor to Turkey was hard put to find a good example of a Turkish rug outside an antique store or museum. Designs had degenerated. Most striking to the eye, the subtle colors of the old natural dyes had been replaced by the harsher tones of the modern chemical dyes that had been invented in Europe in the 1860s and had since swept the world market. The revival in the rug weaver's art since the 1960s results from a complex effort, by experts both Turkish and foreign, to rediscover the secrets of the old natural dyes and revitalize historic design styles. Village dyers and weavers, mostly women, have become intricately tied to the world market; yet they have also gained enlarged possibilities for their creative energies and have accepted major commissions for carpets from European museums and universities. Some have escaped the anonymity of their forebears by accepting invitations to travel to far parts of the world to demonstrate their art. Like the persistence of traditional musical styles, the contemporary revival in carpet making illustrates how "premodern elements" may adapt and survive to "form the pattern of the carpet of modernity" from which they "cannot be brushed away."[15] This is a significant reminder that tradition and modernity interact benignly and constructively even as their clashes attract more attention.

In such ways, space-time compression and the countercurrents of globalism and localism come even to the world of the village. As one sensitive observer has said:

> [W]e cannot think about the globalization of communications and exchange as a linear and successive process; rather it presents itself as an arborescent reality in which the unlimited hybridization of

**Carpet Weaving in Contemporary Turkey.** A heroine in the modern revival of an ancient art, Kıymet Acarçok works at her loom in Örselli, Turkey. Even in black and white, the picture hints at the virtuosic sense of color and pattern expressed in her costume as much as in her carpets. Consisting of a dress (*entari*), pants (*şalvar*, covering the lower part of the dress), possibly a vest (*yelek*), and headscarf (*yemeni*), her ensemble combines pattern contrast with color coordination, as do her rugs. Photo by Charlotte Fiorito, copyrighted by the California Academy of Sciences, 1994.

both worlds continues unrelentingly. The modern world subverts and disintegrates traditional societies. But in the process of doing so, it interiorizes them as well, unknowingly receiving their practical and silent forms of critique; and this presence alters the modern world's manner of being. Combat, conflict, and suffering preside over this blind, unequal, and (today) universal process. . . . What the results of that process will be . . . [is] unknowable and unforeseeable.[16]

Unpredictable and unknowable though its results may be, and conflictive though the process sometimes is, the arborescent penetration of old and new, the "hybridization of both worlds," recalls the metaphorical loom—on which the horizontal fibers represent continuities across space, the vertical fibers represent continuities through time, and the surface designs created by the peaceable act of knotting colored fibers define the patterns that bearers of Turkish culture, wherever they may be, make in the new world of globalization and identity politics.[17]

# NOTES

Preface

    1. Cahen, *Pre-Ottoman Turkey*, xiii.

Introduction

    1. Huntington, *Clash of Civilizations*; B. Lewis, *What Went Wrong?*

    2. Huntington, *Clash of Civilizations*, 184.

    3. For example, see Bentley, *Old World Encounters*.

    4. Juergensmeyer, *Terror in the Mind of God*.

    5. Findley, "Türklük," 15–22.

    6. Ebulgazi Bahadır Han, *Şecere-i Terakime*, 137, 239.

    7. Alstadt, *Azerbaijani Turks*, xix; Kırımlı, *National Movements and National Identity*, 36–45, 124–49.

    8. Fletcher, "Integrative History," 37, 56.

    9. W. B. Denny, *Classical Tradition in Anatolian Carpets*, 18–19, 23; W. B. Denny, "Türkmen Rugs and Early Rug Weaving," 329–37; Glassie, *Turkish Traditional Art Today*, 199–230, 571–775; Sümer, *Oğuzlar (Türkmenler)*, charts following p. 210, listing tribes and showing their brands; thanks to Sumru Belger Krody for the phrase "art knows no borders."

    10. Apt, "Orbit," 14; Times of London, *Times Atlas of the World*, xxviii–ix and plate 5; Taaffe, "Geographic Setting," *CHEIA*, 19–40.

    11. Christian, *History of Russia, Central Asia and Mongolia*, 3–20; DeWeese, *Islamization and Native Religion in the Golden Horde*, 8; Di Cosmo, *Ancient China and Its Enemies*, 13–14.

    12. Golden, *Introduction to the History of the Turkic Peoples*, 40; Golden, *Nomads and Sedentary Societies in Medieval Eurasia*.

    13. Barfield, *Perilous Frontier*, 20.

    14. Ibn Battuta, *Travels of Ibn Battuta*, II, 473; Bulliet, *Camel and the Wheel*, 7–27; Dunn, *Adventures of Ibn Battuta*, 164–66.

15. Barfield, *Perilous Frontier*, 16.

16. Taaffe, "Geographic Setting," *CHEIA*, 30.

17. Crone, *Slaves on Horses*, 19–20; Golden, *Introduction*, 85–86; McChesney, *Central Asia*, 32.

18. Pritsak, *Origin of Rus'*, I, 10–11, quoting Jordanes, "De Origine Actibusque Getarum" ("On the Origins and Deeds of the Goths"), line 25: *Ex hac igitur Scandza insula quasi officina gentium aut certe velut vagina nationum* ("from this island of Scandza, as if from a workshop of peoples or rather a birth canal of nations"). Scandza includes both Scandinavia and the rest of the barbarian lands outside the "known" world.

19. Taaffe, "Geographic Setting," *CHEIA*, 20.

20. J. Tucker, *Silk Road*; Abu-Lughod, *Before European Hegemony*, 140–45; Frye, *Heritage of Central Asia*, 153–57; Foltz, *Religions of the Silk Road*, 1–21.

21. Hütteroth and Höhfeld, *Türkei*, 129–30.

22. Yü, "Hsiung-nu," *CHEIA*, 130.

23. B. Lewis, *Middle East*, 24–25.

24. Golden, *Introduction*, 15, 37; personal communication from Peter Golden, 26 September 1999.

25. For example, Güvenç, *Türk Kimliği*; personal communications from Dru Gladney and Boğaç Ergene, September and December 2003.

26. Boeschoten, "Speakers of Turkic Languages," *TL*, 1–15; Johansen, "History of Turkic," *TL*, 81–84; Roux, *Histoire des Turcs*, 11–35.

27. Róna-Tas, "Reconstruction of Proto-Turkic and the Genetic Question," *TL*, 67–79.

28. Johanson, "Grenzen der Turcia," 57, citing the Oghuz epic *Dede Korkut* as an example.

29. Georgeon, *Aux origines du nationalisme Turc*, 19; Akçuraoğlu, "Osmanlı Saltanatı Müessesatı Tarihine dair bir Tecrübe," 82–96, 117–34. He is more commonly known as Akçura.

30. Johanson, "Grenzen der Turcia," 51–61; Boeschoten, "Speakers of the Turkic Languages," *TL*, 1–15.

31. Khazanov, *After the USSR*, 184–89.

32. Dolkun Kamberi, a Uyghur from the region and an expert on the Tarim "mummies," visibly owes much of his genetic makeup to people like them; Nicholas Wade, "The Palette of Humankind," *NYT*, 24 December 2002, D3: the Uyghur genome is "a blend of European and East Asian"; Novgorodova, "Problèmes de l'Ethnogenèse des Turcs anciens d'après les nouvelles données archéologiques de l'Asie Centrale," *HTPPP*, 13–28; Barber, *Mummies of Ürümchi*.

33. Johanson, "Grenzen der Turcia," 57.

Chapter One

1. Golden, *Introduction to the History of the Turkic Peoples*, 116, 410; Golden, "Turkic Peoples," *TL*, 16–29.

2. Pulleyblank, "Hsiung-nu," *HTPPP*, 52; Golden, *Introduction*, 57–58; Di Cosmo, *Ancient China and Its Enemies*, 163–66.

3. Christian, *History of Russia, Central Asia and Mongolia*, 58–65.

4. Babur, *Baburnama*, 4–6, 60, 67, 152–70, and many other passages; Steve LeVine, "Eden of Apples Is in Kazakhstan," *WSJ*, 3 July 2003, A1, A5.

5. Christian, *History of Russia, Central Asia, and Mongolia*, 107–15.

6. Ibid., 81.

7. Anthony and Brown, "Origins of Horseback Riding," 22–38; Anthony, "Horses and Prehistoric Chronology," 131–33 (evidence of bit-wear first occurs on horse teeth in the Ukraine about 4000 B.C.E., and wheeled vehicles appear about 3500 B.C.E.); Bulliet, *Camel and the Wheel*, 56, 148–49.

8. Christian, *History of Russia, Central Asia and Mongolia*, 85.

9. Frye, *Heritage of Central Asia*, 34.

10. Di Cosmo, *Ancient China and Its Enemies*, 24–30.

11. Frye, *Heritage of Central Asia*, 62; Mair, "Mummies of the Tarim Basin," 28–35; Barber, *Mummies of Ürümchi*.

12. Christian, *History of Russia, Central Asia and Mongolia*, 124–57; Herodotus, *History*, 279–332; Di Cosmo, *Ancient China and Its Enemies*, 13–43.

13. Di Cosmo, *Ancient China and Its Enemies*, chs. 1 and 2.

14. Ibid., 32; Novgorodova, "Problèmes de l'Ethnogenèse des Turcs anciens," *HTPPP*, 13–21.

15. Bunker et al., *Nomadic Art of the Eastern Eurasian Steppes*, 15.

16. Herodotus, *History*, 307.

17. Bunker et al., *Ancient Bronzes of the Eastern Eurasian Steppes*, 8.

18. Barkova, "Pazyryk Fifty Years On," 64–65, 67, 69, 110, with cover showing the complete carpet in color; Kuban, *Batıya Göçün Sanatsal Evreleri*, 48 (the "Gördes knot").

19. A few fragments of knotted carpets from sites in eastern Turkistan do survive from the third to the sixth century C.E.: Erdmann, *Oriental Carpets*, 14.

20. Quoted in Christian, *History of Russia, Central Asia and Mongolia*, 144–45; Frye, *Heritage of Central Asia*, 111–18.

21. Di Cosmo, *Ancient China and Its Enemies*, 89.

22. Frye, *Heritage of Central Asia*, 68–69; Foltz, *Religions of the Silk Road*, 27–30.

23. Frye, *Heritage of Central Asia*, 91, 99–108.

24. Golden, "Imperial Ideology," 41–42, quoting Mahmud al-Kashgari, *Divanü lûgat-it-Türk*, ed. Atalay, 407: "Tatsız Türk bolmas, başsız börk bolmas."

25. Di Cosmo, *Ancient China and Its Enemies*, 127–58; the quotation about "changing our garments" is on p. 135.

26. Pulleyblank, "Hsiung-nu," *HTPPP*, 71–75; Pulleyblank, "Nomads in China and Central Asia in the Post-Han Period," *HTPPP*, 85–89; Klyashtornii, "Les Points Litigieux dans l'Histoire des Turcs Anciens," *HTPPP*, 146–47; Golden, *Introduction*, 57, 59; Di Cosmo, *Ancient China and Its Enemies*, 163–66.

27. Di Cosmo, *Ancient China and Its Enemies*, 178–86.

28. Ibid., 174–75.

29. Bunker et al., *Nomadic Art of the Eastern Eurasian Steppes*, 199.

30. Pulleyblank, "Hsiung-nu," *HTPPP*, 54, on the title *chanyu*, often erroneously rendered as *shanyu* (*shan-yü*); Ögel, *Türk Mitolojisi*, 5.

31. Qian, *Records of the Grand Historian of China*, II, 160–62, emending *shan-yü* to *chanyu*. Sima Qian follows this story immediately with a second episode, in parallel format, in which Modun consults his ministers about how to respond to a mounting series of demands from a neighboring ruler. Only then does Sima Qian describe the organization of Xiongnu power.

32. Ibid., 155.

33. Ibid., 162–63. Modun had more than regained the lands that Chinese general Meng Tian had taken from the Xiongnu.

34. Di Cosmo, *Ancient China and Its Enemies*, 183–90.

35. Ibid., 171–72, mentioning terminological, as well as conceptual, resemblances; Frye, *Heritage of Central Asia*, 44.

36. Barfield, *Perilous Frontier*, 36.

37. Qian, *Records of the Grand Historian of China*, II, 164; Christian, *History of Russia, Central Asia and Mongolia*, 194.

38. Barfield, *Perilous Frontier*, 41–45.

39. Qian, *Records of the Grand Historian of China*, II, 163–64.

40. Di Cosmo, *Ancient China and Its Enemies*, 188–205.

41. Barfield, *Perilous Frontier*, 47–49; Yü, "Hsiung-nu," *CHEIA*, 122.

42. Qian, *Records of the Grand Historian of China*, II, 168, 174.

43. Di Cosmo, *Ancient China and Its Enemies*, 206–52.

44. Christian, *History of Russia, Central Asia and Mongolia*, 198.

45. Barfield, *Perilous Frontier*, 60, 64–65, 78.

46. Golden, *Introduction*, 71; Barfield, *Perilous Frontier*, 86.

47. Golden, *Introduction*, 76.

48. Di Cosmo, "State Formation and Periodization in Inner Asian History," 29–30.

49. Golden, *Introduction*, 2.

50. Yü, "Hsiung-nu," *CHEIA*, 135–38: with the left to the east and the right to the west.

51. Golden, *Introduction*, 86–90; Golden, "Nomads of the Western Eurasian Steppes," *HTPPP*, 282; Denis Sinor, "Hun Period," *CHEIA*, 177, 180, 182.

52. Golden, *Introduction*, 91; Maenchen-Helfen, *World of the Huns*, 125–26.

53. Sinor, "Hun Period," *CHEIA*, 204.

54. Maenchen-Helfen, *World of the Huns*, 376–443, linguistic evidence including Turkic, Iranian, and Germanic elements and some of undetermined origin.

55. Golden, *Introduction*, 86–87.

56. Pulleyblank, "Hsiung-nu," *HTPPP*, 72–75; Pulleyblank, "Nomads in China and Central Asia in the Post-Han Period," *HTPPP*, 85–89 (the Gaoche, "High Carts").

57. Di Cosmo, "State Formation and Periodization," 30.

58. DeWeese, *Islamization and Native Religion*, 275–78; Golden, "Imperial Ideology," 42; Golden, *Introduction*, 117–20; Liu, *Die chinesischen Nachrichten zur Geschichte der Ost-Türken*, I, 5–6; Ögel, *Türk Mitolojisi*, 13–71; Haussig, "Herkunft, Wesen und Schicksal der Hunnen," *HTPPP*, 265–66 (this Türk origin myth may trace back to an earlier one of the Huns).

59. Golden, "Religion Among the Qipçaks of Medieval Eurasia," 188; Scharlipp, "Leben und Kultur der alten Türken," *HTPPP*, 135–36; Klyashtornii, "Les Points Litigieux," *HTPPP*, 163.

60. Allsen, *Culture and Conquest in Mongol Eurasia*, 201–2; Wagner, *Iron and Steel in Ancient China*, 191–99, 267–335; DeWeese, *Islamization and Native Religion*, 235, 275.

61. Klyashtorny, "Royal Clan of the Turks," 445–47; Harmatta, *Prolegomena to the Sources of Pre-Islamic Central Asia* (see Hausigg, "Byzantinische Quellen über Mittelasien in ihrer historischen Aussage," 54–57); Golden, *Introduction*, 115–17.

62. DeWeese, *Islamization and Native Religion*, 276–77; Tekin, *Grammar of Orkhon Turkic*, 261–62 (Kül Tigin inscription: "If the Turkish kagan rules from the Ötükän mountains there will be no trouble in the realm. . . . The place from which the tribes can be [best] controlled is the Ötükän mountains. . . . If you stay at the Ötükän mountains, you will live forever dominating the tribes."), 267 ("You, people of the sacred Ötükän mountains"); from the Tonyukuk inscription, 285 (". . . I led them toward the Ötükän mountains"). Golden, "Imperial Ideology," 48–49; Drompp, "Breaking the Orkhon Tradition," 391, identifies the Ötüken with the "modern Khangay Mountains, from which the Orkhon and Selenga flow," the latter emptying into Lake Baikal.

63. DeWeese, *Islamization and Native Religion*, 275–77; Golden, *Introduction*, 177 (Kırghız myth of descent from the mating of a god and a cow), 235 (origin for the Khazars and Bulghars as recorded in Syriac sources, which describe the Khazars as descended from Khazarîg, one of three brothers, of whom another was named Bulgariôs or Bulgaris).

64. Sinor, "Establishment and Dissolution of the Türk Empire," *CHEIA*, 285–91; Golden, *Introduction*, 120–24; Beckwith, *Tibetan Empire in Central Asia*, 206–208.

65. Golden, "Imperial Ideology," 40–42; Geng, "Die alttürkischen Steppenreiche (552–745)," *HTPPP*, 102–22.

66. Geng, "Die alttürkischen Steppenreiche," 115–16; Frye, *Heritage of Central Asia*, 183–98; Di Cosmo, "State Formation and Periodization," 30–31.

67. Barfield, *Perilous Frontier*, 140.

68. Liu, *Die chinesischen Nachrichten*, I, 465–72.

69. Ibid., I, 137–38, 147.

70. Sinor, "Establishment and Dissolution of the Türk Empire," *CHEIA*, 308.

71. Liu, *Die chinesischen Nachrichten*, I, 392; in some cases, Chinese princes were sent or Turkish princesses were sent in the opposite direction.

72. Ibid., I, 144–57, 194–210, 283–87.

73. Whitfield et al., *Cave Temples of Mogao*, 51–85; Tucker, *Silk Road*.

74. Liu, *Die chinesischen Nachrichten*, I, 283, 467.

75. The quoted passage comes from the Kül Tigin inscription; Tekin, *Grammar of Orkhon Turkic*, 233, 264; Tekin, *Orhon Yazıtları*, 40–41; Sinor, "Establishment and Dissolution of the Türk Empire," *CHEIA*, 310.

76. Golden, *Introduction*, 144, 146, 152–53; Geng, "Die alttürkischen Steppenreiche," *HTPPP*, 104–22; Klyashtornii, "Les Points Litigieux," *HTPPP*, 148–151.

77. Golden, *Introduction*, 71, 146–53 (the origins of the title *kaghan* and its relationship to *kan/qan* or *khan* are unclear); Golden, "Imperial Ideology," 39–73;

Sinor, "Establishment and Disintegration of the Türk Empire," *CHEIA*, 313–16.

78. Tekin, *Grammar of Orkhon Turkic*, 232, 263–64 (Kül Tigin inscription, E 1–3); Tekin, *Orhon Yazıtları*, 38–39; Ögel, "Tuğ," *İA*, Ankara, XII, 1–5.

79. Tekin, *Grammar of Orkhon Turkic*, 250, 258, 285, 294.

80. Barfield, *Perilous Frontier*, 132–33.

81. Frye, *Heritage of Central Asia*, 195–96.

82. Scharlipp, "Leben und Kultur der alten Türken in der Steppe," *HTPPP*, 140–44; Klyashtornii, "Les Points Litigieux," *HTPPP*, 151–60; Golden, "Wolves, Dogs and Qipchaq Religion," 88–93.

83. Wagner, *Iron and Steel in Ancient China*; Klopsteg, *Turkish Archery and the Composite Bow*, xv, 15–32; personal communication from John Guilmartin (September 2003).

84. Scharlipp, "Leben und Kultur der alten Türken in der Steppe," *HTPPP*, 135–40; Klyashtornii, "Les Points Litigieux," *HTPPP*, 163–70.

85. DeWeese, *Islamization and Native Religion*, 27–50; Novgorodova, "Problèmes de l'Ethnogenèse des Turcs Anciens," *HTPPP*, 22–28; Ocak, *Alevî ve Bektaşî İnançlarının İslâm Öncesi Temelleri*, 37–56.

86. Golden, "Imperial Ideology," 48–49; Liu, *Die chinesischen Nachrichten*, I, 458–61.

87. Klyashtornii, "Les Points Litigieux," *HTPPP*, 166–70.

88. Scharlipp, "Leben und Kultur der alten Türken," *HTPPP*, 136–40; Golden, "Religion Among the Qipčaqs," 194–96, 205–7, 211–16; Allsen, *Culture and Conquest*, 203–6.

89. Foltz, *Religions of the Silk Road*, 61–87; Golden, "Religion Among the Qipčaqs," 181–82, 237.

90. Barfield, *Perilous Frontier*, 152–53; Liu, *Die chinesischen Nachrichten*, I, 449–51; Sinor, "Uighur Empire in Mongolia," *CHEIA*, 187–203.

91. Mackerras, *Uighur Empire According to the T'ang Dynastic Histories*, 42–50, 64–65; Hamilton, *Les Ouïghours à l'époque des cinq dynasties*.

92. Barfield, *Perilous Frontier*, 159.

93. Foltz, *Religions of the Silk Roads*, 20, 73–87; Klimkeit, *Gnosis on the Silk Road*; Mackerras, *Uighur Empire*, 9–10.

94. Golden, *Introduction*, 172–76.

95. K. M. Baypakov, "Les Tribus Turques de la Sibérie et de l'Altaï," *HTPPP*, 39–40; Whitfield, *Life Along the Silk Road*, 79–81.

96. Golden, *Introduction*, 155–76, 183–87, 282–85; Drompp, "Breaking the Orkhon Tradition," 390–403.

97. Beckwith, "Impact of the Horse and Silk Trade," 183–198.

98. Zieme, "Die uigurische Königreich von Qočo," *HTPPP*, 205–12; Hamilton, "Le Royaume Ouïgour de Kan-tcheou," *HTPPP*, 205–18.

99. Golden, *Introduction*, 188–94, 205–11; Kafadar, *Between Two Worlds*, 122.

100. Golden, *Introduction*, 233–58.

101. Golden, *Khazar Studies*; Golden, "Imperial Ideology," 60–61; Golden, "Nomads of the Western Eurasian Steppes," *HTPPP*, 291–98.

102. Golden, "Imperial Ideology," 38–39.

103. Ibid., 59.

104. Golden, *Introduction*, 281; Golden, "Religion Among the Qıpčaqs," 186–92; Golden, "Imperial Ideology," 71–72.

105. Bunker et al., *Nomadic Art of the Eastern Eurasian Steppes*, 198, 204, 206–8.

106. Liu, *Die chinesischen Nachrichten*, I, 402–417; Geng, "Die alttürkischen Steppenreiche," *HTPPP*, 105, 107, 108, 111, 113.

107. Quoted in Millward, *Beyond the Pass*, 232.

108. Qian, *Records of the Grand Historian of China*, II, 166.

109. Barfield, *Perilous Frontier*, 54, 99.

110. Liu, *Die chinesischen Nachrichten*, I, 165, 392–93; Sinor, "Uighur Empire of Mongolia," *HTPPP*, 191–93.

111. Bunker et al., *Ancient Bronzes of the Eastern Eurasian Steppes*, 16; Compare Qian, *Records of the Grand Historian of China*, II, 130.

112. Mackerras, *Uighur Empire*, 17, 23, 66–69, 129 n. 16; Sinor, "Uighur Empire of Mongolia," *HTPPP*, 191–92.

113. Whitfield, *Life Along the Silk Road*, 95–112.

Chapter Two

1. Barthold, *Zwölf Vorlesungen über die Geschichte der Türken Mittelasiens*, 86; Kashghari, *Compendium of the Turkic Dialects*, I, 274; see also B. Lewis, *IPMCC*, II, 208.

2. Allsen, *Mongol Imperialism*, 7; Abu-Lughod, *Before European Hegemony*, 32–39, 352–73; Adshead, *Central Asia in World History*, 3–4.

3. Denny, *Classical Tradition in Anatolian Carpets*, 22.

4. Hodgson, *Venture of Islam*, II, 63–69, 131–35, 400–10.

5. Di Cosmo, "State Formation and Periodization," 32–34.

6. F. Denny, *Introduction to Islam*, 69–70.

7. Bulliet, *Islam, the View from the Edge*, 67–179.

8. Hurvitz, "From Scholarly Circles to Mass Movements," 985–1008.

9. Karamustafa, *God's Unruly Friends*.

10. DeWeese, *Islamization and Native Religion*, 51.

11. Ibid., 541–63.

12. Ibid., 323–36.

13. Ibid., 233, 241–43.

14. Ibid., 363–64, 483–88; McChesney, *Central Asia*, 83.

15. Schamiloglu, "Preliminary Remarks on the Role of Disease," 451.

16. DeWeese, *Islamization and Native Religion*, 61, 85–86.

17. Ebulgazi Bahadır Han, *Şecere-i Terâkime*, 122–37, 159–61, 235–39, 247–48; Sümer, *Oğuzlar*, charts following p. 210.

18. The Kur'an also recognizes Sabians, an imprecisely defined third category, alongside Jews and Christians. F. Denny, *Introduction to Islam*, 85–86; B. Lewis, *Jews of Islam*.

19. Idrisi, *Kitab Nuzhat al-Mushtaq fi Ikhtiraq al-Afaq*, 518: the Turks "follow different faiths; they raid (*yaghzuna*) the Muslims; the Muslim Turks, whom Islam

has reached and they have converted, raid them and enslave them (*yaghzunahum wa yasbunahum*), and the alarm goes out to all the Muslims who are beyond the river [the Oxus, or Amu Darya]."

20. Golden, *Introduction to the History of the Turkic Peoples*, 191–94, 211–12.

21. Crone, *Slaves on Horses*, 74–75; Frye, *Heritage of Central Asia*, 195–96.

22. Jahiz, *Life and Works of Jahiz*, 91–95.

23. Nizam al-Mulk, *Book of Government*, 117.

24. Ibid., 103–4, 105–17; Golden, *Introduction*, 216.

25. Crone, *Slaves on Horses*, 79; Golden, *Introduction*, 348–50.

26. Golden, *Introduction*, 217–18; K. M. Bajpakov [Baypakov], "Les Tribus Turques de la Sibérie et de l'Altaï," *HTPPP*, 37; B. Lewis, *IPMCC*, I, 68–69.

27. Golden, "Imperial Ideology," 75.

28. B. Lewis, *Middle East*, 90.

29. Bulliet, *Islam*, 101–2, 122–23, 126–27; Hodgson, *Venture of Islam*, II, 36–39.

30. B. Lewis, *Middle East*, 88.

31. Ibid., 94.

32. Ibid., 148; compare Barthold, *Turkestan Down to the Mongol Invasion*, 347.

33. Hodgson, *Venture of Islam*, II, 63–69.

34. Nizam al-Mulk, *Book of Government*, 32.

35. Kai Ka'us ibn Iskandar, *Mirror for Princes*, 213; Mardin, *Genesis of Young Ottoman Thought*, 95–100; Yusuf Khass Hajib, *Wisdom of Royal Glory*, 107, lines 2057–59; Yusuf Has Hâcib, *Kutadgu Bilig*, I, 222–23.

36. Golden, *Introduction*, 218–19; B. Lewis, *Middle East*, 88–89; Lapidus, *History of Islamic Societies*, 144–52; Ebulgazi, *Şecere*, 272 on Oghuz women rulers.

37. Bonner, *Aristocratic Violence and Holy War*, xiii, 85–92, 107–56; Hütteroth and Höhfeld, *Türkei*, 128–32; B. Lewis, *Middle East*, 95.

38. Cahen, *Pre-Ottoman Turkey*, 37 (noting lack of evidence of *atabegs* among earlier Turks); Lapidus, *History of Islamic Societies*, 144–46.

39. Golden, *Introduction*, 224–25.

40. Cahen, *La Turquie Pré-Ottomane*, 16–21, 26–33.

41. Banarlı, *Resimli Türk Edebiyâtı Târihi*, I, 300–3; Pertev N. Boratav, "Battal," *İA*, II, 344–51.

42. Mélikoff, *La geste de Melik Danişmend*; Bombaci, *Histoire de la littérature turque*; Mas'udi, *Muruj al-Dhahab wa-Ma'adin al-Jawhar*, V, 122–23 (report from a Greek convert about Greek churches, in which ten heroes, including Abdullah al-Battal and various Muslims, Greeks, Paulicians, and Armenians were portrayed); Marius Canard, "al-Battal," *EI2*, I, 1102–3; Irène Melikoff, "Al-Battal," *EI2*, I, 1103–4; M. Canard, "Dhu 'l-Himma or Dhat al-Himma," *EI2*, II, 233–39.

43. *Book of Dede Korkut*, trans. G. Lewis, 9–10.

44. Vryonis, *Decline of Medieval Hellenism in Asia Minor*.

45. *Digenes Akrites*, xxx, xxxii, 3–7, 19–23, 63; *Book of Dede Korkut*, trans. G. Lewis, 86–87, 131–32.

46. Mélikoff, *La geste de Melik Danişmend*, I, 106.

47. Güvenç, *Türk Kimliği*, 48, 121, passim; Balivet, *Romanie byzantine et pays de Rûm turc*, 27–178.

48. Dols, *Black Death in the Middle East*, 46, 51, 58, 62; McNeill, *Plagues and Peoples*, 132–75; Halman, *Yunus Emre and His Mystical Poetry* (see Ilhan Başgöz, "The Human Dimension of Yunus Emre's Transformation," 27).

49. "In those days lived Melik Danişmend. He came to the land of Rum. First, he met Artuhi; they exchanged blows, and he made a Muslim of him; then they went to the land of Rum to open the way of the religion. . . . Artuhi . . . loved a young girl . . . named Efromiya. . . . They abducted her, and the two of them converted her to Islam; she too wrought much on the way of the faith. . . . Finally, [Muhammad] Mustafa gave Efromiya to Artuhi in a dream, what joy!" (Mélikoff, *La Geste de Melik Danişmend*, I, 318–19; II, 132–33). See also Köprülü, *Osmanlı İmparatorluğun Kuruluşu*, 144–71; Köprülü, *Islam in Anatolia After the Turkish Invasion*, 26–31; Mélikoff, *La geste de Melik Danişmend*, I, 129, 164–65.

50. Karamustafa, *God's Unruly Friends*; Enveri, *Le Destan d'Umur Pacha*, 30, 38–42 (a fifteenth-century work recounting events of 1307–48); Lemerle, *L'émirat d'Aydin*; İnalcık, *Middle East and Balkans Under the Ottoman Empire*, 309–41; DeWeese, *Islamization and Native Religion*, 251–55; Kafadar, *Between Two Worlds*, 64.

51. Banarlı, *Resimli Türk Edebiyâtı Târihi*, I, 299: "Bugünden sonra, dîvan ü dergâh ü bargâhda, meclisde ve meydanda Türkçe'den başka dil kullanılmayacaktır"; Golden, *King's Dictionary*, 2; Cahen, *Pre-Ottoman Turkey*, 290; Güvenç, *Türk Kimliği*, 158.

52. Halman, *Yunus Emre and His Mystical Poetry* (see Başgöz, "Human Dimension of Yunus Emre's Transformation," 25, 27–28); Karamustafa, *God's Unruly Friends*, 63, 81–82: Yunus Emre and Taptuk Emre, Jelaleddin Rumi and Shams-i Tabriz.

53. Golden, *Introduction*, 214–16.

54. Yusuf Khass Hajib, *Wisdom of Royal Glory*, 253.

55. Ibid., 218, lines 5484–89; Yusuf Has Hâcib, *Kutadgu Bilig*, I, 545.

56. Yusuf Khass Hajib, *Book of Royal Glory*, 32.

57. Ibid., 258.

58. Golden, *Introduction*, 229; Kashghari, *Compendium of the Turkic Dialects*.

59. Kashghari, *Compendium*, I, 70.

60. Golden, "Imperial Ideology," 72, 76; Golden, *Introduction*, 283–87.

61. Onon, *History and Life of Chinggis Khan*; Bahaeddin Ögel, "Tuğ," *İA*, XII, 2; Adshead, *Central Asia*, 53–59.

62. Allsen, *Culture and Conquest*, 211; Adshead, *Central Asia*, 63, 70–71.

63. McNeill, *Plagues and Peoples*, 132–75; Schamiloglu, "Preliminary Remarks on the Role of Disease," 447–57; Morgan, *Mongols*, 132–35; Dunn, *Adventures of Ibn Battuta*, 269–74.

64. Allsen, *Culture and Conquest*, 17–23, 51–56.

65. Allsen, *Mongol Imperialism*, 21–44; Golden, *King's Dictionary*, 4; Clauson, *Etymological Dictionary of Pre-Thirteenth-Century Turkish*, 152: the Mongols borrowed the originally Turkic word *ulus* to refer to Chinggis Khan's Great Mongol Empire (*Yeke Monggol Ulus*), and subsequently to the four parts into which that was divided after him; thinking more in terms of people than territory, the Mongols later began to use the word for a confederation of peoples; Turkic borrowed back the

word in its acquired Mongol meaning; in modern Turkish, *ulus* means nation, in the social rather than territorial sense.

66. Adshead, *Central Asia*, 60.

67. Togan, *Flexibility and Limitation in Steppe Formations*, 11, 131–36.

68. Ibid., 142; Allsen, *Culture and Conquest*, 19.

69. Togan, *Flexibility and Limitation*, 156; Allsen, *Mongol Imperialism*, 18–20.

70. Zerjal et al., "Genetic Legacy of the Mongols," 717–21; Nicholas Wade, "A Prolific Genghis Khan, It Seems, Helped People the World," *NYT*, 11 February 2003, F3.

71. Allsen, *Mongol Imperialism*, 45–63; Allsen, *Culture and Conquest*, 18.

72. Allsen, *Mongol Imperialism*, 63–76; DeWeese, *Islamization and Native Religion*, 118; Ertürk, *Rethinking Central Asia* (see Togan, "In Search of an Approach to the History of Women in Central Asia," 163–95).

73. Allsen, *Mongol Imperialism*, 77–115; Allsen, *Culture and Conquest*, 63–64, 127–28.

74. Allsen, *Mongol Imperialism*, 116–20, 144–88.

75. Ibid., 189–216.

76. Morgan, *Mongols*, 84.

77. Cited in Allsen, "Mongolian Princes and Their Merchant Partners," 84; Adshead, *Central Asia*, 178–79.

78. Allsen, "Mongolian Princes and Their Merchant Partners," 83–126.

79. Ibid., 112; Allsen, *Culture and Conquest*, 175.

80. Dols, *Black Death*, 49, quoting Pegolotti, *Pratica della Mercatura*, written in Florence between 1335 and 1343.

81. Kessler, *Empires Beyond the Great Wall*, 15 (color picture of a bronze *paizeh* with inscription in the Mongol 'Phags-pa script); Morgan, *Mongols*, 105 (line drawing of a *paizeh* inscribed in Uyghur script).

82. Allsen, *Commodity and Exchange in the Mongol Empire*, 12; Komaroff and Carboni, *Legacy of Genghis Khan*; Pulleyblank, "Tribal Confederations of Uncertain Identity," *HTPPP*, 72, 92.

83. Kessler, *Empires Beyond the Great Wall*, 158–59 (photograph of a fourteenth-century robe excavated in Inner Mongolia); Hearn, *Splendors of Imperial China*, 67 (Liu Kuan-tao, "Khubilai Khan Hunting," detail of hanging scroll dated 1280, showing Khubilai on horseback in a gold-brocaded red robe and trousers and an ermine overcoat).

84. Allsen, *Commodity and Exchange*, 20.

85. Allsen, *Culture and Conquest*, 4, 175, chaps. 12–22.

86. Golden, *King's Dictionary*, 1–49.

87. Allsen, *Commodity and Exchange*, 52.

88. DeWeese, *Islamization and Native Religion*, 224, 257; Ibn Battuta, *Travels of Ibn Battuta*, 480–89.

89. Togan, *Flexibility and Limitation*, 60–103, 121, 156; Tôru Saguchi, "Uyghurs and other Non-Muslim Turks Under Mongol Domination, 1200–1350," *HTPPP*, 219–29, discussing the Uyghurs, Keraits, Naimans, Öngüts, and Kırghız.

90. Golden, *Introduction*, 305–6.

91. Ibid., 297.

92. Southern, *Western Views of Islam in the Middle Ages*, 47–50.

93. Quoted in DeWeese, *Islamization and Native Religion*, 260 (amending transliteration of Mongol terms to conform to usage here).

94. Adshead, *Central Asia*, 70–77.

95. Hodgson, *Venture of Islam*, II, 13.

96. Abu-Lughod, *Before European Hegemony*, 32–38.

97. Cited in Adshead, *Central Asia*, 95–102; Dols, *Black Death in the Middle East*, 13–67, 70–71.

98. McNeill, *Plagues and Peoples*, 144–46, 170–72; Abu-Lughod, *Before European Hegemony*, 170–75.

99. Allsen, *Culture and Conquest*, 63–80, 127.

100. Ibid., 83–92, 116–18, 143–44; Rashiduddin, *Rashiduddin Fazlullah's Jami'u't-tawarikh*.

101. Blair, *Compendium of Chronicles*, 13–14, 114–15 ("articles of endowment of the Rab'-i Rashidi," trans. Wheeler Thackston).

Chapter Three

1. Di Cosmo, "State Formation and Periodization in Inner Asian History," 34–37.

2. Murphey, *Ottoman Warfare*, 14; McNeill, *Pursuit of Power*, 95–102.

3. Adshead, *Central Asia in World History*, 119–26, 144–49, 163–74, 178–79; McChesney, *Central Asia*, 42, on trade.

4. Parker and Smith, *General Crisis of the Seventeenth Century*, 22–23; Khodarkovsky, *Russia's Steppe Frontier*, 126; İnalcık and Quataert, *ESHOE*, 165–66, 416–17; Geraci, *Window on the East*, 19–20.

5. W. B. Denny, "Türkmen Rugs and Early Rug Weaving in the Western Islamic World," 329–37; W. B. Denny, *Classical Tradition in Anatolian Carpets*; see also Sümer, *Oğuzlar*.

6. W. B. Denny, *Classical Tradition in Anatolian Carpets*, 46–55.

7. B. Lewis, *IPMCC*, I, 97–99 (passage from Ibn Khaldun); Crone, *Slaves on Horses*, 90–91.

8. Manz, *Rise and Rule of Tamerlane*, 27–28. Temür's name is linguistically Turkic, and Temür is its proper form. The commonly used term "Timurid," based on the Persian form of the name, has been retained for his descendants to avoid confusion for readers who do not know Turkish.

9. Golden, *Introduction to the History of the Turkic Peoples*, 309–13; Adshead, *Central Asia*, 103–26; B. Lewis, *IPMCC*, I, 102–3.

10. Adshead, *Central Asia*, 107–9; Manz, *Rise and Rule of Tamerlane*, 80.

11. Adshead, *Central Asia*, 103, 119–26.

12. Manz, *Rise and Rule of Tamerlane*, 140.

13. Köprülü, *Islam in Anatolia After the Turkish Invasion*, 40; Neşrî, *Kitâb-ı Cihan-Nümâ*, I, 348–60.

14. Adshead, *Central Asia*, 127.

15. Ibid., 131.

16. Bombaci, *Histoire de la littérature turque*, 118–35.

17. Nava'i, *Muhakemat al-Lughatain*; Bombaci, *Histoire*, 118, 132; Light, "Slippery Paths," 157–67.

18. Light, "Slippery Paths," 60, 92–120, 196–98.

19. Adshead, *Central Asia*, 144–49.

20. Morgan, *Medieval Persia*, 96.

21. Adshead, *Central Asia*, 150–58; Golden, *Introduction*, 313–45.

22. İnalcık, "Khan and Tribal Aristocracy," 452; personal communication from Peter Golden, 26 September 2003; Khodarkovsky, *Russia's Steppe Frontier*, 82–83, 224.

23. Babur, *Baburnama*, 24, 134–35; Dale, *Garden of the Eight Paradises*, 67–68, 87–94, 98–101.

24. Golden, *Introduction*, 330–38; McChesney, *Central Asia*, 119–41.

25. Dale, *Garden of the Eight Paradises*, 21; McChesney, *Central Asia*, 119–41.

26. Dale, *Garden of the Eight Paradises*, 68–86.

27. Khodarkovsky, *Russia's Steppe Frontier*; Bergholz, *Partition of the Steppe*.

28. Richards, *Unending Frontier*, 17.

29. Khodarkovsky, *Russia's Steppe Frontier*, 7–45; Millward, *Beyond the Pass*, 5–13, 156–59, 197–203, 233–34, 250.

30. Millward, *Beyond the Pass*, 28, 32–34, 171–72.

31. McChesney, *Waqf in Central Asia*.

32. McChesney, *Central Asia*, 83, 92–98; Frank, *Islamic Historiography and 'Bulghar' Identity*, 67–76, 82–83, 115–22; Frank, *Muslim Religious Institutions in Imperial Russia*, 268–72, 297–99.

33. McChesney, *Central Asia*, 42–47.

34. Adshead, *Central Asia*, 177–201.

35. Dale, *Indian Merchants and Eurasian Trade*, 108–12; Markovits, *Global World of Indian Merchants*; Levi, *Indian Diaspora in Central Asia and Its Trade*.

36. Frank, *Muslim Religious Institutions in Imperial Russia*, 170, 76.

37. Millward, *Beyond the Pass*, 175–93; Gunder Frank, *ReOrient*, 121–23.

38. Millward, *Beyond the Pass*, 57–63, 98–101, 115, 125, 126; compare Fairbank, Reischauer, and Craig, *East Asia, Tradition and Transformation*, 256–57 Millward strongly criticizes Fairbank on Qing trade policy.

39. Golden, *Introduction*, 347–50.

40. Woods, *Aqquyunlu, Clan, Confederation, Empire*.

41. Köprülü, *Les origines de l'Empire ottoman*; Wittek, *Rise of the Ottoman Empire*; Lindner, *Nomads and Ottomans in Medieval Anatolia*; Cahen, *La Turquie pré-ottomane*, 53, 107, 163, 180, 335; Heywood, "Wittek and the Austrian Tradition"; Heywood, "Boundless Dreams of the Levant"; Imber, "What Does *Ghazi* Actually Mean?"; Kafadar, *Between Two Worlds*, 12, 45–59, 62–90; İnalcık and Renda, *Ottoman Civilization*, I, 34–59; Lowry, *Nature of the Early Ottoman State*; Golden, *Introduction*, 305, 312, 317, 330, 357.

42. Compare Lowry, *Nature of the Early Ottoman State*, 57, 69, 77, 95, with Golden, *Introduction*, 305–6, 312, 317, 330, 356–66.

43. Ibn Battuta, *Travels of Ibn Baṭṭūṭa*, II, 418–20; Köprülü, *Osmanlı İmparatorluğunun Kuruluşu*, 85–103, 128, 144–71; Köprülü, *Origins of the Ottoman Empire*, 77–108.

44. Lowry, *Nature of the Early Ottoman State*, 92, 96, 131, 134, 139, cites evidence of a "manpower shortage" but does not mention the plague, except to note one death in Byzantium (137); Dols, *Black Death in the Middle East*, 46, 51, 58, 62; Schamiloglu, "Preliminary Remarks on the Role of Disease in the History of the Golden Horde," 452, comparing the decline of literary Latin in Europe after the Black Death to the extinction of Volga Bulgharian as a Turkic literary language.

45. Aşıkpaşazade, *Tevarih-i Âl-i Osman*, 6: "Padişahlık sana ve senin nesline mübarek olsun."

46. Ocak, *La révolte de Baba Resul*, 83–84, 160–61.

47. Deny, "Tuğra," *İA*, XII, 6; Ögel, "Tuğ," *İA*, XII, 4. Chinggis Khan and the Moghul Emperors of India also used nine *tugh*: McChesney, *Central Asia*, plate 23; Zygulski, *Ottoman Art in the Service of Empire*, 5, 72–73, 84.

48. Kafadar, *Between Two Worlds*, 60–61, 136.

49. Wittek, *Rise of the Ottoman Empire*, 17–25; Kafadar, *Between Two Worlds*, 85; Anon., *Digenes Akrites*.

50. Imber, *The Ottoman Empire*, 193–206, 252–57.

51. Ibid., 134–42.

52. Ibid., 194–95; Berktay, *Cumhuriyet İdeolojisi ve Fuat Köprülü*, 19–23; Lowry, *Nature of the Early Ottoman State*, 55–143.

53. Kafadar, *Between Two Worlds*, 120, 136–38; İnalcık and Renda, *Ottoman Civilization*, I, 48.

54. Vatin, "L'ascension des Ottomans (1362–1451)," *HEO*, 45–46; B. Lewis, *IPMCC*, I, 135–141.

55. Kafadar, *Between Two Worlds*, 135; Singer, *Constructing Ottoman Beneficence*.

56. Southern, *Western Views of Islam in the Middle Ages*, 100; Bisaha, "Pius II's Letter to Sultan Mehmed II," 183–201; Necipoğlu, *Architecture, Ceremonial and Power*.

57. Murphey, *Ottoman Warfare*, 144.

58. Peirce, *Imperial Harem*; Fleischer, *Bureaucrat and Intellectual in the Ottoman Empire*.

59. In contrast to English-language usage, which refers to the Ottoman rulers as "sultans," the Ottomans also used *sultan* as a princely form of address before the name for males (Sultan Murad, "Prince Murad"), and after it for females (Fatma Sultan, "Princess Fatma"). The same term was used for the monarch before his name with *khan* after it: Sultan Süleyman Khan. Numerous synonyms were used to convey the idea of "monarch," including *khakan*, *padişah*, *hüdavendigâr*, and *hünkar*. All of these stem from Iranian tradition, although *khakan* also corresponds to *kaghan* as used among the Turks and Mongols of Inner Asia. See İnalcık, "Padişah," *İA*, IX, 491–95; Peirce, *Imperial Harem*, 18.

60. İnalcık and Renda, *Ottoman Civilization*, I, 137–51; Veinstein, "L'empire dans sa grandeur (XVIe siècle)," *HEO*, 159–226; Necipoğlu, *Architecture, Ceremonial and Power*, 111–14.

61. Schacht, *Introduction to Islamic Law*, 89; İnalcık and Renda, *Ottoman Civilization*, I, 160–68; Ortaylı, *İmparatorluğun En Uzun Yüzyılı*, 137; Imber, *Ebu's-Su'ud*.

62. Murphey, *Ottoman Warfare*, 179–80; Genç, *Osmanlı İmparatorluğunda Devlet ve Ekonomi*, 211–25.

63. Richards, *Unending Frontier*, 517–46.

64. İnalcık and Renda, *Ottoman Civilization*, I, 172–78; İnalcık and Quataert, *ESHOE*, 143–54; Imber, *Ottoman Empire*, 193–206; Barkan, *Türkiye'de Toprak Meselesi*; Singer, *Palestinian Peasants and Ottoman Officials*.

65. Abou-El-Haj, *The 1703 Rebellion and the Structure of Ottoman Politics*, 10, 31, 43–48, 51–56, 82, 87, 90.

66. İnalcık, "Centralization and Decentralization in Ottoman Administration," 39–40, 48–52; Khoury, *State and Provincial Society in the Ottoman Empire*, 43.

67. Khoury, *State and Provincial Society*, 56–58, 123; Tabakoğlu, *Gerileme Dönemine Girerken Osmanlı Maliyesi*, 222–26.

68. B. Lewis, "Dustur," *EI2*, II, 640–41.

69. Zilfi, *Politics of Piety*, 43–80, 183–225; Findley, *Bureaucratic Reform in the Ottoman Empire*, 41–111.

70. Murphey, *Ottoman Warfare*, passim; Finkel, *Administration of Warfare*.

71. Murphey, *Ottoman Warfare*, 190–91.

72. Ibid., 145, 173, 190; Aksan, "Whatever Happened to the Janissaries?" 23–36; McNeill, *Pursuit of Power*, chs. 4–5.

73. Arjomand, *Shadow of God and the Hidden Imam*, 66–84; Morgan, *Medieval Persia*, 107–14; Köprülü, *Islam in Anatolia After the Turkish Invasion*, 50–51.

74. Ocak, *La révolte de Baba Resul*, 132: "Shahuning evladina iqrar edenler / Ahiler Gaziler Abdallar oldı."

75. Richards, *Mughal Empire*, 6–12.

76. Ibid., 219 (example from reign of Aurangzeb, 1658–1707); among the Ottomans, the central administration accompanied the army to the front as late as the Napoleonic wars.

77. Ibid., 24–25, 143–48; Richards, *Unending Frontier*, 25–38.

78. Morgan, *Medieval Persia*, 119.

79. Arjomand, *Shadow of God and the Hidden Imam*, 70.

80. Morgan, *Medieval Persia*, 128–29.

81. Richards, *Mughal Empire*, 19–24, 60–64.

82. Minorsky, "Poetry of Shah Ismail," 1007–53a; Morgan, *Medieval Persia*, 110, 114–18, 120–23.

83. Arjomand, *Shadow of God and the Hidden Imam*, 109–21, 243–44.

84. Richards, *Mughal Empire*, 12–57.

85. Ibid., 94–100.

86. Ibid., 119–23, 148–50.

87. Ibid., 151–84.

88. Aksan, "Ottoman Historical Writing," 53–69; Findley, "Ebu Bekir Ratib's

Vienna Embassy Narrative," 41–80; Findley, "Osmanlı Siyasal Düşüncesinde Devlet ve Hukuk," 1195–1202.

89. Richards, *Mughal Empire*, 100.

90. Hodgson, *Venture of Islam*, III, 55–58, 103–4, 127–30.

91. Morgan, Medieval Persia, 158–61; Arjomand, *Shadow of God and the Hidden Imam*, 105–212.

92. Richards, *Mughal Empire*, 127, 292–94.

93. Babur, *Baburnama*, 116–17, 119–22.

94. For example, ibid., 105, 129; Dale, *Garden of the Eight Paradises*, 117, 135, 164, 170–71, 246.

95. Silahdar Fındıklı Mehmed Ağa, *Silahdar Tarihi*, II, 85–93.

96. Golden, *Introduction*, 384.

97. Dale, *Garden of the Eight Paradises*, 23–24.

98. Ibid., 61.

99. Ibid., 71–75; Babur, *Baburnama*, trans. Thackston, 192–219.

100. Dale, *Garden of the Eight Paradises*, 94.

Chapter Four

1. Therborn, *European Modernity and Beyond*, xi, 4–5.

2. Said, *Culture and Imperialism*, 329; compare Jusdanis, *Necessary Nation*, ch. 4, "Progress and Belatedness."

3. Khalid, *Politics of Muslim Cultural Reform*, 2.

4. Quataert, *Ottoman Manufacturing in the Age of the Industrial Revolution*, 134–60.

5. Therborn, *European Modernity and Beyond*, 3–5.

6. Touraine, *Critique of Modernity*, 95–103, 134–35, 144–45.

7. Therborn, *European Modernity and Beyond*, 5–7.

8. Khater, *Inventing Home*.

9. Jusdanis, *Necessary Nation*, ch. 4.

10. Golden, *Introduction to the History of the Turkic Peoples*, 317, 376, 384.

11. Soucek, *History of Inner Asia*, 200–8; Daulet, *Kazan and Moscow*.

12. Fisher, *Crimean Tatars*, 8; Kırımlı, *National Movements and National Identity Among the Crimean Tatars*, 7; Williams, *Crimean Tatars*.

13. Kırımlı, *National Movements and National Identity Among the Crimean Tatars*, 32–55, 116–49; Brower and Lazzerini, *Russia's Orient* (see "Local Accommodation and Resistance to Colonialism in Nineteenth-Century Crimea," 169–87).

14. Frank, *Islamic Historiography and 'Bulghar' Identity*, 21–91; Geraci, *Window on the East*, 22, 180–94.

15. Georgeon, *Aux origines du nationalisme turc*; Geraci, *Window on the East*, 279–80.

16. Swietochowski, *Russia and Azerbaijan*, 3–5; Alstadt, *Azerbaijani Turks*, 15–19.

17. Swietochowski, *Russia and Azerbaijan*, 6–10.

18. Beydilli, "1828–1829 Osmanlı-Rus Savaşında Doğu Anadolu'dan Rusya'ya Göçürülen Ermeniler," 365–67, 403–8.

19. Swietochowski, *Russia and Azerbaijan*, 10–12.

20. Ibid., 25–36.

21. Ibid., 52–56; Khalid, *Politics of Muslim Cultural Reform*, 211–14.

22. Swietochowski, *Russia and Azerbaijan*, 37–42; Suny, *Revenge of the Past*, 38–43.

23. Swietochowski, *Russian Azerbaijan*, 42–49.

24. Quoted in Alstadt, *Azerbaijani Turks*, 77.

25. Swietochowski, *Russia and Azerbaijan*, 61–65.

26. Alstadt, *Azerbaijani Turks*, 86–87.

27. Swietochowski, *Russia and Azerbaijan*, 69.

28. Ibid., 85.

29. Ibid., 92–94; Alstadt, *Azerbaijani Turks*, 99.

30. Swietochowski, *Russia and Azerbaijan*, 104–5.

31. Ibid., 94–100.

32. Allworth, *Central Asia*, chs. 4–8.

33. DeWeese, "Politics of Sacred Lineages in 19th-Century Central Asia," 507–30; Frank, *Muslim Religious Institutions in Imperial Russia*, 274–89.

34. Soucek, *History of Inner Asia*, 211; Allworth, *Central Asia*, chs. 8–10.

35. Soucek, *History of Central Asia*, 211–12.

36. Khalid, *Politics of Muslim Cultural Reform*, 19–44; Levin, *Hundred Thousand Fools of God*; Light, "Slippery Paths."

37. Khalid, *Politics of Muslim Cultural Reform*, 160–62; Geraci, *Window on the East*, 264 (But it is not exact to say that Muslims in the Russian Empire were "on the forefront of a cultural trend that had begun to sweep the Muslim world." Rather, educational methods pioneered by Muslims elsewhere assumed exceptional significance for those under Russian rule). In the first phase of a nationalist movement arising under foreign rule, concentration on cultural issues is normal: Jusdanis, *Necessary Nation*, 119; Chatterjee, *Nation and Its Fragments*, 3–13.

38. Khalid, *Politics of Muslim Cultural Reform*, 102; Geraci, *Window on the East*, 277–85, on Russian fears of pan-Islamism and pan-Turkism.

39. Khalid, *Politics of Muslim Cultural Reform*, 223.

40. Manz, *Central Asia in Historical Perspective* (see Subtelny, "Symbiosis of Turk and Tajik," 45–61).

41. Khalid, *Politics of Muslim Cultural Reform*, 187–215; the quoted passage is on p. 208.

42. Karpat, *Politicization of Islam*, 305–6, 375–76; Alstadt, *Azerbaijani Turks*, 69–70, 274 n. 90.

43. Millward, *Beyond the Pass*, 20–43, 194–252; Soucek, *History of Inner Asia*, 262–70; Rudelson, *Oasis Identities*, 17–38.

44. Karpat, *Ottoman Population*, 55.

45. Pamuk, *Monetary History of the Ottoman Empire*, 188–204.

46. Khoury, *State and Provincial Society in the Ottoman Empire*, 156–87.

47. S. J. Shaw, *Between Old and New*, chs. 8–14; Aksan, "Selim III," *EI2*, IX, 132–34; Levy, "Military Policy of Sultan Mahmud II"; Cezar, *Osmanlı Maliyesinde Bunalım ve Değişim Dönemi)*, 155–207.

48. Findley, *Bureaucratic Reform in the Ottoman Empire*, 42–43.

49. A. Levy, "Mahmud II," *EI2*, VI, 58; Khoury, *State and Provincial Society*, 166–78; Hourani, Khoury, and Wilson, *Modern Middle East* (see Hourani, "Ottoman Reform and the Politics of Notables," 83–109); Meeker, *Nation of Modernity*.

50. Fahmy, *All the Pasha's Men*; Cuno, *Pasha's Peasants*.

51. Findley, *Bureaucratic Reform*, 63, 140–47; Findley, *Ottoman Civil Officialdom*, 20–28; Levy, "Military Policy," 479–89.

52. Göçek, *Rise of the Bourgeoisie, Demise of Empire*, 45, 67.

53. Wilhite, "Guerrilla War, Counterinsurgency, and State Formation in Ottoman Yemen."

54. Ortaylı, *İmparatorluğun En Uzun Yüzyılı*, 77, 179–80; Rumpf, *Das Rechtsstaatsprinzip in der türkischen Rechtsordnung*.

55. Findley, *Ottoman Civil Officialdom*, 23; Ortaylı, *İmparatorluğun En Uzun Yüzyılı*, 106–32.

56. Pamuk, *Monetary History of the Ottoman Empire*, 205–24.

57. This opinion derives from my research in the registers on the tax reform of the mid-1840s (Başbakanlık Osmanlı Arşivi, Istanbul, Temettuat defterleri for Sivas and Skopje); see also Khater, *Inventing Home*, 30–31, on "artificially low taxes" in Mount Lebanon.

58. İnalcık and Quataert, *ESHOE*, 759–933.

59. Berkes, *Development of Secularism in Turkey*.

60. Mardin, *Genesis of Young Ottoman Thought*.

61. The Ottoman Empire thus acquired a constitution before Russia ever did: Ortaylı, *İmparatorluğun En Uzun Yüzyılı*, 216.

62. Deringil, *Well-Protected Domains*.

63. Beatrice Saint Laurent, personal communication; Saint Laurent, "Ottoman Power and Westernization," 222–26.

64. Findley, "Ottoman Occidentalist in Europe," 15–49; Findley, "La soumise, la subversive," 153–76.

65. Karpat, *Politicization of Islam*, 176–82.

66. Hanioğlu, *Young Turks in Opposition*; Hanioğlu, *Preparation for a Revolution*; Sohrabi, "Global Waves, Local Actors," 45–79; Zürcher, *Unionist Factor*.

67. Kayalı, *Arabs and Young Turks*, 207–12; Karpat, *Politicization of Islam*, 353–73.

68. Berkes, *Development of Secularism in Turkey*, 411–28; Toprak, *Milli İktisat—Milli Burjuvazi*.

69. Erickson, *Ordered to Die*; Yanıkdağ, "Ill-Fated Sons of the Nation" and personal communication, 30 September 2003.

70. B. Lewis, *Middle East*, 338–41; McCarthy, *Muslims and Minorities*, 118, 135, 138–39; McCarthy, *Ottoman Peoples and the End of Empire*, 106–12; Zürcher, *Turkey*, 171; Suny, *Revenge of the Past*, 72–76; Erickson, *Ordered to Die*, 95–104; Akçam, *Armenien und der Völkermord*; Akçam, *İnsan Hakları ve Ermeni Sorunu*.

71. Kayalı, *Arabs and Young Turks*.

72. Among many standard treatments, see Hourani, *History of the Arab Peoples*, 315–19; Cleveland, *History of the Modern Middle East*, 146–67.

73. Zürcher, *Unionist Factor*, 106–17.

74. E. J. Hobsbawm missed this point. Of the defeated belligerents of World War I, only the Turks succeeded in forcing a renegotiation of the peace terms imposed on them. Compare Hobsbawm, *Nations and Nationalism Since 1780*, 134: "In spite of various shortlived attempts to redraw the frontiers of the succession states of the Austrian and Turkish empires, they are still more or less where they ended up after World War I, at least south and west of the Soviet borders."

75. Hanioğlu, *Young Turks in Opposition*, 32, 213–16.

76. Findley, "Ottoman Occidentalist in Europe," 15–49.

77. Karpat, *Politicization of Islam*, 155–82.

78. Georgeon, *Aux origines du nationalisme turc*; Karpat, *Politicization of Islam*, 388–96; Zürcher, *Turkey*, 134.

79. Findley, "La soumise, la subversive," 153–75; Çakır, *Osmanlı Kadın Hareketi*.

80. Khalid, *Politics of Muslim Cultural Reform*, 112.

81. Kırımlı, *National Movements and National Identity Among the Crimean Tatars*, 34–35.

82. Ibid., 47; Siyavuşgil, "Ahmed Midhat," *İA*, I, 185; Khalid, *Politics of Muslim Cultural Reform*, 159.

83. İnal, *Son Asır Türk Şairleri*, 1834: "Paris'e git hey efendi akl-ü-fikrin var ise / Âleme gelmiş sayılmaz gitmeyenler Paris'e"; Khalid, *Politics of Muslim Cultural Reform*, 138–39.

84. Huseinzade's original is *Türkleshtirmek, Islamlashtirmak, Avrupalilashtirmak*. Gökalp's is *Türkleşmek, İslamlaşmak, Muasırlaşmak*. See Karpat, *Politicization of Islam*, 305–6, 375–76; Alstadt, *Azerbaijani Turks*, 69–70, 254 n. 90.

85. Akçuraoğlu, *Türkçülük ve Dış Türkler*; Kırımlı, *National Movements and National Identity Among the Crimean Tatars*; Shissler, *Between Two Empires*; Adam, *Russlandmuslime in Istanbul am Vorabend des Ersten Weltkrieges*; Georgeon, *Des Ottomans aux Turcs*, 109–23; Arai, *Turkish Nationalism in the Young Turk Era*; Landau, *Pan-Turkism*.

Chapter Five

1. Jusdanis, *Necessary Nation*, 162–65.

2. Neil J. Smelser, "Uncertain Connections: Globalization, Localization, Identities, and Violence," presentation at the conference on "Deprivation, Violence, and Identities: Mapping Contemporary World Conflicts," Mershon Center, Ohio State University, 3 October 2003.

3. Georgeon, *Des Ottomans aux Turcs*, "Le rêve panturc," 109–23; Akçuraoğlu, *Türkçülük ve Dış Türkler*; Kırımlı, *National Movements and National Identity Among the Crimean Tatars*.

4. Hale, *Turkish Foreign Policy*, 287–96.

5. Suny and Martin, *State of Nations*, 67–90; Martin, *Affirmative Action Empire*; Eley and Suny, *Becoming National* (see Slezkine, "USSR as a Communal Apartment," 202–38); Khazanov, *After the USSR*, 4–21.

6. Suny and Martin, *State of Nations*, 78; communication from Adeed Khalid, 30 October 2003.

7. Suny and Martin, *State of Nations*, 79.

8. Ibid. (see Northrop, "Nationalizing Backwardness," 191–220).

9. Levin, *Hundred Thousand Fools of God*, 10–22, 46–47.

10. Williams, *Crimean Tatars*, 334–464.

11. Khazanov, *After the USSR*, 193–210; Dan Brennan, "Meskhetian Turks: Still Struggling to Return to Their Homeland," EN, 25 March 2003.

12. Gorenburg, "Nationalism for the Masses," 49–59; Khazanov, *After the USSR*, 175–91; Lydolph, *Geography of the U.S.S.R.*, 19–30; Slezkine, *Arctic Mirrors*, 1–3; Daulet, *Kazan and Moscow*, Bukharaev, *The Model of Tatarstan*; Kondrashov, *Nationalism and the Drive for Sovereignty in Tatarstan*.

13. Soucek, *History of Inner Asia*, 232.

14. Alstadt, *Azerbaijani Turks*, 108–10; van der Leeuw, *Azerbaijan*, 125.

15. Alstadt, *Azerbaijani Turks*, 121.

16. Swietochowski, *Russia and Azerbaijan*, 108–18.

17. Van der Leeuw, *Azerbaijan*, 155.

18. Alstadt, *Azerbaijani Turks*, 123.

19. Ibid., 140.

20. Swietochowski, *Russia and Azerbaijan*, 124–28; van der Leeuw, *Azerbaijan*, 128.

21. Swietochowski, *Russia and Azerbaijan*, 118–24.

22. Ibid., 135–62.

23. Alstadt, *Azerbaijani Turks*, 165, 175–76.

24. Ibid., 181.

25. Swietochowski, *Russia and Azerbaijan*, 211, quoting *Stolitsa* (Moscow), 1 (1990), n.p.

26. Ibid., 177–82.

27. Van der Leeuw, *Azerbaijan*, 132.

28. Swietochowski, *Russia and Azerbaijan*, 183.

29. Alstadt, *Azerbaijani Turks*, 209, 211; van der Leeuw, *Azerbaijan*, 173, 181–82, 187.

30. Van der Leeuw, *Azerbaijan*, 159–60.

31. Ibid., 162; Swietochowski, *Russia and Azerbaijan*, 205–6.

32. Van der Leeuw, *Azerbaijan*, 166–68.

33. Swietochowski, *Russia and Azerbaijan*, 213, 218–19.

34. Van der Leeuw, *Azerbaijan*, 183–88; Swietochowski, *Russia and Azerbaijan*, 212; Emil Danielyan, "Summit Offers No Quick Fix for Karabakh Conflict," 19 August 2002, and Fariz Ismailzade, "Tension between Armenia, Azerbaijan Rising Over Nagorno-Karabakh," 29 July 2003, EN.

35. Swietochowski, *Russia and Azerbaijan*, 167–78, 184–90.

36. The Russians used the term "Kirgiz" to refer to both Kazakhs and Kyrgyz; on this terminology, see Soucek, *History of Inner Asia*, 216, 224; Golden, *Introduction to the History of the Turkic Peoples*, 401, 404–5.

37. Olcott, *Kazakhs*, 160–65, 193–98.

38. Eley and Suny, *Becoming National* (see Slezkine, "USSR as a Communal Apartment," 203, 221); compare Soucek, *History of Inner Asia*, 225.

39. Soucek, *History of Inner Asia*, 228, quoting the description of the Uzbek constitution of 1978 in the *Uzbek Sovet Entsiklopediyasi* (Tashkent, 1980), 490–91: "pivot" is *özak*; "one of its advance platoons" is *avangard otryadlaridan biri.*

40. Soucek, *History of Inner Asia*, 230, 311.

41. Khalid, "Secular Islam," 576–77; Kemp, "Pilgrimage and Performance," 263–78; Ro'i, *Islam in the Soviet Union*, 535–49.

42. Olcott, *Kazakhs*, 175–87; Khazanov, *After the USSR*, 156–73.

43. Soucek, *History of Inner Asia*, 232.

44. Olcott, *Kazakhs*, 187–93.

45. Soucek, *History of Central Asia*, 234, 237; Khalid, *Politics of Muslim Cultural Reform*, 111–12, 140–43.

46. Eley and Suny, *Becoming National* (see Slezkine, "USSR as a Communal Apartment," 222); Soucek, *History of Inner Asia*, 232; Olcott, *Kazakhstan* 15, 54–55.

47. Aitmatov, *White Ship*.

48. Olcott, *Kazakhstan*, 124, 128–71, 204.

49. Ilkhamov, "Nation-State Formation," 317–35; Eley and Suny, *Becoming National* (see Slezkine, "USSR as a Communal Apartment," 228–30); Olcott, *Kazakhs*, 253 quoting *Pravda*, 25 October 1986, 6.

50. Olcott, *Kazakhstan*, 10–17, 24–25; Khazanov, *After the USSR*, 115–73; Soucek, *History of Inner Asia*, 262.

51. Soucek, *History of Inner Asia*, 282, 286; Khazanov, *After the USSR*, 138, 141–42; Mango, *Atatürk*, 498.

52. Levin, *Hundred Thousand Fools of God*, 228–29; Allworth, *Central Asia*, 527–607.

53. Hugh Pope, "Back on the Silk Road," *Middle East International*, no. 487 (4 November 1994), 13.

54. Khalid, "Secular Islam," 583, 587, 590–92; Khazanov, *After the USSR*, 146–47; Hassan, *Faithlines*.

55. Olcott, *Kazakhstan*, 3–10; Patrick E. Tyler, "Kazakh Leader Urges Iran Pipeline Route," *NYT*, 10 Dec. 2001.

56. Khazanov, *After the USSR*, 26, 115–55; Olcott, *Kazakhstan*, 174–77, 203–4.

57. Soucek, *History of Inner Asia*, 270; Rudelson, *Oasis Identities*, 7, 55–57.

58. Rudelson, *Oasis Identities*, 101–2, 105–8, 131, 133–37.

59. Ibid., 22–24, 34–38.

60. Ibid., 14; Sponsel, *Endangered Peoples of Southeast and East Asia* (see Gladney, "Uyghur of China," 233–51); Soucek, *History of Inner Asia*, 274, 290.

61. Rudelson, *Oasis Identities*, 33, 116–20, 131–32, 144; Esposito, *Oxford History of Islam* (see Gladney, "Central Asia and China," 462–73); Sponsel, *Endangered Peoples of Southeast and East Asia* (see Gladney, "Uyghur of China," 245).

62. Rudelson, *Oasis Identities*, 167–71; Craig J. Smith, "China, in Harsh Crackdown, Executes Muslim Separatists," *NYT*, 16 December 2001, A1, A8.

63. Rudelson, *Oasis Identities*, 153–54; Light, "Slippery Paths," 196–98, 299–301.

64. C. J. Chivers, "In Home Called Base of Jihad Teacher, the Lessons of Terror," *NYT*, 1 December 2001, B1, B3; David Rohde, "Taliban Enlisting Eager Recruits of Many Lands," *NYT*, 28 September 2001, p. B3; Levin, *Hundred Thou-*

*sand Fools of God*, 149, 236; Olcott, *Kazakhstan*, 184; Aitmatov, *White Ship*, 109–10.

65. Levin, *Hundred Thousand Fools of God*, 10, 44, 49, 260–87; Light, "Slippery Paths."

66. For example, Adıvar, *Ateşten Gömlek*, 84, 90–91, 98, 99, 101, 104, 109, 121–23 (*ihtilal*). Compare Karaosmanoğlu, *Panorama*, 43, 44, 45, 53, 56, 62, 65, 108, 109, 111–14, 118, 121–22, 125, 148, 150, 175, 211, 215, 218, 222, 277, 301, 337, 350, 366, 484, 487, 494–96, 500, 551–53, 555–57, 572 (*inkilap*).

67. Berkes, *Development of Secularism in Turkey*, 106, 155, 159, 174, 217, 467–78.

68. Schick and Tonak, *Turkey in Transition* (see Toprak, "Religious Right," 218–35).

69. Zürcher, *Turkey* 163–67, 173–75.

70. Zürcher, *Unionist Factor*, 68–173; Zürcher, *Turkey*, 175–83.

71. Zürcher, *Unionist Factor*, 142–67 (especially 160).

72. See Duara, *Rescuing History from the Nation*. Published versions of the speech include Kemal, *Nutuk* (543 pages); Kemal, *Speech Delivered by Ghazi Mustapha Kemal* (724 pages).

73. Hourani, Khoury, and Wilson, *Modern Middle East* (see Toprak, "Religious Right," 630–31, a thorough list of the secularizing reforms).

74. Karaömlerlioğlu, "Cult of the Peasant," 65–158.

75. Allworth, *Central Asia* (see Menges, "People, Languages, and Migrations," 60–91).

76. G. Lewis, *Turkish Language Reform*.

77. Hansen, *Political Economy of Poverty, Equity, and Growth*, 319–35.

78. Heper, *İsmet İnönü*, 187–93.

79. Ibid., 140–41, 184–85; Karaömerlioğlu, "Cult of the Peasant," 112–58; Karaömerlioğlu, "People's Houses and the Cult of the Peasant in Turkey," 67–91; Karaömerlioğlu, "Village Institutes Experience in Turkey," 47–73.

80. Zürcher, *Turkey*, 228: parliamentary elections first occurred in 1876, and there had been three periods of multiparty politics (1908–13, 1924–26, and 1930).

81. Özbudun, "Paradoxes of Turkish Democratic Development," 297–309.

82. Heper and Güney, "Military and the Consolidation of Democracy," 635–57; Sakallıoğlu, "Anatomy of the Turkish Military's Political Autonomy," 151–66.

83. Sakallıoğlu, "Anatomy of the Turkish Military's Political Autonomy," 157.

84. Yavuz, *Islamic Political Identity in Turkey*, 75–79, 121–28.

85. Heper and Keyman, "Double-Faced State," 259–77.

86. Cizre, "Demythologizing the National Security Concept," 213–29.

87. Schmalz-Jacobsen and Hansen, *Kleines Lexikon der ethnischen Minderheiten in Deutschland*; van der Leeuw, *Azerbaijan*, 19; Olcott, *Kazakhstan*, 176.

88. Leggewie and Şenocak, *Deutsche Türken*; Yerasimos, *Les Turcs* (see Kastoryano, "Les émigrés," 96–99); Horrocks and Kolinsky, *Turkish Culture in German Society Today*, "Non-German Minorities in Contemporary German Society," 71–81; Nonneman, Niblock, and Szajkowski, *Muslim Communities in the New Europe*; Heine,

*Halbmond über deutschen Dächern*, 299–302, 312; Dassetto and Conrad, *Musulmans en Europe occidentale*.

89. Stephens, *Children and the Politics of Culture* (see Mandel, "Second-Generation Noncitizens," 278–79).

90. Horrocks and Kolinsky, *Turkish Culture*, "Non-German Minorities in German Society," 83–89; Sevimli, *Kimliksiz Cemaatler*, 12; Yerasimos, *Les Turcs* (see Kastoryano, "Les émigrés," 98).

91. White, "Turks in the New Germany," 755; Yerasimos, *Les Turcs* (see Kastoryano, "Les émigrés," 107).

92. Tietze, "La Turcité allemande," 252–70.

93. Horrocks and Kolinsky, *Turkish Culture* (see Karakaşoğlu, "Turkish Cultural Orientations in Germany and the Rise of Islam," 170–71); Aslan et al., *Graue Wölfe heulen wieder*; Schiffauer, *Die Gottesmänner*; Heitmeyer, Müller, and Schröder, *Verlockender Fundamentalismus*; Douglas Frantz, "Terror Plan Born in Germany and Aimed at Turkey Gets New Scrutiny," *NYT*, 5 February 2002, A13 (a plan to crash a plane into Atatürk's mausoleum in Ankara).

94. Björgo and Witte, *Racist Violence in Europe*; Heitmeyer and Anhut, *Bedrohte Stadtgesellschaft*.

95. SOPEMI, *Trends in International Migration*, 263–64; Hansen and Weil, *Towards a European Nationality* (see Green, "Citizenship Policy in Germany," 24–51); Mandel, "Second-Generation Noncitizens," 165–81.

96. Horrocks and Kolinsky, *Turkish Culture* (see Karakaşoğlu, "Turkish Cultural Orientations in Germany and the Role of Islam," 173); *Was ist ein Deutscher? Was ist ein Türke?*; Koçtürk, *Matter of Honour*; Ferrari and Bradney, *Islam and European Legal Systems*; Polat, *Soziale und kulturelle Identität*; Alacacıoğlu, *Deutsche Heimat Islam*.

97. White, "Turks in the New Germany," 762.

Conclusion

1. Communication from Dru Gladney and Boğaç Ergene; compare Clause Schöning, "South Siberian Turkic," *TL*, 403–16, discussing Tuvan Turkic; Levin, *Hundred Thousand Fools of God*, 154–55 on singing styles.

2. Golden, *Introduction to the History of the Turkic Peoples*, 2.

3. Nicholas Wade, "Palette of Humankind," *NYT*, 24 December 2002, D 3.

4. Louis Bazin, "La Turcologie et l'histoire," *HTPPP*, 5.

5. Güvenç, *Türk Kimliği*, 48, 121 (quoting Sabahattin Eyuboğlu), and chs. 2–4.

6. Dru Gladney, "Cyber-Separatism, Islam, and the State in China," presentation at the Conference on "Deprivation, Violence, and Identities: Mapping Contemporary World Politics," Mershon Center, Ohio State University, 3 October 2003.

7. Ali Bulaç, "'Islami terör' mümkün mü?" *Zaman*, 3 December 2003 ("Is 'Islamic Terror' Possible?"), in comment on four suicide bombings that occurred in Istanbul in November 2003, first at two synagogues, then at the British consulate-general and the offices of a British bank; Craig S. Smith, "Turkey Says Foreign Terrorists May Be Behind Suicide Blasts" and "Turkey Expects to Identify Synagogue Bombers Soon," *NYT*, 17 November 2003; Craig S. Smith, "Turks Say to

Europe: Can't We Just Come as We Are?" *NYT*, 24 November 2003; Frank Bruni, "Turkish Town's Despair Breeds Terrorists, Residents Fear," *NYT*, 27 November 2003, about the town of Bingöl, from which at least two of the bombers came.

8. Khazanov, *After the USSR*, 184–89.

9. Di Cosmo, "State Formation and Periodization," 1–40.

10. Wilhite, "Guerrilla War, Counterinsurgency, and State Formation in Ottoman Yemen," 26–29, 291.

11. Navaro-Yashin, *Faces of the State*, 185.

12. Ortaylı, *İmparatorluğun En Uzun Yüzyılı*, 77.

13. Navaro-Yashin, *Faces of the State*, 132; Meeker, *Nation of Empire*.

14. Navaro-Yashin, *Faces of the State*, 171–80.

15. Jusdanis, *Necessary Nation*, 17, the "carpet of modernity"; Anderson, *Return to Tradition*, 3ff., 49; Glassie, *Turkish Traditional Art Today*, 571–775.

16. Gilly, "Chiapas and the Rebellion of the Enchanted World," in Nugent, *Rural Revolt in Mexico*, 319.

17. Fletcher, "Integrative History," 37, 56.

# BIBLIOGRAPHY

Abou-El-Haj, Rifa'at. *The 1703 Rebellion and the Structure of Ottoman Politics*. Leiden: Nederlands Historisch-Archologisch Instituut te Istanbul, 1984.

Abu-Lughod, Janet. *Before European Hegemony: The World System, A.D. 1250–1350*. Oxford: Oxford University Press, 1989.

Adam, Volker. *Russlandmuslime in Istanbul am Vorabend des Ersten Weltkrieges: Die Berichterstattung osmanischer Periodika über Russland und Zentralasien*. Frankfurt-am-Main: Peter Lang, 2002.

Adıvar, Halide Edib. *Ateşten Gömlek*. Istanbul: Özgür, 1997. ("Shirt of Flame," about the national struggle)

Adshead, S. A. M. *Central Asia in World History*. New York: St. Martin, 1993.

Ahmad, Feroz. *The Making of Modern Turkey*. London: Routledge, 1993.

Aitmatov, Chingiz. *The White Ship*. Trans. Mirra Ginsburg. New York: Crown, 1972.

Akarlı, Engin. *The Long Peace: Ottoman Lebanon, 1861–1920*. Berkeley and Los Angeles: University of California Press, 1993.

Akçam, Taner. *Armenien und der Völkermord: Die Istanbuler Prozesse und die türkische Nationalbewegung*. Hamburg: Hamburger Edition, 1996.

———. *Insan Hakları ve Ermeni Sorunu: İttihad ve Terakki'den Kurtuluş Savaşı'na*. Ankara: İmge, 1999.

Akçura, Yusuf. *Türkçülüğün Tarihi*. Istanbul: Analiz, 1998. ("History of Turkism")

Akçuraoğlu, Yusuf. "Osmanlı Saltanatı MüessesatıTarihine dair bir Tecrübe," *Bilgi Mecmuası*, 1.1–2 (1329/1913), 82–96, 117–34.

———. *Türkçülük ve Dış Türkler*. Istanbul: Toker Yayınları, 1990. (Turkism and Turks Abroad)

Aksan, Virginia H. "Ottoman Historical Writing, 1768–1808." *International Journal of Middle East Studies* 25 (1993): 53–69.

———. "Whatever Happened to the Janissaries? Mobilization for the 1768–1774 Russo-Ottoman War," *War in History* 5.1 (1998): 23–36.

Alacacıoğlu, Hasan. *Deutsche Heimat Islam*. Munich and Berlin: Waxmann, 2000.

Allsen, Thomas T. *Commodity and Exchange in the Mongol Empire: A Cultural History of Islamic Textiles*. Cambridge: Cambridge University Press, 1997.

———. *Culture and Conquest in Mongol Eurasia*. Cambridge: Cambridge University Press, 2001.

———. "Ever Closer Encounters: The Appropriation of Culture and the Apportionment of Peoples in the Mongol Empires." *Journal of Early Modern History* 1 (1997).

———. "Mongolian Princes and Their Merchant Partners, 1200–1260." *Asia Major* 2 (third series), no. 2 (1989): 83–126.

———. *Mongol Imperialism: The Policies of the Grand Qan Möngke in China, Russia, and the Islamic Lands, 1251–1259*. Berkeley and Los Angeles: University of California Press, 1987.

Allworth, Edward A. *The Modern Uzbeks: From the Fourteenth Century to the Present, A Cultural History*. Stanford, Cal.: Hoover Institution Press, 1990.

Allworth, Edward A., ed. *Central Asia: 130 Years of Russian Dominance: A Historical Overview*. 3d ed., Durham, N.C.: Duke University Press, 1994.

Altstadt, Audrey L. *The Azerbaijani Turks: Power and Identity under Russian Rule*. Stanford, Cal.: Hoover Institution Press, 1992.

Anderson, June. *Return to Tradition: The Revitalization of Turkish Village Carpets*. Seattle: California Academy of Sciences in Association with Washington University Press, 1998.

Anthony, David W. "Horses and Prehistoric Chronology of Eastern Europe and Western Central Asia." *The Journal of Ancient Near Eastern Society* 21 (1992): 131–33.

Anthony, David W., and Dorcas R. Brown. "The Origins of Horseback Riding." *Antiquity* 65, no. 246 (March 1991): 22–38.

Apt, Jay. "Orbit: The Astronaut's View of Home." *National Geographic* 190, no. 5 (November 1996): 4–27.

Arai, Masami. *Turkish Nationalism in the Young Turk Era*. Leiden: Brill, 1992.

Arjomand, Said Amir. *The Shadow of God and the Hidden Imam: Religion, Social Order, and Societal Change in Shi'ite Iran from the Beginning to 1890*. Chicago: University of Chicago Press, 1984.

Aşıkpaşazade. *Tevarih-i Âl-i Osman: Aşıkpaşazade Tarihi*. Ed. Âli. Istanbul: Matbaa-ı Amire, [1332] 1913–14. (History of Ottoman dynasty, fifteenth century)

Aslan, Fikret, Kemal Bozay, et al. *Graue Wölfe heulen wieder: Türkische Faschisten und ihre Vernetzung in der BRD*. Münster: Unrast, 1997.

Atatürk. See Kemal, Mustafa.

Babur. *The Baburnama: Memoirs of Babur, Prince and Emperor*. Ed. and trans. Wheeler M. Thackston. New York: Oxford University Press, 1996. Published in association with the Freer Gallery of Art

———. *The Baburnama: Memoirs of Babur, Prince and Emperor*. Ed. and trans. Wheeler M. Thackston. New York: Modern Library, 2002. (This edition is cited in the notes.)

Balivet, Michel. *Islam mystique et révolution armée dans les Balkans ottomans: Vie du Cheikh Bedreddîn, le "Hallâj des Turcs" (1358/59–1416)*. Istanbul: Isis, 1995.

———. *Romanie byzantine et pays de Rûm turc: Histoire d'un espace d'imbrication gréco-turque*. Istanbul: Isis, 1994.

Banarlı, Nihad Sâmi. *Resimli Türk Edebiyâtı Târihi: Destanlar Devrinden Zamanımıza Kadar*. 2 vols. Istanbul: Milli Eğitim Basımevi, 1987. (History of Turkish Literature).

Barber, Elizabeth Wayland. *The Mummies of Ürümchi*. New York: Norton, 1999.

Barfield, Thomas J. *The Perilous Frontier: Nomadic Empires and China*. Cambridge: Blackwell, 1996.

Barkan, Ömer Lûtfi. *Türkiye'de Toprak Meselesi*. Istanbul: Gözlem Yayınları, 1980. (Land Tenure in Turkey)

Barkova, Ludmila. "The Pazyryk Fifty Years On." *Halı* 107 (1999): 64–69, 110.

Barthold, W. *Turkestan Down to the Mongol Invasion*. 4th ed. London: E. J. W. Gibb Memorial Trust, 1977.

———. *Zwölf Vorlesungen über die Geschichte der Türken Mittelasiens*. Hildesheim: Georg Olms Verlag, 1962.

Beckwith, Christopher I. "The Impact of the Horse and Silk Trade on the Economies of T'ang China and the Uighur Empire: On the Importance of International Commerce in the Early Middle Ages." *Journal of the Economic and Social History of the Orient* 34, no. 2 (June 1991): 183–98.

———. *The Tibetan Empire in Central Asia: A History of the Struggle for Great Power Among Tibetans, Turks, Arabs, and Chinese during the Early Middle Ages*. Princeton, N.J.: Princeton University Press, 1993.

Bentley, Jerry H. *Old World Encounters: Cross-Cultural Contacts and Exchanges in Pre-Modern Times*. New York: Oxford University Press, 1993.

Bergholz, Fred W. *The Partition of the Steppe: The Struggle of the Russians, Manchus, and the Zunghar Mongols for Empire in Central Asia, 1619–1758, A Study in Power Politics*. New York and Frankfurt am Main: Peter Lang, 1993.

Berkes, Niyazi. *The Development of Secularism in Turkey*. Montreal: McGill University Press, 1964.

Berktay, Halil. *Cumhuriyet İdeolojisi ve Fuat Köprülü*. Istanbul: Kaynak, 1983.

Beydilli, Kemal. "1828–1829 Osmanlı-Rus Savaşında Doğu Anadolu'dan Rusya'ya Göçürülen Ermeniler." *Belgeler: Türk Tarih Belgeleri Dergisi* 13, no. 17 (1988): 365–434. (Armenians Transferred from Eastern Anatolia to Russia in the 1828–29 War)

Biran, Michal. "The Chaghadaids and Islam: The Conversion of Tarmashirin Khan (1331–34)." *Journal of the American Oriental Society* 122.4 (October–December 2002): 742–52.

———. *Qaidu and the Rise of the Independent Mongol State in Central Asia*. Richmond, UK: Curzon, 1997.

Bisaha, Nancy. "Pius II's Letter to Sultan Mehmed II: A Reexamination." *Crusades* 1 (2002): 183–201.

Björgo, Tore, and Rob Witte, eds. *Racist Violence in Europe.* New York: St. Martin, 1993.

Blair, Sheila S. *A Compendium of Chronicles: Rashid al-Din's Illustrated History of the World.* London: The Nour Foundation in association with Azimuth Editions and Oxford University Press, 1995.

Bombaci, Alessio. *Histoire de la littérature turque.* Trans. Irène Melikoff. Paris: Librairie C. Klincksieck, 1968.

Bonner, Michael. *Aristocratic Violence and Holy War: Studies in the Jihad and the Arab-Byzantine Frontier.* New Haven, Conn.: American Oriental Society, 1996.

*The Book of Dede Korkut.* Trans. Ahmet E. Uysal, Faruk Sümer, and Warren S. Walker. Austin: University of Texas Press, 1972.

*The Book of Dede Korkut.* Trans. Geoffrey Lewis. Harmondsworth, UK: Penguin, 1974.

Bozdoğan, Sibel. *Modernism and Nation Building: Turkish Architectural Culture in the Early Republic.* Seattle: University of Washington Press, 2001.

Bozdoğan, Sibel, and Reşat Kasaba, eds. *Rethinking Modernity and National Identity in Turkey.* Seattle: University of Washington Press, 1997.

Bregel, Yuri. *Historical Maps of Central Asia, 9th–19th Centuries A.D.* Bloomington: Indiana University Research Institute for Inner Asian Studies, 2000.

Brower, Daniel R., and Edward J. Lazzerini, eds. *Russia's Orient: Imperial Borderlands and Peoples, 1700–1917.* Bloomington: Indiana University Press, 1997.

Bukharaev, Ravil. *The Model of Tatarstan Under President Mintimer Shaimev.* Richmond, UK: Curzon, 1999.

Bulliet, Richard W. *The Camel and the Wheel.* New York: Columbia University Press, 1990.

———. *Islam, the View from the Edge.* New York: Columbia University Press, 1994.

Bunker, Emma C., with contributions by James C. Y. Watt and Zhixin Sun. *Nomadic Art of the Eastern Eurasian Steppes: The Eugene V. Thaw and Other New York Collections.* New York: Metropolitan Museum of Art, 2002.

Bunker, Emma C., with Trudy S. Kawami, Katheryn M. Linduff, and Wu En. *Ancient Bronzes of the Eastern Eurasian Steppes from the Arthur M. Sackler Collections.* New York: The Arthur M. Sackler Foundation, 1997.

Çağatay, Neşet. *Bir Türk Kurumu Olan Ahilik.* Ankara: Ankara Üniversitesi, 1974.

Cahen, Claude. *Pre-Ottoman Turkey: A General Survey of the Material and Spiritual Culture and History c. 1071–1330.* Trans. J. Jones-Williams. New York: Taplinger, 1968.

———. *La Turquie pré-Ottomane.* Istanbul-Paris: Institut Français d'Etudes Anatoliennes, 1988.

Çakır, Serpil. *Osmanlı Kadın Hareketi.* Istanbul: Metis Yayınları, 1993. (The Ottoman Women's Movement)

Canfield, Robert L., ed. *Turko-Persia in Historical Perspective.* Cambridge: Cambridge University Press, 1991.

Cezar, Yavuz. *Osmanlı Maliyesinde Bunalım ve Değişim Dönemi (XVIII yy'dan Tanzimat'a Mali Tarih).* Istanbul: Alan, 1986. (The Period of Crisis and Change in Ottoman Finance.)

Chadwick, Nora K., and Victor Zhirmunsky. *Oral Epics of Central Asia.* Cambridge: Cambridge University Press, 1969.

Chaliand, Gérard. *Les empires nomades de la Mongolie au Danube (Ve–IVe siècles av. J.-C. Xve–XVe siècles ap. J.-C.).* Paris: Perrin, 1995.

Chatterjee, Partha. *The Nation and Its Fragments: Colonial and Postcolonial Histories.* Princeton, N.J.: Princeton University Press, 1993.

Christian, David. *A History of Russia, Central Asia and Mongolia, Volume I: Inner Eurasia from Prehistory to the Mongol Empire.* Oxford: Blackwell, 1998.

Cizre, Ümit. "Demythologizing the National Security Concept: The Case of Turkey." *Middle East Journal* 57, no. 2 (Spring 2003): 213–29. See also Sakallıoğlu, Ümit Cizre.

Clauson, Sir Gerard. *An Etymological Dictionary of Pre-Thirteenth-Century Turkish.* Oxford: Oxford University Press, 1972.

Cleaves, Francis Woodman, trans. *The Secret History of the Mongols.* Cambridge, Mass.: Harvard University Press, 1982. See also Onon, Urgunge.

Cleveland, William L. *A History of the Modern Middle East.* 2d ed. Boulder: Westview, 2000.

Crone, Patricia. *Slaves on Horses: The Evolution of the Islamic Polity.* Cambridge: Cambridge University Press, 1980.

Cuno, Kenneth M. *The Pasha's Peasants: Land, Society, and Economy in Lower Egypt, 1740–1858.* Cambridge: Cambridge University Press, 1992.

Czeglédy, K. "From East to West: The Age of Nomadic Migrations in Eurasia." *Archivum Eurasiae Medii Aevi* 3 (1983): 25–125, Trans. Peter B. Golden.

———. "Das Sakrale Königtum bei Den Steppen-Völkern." *Numen: International Review for the History of Religions* 13 (1966): 14–26.

Dale, Stephen Frederic. *The Garden of the Eight Pardises: Bâbur and the Culture of Empire in Central Asia, Afghanistan and India, 1483–1530.* Leiden: Brill, 2004.

———. *Indian Merchants and Eurasian Trade, 1600–1750.* Cambridge: Cambridge University Press, 1994.

Dankoff, Robert. See Evliya, Mahmud al-Kashghari, and Yusuf Khass Hacib.

Dassetto, Felice, and Yves Conrad, eds. *Musulmans en Europe occidentale: Bibliographie commentée; Muslims in Western Europe, An Annotated Bibliography.* Paris: Editions L'Harmattan, 1996.

Daulet, Shafiga, *Kazan and Moscow: Five Centuries of Crippling Coexistence, 1552–2002,* Palm Beach, Fla.: SDR, 2003.

Davison, Roderic H. *Turkey: A Short History.* 3d ed., Updated by Clement H. Dodd. Huntingdon, UK: Eothen, 1998.

Dawisha, Adeed. *Arab Nationalism in the Twentieth Century: From Triumph to Despair.* Princeton, N.J.: Princeton University Press, 2003.

Denny, Frederick Matthewson. *An Introduction to Islam.* 2d ed. New York: Macmillan, 1994.

Denny, Walter B. "Türkmen Rugs and Early Rug Weaving in the Western Islamic World." *Halı* 4, no. 4 (Spring 1982): 329–36.

Denny, Walter B., with contributions by Sumru Belger Krody. *The Classical Tradition in Anatolian Carpets.* Washington: Textile Museum, 2002.

Deringil, Selim. *The Well-Protected Domains: Ideology and the Legitimation of Power in the Ottoman Empire, 1876–1909*. London: I. B. Tauris, 1998.

DeWeese, Devin. *Islamization and Native Religion in the Golden Horde: Baba Tükles and Conversion to Islam in Historical and Epic Tradition*. University Park: Pennsylvania State University Press, 1994.

———. "The Politics of Sacred Lineages in 19th-Century Central Asia: Descent Groups Linked to Khwaja Ahmad Yasavi in Shrine Documents and Genealogical Charters." *International Journal of Middle East Studies* 31, no. 4 (November 1999): 507–30.

Di Cosmo, Nicola. *Ancient China and Its Enemies: The Rise of Nomadic Power in East Asian History*. Cambridge: Cambridge University Press, 2002.

———. "State Formation and Periodization in Inner Asian History." *Journal of World History* 10, no. 1 (Spring 1999): 1–40.

*Digenes Akrites*. Ed. and trans. John Mavrogordato. Oxford: Clarendon, 1956.

Ding Xueyun. "Butumuji Jindai Shi Ji Qi Yanjiu." In *Neimenggu Wenwu Gaogu Wenji: Di Erh Ji*, Ed. Wei Jian. Vol. II, 463–73. Beijing: Encyclopedia of China Publishing House, 1997. ("Gold Belt Ornaments from Butumuji and Their Study," in Wei Jian, ed., *Collected Papers on Inner Mongolian Relics and Archeology*; about the belt illustrated in chapter one)

Dodd, Clement H. *Storm Clouds Over Cyprus: A Briefing*. Huntingdon, UK: Eothen, 2001.

Dodd, Clement H., ed. *Cyprus: The Need for New Perspectives*. Huntingdon, UK: Eothen, 1999.

Dols, Michael. *The Black Death in the Middle East*. Princeton, N.J.: Princeton University Press, 1977.

Drompp, Michael R. "Breaking the Orkhon Tradition: Kirghiz Adherence to the Yenisei Region after A.D. 840." *Journal of the American Oriental Society* 119, no. 3 (1999): 390–403.

Duara, Prasenjit. *Rescuing History from the Nation: Questioning Narratives of Modern China*. Chicago: University of Chicago Press, 1995.

Duben, Alan, and Cem Behar. *Istanbul Households: Marriage, Family, and Fertility, 1880–1940*. Cambridge: Cambridge University Press, 1991.

Dunn, Ross E. *The Adventures of Ibn Battuta: A Muslim Traveler of the 14th Century*. Berkeley and Los Angeles: University of California Press, 1989.

Ebulgazi Bahadır Han. *Şecere-i Terâkime (Türkmenlerin Soykütüğü)*. Ed. Zuhal Kargı Ölmez. Ankara: Simurg, 1996. (Genealogy of the Türkmen)

Eley, Geoff, and Ronald Grigor Suny, eds. *Becoming National: A Reader*. New York: Oxford University Press, 1996.

*Encyclopaedia of Islam*. 2d ed. 11 vols. Leiden: Brill, 1960–2002.

Endicott-West, Elizabeth. "Merchant Associations in Yüan China: The *Ortogh*." *Asia Major* 2 (third series), no. 2 (1989): 127–54.

Enveri. *Le Destan d'Umur Pacha (Düsturname-i Enveri)*. Ed. and trans. Irène Mélikoff-Sayar. Paris: Presses Universitaires de France, 1954.

Erdmann, Kurt. *Oriental Carpets, an Essay on Their History*. Trans. Charles Grant Ellis. New York: Universe Books, 1962.

Ergene, Boğaç A. *Local Court, Provincial Society, and Justice in the Ottoman Empire: Legal Practice and Dispute Resolution in Çankırı and Kastamonu (1652–1744)*. Leiden: Brill, 2003.

Erickson, Edward J. *Ordered to Die: A History of the Ottoman Army in the First World War*. Westport, Conn.: Greenwood Press, 2001.

Ertürk, Korkut A., ed. *Rethinking Central Asia: Non-Eurocentric Studies in History, Social Structure and Identity*. Reading, UK: Ithaca Press, 1999.

Erzurumi, Hüseyin ibn Ahmet el-, *Hulasa, Okçuluk ve Atçılık: Kitb fî-İlm'n-Nüşşab, Kitab fî-Riyâzâti'l-Hayl, Kitâb fî'l-İlmi'l-Musâbaka*. Ed. H. İbrahim Delice. Istanbul: Kitabevi, 2003. (Sources on Archery and Horsemanship)

Esin, Emel. *A History of Pre-Islamic and Early Islamic Turkish Culture*. Istanbul: Ünal, 1980.

Esposito, John, ed. *The Oxford History of Islam*. Oxford: Oxford University Press, 1999.

Evliya. *The Intimate Life of an Ottoman Statesman, Melek Ahmed Pasha (1588–1662), as Portrayed in Evliya Çelebi's Book of Travels (Seyahatname)*. Ed. and trans. Robert Dankoff, with historical introduction by Rhoads Murphey. Albany: State University of New York Press, 1991.

Fahmy, Khaled. *All the Pasha's Men: Mehmed Ali, His Army and the Making of Modern Egypt*. Cambridge: Cambridge University Press, 1997.

Fairbank, John K., Edwin O. Reischauer, and Albert M. Craig. *East Asia, Tradition and Transformation*. Boston: Houghton Mifflin, 1978.

Faroqhi, Suraiya. *Men of Modest Substance: House Owners and House Property in Seventeenth-Century Ankara and Kayseri*. Cambridge: Cambridge University Press, 1987.

———. *Pilgrims and Sultans: The Hajj Under the Ottomans, 1517–1683*. London: I. B. Tauris, 1994.

———. *Towns and Townsmen of Ottoman Anatolia: Trade, Crafts and Food Production in an Urban Setting, 1520–50*. Cambridge: Cambridge University Press, 1984.

Ferdinand, Peter, ed. *The New States of Central Asia and Their Neighbors*. New York: Council on Foreign Relations, 1994.

Ferrari, Silvio, and Anthony Bradney. *Islam and European Legal Systems*. Aldershot, UK: Ashgate-Dartmouth, 2000.

Findley, Carter Vaughn. *Bureaucratic Reform in the Ottoman Empire: The Sublime Porte, 1789–1922*. Princeton, N.J.: Princeton University Press, 1980.

———. "Ebu Bekir Ratib's Vienna Embassy Narrative: Discovering Austria or Propagandizing for Reform in Istanbul?" *Wiener Zeitschrift für die Kunde des Morgenlandes* 85 (1995): 41–80.

———. "Economic Bases of Revolution and Repression in the Late Ottoman Empire." *Comparative Studies in Society and History* 28 (1986): 81–106.

———. "Fatma Aliye: First Ottoman Woman Novelist, Pioneer Feminist." In *Histoire économique et sociale de l'Empire ottoman et de la Turquie (1326–1960), Actes du sixième congrès international tenu à Aix-en-Provence du 1er au 4 juillet 1992*, ed. Daniel Panzac, 783–89. Paris: Peeters, 1995.

———. "Osmanlı Düşüncesinde Devlet ve Hukuk: İnsan Hakları mı, Hukuk

Devleti mi?" In *XII. [Onikinci] Türk Tarih Kongresi*. Ankara: Türk Tarih Kurumu, 2000. (Human Rights or *Rechtsstaat:* State and Law in Ottoman Thought)

————. *Ottoman Civil Officialdom: A Social History*. Princeton, N.J.: Princeton University Press, 1989.

————. "An Ottoman Occidentalist in Europe: Ahmed Midhat Meets Madame Gülnar, 1889." *The American Historical Review* 103, no. 1 (February 1998): 15–49.

————. "Problems of Educational Democratization in an Era of Explosive Population Growth." *Journal of the Japan-Netherlands Institute* 6 (1996): 257–76.

————. "La soumise, la subversive: Fatma Aliye, romancière et féministe." *Turcica* 27 (1995): 153–76.

————. "Türklük: Zamanda ve Zeminde Kültür Dönüşümleri." Trans. Boğaç Ergene. *Tarih ve Toplum* 29, no. 169 (January 1998): 15–22.

Finkel, Caroline. *The Administration of Warfare: The Ottoman Military Campaigns in Hungary, 1593–1606*. Vienna: Verein der wissenschaftlichen Gesellschaften Österreichs, 1988.

Fisher, Alan W. *The Crimean Tatars*. Stanford, Cal.: Hoover Institution, 1978.

Fleischer, Cornell H. *Bureaucrat and Intellectual in the Ottoman Empire: The Historian Mustafa Âli (1541–1600)*. Princeton, N.J.: Princeton University Press, 1986.

Fletcher, Joseph. "Integrative History: Parallels and Interconnections in the Early Modern Period, 1500–1800." *Journal of Turkish Studies—Türklük Bilgisi Araştırmaları* 9 (1985): 37–57.

————. "Turco-Mongolian Monarchic Tradition in the Ottoman Empire." *Harvard Ukrainian Studies* 3–4, Part 1 (1979–80): 236–51.

Foltz, Richard C. *Religions of the Silk Road: Overland Trade and Cultural Exchange from Antiquity to the Fifteenth Century*. New York: St. Martin, 1999.

Fortna, Benjamin. *Imperial Classroom: Islam, the State, and Education in the Late Ottoman Empire*. Oxford: Oxford University Press, 2002.

Frank, Allen J. *Islamic Historiography and 'Bulghar' Identity Among the Tatars and Bashkirs of Russia*. Leiden: Brill, 1998.

————. *Muslim Religious Institutions in Imperial Russia: The Islamic World of Novouzensk District and the Kazakh Inner Horde, 1780–1910*. Leiden: Brill, 2001.

Frye, Richard N. *The Heritage of Central Asia: From Antiquity to the Turkish Expansion*. Princeton, N.J.: Markus Wiener, 1996.

Genç, Mehmet. *Osmanlı İmparatorluğunda Devlet ve Ekonomi*. Istanbul: Ötüken, 2000. (State and Economy in the Ottoman Empire)

Georgeon, François. *Abdulhamid II, le sultan calife*. Paris: Fayard, 2003.

————. *Aux origines du nationalisme turc, Yusuf Akçura (1876–1935)*. Paris: Editions ADPF, 1980.

————. *Des Ottomans aux Turcs, naissance d'une nation*. Istanbul: Isis, 1995.

Geraci, Robert P. *Window on the East: National and Imperial Identities in the Late Tsarist Russia*. Ithaca, N.Y.: Cornell University Press, 2001.

Giraud, René. *L'Empire des Turcs célestes: Les règnes d'Elterich, Qapghan et Bilgä (680–734)*. Paris: Adrien-Maisonneuve, 1960.

Gladney, Dru C. "Central Asia and China: Transnationalization, Islamization, and Ethnicization." In *The Oxford History of Islam*, ed. John L. Esposito. New York: Oxford University Press, 1999.

———. *Muslim Chinese: Ethnic Nationalism in the People's Republic*. Cambridge, Mass.: Harvard University Press, 1991.

———. "The Uyghur of China." In *Endangered Peoples of Southeast and East Asia*, ed. Leslie E. Sponsel, 233–50. Westport, Conn.: Greenwood Press, 2000.

Glassie, Henry. *Turkish Traditional Art Today*. Bloomington: Indiana University Press, 1993.

Göçek, Fatma Müge. *Rise of the Bourgeoisie, Demise of Empire: Ottoman Westernization and Social Change*. New York: Oxford University Press, 1996.

Goffman, Daniel. *Izmir and the Levantine World*. Seattle: University of Washington Press, 1990.

Golden, Peter B. "Central Asia." In *The American Historical Association's Guide to Historical Literature*, ed. Pamela Gerardi and Mary Beth Norton, vol. I, 259–82. New York: Oxford University Press, 1995. The *AHA Guide* also includes bibliographies on the Islamic world to 1500, the Middle East and North Africa since 1500, and other relevant themes.

———. "Imperial Ideology and the Sources of Political Unity Amongst the Pre-Činggisid Nomads of Western Eurasia." *Archivum Eurasiae Medii Aevi* 2 (1982): 37–76.

———. *An Introduction to the History of the Turkic Peoples: Ethnogenesis and State-Formation in Medieval and Early Modern Eurasia and the Middle East*. Wiesbaden: Otto Harrassowitz, 1992.

———. "'I Will Give the People Unto Thee': The Činggisid Conquests and Their Aftermath in the Turkic World." *Journal of the Royal Asiatic Society* series 3, 10, no. 1 (2000): 21–41.

———. *Khazar Studies: An Historico-Philological Inquiry into the Origins of the Khazars*. 2 vols. Budapest: Akadémiai Kiadó, 1980.

———. "The Migrations of the Oğuz." *Archivum Ottomanicum* 4 (1972): 45–84.

———. *Nomads and Sedentary Societies in Medieval Eurasia*. Washington, D.C.: American Historical Association, 1998.

———. "Religion Among the Qıpčaqs of Medieval Eurasia." *Central Asiatic Journal: International Periodical for the Languages, History and Archaeology of Central Asia* 42, no. 2 (1998): 180–237.

———. "Wolves, Dogs and Qipčaq Religion." *Acta Orientalia Academiae Scientiarum Hungaricae* 50, nos. 1–3 (1997): 87–97.

Golden, Peter B., ed. *The King's Dictionary, The Rasûlid Hexaglot: Fourteenth Century Vocabularies in Arabic, Persian, Turkic, Greek, Armenian and Mongol*. Trans. Tibor Halas-Kun, Peter B. Golden, Louis Ligeti, and Edmund Schutz. Introductory essays by Peter B. Golden and Thomas T. Allsen. Leiden: Brill, 2000.

Göle, Nilüfer. *The Forbidden Modern: Civilization and Veiling*. Ann Arbor: University of Michigan Press, 1996.

———. *Modern Mahrem: Medeniyet ve Örtünme*. Istanbul: Metis Yayınları, 1991. (Civilization and Veiling)

Gorenburg, Dimitry Primus. "Nationalism for the Masses: Minority Ethnic Mobilization in the Russian Federation." Ph.D. diss. Cambridge, Mass.: Harvard University, 1999.

Gross, Jo-Ann, ed. *Muslims in Central Asia: Expressions of Identity and Change.* Durham, N.C.: Duke University Press, 1992.

Gunder Frank, André. *ReOrient: Global Economy in the Asian Age.* Berkeley and Los Angeles: University of California Press, 1998.

Güran, Tevfik. *19. Yüzyıl Osmanlı Tarımı üzerine Araştırmalar.* Istanbul: Eren, 1998. (Researches on Nineteenth-Century Ottoman Agriculture)

Güvenç, Bozkurt. *Türk Kimliği: Kültür Tarihinin Kaynakları.* Ankara: Kültür Bakanlığı, 1993. (Turkish Identity: Sources of Cultural History)

Hale, William. *Turkish Foreign Policy, 1774–2000.* London: Frank Cass, 2000.

———. *Turkish Politics and the Military.* London: Routledge, 1994.

Halman, Talât Said, ed. *Yunus Emre and His Mystical Poetry.* Bloomington: Indiana University Turkish Studies, 1981.

Hamilton, James Russell. *Les Ouïghours à l'époque des cinq dynasties d'après les documents chinois.* Paris: Imprimerie Nationale, 1955.

Hanioğlu, M. Şükrü. *Preparation for a Revolution: The Young Turks, 1902–1908.* New York: Oxford University Press, 2001.

———. *The Young Turks in Opposition.* New York: Oxford University Press, 1995.

Hansen, Bent. *The Political Economy of Poverty, Equity, and Growth: Egypt and Turkey.* Oxford: Oxford University Press for the World Bank, 1991.

Hansen, Randall, and Patrick Weil. *Towards a European Nationality: Citizenship, Immigration and Nationality Law in the EU.* Houndsmills, UK: Palgrave, 2001.

Harmatta, J., ed. *Prolegomena to the Sources of Pre-Islamic Central Asia.* Budapest: Akadémiai Kiadó, 1979.

Hassan, Riaz. *Faithlines: Muslim Conceptions of Islam and Society.* Oxford: Oxford University Press, 2002.

Hathaway, Jane. *The Politics of Households in Ottoman Egypt: The Rise of the Qazdağlıs.* Cambridge: Cambridge University Press, 1997.

———. *A Tale of Two Factions: Myth, Memory, and Identity in Ottoman Egypt and Yemen.* Albany: State University of New York Press, 2003.

Hatto, Arthur T. *The Manas of Wilhelm Radloff: Re-Edited, Newly Translated and with a Commentary.* Wiesbaden: Otto Harrassowitz, 1990.

Hearn, Maxwell K. *Splendors of Imperial China: Treasures from the National Palace Museum, Taipei.* New York: Metropolitan Museum of Art, 1996.

Heine, Peter. *Halbmond über deutschen Dächern: Muslimisches Leben in unserem Land.* Munich-Leipzig: List, 1997.

Heitmeyer, Wilhelm, and Reimund Anhut, eds. *Bedrohte Stadtgesellschaft: Soziale Desintegrationsprozesse und ethnisch-kulturelle Konfliktkonstellationen.* Weinheim and Munich: Juventa, 2000.

Heitmeyer, Wilhelm, Joachim Müller, and Helmut Schröder. *Verlockender Fundamentalismus: Türkische Jugendliche in Deutschland.* Frankfurt am Main: Suhrkamp, 1997.

Heper, Metin. *Historical Dictionary of Turkey*. Lanham, Md.: Scarecrow Press, 2002.

———. *Ismet Inönü: The Making of a Turkish Statesman*. Leiden: Brill, 1998.

Heper, Metin, and Ahmed Evin, eds. *Politics in the Third Turkish Republic*. Boulder, Col.: Westview Press, 1994.

Heper, Metin, and Aylin Güney. "The Military and the Consolidation of Democracy: The Recent Turkish Experience." *Armed Forces and Society* 26, no. 4 (Summer 2000): 635–57.

Heper, Metin, Ali Kazancıgil, and Bert A. Rockman. *Institutions and Democratic Statecraft*. Boulder, Col.: Westview, 1997.

Heper, Metin, and E. Fuat Keyman. "Double-Faced State: Political Patronage and the Consolidation of Democracy in Turkey." In *Turkey Before and After Atatürk, Internal and External Affairs*, ed. Sylvia Kedourie, 259–77. London: Frank Cass, 1999.

Heper, Metin, and Sabri Sayarı, eds. *Political Leaders and Democracy in Turkey*. Lanham, Md.: Lexington Books, 2002.

Herodotus. *The History*. Trans. David Grene. Chicago: University of Chicago Press, 1987.

Heywood, Colin. "Boundless Dreams of the Levant: Paul Wittek, the George-Kreis, and the Writing of Ottoman History." *Journal of the Royal Asiatic Society*, no. 1 (1989): 32–50.

———. "Wittek and the Austrian Tradition." *Journal of the Royal Asiatic Society*, no. 1 (1988): 7–25.

Hobsbawm, E. J. *Nations and Nationalism Since 1780: Programme, Myth, Reality*. Cambridge: Cambridge University Press, 1992.

Hodgson, Marshall G. S. *The Venture of Islam*. 3 vols. Chicago: University of Chicago Press, 1974.

Horrocks, David, and Eva Kolinsky, eds. *Turkish Culture in German Society Today*. Providence, R.I.: Berghahn, 1996.

Hourani, Albert. *A History of the Arab Peoples*. Cambridge, Mass.: Harvard University Press, 1991.

Hourani, Albert, Philip S. Khoury, and Mary C. Wilson, eds. *The Modern Middle East: A Reader*. Berkeley and Los Angeles: University of California Press, 1993.

Huntington, Samuel. *The Clash of Civilizations: Remaking of World Order*. New York: Touchstone, 1996.

Hurvitz, Nimrod. "From Scholarly Circles to Mass Movements: The Formation of Legal Communities in Islamic Societies." *American Historical Review* 108, no. 4 (October 2003): 985–1008.

Hütteroth, Wolf-Dieter, and Volker Höhfeld. *Türkei*. Darmstadt: Wissenschaftliche Buchgesellschaft, 2002.

Ibn Battuta. *The Travels of Ibn Battuta, A.D. 1325–1354*. 5 vols. Ed. C. Defremery and B. R. Sanguinetti. Trans. H. A. R. Gibb. Cambridge: Published for the Hakluyt Society at the University Press, 1958–2000.

Idrisi, Al- (Abu Abdullah Muhammad ibn Muhammad ibn Abdullah ibn Idris al-Hammudi al-Hasani). *Kitab Nuzhat al-Mushtaq fi Ikhtiraq al-Afaq: Opus Geographicum sive 'Liber ad Eorum Delectationem qui Terras Peragrare Studeant'*.

Ed. A. Bombaci, U. Rizzitano, R. Rubinacci, and L. Veccia Vagliera. Leiden: Brill, 1974.

Ilkhamov, Alisher. "Nation-State Formation: Features of Social Stratification in the Late Soviet Era." *International Journal of Middle East Studies* 34, no. 2 (2002): 317–35.

Imber, Colin. *Ebu's-Su'ud, The Islamic Legal Tradition*. Stanford, Cal.: Stanford University Press, 1997.

———. *The Ottoman Empire, 1300–1650*. New York: Palgrave Macmillan, 2002.

———. "What Does *Ghazi Really Mean?*" In *The Balance of Truth: Essays in Honour of Professor Geoffrey Lewis*, ed. Çiğdem Balım-Harding and Colin Imber, 165–78. Istanbul: Isis, 2000.

İnal, İbnülemin Mahmud Kemal. *Son Asır Türk Şairleri*. Istanbul: Milli Eğitim Basımevi, 1969. (Lives of Late Ottoman Literati)

İnalcık, Halil. "Adaletnameler." *Belgeler* 2 (1965): 49–145. (Justice Decrees)

———. "Bursa and the Commerce of the Levant." *Journal of the Social and Economic History of the Orient* 3 (1960): 131–47.

———. "Centralization and Decentralization in Ottoman Administration." In *Studies in Eighteenth Century Islamic History*, ed. Thomas Naff and Roger Owen, 27–52. Carbondale: Southern Illinois University Press, 1977.

———. *Fâtih Devri üzerinde Tetkikler ve Vesikalar*. Ankara: Türk Tarih Kurumu, 1954. (Studies and Documents on the Period of Mehmed the Conqueror)

———. *Hicrî 835 Tarihli Sûret-i Defter-i Sancak-ı Arvanid*. Ankara: Türk Tarih Kurumu, 1954. (The Albanian Land Tenure Register of 835/1431–32)

———. "The Khan and the Tribal Aristocracy: The Crimean Khanate Under Sahib Giray I." *Harvard Ukrainian Studies* 3–4, Part 1 (1979–80): 445–66.

———. *The Middle East and the Balkans Under the Ottoman Empire: Essays on Economy and Society*. Bloomington: Indiana University Turkish Studies, 1993.

———. "Military and Fiscal Transformation in the Ottoman Empire, 1600–1700." *Archivum Ottomanicum* 6 (1980): 283–337.

———. "Osmanlılar'da Raiyyet Rüsumu." *Belleten* 23 (1959): 575–608. (Tax Obligations of the Peasantry)

———. *The Ottoman Empire, the Classical Age 1300–1600*. London: Weidenfeld and Nicholson, 1973.

İnalcık, Halil, and Günsel Renda, eds. *Ottoman Civilization*. 2 vols. Ankara: Ministry of Culture, 2002.

İnalcık, Halil, with Donald Quataert, eds. *An Economic and Social History of the Ottoman Empire, 1300–1914*. Cambridge: Cambridge University Press, 1994.

*Islâm Ansiklopedisi*. 13 vols. Istanbul: Milli Eğitim Basımevi, 1940–88.

Jahiz, Abu 'Uthman 'Amr ibn Bahr, al-. *Hilâfet Ordusunun Menkibeleri ve Türkler'in Fazîletleri*. Trans. Ramazan Şeşen. Ankara: Türk Kültürünü Araştırma Enstitüsü, 1967. (Deeds of the Caliphal Army and Virtues of the Turks)

———. *The Life and Works of Jahiz*. Ed. Charles Pellat. Trans. D. M. Hawke. Berkeley and Los Angeles: University of California Press, 1969.

Jarring, Gunnar. *Return to Kashgar: Central Asian Memoirs in the Present*. Durham, N.C.: Duke University Press, 1986.

Jarring, Gunnar, ed. and trans. *Literary Texts from Kashghar.* Lund, Sweden: C. W. K. Gleerup, 1980.

Johanson, Lars. "Grenzen der Turcia: Verbindendes und Trennendes in der Entwicklung der Türkvölker." In *Turcica et Orientalia: Studies in Honour of Gunnar Jarring on His Eightieth Birthday, 12 October 1987,* ed. Ulla Ehrensvärd, 51–61. Stockholm: Swedish Research Institute in Istanbul, 1988.

Johanson, Lars, and Éva Á. Csató, eds. *The Turkic Languages.* London: Routledge, 1998.

Juergensmeyer, Mark. *Terror in the Mind of God: The Global Rise of Religious Violence.* Berkeley and Los Angeles: University of California Press, 2000.

Jusdanis, Gregory. *The Necessary Nation.* Princeton, N.J.: Princeton University Press, 2001.

Juvaini, 'Ala-ad-Din 'Ata-Malik. *The History of the World-Conqueror.* 2 vols. Trans. John Andrew Boyle. Cambridge, Mass.: Harvard University Press, 1958.

Kafadar, Cemal. *Between Two Worlds: The Construction of the Ottoman State.* Berkeley and Los Angeles: University of California Press, 1995.

Kafesoğlu, Ibrahim. *Eski Türk Dini.* Ankara: Kültür Bakanlığı, 1980. (Ancient Turkic Religion)

Kağıtçıbaşı, Çiğdem. "Women and Development in Turkey." *International Journal of Turkish Studies* 2, no. 2 (Winter 1982): 59–70.

Kai Ka'us ibn Iskandar. *A Mirror for Princes: The Qabus Nama.* Trans. Reuben Levy. New York: Dutton, 1951.

Karakaya-Stump, Ayfer. "Debating Progress in a 'Serious Newspaper for Muslim Women': The Periodical *Kadın* of the Post-Revolutionary Salonica, 1908–1909." *British Journal of Middle East Studies* 30, no. 2 (November 2003): 155–81.

Karamustafa, Ahmet T. *God's Unruly Friends: Dervish Groups in the Islamic Later Middle Period, 1200–1550.* Salt Lake City: University of Utah Press, 1994.

Karaömerlioğlu, M. Asım. "The Cult of the Peasant: Ideology and Practice, Turkey, 1930–1946." Ph.D. diss., Ohio State University, Columbus, 1999.

———. "The People's Houses and the Cult of the Peasant in Turkey." *Middle Eastern Studies* 34, no. 4 (October 1998): 67–91. Special Issue, *Turkey Before and After Atatürk: Internal and External Affairs,* ed. Sylvia Kedourie

———. "The Village Institutes Experience in Turkey." *British Journal of Middle Eastern Studies* 25, no. 1 (1998): 47–73.

Karaosmanoğlu, Yakup Kadri. *Panorama.* Istanbul: İletişim, 1987.

Karpat, Kemal H. *Ottoman Population, 1830–1914.* Madison: University of Wisconsin Press, 1985.

———. *The Politicization of Islam: Reconstructing Identity, State, Faith, and Community in the Late Ottoman State.* New York: Oxford University Press, 2001.

Kaşgari, Mahmud al-. *Divanü Lûgat-it-Türk. Tıpkıbasımı: "Faksimile."* Ed. Besim Atalay. Ankara: Alâeddin Kıral Basımevi, 1941.

Kashghari, Mahmud al-. *Compendium of the Turkic Dialects (Diwan Lughat al-Turk).* 3 vols. Ed. and trans. Robert Dankoff and James Kelly. Cambridge, Mass.: Harvard University, Office of the University Printer, 1982–85.

Kayalı, Hasan. *Arabs and Young Turks: Ottomanism, Arabism, and Islamism in the*

*Ottoman Empire, 1908–1918.* Berkeley and Los Angeles: University of California Press, 1997.

Kemal, Mustafa. *Nutuk.* Ankara: Türk Tayyare Cemiyeti, 1927. ("The Speech")

———. *A Speech Delivered by Ghazi Mustapha Kemal, President of the Turkish Republic.* Leipzig: K. F. Koehler, 1929.

Kemp, Marianne. "Pilgrimage and Performance: Uzbek Women and the Imagining of Uzbekistan in the 1920s." *International Journal of Middle East Studies* 34, no. 2 (2002): 263–78.

Kennedy, Hugh, ed. *An Historical Atlas of Islam, Atlas Historique de l'Islam.* 2d ed., rev. Leiden: Brill, 2002.

Kessler, Adam T. *Empires Beyond the Great Wall: The Heritage of Genghis Khan.* Los Angeles: Natural History Museum of Los Angeles County, 1993.

Keyder, Çağlar, ed. *Istanbul Between the Global and the Local.* Lanham, Md.: Rowman and Littlefield, 1999.

Khalid, Adeeb. *The Politics of Muslim Cultural Reform: Jadidism in Central Asia.* Berkeley and Los Angeles: University of California Press, 1998.

———. "A Secular Islam: Nation, State, and Religion in Uzbekistan." *International Journal of Middle East Studies* 35, no. 4 (November 2003): 573–98.

Khater, Akram Fouad. *Inventing Home: Emigration, Gender, and the Middle Class in Lebanon, 1870–1920.* Berkeley and Los Angeles: University of California Press, 2001.

Khazanov, Anatoly M. *After the USSR: Ethnicity, Nationalism, and Politics in the Commonwealth of Independent States.* Madison: University of Wisconsin Press, 1995.

———. *Nomads and the Outside World.* Trans. Julia Crookenden. Madison: University of Wisconsin Press, 1983.

Khodarkovsky, Michael. *Russia's Steppe Frontier: The Making of a Colonial Empire, 1500–1800.* Bloomington: Indiana University Press, 2002.

Khoury, Dina Rizk. *State and Provincial Society in the Ottoman Empire: Mosul, 1540–1834.* Cambridge: Cambridge University Press, 1997.

Kinzer, Stephen. *Crescent and Star: Turkey Between Two Worlds.* New York: Farrar, Straus and Giroux, 2001.

Kırımlı, Hakan. *National Movements and National Identity Among the Crimean Tatars (1905–1916).* Leiden: Brill, 1996.

Klimkeit, Hans-Joachim, trans. and ed. *Gnosis on the Silk Road: Gnostic Texts from Central Asia.* San Francisco: Harper, 1993.

Klopsteg, Paul E. *Turkish Archery and the Composite Bow.* Manchester: Simon Archery Foundation, 1987.

Klyashtorny, S. G. "The Royal Clan of the Turks and the Problem of Early Turkic-Iranian Contacts." *Acta Orientalia Hungarica* 47, no. 3 (1994): 445–47.

Koçtürk, Tahire. *A Matter of Honour: Experiences of Turkish Women Immigrants.* London: Zed Books, 1992.

Komaroff, Linda, and Stefano Carboni. *The Legacy of Genghis Khan: Courtly Art and Culture in Western Asia, 1256–1353.* New York: Metropolitan Museum of Art, 2002.

Kondrashov, Sergei. *Nationalism and the Drive for Sovereignty in Tatarstan, 1988–92: Origins and Development.* Houndmills, UK: Macmillan, 2000.

Köprülü, Mehmed Fuad. *Islam in Anatolia After the Turkish Invasion (Prolegomena)*. Trans. Gary Leiser. Salt Lake City: University of Utah Press, 1993.

———. *Les origines de l'Empire ottoman*. Paris: E. de Boccard, 1935

———. *Osmanlı İmparatorluğunun Kuruluşu*. Ed. Orhan Köprülü. Istanbul: Ötüken, 1981.

———. *The Seljuks of Anatolia*. Trans. Gary Leiser. Salt Lake City: University of Utah Press, 1992.

Köseoğlu, Nevzat. *Devlet, Eski Türklerde, İslâm'da, ve Osmanlı'da*. Istanbul: Ötüken, 1997. (The State, Among the Early Turks, in Islam, and Among the Ottomans)

Kreiser, Klaus, and Christoph K. Neumann, *Kleine Geschichte der Türkei*. Stuttgart: Philipp Reclam jun., 2003.

Kuban, Doğan. *Batıya Göçün Sanatsal Evreleri: Anadoludan Önce Türklerin Sanat Ortaklıkları*. Istanbul: Cem Yayınevi, 1993. (Artistic Stages in the Westward Migration: The Shared Artistic Inheritance of the Pre-Anatolian Turks)

———. *Sinan's Art: Selimiye*. Istanbul: Economic and Social History Foundation of Turkey, 1997.

Küçükcan, Talip. *Politics of Ethnicity, Identity, and Religion: Turkish Muslims in Britain*. Aldershot: Ashgate, 1999.

Landau, Jacob. *Pan-Turkism: From Irredentism to Cooperation*. Bloomington: Indiana University Press, 1995.

Lapidus, Ira M. *A History of Islamic Societies*. Cambridge: Cambridge University Press, 1988.

Lattimore, Owen. *Inner Asian Frontiers of China*. Hong Kong: Oxford University Press [1940], 1988.

Leeuw, Charles van der. *Azerbaijan, A Quest for Identity: A Short History*. New York: St. Martin, 2000.

Leggewie, Claus, and Zafer Şenocak. *Deutsche Türken, Das Ende der Geduld; Türk Almanlar, Sabrın Sonu*. Reinbek bei Hamburg: Rowohlt, 1993.

Leiser, Gary. *A History of the Seljuks: Ibrahim Kafesoğlu's Interpretation and the Resulting Controversy*. Carbondale and Edwardsville: Southern Illinois University Press, 1988.

Lemerle, Paul. *L'émirat d'Aydin, Byzance et l'Occident, Recherches sur "La geste d'Umur Pacha."* Paris: Presses universitaires de France, 1957.

Levi, Scott C. *The Indian Diaspora in Central Asia and Its Trade, 1550–1900*. Leiden: Brill, 2002.

Levin, Theodore. *The Hundred Thousand Fools of God: Musical Travels in Central Asia (and Queens, New York)*. Bloomington: Indiana University Press, 1996.

Levy, Avigdor. "The Military Policy of Sultan Mahmud II, 1808–1839." Ph.D. diss., Harvard University, Cambridge, Mass., 1968.

Lewis, Bernard. *Islam from the Prophet Muhammad to the Capture of Constantinople*. 2 vols. New York: Oxford University Press, 1987.

———. *The Jews of Islam*. Princeton, N.J.: Princeton University Press, 1984.

———. *The Middle East: A Brief History of the Last 2,000 Years*. New York: Oxford University Press, 1995.

———. *What Went Wrong? Western Impact and Middle Eastern Response*. New York: Oxford University Press, 2002.

Lewis, Geoffrey. *The Turkish Language Reform: A Catastrophic Success*. Oxford: Oxford University Press, 1999. See also *The Book of Dede Korkut*.

Light, Nathan. "Slippery Paths: The Performance and Canonization of Turkic Literature and Uyghur Muqam Song in Islam and Modernity." Ph.D. diss., Indiana University, Bloomington, 1998.

Lindner, Rudi Paul. *Nomads and Ottomans in Medieval Anatolia*. Bloomington, Ind.: Research Institute for Inner Asian Studies, 1983.

Liu, Mau-tsai. *Die chinesischen Nachrichten zur Geschichte der Ost-Türken (T'u-Küe)*. 2 vols. Wiesbaden: Otto Harrassowitz, 1958.

Lowry, Heath W. *The Nature of the Early Ottoman State*. Albany: State University of New York, 2003.

Lydolph, Paul E. *Geography of the U.S.S.R.* 5th ed. Elkhart Lake, Wisc.: Misty Valley, 1990.

Mackerras, Colin. *The Uighur Empire According to the T'ang Dynastic Histories: A Study in Sino-Uighur Relations, 744–840*. Columbia: University of South Carolina Press, 1972.

Maenchen-Helfen, O. *The World of the Huns*. Berkeley and Los Angeles: University of California Press, 1973.

Mair, Victor H. "Mummies of the Tarim Basin: Dessicated Remains Found in Western China Point to the Spread of Indo-Europeans Some 4,000 Years Ago." *Archeology* 48, no. 2 (1995): 28–35.

Mango, Andrew. *Atatürk*. London: John Murray, 1999.

Mantran, Robert, ed. *Histoire de l'Empire ottoman*. Paris: Fayard, 1989.

Manz, Beatrice F. *The Rise and Rule of Tamerlane*. Cambridge: Cambridge University Press, 1989.

Manz, Beatrice F., ed. *Central Asia in Historical Perspective*. Boulder, Col.: Westview Press, 1994.

Mardin, Şerif. *The Genesis of Young Ottoman Thought: A Study in the Modernization of Turkish Political Ideas*. Princeton, N.J.: Princeton University Press, 1962.

———. *Religion and Social Change in Modern Turkey*. Albany: State University of New York Press, 1989.

Markovits, Claude. *The Global World of Indian Merchants, 1750–1947: Traders of Sind from Bukhara to Panama*. Cambridge: Cambridge University Press, 2000.

Martin, Terry. *The Affirmative Action Empire: Nations and Nationalism in the Soviet Union, 1923–1939*. Ithaca, N.Y.: Cornell University Press, 2001.

Masters, Bruce. *Christians and Jews in the Ottoman Arab World: The Roots of Sectarianism*. Cambridge: Cambridge University Press, 2001.

Mas'udi, Al-. *Muruj al-Dhahab wa Ma'adin al-Jawhar*. 7 vols. Ed. Charles Pellat. Beirut: Manshurat al-Jami'at al-Lubnaniyya, 1966–79.

Matthee, Rudolph P. *The Politics of Trade in Safavid Iran: Silk for Silver, 1600–1730*. Cambridge: Cambridge University Press, 1999.

McCarthy, Justin. *Death and Exile: The Ethnic Cleansing of Ottoman Muslims, 1821–1922*. Princeton, N.J.: Darwin Press, 1995.

McCarthy, Justin. *Muslims and Minorities: The Population of Ottoman Anatolia and the End of the Empire*. New York: New York University Press, 1983.

────. *The Ottoman Peoples and the End of Empire*. London: Arnold, 2001.

McCarthy, Justin, and Carolyn McCarthy. *Who Are the Turks? A Manual for Teachers*. New York: American Forum for Global Education, 2003.

McChesney, R. D. *Central Asia: Foundations of Change*. Princeton, N.J.: Darwin Press, 1996.

────. *Waqf in Central Asia: Four Hundred Years in the History of a Muslim Shrine, 1480–1889*. Princeton, N.J.: Princeton University Press, 1991.

McNeill, William H. *Plagues and Peoples*. New York: Doubleday, 1977.

────. *The Pursuit of Power: Technology, Armed Force, and Society Since A.D. 1000*. Chicago: University of Chicago Press, 1982.

Meeker, Michael E. *A Nation of Empire: The Ottoman Legacy of Turkish Modernity*. Berkeley and Los Angeles: University of California Press, 2002.

Menges, Karl. *The Turkic Languages and Peoples, an Introduction to Turkic Studies*. Wiesbaden: Harrassowitz, 1995.

Mélikoff, Irène. *La geste de Melik Danişmend: Étude critique du Danişmendname*. 2 vols. Paris: Adrien Maisonneuve, 1960. See also Enveri.

Millward, James A. *Beyond the Pass: Economy, Ethnicity, and Empire in Qing Central Asia, 1759–1864*. Stanford, Cal.: Stanford University Press, 1998.

Minorsky, Vladimir. "The Poetry of Shah Ismail." *Bulletin of the School of Oriental and African Studies* 10 (1940–42): 1007–53a.

Morgan, David. *Medieval Persia 1040–1797*. London: Longman, 1988.

────. *The Mongols*. Oxford: Blackwell, 1986.

Murphey, Rhoads. *Ottoman Warfare 1500–1700*. New Brunswick, N.J.: Rutgers University Press, 1999.

Nava'i, Ali Shir. *Muhakemat al-Lughatain, by Mir 'Ali Shir*. Ed. and trans. Robert Devereux. Leiden: Brill, 1966.

Navaro-Yashin, Yael. *Faces of the State: Secularism and Public Life in Turkey*. Princeton, N.J.: Princeton University Press, 2002.

Necipoğlu, Gülru. *Architecture, Ceremonial and Power: The Topkapı Palace in the Fifteenth and Sixteenth Centuries*. Cambridge, Mass.: MIT Press, 1991.

Neşrî, Mehmed. *Kitâb-ı Cihan-Nümâ, Neşrî Tarihi*. 2 vols. Ed. Faik Reşit Unat and Mehmed A. Köymen. Ankara: Türk Tarih Kurumu, 1949-57. (Ottoman chronicle)

Nizam al-Mulk. *The Book of Government or Rules for Kings: The Siyar al-Muluk or Siyasat-Nama*. 2d ed. Trans. Hubert Darke. London: Routledge and Kegan Paul, 1978.

Nonneman, Gerd, Tim Niblock, and Bogdan Szajkowski, eds. *Muslim Commuinities in the New Europe*. Reading, UK: Ithaca Press, 1996.

Nugent, Daniel, ed. *Rural Revolt in Mexico: U.S. Intervention and the Domain of Subaltern Politics*. Durham, N.C.: Duke University Press, 1998.

Ocak, Ahmet Yaşar. *Alevî ve Bektaşî İnançlarının İslâm Öncesi Temelleri*. Istanbul: İletişim, 2000. (Pre-Islamic Bases of Alevi and Bektaşi Beliefs; originally published Istanbul: Enderun, 1983)

────. *Osmanlı Toplumunda Zındıklar ve Mülhidler, 15.-17. Yüzyıllar*. Istanbul: Türkiye Ekonomik ve Toplumsal Tarih Vakfı, 1998. (Religious Dissent in Ottoman Society)

————. *La révolte de Baba Resul ou la formation de l'heterodoxie musulmane en Anatolie au XIIIe siècle.* Ankara: Türk Tarih Kurumu, 1989.

————. *Sarı Saltık: Popüler İslâm'ın Balkanlar'daki Destanî Öncüsü (XIII. Yüzyıl).* Ankara: Türk Tarih Kurumu, 2002. (S.S., Epic Precursor of Popular Islam in the Balkans)

Olcott, Martha Brill. *The Kazakhs.* Stanford, Cal.: Hoover Institution Press, 1995.

————. *Kazakhstan: Unfulfilled Promise.* Washington, D.C.: Carnegie Endowment for International Peace, 2002.

Onon, Urgunge, trans. *The History and the Life of Chinggis Khan (The Secret History of the Mongols).* Leiden: Brill, 1990. See also Cleaves, Francis Woodman.

Ortaylı, İlber. *İmparatorluğun En Uzun Yüzyılı.* Istanbul: Hil Yayın, 1987. (The Empire's Longest Century)

————. *Osmanlı İmparatorluğunda Alman Nüfuzu.* Istanbul: Kaynak Yayınları, 1983. (German Influence in the Ottoman Empire)

Ögel, Bahaeddin. *Türk Mitolojisi (Kaynakları ve Açıklamaları ile Destanlar).* Ankara: Türk Tarih Kurumu, 1989. (Turkic Mythology)

Özbudun, Ergun. "Paradoxes of Turkish Democratic Development: The Struggle Between the Military-Bureaucratic 'Founders' of Democracy and New Democratic Forces." In *Politics, Society, and Democracy: Comparative Studies,* eds. H. E. Chehabi and Alfred Stepan, 297–309. Boulder, Col.: Westview Press, 1995.

Pamuk, Şevket. *A Monetary History of the Ottoman Empire.* Cambridge: Cambridge University Press, 2000.

Parker, Geoffrey, and Lesley M. Smith, eds. *The General Crisis of the Seventeenth Century.* London: Routledge, 1997.

Peirce, Leslie P. *The Imperial Harem: Women and Sovereignty in the Ottoman Empire.* New York: Oxford University Press, 1993.

————. *Morality Tales: Law and Gender in the Ottoman Court of Aintab.* Berkeley and Los Angeles: University of California Press, 2003.

Polat, Ülger. *Soziale und kulturelle Identität türkischer Migranten der zweiten Generation in Deutschland.* Hamburg: Verlag Dr. Kovač, 1997.

Pope, Nicole, and Hugh Pope. *Turkey Unveiled: A History of Modern Turkey.* Woodstock, NY: Overlook Press, 1998.

Pritsak, Omeljan. *The Origin of Rus'. Volume 1: Old Scandinavian Sources Other Than the Sagas.* Cambridge, Mass.: Harvard Ukrainian Research Institute–Harvard University Press, 1981.

Qian, Sima (Ssu-ma Ch'ien). *Records of the Grand Historian of China, Translated from the Shi Chi of Ssu-Ma Ch'ien.* 2 vols. Trans. Burton Watson. New York: Columbia University Press, 1961.

Quataert, Donald. *The Ottoman Empire, 1700–1922.* Cambridge: Cambridge University Press, 2000.

————. *Ottoman Manufacturing in the Age of the Industrial Revolution.* Cambridge: Cambridge University Press, 1993.

*Al-Qur'an, a Contemporary Translation.* Trans. Ahmed Ali. Princeton, N.J.: Princeton University Press, 1988.

Rashiduddin, *Rashiduddin Fazlullah, Jam'u't-tawarikh* (*Compendium of chronicles*): *A Histroy of the Mongols*. 3 vols. Trans. W. M. Thackston. Cambridge, Mass.: Harvard University, Dept. of Near Eastern Languages and Civilizations, 1998–99.

Rásonyi, László. *Türk Devletinin Batıdaki Vârisleri ve İlk Müslüman Türkler*. Trans. Ş. K. Seferoğlu and Adnan Müderrisoğlu. Ankara: Türk Kültürünü Araştırma Enstitüsü, 1983. (The Western Heirs of the Türk Empire and the First Muslim Turks)

Ratchnevsky, Paul. *Genghis Khan, His Life and Legacy*. Ed. and trans. Thomas Nivison Harding. Oxford: Blackwell, 1992.

Raymond, André. *The Great Arab Cities in the 16th–18th Centuries: An Introduction*. New York: New York University Press, 1984.

Richards, John F. *The Mughal Empire*. Cambridge: Cambridge University Press, 1993. (*The New Cambridge History of India*, vol. I.5)

———. *The Unending Frontier: An Environmental History of the Early Modern World*. Berkeley and Los Angeles: University of California Press, 2003.

Roemer, Hans Robert, ed., with the assistance of Wolfgang-Ekkehard Scharlipp. *History of the Turkic Peoples in the Pre-Islamic Period; Histoire des peuples turcs à l'époque pré-Islamique*. Berlin: Klaus Schwarz Verlag, 2000.

Rogers, J. M. *The Topkapı Saray Museum*. 4 vols. Boston: Little Brown, 1986. From the Turkish original by Filiz Çağman and Zeren Tanındı.

Ro'i, Yaacov. *Islam in the Soviet Union: From the Second World War to Gorbachev*. New York: Columbia University Press, 2000.

Rossabi, Morris. *Khubilai Khan: His Life and Times*. Berkeley and Los Angeles: University of California Press, 1988.

Roux, Jean-Paul. *Histoire des Turcs: Deux mille ans du Pacifique à la Méditerranée*. Paris: Fayard, 1984.

Roy, Olivier. *La nouvelle Asie Centrale, ou la fabrication des nations*. Paris: Éditions du Seuil, 1997.

Rudelson, Justin Jon. *Oasis Identities: Uyghur Nationalism Along China's Silk Road*. New York: Columbia University Press, 1997.

Rumpf, Christian. *Das Rechtsstaatsprinzip in der türkischen Rechtsordnung: Ein Beitrag zum türkischen Verfassungsrecht und zur europäischen Rezeptionsgeschichte*. Bonn: Bouvier, 1992.

Said, Edward W. *Culture and Imperialism*. New York: Random House, 1994.

Saint Laurent, Beatrice. "Ottoman Power and Westernization: The Architecture and Urban Development of Nineteenth and Early Twentieth Century Bursa." *Anatolia Moderna, Yeni Anadolu V* (1994): 199–232.

Sakallıoğlu, Ümit Cizre. "The Anatomy of the Turkish Military's Political Autonomy." *Comparative Politics* 29, no. 2 (1997): 151–66. See also Cizre, Ümit.

Saray, Mehmet. *The Turkmens in the Age of Imperialism: A Study of the Turkmen People and Their Incorporation into the Russian Empire*. Ankara: Turkish Historical Society, 1989.

Schacht, Joseph. *An Introduction to Islamic Law*. Oxford: Oxford University Press, 1964.

Schamiloglu, Uli. "Preliminary Remarks on the Role of Disease in the History of the Golden Horde." *Central Asian Survey* 12.4 (1993): 447–57.

———. "Tribal Politics and Social Organization in the Golden Horde." Ph.D. diss., Columbia University, New York, 1986.

Scharlipp, Wolfgang-Ekkehard. *Die frühen Türken in Zentralasien, Eine Einführung in ihre Geschichte und Kultur.* Darmstadt: Wissenschaftliche Buchgesellschaft, 1992.

Schick, İrvin Cemil, and Ahmet Tonak Ertuğrul, eds. *Turkey in Transition: New Perspectives.* New York: Oxford University Press, 1987.

Schiffauer, Werner. *Die Gottesmänner: Türkische Islamisten in Deutschland.* Frankfurt am Main: Suhrkamp, 2000.

Schmalz-Jacobsen, Cornelia, and Georg Hansen. *Kleines Lexikon der ethnischen Minderheiten in Deutschland.* Munich: Beck, 1997.

Şeşen, Ramazan. *İslâm Coğrafyacılarına göre Türkler ve Türk Ülkeleri.* Ankara: Türk Kültürünü Araştırma Enstitüsü, 1985. (The Turks and the Turkic Lands according to the Arab Geographers)

Sevimli, İbrahim. *Kimliksiz Cemaatler: Konumları, Sorunları ve Gelenekleriyle Avrupa'daki Anadolu Kökenliler.* Istanbul: Alan, 2000. (Communities without Identity: Communities of Anatolian Origin in Europe)

Seyitdanlıoğlu, Mehmet. *Tanzimat Devrinde Meclis-i Vâlâ (1838–1868).* Ankara: Türk Tarih Kurumu, 1994. (The Meclis-i Vala during the Tanzimat)

Shankland, David. *Islam and Society in Turkey.* Huntingdon, UK: Eothen, 1999.

Shaw, Stanford J. *Between Old and New: The Ottoman Empire Under Sultan Selim III, 1789–1807.* Cambridge, Mass.: Harvard University Press, 1971.

Shaw, Stanford J., and Ezel Kural Shaw. *History of the Ottoman Empire and Modern Turkey. Vol. II, Reform, Revolution, and Republic: The Rise of Modern Turkey, 1808–1975.* Cambridge: Cambridge University Press, 1977.

Shaw, Wendy M. K. *Possessors and Possessed: Museums, Archaeology, and the Visualization of History in the Late Ottoman Empire.* Berkeley and Los Angeles: University of California Press, 2003.

Shir, Mir Ali. *Muhakamat al-Lughatain by Mir Ali Shir.* Ed. and trans. Robert Devereux. Leiden: Brill, 1966. (The Judgement between the Two Languages)

Shissler, Holly. *Between Two Empires: Ahmet Ağaoğlu and the New Turkey.* London: I. B. Tauris, 2003.

Silahdar Fındıklı Mehmed Ağa. *Silahdar Tarihi.* 2 vols. Istanbul: Orhaniye Matbaası, 1928.

Singer, Amy. *Constructing Ottoman Beneficence: An Imperial Soup Kitchen in Jerusalem.* Albany: State University of New York Press, 2002.

———. *Palestinian Peasants and Ottoman Officials: Rural Administration around Sixteenth-Century Jerusalem.* Cambridge: Cambridge University Press, 1994.

Sinor, Denis, ed. *The Cambridge History of Early Inner Asia.* Cambridge: Cambridge University Press, 1990.

Slezkine, Yuri. *Arctic Mirrors: Russia and the Small Peoples of the North.* Ithaca, N.Y.: Cornell University Press, 1994.

Sohrabi, Nader. "Global Waves, Local Actors: What the Young Turks Knew About Other Revolutions and Why It Mattered." *Comparative Studies in Society and History* 44, no. 1 (January 2002): 45–79.

SOPEMI. *Trends in International Migration, Annual Report, 2000 Edition.* Paris: SOPEMI, 2001. (SOPEMI is the French acronym for the Continuous Reporting System on Migration of the OECD [Organization for Economic Cooperation and Development]).

Soucek, Svat. *A History of Inner Asia.* Cambridge: Cambridge University Press, 2000.

Southern, R. W. *Western Views of Islam in the Middle Ages.* Cambridge, Mass.: Harvard University Press, 1962.

Sponsel, Leslie E., ed. *Endangered Peoples of Southeast and East Asia: Struggles to Survive and Thrive.* Westport, Conn.: Greenwood Press, 2000.

Stephens, Sharon, ed. *Children and the Politics of Culture.* Princeton, N.J.: Princeton University Press, 1995.

Sümer, Faruk. *Oğuzlar (Türkmenler): Tarihleri, Boy Teşkilâtı, Destanları.* Istanbul: Ana Yayınları, 1980. (The Oghuz [Türkmens]: Their History, Tribal Organization, and Epics)

Suny, Ronald Grigor. *The Revenge of the Past: Nationalism, Revolution, and the Collapse of the Soviet Union.* Stanford, Cal.: Stanford University Press, 1993.

Suny, Ronald Grigor, and Terry Martin. *A State of Nations: Empire and Nation-Making in the Age of Lenin and Stalin.* New York: Oxford University Press, 2001.

Swietochowski, Tadeusz. *Russia and Azerbaijan: A Borderland in Transition.* New York: Columbia University Press, 1995.

Tabakoğlu, Ahmet. *Gerileme Dönemine Girerken Osmanlı Maliyesi.* Istanbul: Dergâh, 1985. (Ottoman Finance as It Entered the Period of Retraction)

Taşağıl, Ahmet. *Gök-Türkler.* Ankara: Türk Tarih Kurumu, 1995.

Tekin, Şinasi. "XIV. Yüzyılda Yazılmış Gazilik Tarikası 'Gâziliğin Yolları' adlı bir Eski Anadolu Türkçesi Metni ve Gazâ/Cihâd Kavramları Hakkında." *Journal of Turkish Studies—Türklük Bilgisi Araştırmaları* 13 (1989): 139–204. (A Fourteenth-Century Anatolian Text on the Way of the Ghazi)

———. "XIVüncü Yüzyıla ait bir *Ilm-i Hâl:* Risâletü'l-Islâm." *Wiener Zeitschrift Für die Kunde Des Morgenlandes* 76 (1986): 279–92. (A Fourteenth-Century Catechism)

Tekin, Talat. *A Grammar of Orkhon Turkic.* Bloomington: Indiana University Press, 1968. Includes the Orkhon inscriptions in Turkic and in translation.

———. *Orhon Yazıtları: Kül Tigin, Bilge Kağan, Tunyukuk.* Istanbul: Simurg, 1995. (The Orkhon Inscriptions)

———. *Tunyukuk Yazıtı.* Ankara: Simurg, 1994. (The Tunyukuk Inscription)

Tezel, Yahya S. *Cumhuriyet Döneminin İktisadi Tarihi (1923–1950).* Rev. ed. Ankara: Yurt Yayınları, 1986. (Economic History of the Turkish Republic)

Therborn, Göran. *European Modernity and Beyond: The Trajectory of European Societies, 1945–2000.* London: Sage, 1995.

Tietze, Andreas. *Tarihi ve Etimolojik Türkiye Türkçesi Lugati, Sprachgeschichtliches und Etymologisches Wörterbuch Des Türkei-Türkischen, I: A-E.* Istanbul-Vienna: Österreichisches Akademie der Wissenschaften, 2001.

Tietze, Nikola. "La Turcité allemande: Les difficultés d'une nouvelle construction identitaire." *Cahiers d'Études sur la Méditerranée Orientale et le Monde Turco-Iranien* 24 (1997): 252–70.

Times of London. *The Times Atlas of the World.* Boston: Houghton Mifflin, 1967.

Togan, İsenbike. *Flexibility and Limitation in Steppe Formations: The Kerait Khanate and Chinggis Khan.* Leiden: Brill, 1998.

Toprak, Zafer. *İttihat-Terakki ve Devletçilik. Türkiye'de Ekonomi ve Toplum (1908–1950).* Istanbul: Tarih Vakfı Yurt Yayınları, 1995. (Statism in the Young Turk Period)

———. *Milli İktisat—Milli Burjuvazi. Türkiye'de Ekonomi ve Toplum (1908–1950).* Istanbul: Tarih Vakfı Yurt Yayınları, 1995. (National Economy, National Bourgeoisie)

Touraine, Alain. *Critique of Modernity.* Trans. David Macey. Cambridge: Blackwell, 1995.

Tucker, Jonathan. *The Silk Road: Art and History.* London: Art Media Resources, 2003.

Tucker, Judith E. *In the House of the Law: Gender and Islamic Law in Ottoman Syria and Palestine.* Berkeley and Los Angeles: University of California Press, 1998.

Tunçay, Mete. *T.C.'nde Tek-Parti Yönetimi'nin Kurulması (1923–1931).* 2d ed. Ankara: Yurt Yayınları, 1989. (The Foundation of Single-Party Rule in the Turkish Republic)

*Turkologischer Anzeiger.* Vienna: Orientalisches Institut, 1975. (Bibliography published annually since 1975, includes books and articles in all languages, on all aspects of Turkish studies.)

Vatin, Nicolas, and Gilles Veinstein. *Le Sérail ébranlé: Essai sur les morts, dépositions et avènements des sultans ottomans (XIVe–XIXe siècle).* Paris: Fayard, 2003.

Vryonis, Speros, Jr. *The Decline of Medieval Hellenism and the Process of Islamization from the Eleventh Through the Fifteenth Century.* Berkeley and Los Angeles: University of California Press, 1971.

Wagner, Donald B. *Iron and Steel in Ancient China.* Leiden: Brill, 1993.

*Was ist ein Deutscher? Was ist ein Türke? Alman Olmak Nedir? Türk Olmak Nedir? Deutsch-Türkisches Symposium 1997, Türk-Alman Sempozyumu 1997.* Hamburg: Körber Stiftung, 1998.

White, Jenny B. *Islamist Mobilization in Turkey: A Study in Vernacular Politics.* Seattle: University of Washington Press, 2002.

———. "Turks in the New Germany." *American Anthropologist* 99, no. 4 (1997): 754–69.

Whitfield, Roderick, Susan Whitfield, and Neville Agnew. *Cave Temples of Mogao: Art and History on the Silk Road.* Los Angeles: The Getty Conservation Institute and the J. Paul Getty Museum, 2000.

Whitfield, Susan. *Life Along the Silk Road.* Berkeley and Los Angeles: University of California Press, 1999.

Wilhite, Vincent. "Guerrilla War, Counterinsurgency, and State Formation in Ottoman Yemen." Ph.D. diss., Ohio State University, Columbus, 2003.

Williams, Brian Glyn. *The Crimean Tatars: The Diaspora Experience and the Forging of a Nation.* Leiden: Brill, 2001.

Wittek, Paul. *The Rise of the Ottoman Empire.* London: Luzac, 1938.

Woods, John E. *The Aqquyunlu, Clan, Confederation, Empire: A Study in 15th/9th Century Turko-Iranian Politics.* Minneapolis and Chicago: Bibliotheca Islamica, 1976.

Yanıkdağ, Yücel. "Ill-Fated Sons of the Nation: Ottoman Prisoners of War in Russia and Egypt, 1914–1922." Ph.D. diss., Ohio State University, Columbus, 2001.

Yavuz, M. Hakan. *Islamic Political Identity in Turkey.* New York: Oxford University Press, 2003.

Yerasimos, Stéphane, ed. *Les Turcs: Orient et Occident, Islam et laïcité.* Paris: Editions Autrement, 1994.

Yücel, Ünsal. *Türk Okçuluğu.* Ankara: Atatürk Kültür Merkezi, 1999. (Turkish Archery)

Yusuf Has Hâcib. *Kutadgu Bilig.* 2 vols. Ed. and trans. Reşid Rahmeti Arat. Ankara: Türk Tarih Kurumu, 1947–59.

Yusuf Khass Hajib. *Wisdom of Royal Glory (Kutadgu Bilig), A Turko-Islamic Mirror for Princes.* Ed. and trans. Robert Dankoff. Chicago: University of Chicago Press, 1983.

Zachariadou, Elizabeth. *Trade and Crusade: Venetian Crete and the Emirates of Menteshe and Aydin (1300–1415).* Venice: Istituto Ellenico di Studi Bizantini e Postbizantini di Venezia, 1983.

Ze'evi, Dror. *An Ottoman Century: The District of Jerusalem in the 1600s.* Albany: State University of New York Press, 1996.

Zerjal, Tatiana, Yali Xue, Giorgio Bertorelle, et al. "The Genetic Legacy of the Mongols." *American Journal of Human Genetics* 72 (2003): 717–21.

Zilfi, Madeline C. *The Politics of Piety: The Ottoman Ulema in the Postclassical Age.* Minneapolis: Bibliotheca Islamica, 1988.

Zürcher, Erik Jan. *Turkey: A Modern History.* Rev. ed. London: I. B. Tauris, 1998.

———. *The Unionist Factor: The Rôle of the Committee of Union and Progress in the Turkish National Movement.* Leiden: Brill, 1984.

Zygulski, Zdzislaw, Jr. *Ottoman Art in the Service of Empire.* New York: New York University Press, 1992.

# INDEX

287